ORACLE®

Oracle Press™

Implementing Oracle Fusion General Ledger and Oracle Fusion Accounting Hub

Anil Passi
Nivas Ramanathan
Vladimir Ajvaz

 Mc Graw Hill Education

New York   Chicago   San Francisco
Athens   London   Madrid   Mexico City
Milan   New Delhi   Singapore   Sydney   Toronto

Library of Congress Cataloging-in-Publication Data

Names: Passi, Anil, author. | Ramanathan, Nivas, author. | Ajvaz, Vladimir, author.
Title: Implementing Oracle Fusion general ledger and Oracle Fusion accounting hub / Anil Passi, Nivas Ramanathan, Vladimir Ajvaz.
Description: New York : McGraw-Hill Education, 2016. | Includes index.
Identifiers: LCCN 2016001443 (print) | LCCN 2016008600 (ebook) | ISBN 9780071846622 (paperback) | ISBN 9780071846639 ()
Subjects: LCSH: Oracle (Computer file) | Accounting—Data processing. | Management information systems. | BISAC: COMPUTERS / Enterprise Applications / Business Intelligence Tools.
Classification: LCC HF5679 .P3147 2016 (print) | LCC HF5679 (ebook) | DDC 657.0285/53—dc23
LC record available at http://lccn.loc.gov/2016001443

McGraw-Hill Education books are available at special quantity discounts to use as premiums and sales promotions, or for use in corporate training programs. To contact a representative, please visit the Contact Us pages at www.mhprofessional.com.

Implementing Oracle Fusion General Ledger and Oracle Fusion Accounting Hub

1234567890 DOC DOC 109876

ISBN   978-0-07-184662-2
MHID   0-07-184662-X

Sponsoring Editor Brandi Shailer	**Technical Editor** Nicola Orme	**Production Supervisor** Pamela Pelton
Editorial Supervisor Jody McKenzie	**Copy Editor** Margaret Berson	**Composition** Cenveo Publisher Services
Project Manager Moumita Majumdar, Cenveo® Publisher Services	**Proofreader** Lisa McCoy	**Illustration** Cenveo Publisher Services
	Indexer Jack Lewis	**Art Director, Cover** Jeff Weeks

About the Authors

Anil Passi, Oracle ACE, is the founder of www.apps2fusion.com, which helps customers with Oracle training and implementation. Anil has been helping various companies implement a Finance in a Box model on Oracle's cloud, using the implementation accelerators developed in the apps2fusion innovation lab, which includes a data integration hub, EBS, Fusion Financials, and Hyperion suite glued together by Fusion Middleware.

Nivas Ramanathan is an independent Oracle Consultant specializing in the implementation of Oracle E-Business Suite and Oracle Fusion Applications. He started his career with Oracle Corporation and has been advising clients in Oracle technology for the past 15 years. He has successfully delivered many challenging finance transformation and Enterprise Resource Planning projects in EMEA, APAC, and the North American region in the capacity of Solution Architect and Delivery Lead. He holds an MBA in Finance and Business Strategy from the prestigious Imperial Business School in London. He also runs a boutique consulting firm, Bluebells Technology Solutions based in London, which provides expert advice to listed companies and major consulting firms' clients for running optimized Enterprise Resource Planning solutions in the cloud that work seamlessly with existing IT ecosystems.

Vladimir Ajvaz is an Oracle expert and has been working with the Oracle E-Business Suite and, more recently, Oracle Fusion Applications for the past 15+ years. He coauthored *Oracle E-Business Suite Development & Extensibility Handbook* and *Oracle Fusion Applications Development and Extensibility Handbook*, which were published by McGraw-Hill Education (Oracle Press). Vladimir worked at Oracle Corporation for many years and was fortunate enough to work on some of Oracle's best teams across the globe, where he gained in-depth knowledge of Oracle technologies. Today, he provides independent advice and consulting services to companies around the globe in the areas of enterprise, solution, and technical architecture, but he also inspires and participates in the development, creation, and design of new enterprise-class products and services.

About the Technical Reviewer

Nicola Orme received a MEng (Hons) in Aerospace Engineering from UMIST University in 1999 and gained her ACA Qualification in 2002 while working at PwC. She is now a Fellow of the ICAEW. Nicola has worked for a number of large financial services institutions (including a number of global banks), principally in the technology space, for more than 10 years and is currently a program director working on the integration of two large insurance companies. This is her first involvement in a technical publication, and all proceeds received will be going to a charity based in West Yorkshire (http://www.kirkwoodhospice.co.uk), where she was born in 1975.

Contents at a Glance

Contents

Acknowledgments

We owe a debt of gratitude to our families and friends who helped see this book through to completion. Working on the book outside of our consulting and other duties can be an overwhelming challenge, and we are grateful to all who put up with us. We are thankful to Anil's apps2fusion.com team who provided and supported a privately hosted Fusion Financials instance to implement the scenarios that we have covered in this book. We would like to thank Milan Parekh, Group Manager, Fusion Application Product Management with Oracle Corporation, for his review comments and suggestions on key topics of the book. Writing can quickly consume many hours in a day, and we would like to thank the following people for being patient and providing support: Brandi Shailer, Paul Carlstroem, and Amanda Russell, from the McGraw-Hill Education production team, and Moumita Majumdar from Cenveo Publisher Services.

Introduction

Oracle Fusion Applications, including Fusion Financials, are designed from the ground up, and from an architectural viewpoint, they are designed in such a way that they can be used in the Oracle Cloud or deployed on-premise where customers have full control over their deployment. This is an important difference between pure software-as-a-service (SaaS) vendors and Oracle, which provides its customers with a choice of deployment, at least at this time.

This book doesn't discuss the benefits of Cloud over on-premise deployment or the reverse; most of the text covered in this book is applicable to both.

Intended Audience

This book is for chief financial officers (CFOs), implementation consultants, system integrators, solution and enterprise architects, project managers, and other professionals intending to work on implementation projects that relate to Oracle Fusion General Ledger and Financial Accounting Hub.

This book assumes that you have unrestricted access to an on-premise installation, as the SaaS option restricts you from performing some of the tasks and techniques described in this book. If you are a reader with access to an SaaS environment only, we advise you to get in touch with your Oracle account manager or Oracle Support representative to become familiar with what features are available in your environment so that you can follow the examples in the book.

The authors assume that the reader is familiar with financial accounting and control principles, and for those who need a quick refresher on the basics, we have provided an introduction to Oracle Financials in Chapter 2.

What This Book Covers

This book covers the following core modules of Oracle Fusion Financials Suite: Oracle Fusion General Ledger (GL) and Financials Accounting Hub (FAH).

The question that often crops up is this: Which of these modules is available in the Oracle Cloud versus on-premise deployment? The Oracle Financials Cloud offering, at the time of writing this book, in Release 8 covers the General Ledger, Payables, Receivables, Payments, Cash Management, Tax, Expenses, and Assets modules. This means that the core General Ledger concepts explained in this book are equally applicable in both deployment options. It must be noted that Fusion FAH is not available on Oracle Public Cloud at the time of writing this book.

As for the Financial Accounting Hub module, Oracle Fusion Accounting Hub Reporting is available as part of the Oracle Cloud service with out-of-the box synchronization that works with Oracle E-Business Suite GL Balances. This integration enables real-time analysis of financial data and drill-down into Oracle E-Business Suite journal lines from Oracle Fusion General Ledger.

How This Book Is Organized

This book discusses the process of implementing Oracle Fusion General Ledger and Financials Accounting Hub based on use cases and business requirements of a fictional banking organization called ACME Bank.

Chapter 1 outlines the business pains that the fictional bank sets out to solve by embarking on a business transformation program to resolve business-critical issues. Although Chapter 2 can be read in isolation, as it provides the background to some basic concepts that relate to Oracle Fusion Financials, we suggest reading the rest of the chapters in the book in order for a better understanding of the text.

Finally, this book is intended to complement the existing product documentation and other vendor-provided information such as white papers and case studies, and the reader is advised to always consult the product documentation applicable to their release and deployment scenario (Cloud or on-premise), as well as resources provided by Oracle Support.

CHAPTER
1

Project Initiation
and Scope

In this book, we will be implementing Oracle Fusion Financials for a fictitious bank named ACME Bank. This bank does not reflect any real bank in any country.

ACME Bank profits have been decreasing for the past two years even though the name is a very strong and well-known brand. Operating margins are low. Investors are concerned about the opaqueness in their reporting. Auditors are concerned about the lack of control and governance in the bank. The Chief Operating Officer is struggling to pinpoint the areas where there are cost inefficiencies. The Chief Financial Officer is concerned that he does not know the true picture about which lines of businesses within the bank are performing poorly. The operational business users are frustrated that too many of their daily tasks involve manual work. There are too many Microsoft Excel spreadsheets floating around in the shared drives and in the emails, resulting in total lack of governance and controls on the financial data within the organization.

The Chief Executive Officer creates a small team to do an operational analysis of the bank operations and processes. The deliverable from this team is to make recommendations to make the bank more efficient for operations and compliant with regulatory requirements.

Listing the Bank's Pain Points

The operational efficiency analysis team performs a detailed analysis for a month after interviewing several people within the organization. The people interviewed are primarily in the Information Technology (IT), Finance, and Investment Banking departments. The key finding of the team is that the bank's IT architecture is fragmented, with each division making its own decisions for implementing the software solutions. The bank lacks a centralized finance platform. There is no centralized IT control of the architecture, and this has resulted in highly fragmented systems and processes, thus increasing operational costs and reducing efficiencies. This has been further aggravated by the different technical teams working in their silos.

In the past, the bank has grown organically and also by acquisitions. With the economic crisis of 2008, regulatory authorities have cranked up pressure for compliance to their reporting needs. However, the bank is struggling to understand its capital adequacy situation given the lack of a central accounting and reporting platform.

Business Process Pain Points

The team discovers various shortcomings in the operational processes that make the organization inefficient overall. These are listed in Table 1-1.

Area	Problem
Profitability	The bank does not know which lines of business are making profits.
Exposure	The bank has various transactional systems that keep track of their exposures to the counterparties local to that system. However, there is no single unified view of the exposure to counterparties. This hinders efficient decision making when it comes to initiating new deals with the key counterparties.
Cash position	Given that the bank has grown by acquisitions, this has resulted in various different isolated cash management systems. At any given point in time, the bank finds it hard to collate the information about the total cash that exists in the bank across its various divisions and units.
Manual processes	Due to regulatory requirements, the bank should be reporting their General Ledger data in US GAAP (Generally Accepted Accounting Principles), UK GAAP, and IFRS (International Financial Reporting Standards). This is a very manual process because their legacy general ledger creates the accounting using only one of the GAAPs.
Risk of fraud	The lack of segregation of duties management makes it risky to manage the risk of fraudulent activities.
Reputational risk	The company struggles to submit their financial reports on time to the regulatory bodies. The reason for this is that information is collated from various systems and spreadsheets manually and then analyzed. This results in reputational damage and penalties imposed due to late submission.
Expense and cost management	The bank does not have a unified view of their suppliers and does not know the worth of services or supplies that are being consumed from their key vendors globally.
Lacking features and functionality	The financial systems used in the bank lack various features and functionality because some of these systems are custom made and it has not been possible to keep up with the speed of change in the way the bank operates and does international business. Also, investment is required for each new regulatory requirement that must be implemented into the custom financial systems. Therefore, the divisions within the bank have to allocate budgets to fund each such change initiative.
Expensive IT support	Due to the lack of centralized systems, there are multiple systems that need support, some of them running software versions that are no longer supported by the respective vendors. This is resulting in significant maintenance effort by the in-house team to support various legacy systems. The many types of software used in the bank are also resulting in multiple license fees paid to various vendors for tools that have similar functionalities. The cost of maintenance also increases when a standard regulatory change has to be applied to multiple systems coded in different programming languages because different divisions within the banking group use different local systems.

TABLE 1-1.   *Business Process Pain Points at ACME Bank*

Technical Pain Points

The analysis team discovers the various system architecture–related pains suffered by the business and their Information Technology department. The root causes of these pain points are due to the way ACME Bank's legacy systems have evolved over a period of time. Most of the time, the new systems were implemented without proper due diligence and were implemented in a rapid response to a requirement with a narrow and tactical viewpoint. The development processes for these systems lacked any centralized governance. Table 1-2 lists the various technical and architectural pain points identified by the analysis team.

Area	Problem
Data security	The bank has too many stand-alone systems with various databases, with developers having write access to production systems.
Data inconsistency	There are too many copies of the reference data without a single system being the master. Multiple systems maintain their own copy of the reference data in each system locally, resulting in inconsistency in descriptions of the various reference codes used in the bank.
Reconciliation	Given that there are various systems that are not integrated seamlessly, it leaves the onus on the staff to take extracts from individual systems and to reconcile the data in Microsoft Access database or Excel spreadsheets.
Lack of centralized reporting	The bank does not have a single enterprise reporting system. Each legacy system has its very own reports facility. Historically it was easy to build stand-alone reports in Excel, because the mainframe reports lacked any analytic capabilities. This has resulted in finance-related data being held in multiple legacy systems with no enterprise reporting solution implemented. Therefore, the users have to manually join the results from various reports in Excel to meet their group-wide reporting needs.
Lack of any real-time integration on time-critical data flows	The existing systems do not have real-time integration capability. Every single interface is a batch process. It means that the end-to-end flow of data for its transaction lifecycle takes much longer than it would if it had been integrated in real time. This lack of capability makes the bank's operations inefficient.

TABLE 1-2. *Technical Pain Points (Continued)*

Area	Problem
Lack of integration between roles and job positions	Every single legacy system in the bank has its very own security model. It is very difficult to present to the auditors the overall access matrix for users. The bank is under pressure from auditors to implement segregation of duties.
Long time to close finance periods	A large volume of late adjustments are applied to their general ledgers because of the issues encountered during reconciliation.
Lack of documentation	Many of the existing systems are home-grown and lack sufficient documentation. Therefore, improvements are hard to make to these systems because the developers that built these systems no longer work in the organization.
Overlapping toolsets across the organization	Management reporting is available, using a common toolset, based on a controlled, consistent data model that seamlessly aligns a core set of financial control dimensions with the appropriate reference data to manage business performance.
Manual processes for intercompany transactions	The home-grown legacy general ledger system in the bank lacks the features that make automatic elimination of intercompany transactions during consolidation. This requires significant manual work at each month end with dedicated resources to perform these eliminations offline in Microsoft Access databases, which are not governed.
Lack of master data management	Multiple interest rates are used within the different companies within the banking group. The traded instruments are categorized in decentralized ways, causing various interpretations of the master data. This causes significant overhead when doing consolidated operational reporting.
Accounting methodology is black box	The bank is required to produce the accounting results in multiple reporting bases, such as US GAAP and IFRS. These GAAP calculations are performed offline in Excel. Doing so loses the data lineage from the source transactions that have resulted in those accounting entries. The rules for producing these accounting entries are coded within the Excel spreadsheets, and over a period of time, there have been various different versions of these Excel spreadsheets, causing much confusion.
Lack of high availability	The legacy systems used by banks do not have failover architecture. In the event of system failure, the core systems are inaccessible until they are restored from backups.
Heavy customizations	Some of the off-the-shelf products purchased a few decades ago have been customized so much that the vendor refuses to support those systems.

TABLE 1-2.   *Technical Pain Points*

Post-Analysis Decisions

After the analysis work was done, the following action points were captured:

- Implement a new architecture for finance that is superior to the technology stack in legacy systems.

- Implement industry-standard best practices for operational processes.

- Reduce end-user applications and centralize key business applications, starting with finance systems.

- Standardize the technologies that are supported by the business as usual support team.

- Reduce the number of technology vendors.

- Reduce and standardize the number of development tools.

- Implement a platform for centralized security of key applications to ensure segregation of duties.

- Implement best practices for data integration into financial systems.

- Implement a governed release management process.

There has been an increasing amount of pressure from regulatory bodies, and both internal and external auditors, to improve the systems and processes within the bank. As a result of these findings, it was then decided to initiate a new project for financial transformation by introducing an architecture that will help the bank improve processes, technologies, and time to market, and thus become more efficient. In order to meet this objective, industry-standard tools will be considered and decisions will be made to deploy a tool that addresses most of the bank's needs. Given the problems with the bank's past experiences, the possibility of building a home-grown system was left out of the discussions.

Finance System Selection for Finance Transformation

After investigating various products in the market, Oracle Fusion Financials was selected for implementation. This product addresses various business and technical pain points faced by the bank.

Addressing the Business Process Pain Points

Oracle Fusion Financials addresses the business process pain points listed in Table 1-3.

Area	Solution
Profitability	Lines of business can be a segment in the global chart of accounts. Assets, Liabilities, Profit, and Losses can then be tracked by the line of business.
Exposure	Oracle Fusion Financials Accounting Hub allows the business to define an extended chart of accounts that can track balances against the counterparty. The source system feeding into a centralized Financial Accounting hub will show counterparty details in relevant transactions.
Cash position	A proper range of Cash Account definitions in Fusion General Ledger will allow the company to know the cash on hand at any point in time. The system also allows for cash management to be implemented in the future that can facilitate reconciling cash balances in bank statements with the general ledger cash balances.
Manual processes	Accounting rules can be defined in Fusion Financial Accounting Hub to generate US GAAP, UK GAAP, and IFRS accounting automatically. This allows the accounting system to generate additional reporting basis entries for a single transaction. In the old architecture, the accounting process had to be repeated for each additional reporting basis.
Risk of fraud	Oracle Fusion Financials comes integrated with Oracle's Identity & Access Management, allowing segregation of duties to be monitored and enforced.
Reputational risk	Oracle Fusion Accounting Hub will allow the bank to close their periods quickly and thus allow reports to be produced for shareholders and regulatory bodies on time and accurately.
Expense and cost management	The Fusion Financials platform will allow the bank to implement a central vendor management system coupled with a centralized payment system. This will ensure that supplier spending can be centrally tracked.
Lacking features and functionality	Oracle Fusion Financials has been developed by cherry-picking the best-of-breed product features from Oracle EBS, Siebel, PeopleSoft, and many others.
Expensive IT support	Transitioning various legacy systems into a common platform means that the bank does not have to provide support to various in-house teams.

TABLE 1-3. *Addressing the Business Process Pain Points*

Addressing the Technical Pain Points

Implementing the Oracle Fusion Financials system addresses the various technical pain points listed in Table 1-4.

Area	Solution
Data security	Oracle Fusion allows data security to be implemented centrally on database objects using Oracle Authorization Policy Manager (APM).
Data inconsistency	Creating value sets and a common chart of accounts means there is a single code and description for each unique Cost Center, Account Code, Entity, and other segments.
Reconciliation	Extended Chart of Accounts allows the bank to track balances using source system codes. This will allow easy reconciliation back to the source systems.
Lack of centralized reporting	Oracle Fusion Financials comes pre-integrated with Oracle Business Intelligence Enterprise Edition. It contains various data sources out of the box that can be exposed to the user for Self-Service Reporting, subject to Role Based Access Control.
Lack of any real-time integration on time-critical data flows	The foundation of Oracle Fusion Financials is Fusion Middleware. This has Service Oriented Platform installed out of the box.
Lack of integration between roles and job positions	Oracle Fusion Application allows the Joiner, Mover & Leavers process to be integrated with roles allocated to the user. For example, when a user's position changes, it is possible to allocate a new set of roles automatically to this user.
Long time to close finance periods	Given the tight controls and data validations in Oracle Fusion Financials, it is quicker to close the periods because the system performs various validation checks at month end automatically.

TABLE 1-4. *Addressing the Technical Pain Points (Continued)*

Area	Solution
Lack of documentation	Oracle has published detailed documentation on features and processes for Fusion Financials on http://docs.oracle.com. In addition, there are blogs such as blogs.oracle.com and apps2fusion.com that have published extensive white papers on Oracle Fusion Financials. The bank support staff can also rely on the support.oracle.com portal, which is the knowledge base and support portal for Oracle.
Overlapping toolsets across organization	Oracle Fusion Financials presents JDeveloper as the standardized single tool for doing development across all Fusion Middleware technology components.
Manual processes for intercompany entries	Oracle Fusion Financials has a consolidation feature that can perform autoelimination of intercompany entries.
Accounting methodology is black box	Oracle Fusion Financials offers configurable screens to define accounting rules, which the Subject Matter Experts (SMEs) can maintain themselves with minimal training.
Lack of high availability	WebLogic Server as the centerpiece of Oracle Fusion Application allows scalability by clustering the system across various physical machines, while presenting a unified view to the business user.
Heavy customizations	Oracle Fusion Financials is heavily extensible by configurations and personalizations. Changes of this nature are upgrade-safe.

TABLE 1-4. *Addressing the Technical Pain Points*

Scope of Financial Transformation

The CFO has directed that the scope of the initiated project should address most of the pain points. The operational efficiency analysis team prepares a business case for the Financial Transformation project that is presented to the CFO and senior executives in the bank. A consensus is reached, and a budget is allocated for the commencement of this project. Given the large size of the bank, it is decided to restrict the scope of the initial project to deliver major benefits, with measurable success. The project will be done in two phases. In Phase 1, the Financial Systems platform will be implemented, followed by Phase 2, during which other Oracle Fusion Applications subledgers will be implemented.

It was mandated that the standard Oracle Fusion product will not be modified in any way that makes the system unsupportable by Oracle. However, as part of the implementation, there will be a need to extend the system by using the Standard API (Application Programming Interfaces) & Web Services, which Oracle Fusion provides out of the box to design extensions, and interfaces; for example, for importing data into Oracle using File Based Data Import (FBDI) and outbound extracts using BI Publisher. The system will also be configured to implement the various data security rules, approval management rules, and segregation of duties in a manner that meets the acceptable governance requirements on the system.

The ACME Bank is headquartered in the United States with additional operations in the United Kingdom, Japan, and Latin America. The bank's business is divided into four key pillars that are also referenced as a Line of Business (LOB). Some of the key LOBs in ACME Bank are Investment Banking, Commercial Finance, Insurance, and Mortgage, as shown in Figure 1-1. Each of these Lines of Business has various cost centers. Some of the cost centers are shared across these LOBs, whereas some of the cost centers are dedicated to each LOB. Some of the key cost centers in the bank are Human Resources, Tax, Compliance, Training, Customer Services, IT Support, IT Service Delivery, and Finance. The various activities performed in the bank are grouped into projects. One of the examples of these projects is the Financial Transformation project itself, which is the underlying basis of this book. It is expected that the Financial Transformation project will allow the bank to track the revenue, expenses, assets, and liabilities for the U.S., U.K., Japan, and Latin America operations across all lines of business and cost centers.

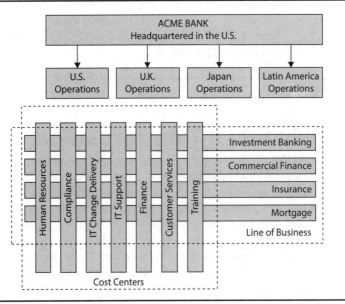

FIGURE 1-1. *ACME Bank's high-level operational structure*

In order to achieve the objectives of this project, the following goals are defined as the high-level scope of this project.

Introduction of Common Global Chart of Accounts

It was decided that even though the U.S., U.K., and Latin American operations will operate with their own separate ledgers, to ease consolidation and procedural consistency across the globe, the same Chart of Accounts (CoA) design will be used in all ledgers. The CoA should allow room for growth and future reporting requirements. Equally, it will be necessary to provide new bases of reporting, that is, US GAAP, UK GAAP, IFRS, and other future requirements, and these should be capable of incorporation with minimal redesign or workarounds. The following principles must be adhered to for the global Chart of Accounts.

Keep the Structure Short and Simple

The Chart of Accounts structure should be kept as simple as possible. In cases where a reporting attribute could be held either as an element in the GL Chart of Accounts or as a reporting attribute in the Fusion Financial Account Hub (FFAH), the intention is that it should be held in the FFAH unless there is a proven and identifiable need to keep the element in the Fusion GL Chart of Accounts.

Keep the Structure Logical

Each element should have a clear and single purpose. We have avoided allowing element values that mix concepts (for example, nominal account codes for Sales Western Region and Sales Eastern Region). These should be dissociated into two separate elements (Account and Region).

Keep the Usage of Each Element Unambiguous

Elements such as Location are open to misinterpretation. For example, having the location segment in Chart of Accounts can raise several questions, such as, is this the location of the investing unit in ACME Bank or the location of the trading counterparty? Or is it the location of the shared service center settling the trade or the location of the trading broker? The aim of the design should be to provide clear and unambiguous definition of the intended usage of each of the proposed segments in the Fusion General Ledger Chart of Accounts.

Introduction of Ledger Strategy

It was decided that all the countries in the ACME Bank would operate with their own ledgers. Even though accounting will be carried out on multiple reporting bases, it was noted that most of the accounting events have the same treatment in GAAPs and IFRS, and therefore, to avoid data duplication, a delta ledger strategy will be implemented. For example, the difference between US GAAP representation and the IFRS regulatory requirements only affects a small section of the ledger, and therefore it would be particularly cumbersome to maintain a full parallel ledger for IFRS reporting.

Introduce Centralized Audits, Governance, and Security

It was decided that the bank must improve and simplify access management of financial systems by consolidating and replacing a number of components that make up ACME Bank's existing Identity Governance framework, including management of access rights (Rules), Entitlements, Reporting, Provisioning, and Role Catalog, as well as the user access to execute various financial processes. The new finance system should provide a number of features, including a number of recertification options (roles, role assignments, rules, movers, non-personal accounts, and data container ownership), reconciliation of financial systems, and provisioning of access rights for finance users. Thus, it should be possible to capture the audit trail of access and to provide the ability to report on audit trails, compliance checking, and violation management to allow faster response to external regulations.

Budgeting, Intercompany, and Consolidation

It was mandated by the CFO that budgets must be defined in the finance systems and enforced during operational activities to control costs and expense. It was also decided that manual processes of consolidation among group companies must be automated, with intercompany entries to be eliminated automatically during consolidation. The system should be able to easily adapt as the organizational structure becomes significantly more complex for consolidations. If new businesses are acquired, those acquired entities should be consolidated quickly without having to be immediately operationally integrated. Consolidated reporting should be possible under multiple accounting bases (that is, US GAAP, UK GAAP, IFRS, and so on). Further, consolidated reporting must be possible under multiple reporting currencies as required.

Fast Close of GL Periods

The system should allow a faster close process while adding more control and automation to the various GAAP submissions and consolidation for group reporting. The system should provide integrity, transparency, auditability, and reduced risk of errors during the period close processes. It should be possible to easily investigate numbers, review and compare results across periods, and reconcile back to source systems as applicable.

Financial Reporting and Dashboards

The bank has been deprived of a centralized financial system that provides reporting dashboards and analytic capabilities. Therefore, the new finance system must have state-of-the-art reporting with dashboards and analytics. Not only must the reports available to the users be secured for access, but the data presented within those reports must be secured by roles as well. The users should also be able to build a dashboard by themselves using the catalog of data sources available to them.

Summary

In this chapter we provided a high-level overview of why a Financial Transformation project has been initiated in ACME Bank. We have also explained why Oracle Fusion Financials was the chosen product to address the problems faced by the bank in financial reporting and governance. Finally, we explained the high-level scope of the Financial Transformation project initiated by the bank while explaining how it addresses the key pain points of the bank for finance operations.

Subsequent chapters will detail the features in Oracle Fusion Financials and how they are implemented in Phase 1 of the project, which is highlighted in this chapter.

CHAPTER
2

Introduction to General Ledger and Fusion Accounting Hub

Oracle Fusion Financials is a product family within the Fusion Applications suite and it consists of products and applications such as General Ledger (GL), Receivables, Payables, Assets, and Cash Management. In addition to the products from the Financials product family, Oracle Fusion Applications can interface financial data and perform accounting integration with other Oracle and non-Oracle systems using a product called Fusion Accounting Hub (FAH). There is far more to FAH than just accounting integration capability; for instance, using FAH can help organizations to efficiently standardize accounting feeds from third-party systems and provide real-time consolidated reporting and analytics, all in one place out of the box.

Since this book focuses primarily on GL and FAH, their capabilities and features will be covered in great detail throughout the book, and in this chapter we'll provide only a brief introduction to some key functional and technical concepts frequently used and referenced in Fusion Applications. This chapter can be read independently from the rest of the book, and we'll introduce some of the language frequently used in the world of Oracle Applications, which we hope should benefit the readers with little or no previous exposure to it. The examples that we use in this chapter are generic, simple, and are not connected directly with the implementation use case from the financial industry as described in the rest of the book. In fact, in this chapter we describe basic concepts using receivables and payables business processes, something that most people can easily relate to.

Overview of General Ledger (GL)

General Ledger in Oracle applications is traditionally defined as a main repository of accounting information. In accounting textbooks and other resources, an often-quoted definition of accounting is "the process of identifying, measuring, and communicating economic information to permit informed judgments and decisions by users of the information."

The key thing to notice in this definition is that accounting is not confined to one particular event, but is a continuous process of capturing, recording, manipulating, and reporting of accounting information and business transactions. An example of such a process is activities and transactions related to Accounts Payable (AP), where invoices for purchased goods and services from suppliers are received by a company or an organization and need to be accounted for, processed, and posted to AP Subledger and General Ledger. The examples of other processes in which transactions ultimately are posted into General Ledger are accounting for Fixed Assets transactions (for example, cost of assets, depreciation, profit or loss on sale, all posted to GL) and Accounts Receivables (AR) transactions that mainly deal with invoices we send to customers for our goods and services provided to them (sales analysis and receipts posted to GL, for example).

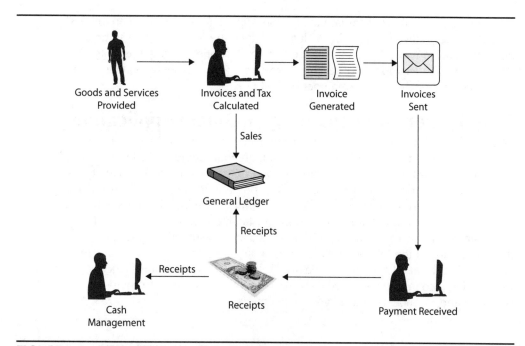

FIGURE 2-1. *Processing invoices in Accounts Receivables*

Let us take a further look at how business transactions that need to be accounted for flow using an Accounts Receivables example to process customer invoices. Figure 2-1 provides an illustration of such a process.

For example, goods can be ordered in the Order Management application and invoice values automatically calculated based on product type and quantity entered. Tax could also be calculated based on the customer profile held in the Receivables application and interfaced into the General Ledger along with debit and sales amounts. Likewise, when we receive payment for provided goods and/or services, the payments are usually matched to invoices, and the payment details, known as receipts, are interfaced to General Ledger.

General Ledger keeps varying levels of information about conducted business transactions. In our example, we would typically send the totals and summary data rather than invoice details such as individual invoice lines to General Ledger. Generally, the detail part of the accounting data is kept in subledgers. A *subledger* is a ledger that resides outside of the general ledger. The Accounts Receivable account is an example of a summary account, also known as a control account in General Ledger. Nonetheless, the balances and totals in General Ledger's control accounts should match those in subledgers when reporting financial statements.

Later in this book we'll explain the Fusion Applications reporting capabilities and how to drill down into the individual and detail transactions from summary accounts. For now, we'll continue to use simple illustrations using Accounts Receivable as an example in order to introduce some fundamental concepts that will be used throughout the remainder of the book.

Introduction of Accounting in Oracle Applications

At a very high level, one of the main aims of accounting is to gather information and data of economic interest and to make it available to individuals, institutions, and regulatory bodies for analysis, reporting, or other purposes. There are many types of reports that target different types of users like company managers and executives, auditors, and business analysts, but the most common are income statement (profit and loss or P&L statement) and balance sheet (statement of financial position).

Business transaction data is recorded in ledgers and subledgers using accounts that can be any of the following basic types: asset, liability, equity, revenue, and expense. The list of all accounts made available for recording of transactions grouped by account type is called the *chart of accounts*. Table 2-1 provides a summary and examples of basic types of accounts.

Type of Account	Description	Examples
Asset	What the business owns.	Equipment, machinery, receivables, cash, office building, inventory.
Liability	Something a business owes to other parties, like cash or other resources.	Loans, bank overdraft, taxes, payables to employees, payables to suppliers.
Equity	What the business is worth after liabilities are deducted from the assets.	Shareholders' equity and capital, retained earnings, revaluation surpluses.
Revenue	What a business earns from sales and other gains.	Income from goods and products, income from services, interest on a bank deposit, rent money received on commercial property lease.
Expense	What a business spends.	Interest on borrowing, salaries, costs of marketing, administrative and utility expenses.

TABLE 2-1. *Types of Accounts*

Basic Accounting Concepts

This book is by no means meant to teach the art of accounting, but merely to provide an overview of some really essential accounting concepts that will lead into a discussion of how these concepts are technically implemented in the context of Fusion Applications. With that said, here is an outline of some fundamental ideas using as an example business transactions that occur in Account Receivables.

In a double-entry accounting system, every transaction has two effects, known as Debit (Dr) and Credit (Cr), and for every Dr entry there is going to be an equal Cr entry that will be posted into a subledger or general ledger. Debits and credits are posted to the ledger as journal lines (entries) into the accounts, which could belong to any of the account types mentioned in the previous section: assets, liabilities, equity, expenses, or revenue. There is a specific set of rules that govern how account balances are affected depending on the account type. The rules are shown in Table 2-2.

Notice that in Table 2-2, each account has a normal balance, which means that to increase the value of an account with a normal balance of credit, we would credit the account or post an entry in the ledger flagged as credit.

Now we can write the ledger-balancing formula:

1   Assets + Expenses = Liabilities + Equity + Revenue
2   Debits = Credits

The accounts on the left side of the equation (1) have a normal balance of debit, while the accounts on the right side have a normal balance of credit. The left side of the equation (2) must be equal to the right side.

Other notable formulas that express profitability of a business are

3   Assets − Liabilities = Equity
4   Income − Expense = Profit (or Loss)

Obviously, one would want assets to exceed liabilities so that we own more than we owe. Likewise, we would like for our business to be profitable: therefore, income should be larger than expenses.

Account Type	Normal Balance	Account Balance Debit	Account Balance Credit
Asset	Debit	Increases	Decreases
Liability	Credit	Decreases	Increases
Equity	Credit	Decreases	Increases
Revenue	Credit	Decreases	Increases
Expense	Debit	Increases	Decreases

TABLE 2-2.   *Rules for Debit and Credit Applications to Ledger Accounts*

An Example: Applying the Accounting Principles to the Receivables Subledger

Remember that the General Ledger typically records a summary or aggregate level of information in control accounts received from subledgers such as Accounts Receivable. We'll now demonstrate how business transactions are recorded on the subledger level using a couple of examples that we can easily relate to.

Accounts Receivable is an asset account in General Ledger and it represents what someone else owes to you. For example, when we invoice a customer, we create a receivable, and through it we track what is owed to us. On the other hand, when we purchase office equipment from suppliers on credit, we create a payable to enable us to track what we owe to that supplier. Payable is a Liability type of account. Once we get paid by our customer, the receivable disappears and the Cash Balance increases; therefore, the receivable represents the expectation of getting paid and converting it into another asset, which is most often cash.

If we recall the ledger-balancing formula (1) from the previous section, assets that are on the left side of the equation need to be in balance with something, and that something is a revenue account, which offsets the receivable. Revenue can be booked as income before we receive the cash from our customer and represents the expectation of what are we about to earn or have already earned for our goods and services. Note that tax and other fees applicable that are owed to us are also tracked by the receivable. Figure 2-2 shows three sample transactions using T-Accounts notation to represent ledger journal entries to create, credit, and pay the invoice.

1. When we invoice the customer for $2400 inclusive of tax, we debit $2400 in the Receivables account and credit Revenue and Tax so that debits are equal to credits for this transaction. Since the balance of the revenue account is positive, we know that someone owes us money and we haven't received the cash for provided goods and/or services yet.

2. Suppose that our customer returned half of our goods and demanded that we credit the invoice proportionally. When we credit the invoice, we credit $1200 in Receivables, which will decrease the total receivables balance by half and debit Revenue and Tax accounts to decrease their balance correspondingly.

3. The invoice is paid for the full amount of the remaining $1200. At this stage we enter a receipt for payment and increase the balance of the Unapplied account by crediting $1200 to it. The Cash account also increases its balance by debiting $1200 as it belongs to the Assets type of accounts.

4. After applying the receipt to the invoice by debiting $1200 to the Unapplied account, the Receivable account balance is also decreased by debiting $1200 to it, which brings its balance to zero, representing that there is no outstanding amount to be paid.

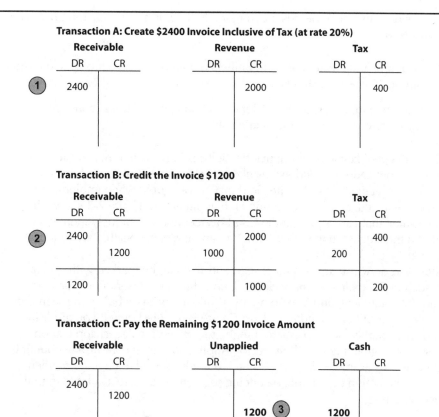

FIGURE 2-2. *Example of receivables transactions*

Ledger Accounts in Oracle Applications

Oracle Fusion Applications is an enterprise class of application software that has to represent General Ledger accounts, accounting rules, and other aspects of financial accounting in such a way as to be very flexible and convenient to configure, set up, and customize in a wide variety of scenarios. For example, every company or organization has its own Chart of Accounts that has to be reflected in accounting software.

Oracle Fusion Applications use the Accounting Flexfield structure to represent and uniquely identify the ledger accounts. But what is a flexfield? From the user interface perspective, a *flexfield* is a configurable field on an application's page that allows users to

- Structure and create unique identifiers required by a specific Oracle Fusion application (key flexfields)

- Capture and display additional information about business entities (descriptive and extensible flexfields)

The concept of key and descriptive flexfields is borrowed from E-Business Suite, and Fusion Applications added extensible flexfields into the mix. An Accounting Flexfield is a specific type of key flexfield that is configured when implementing Oracle General Ledger and Accounting Hub applications. Figure 2-3 shows the example value that can appear in the Chart of Accounts to uniquely identify an account in the ledger along with its structure and the elements that are required to create it.

The Chart of Accounts consists of segments that can be marked with special labels such as Balancing (Primary, Second, and Third), Cost Centre, Natural Account, Management, and Intercompany. While the primary balancing segment and natural account are mandatory, Cost Centre is required only if you are using specific functionality like depreciation in the Oracle Fusion Assets application. These special segment labels allow Fusion Applications to accomplish accounting functionality, for example, ensuring that all journals for each balancing segment value or combination of multiple balancing segment values are available in trial balance reporting.

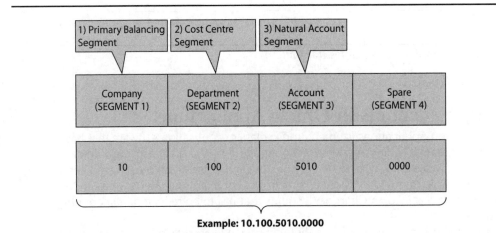

FIGURE 2-3. *Example value from a chart of accounts*

Segments have value sets attached to them, which allows values like "10" for company, "100" for department, and "5010" for natural accounts to be associated with them. In our example in Figure 2-3, we also have a spare segment for potential future use that can be used with the default value "0000". The numbers in this example can have associated meanings, like 10 for Oracle FR and 20 for Oracle UK, 100 for Support and 110 for Human Resources departments, 5010 for Consulting Income, 5105 for Support Renewal, and so forth.

To summarize, 10.100.5010.000 is a particular dot (.)-separated code combination, which in our example, could represent Oracle UK (Company).Support(Department) .Consulting Income Account(Revenue Natural Account).Spare(Spare Segment for Future Use). This code combination is effectively a user-defined composite key that is recorded in the GL_CODE_COMBINATIONS database table, and it is uniquely identified by the value in column CODE_COMBINATION_ID. In turn, this unique composite key can be referenced in many places in Fusion Applications, and it will always be linked with this particular account combination.

An adequate Chart of Accounts design is one of the key implementation activities when configuring General Ledger. The selection of the number of segments, their labels, and associated value sets will determine the granularity of financial reporting capabilities. The primary purpose of ledgers is to track balances in various accounts, and it is up to us to decide the level of detail posted to the General Ledger unless this is dictated by out-of-the-box functionality of other applications that post to it.

The following list summarizes the steps to implement the Chart of Accounts in Fusion Applications:

- Create value sets with no values associated.

- Create the Chart of Accounts structure and designate segment labels.

- Create a Chart of Accounts instance from the structure created in the previous step.

- Create value set values and designate mandatory attributes.

The book will deal in detail with all of the mentioned steps in further chapters, including some additional steps often required to meet the business requirements in a typical enterprise, including the creation of account hierarchies, security rules for segment values, and cross-validation rules. Also, configuration of financial reporting structures is incomplete without setting up calendars and currencies, but this will also be covered when we provide steps to set up ledgers in Fusion Applications.

NOTE
The concept of Chart of Accounts in Fusion Applications is slightly different from the concept in E-Business Suite R12. In Fusion Applications, we first need to design and create a Chart of Accounts structure, which we can think of as a template for multiple other Chart of Accounts instances that share the same structure but differ in some detail to meet the business goals. Also, in E-Business Suite, there is one balancing segment and secondary tracking segment, while in Fusion Applications there are up to three balancing segments.

Overview of Fusion Accounting Hub

Fusion Accounting Hub (FAH) is a collection of software components, applications, and tools that facilitates financial management, reporting, and analytical needs. From a product implementation perspective, it is one of the two offerings predefined for financial implementations, and it includes General Ledger, a Subledger Accounting component, Allocations Manager, and a number of reporting and analytics tools, such as Financial Reporting Center, Oracle Transactional Business Intelligence, Business Intelligence Publisher, Smart View, and others.

Fusion Accounting Hub fulfills two major functions and capabilities:

- As a financial integration platform, it is designed to integrate with non-Fusion systems and external feeds. The transaction data is treated by centrally defined accounting policies and rules in FAH by business users.

- As a financial reporting platform, FAH leverages standard General Ledger reports, custom Business Intelligence dashboards, and use of supporting references to reconcile accounting between the source system and what is derived in FAH.

NOTE
The integration feature of FAH is only available in on-premise deployment at the time of writing this book. The reporting FAH features are available both on-premise and on the cloud (software-as-a-service or SaaS deployment), and there is packaged integration from E-Business Suite and PeopleSoft General Ledger, but other data can also be brought in.

In the sections that follow, we'll provide some more background information about the key benefits of using a product like FAH and the key technology enablers that make it all happen.

Benefits of Using FAH

As we mentioned earlier, FAH is a central place that provides control and visibility of all accounting rules, not only for the third-party financial transaction data feeds, but also for Fusion modules like Fusion Payables and Fusion Receivables, for example. It is easy to understand why this matters in today's world of ever-increasing regulatory pressures on organizations, where accounting rules are often buried and hard-coded within in-house–built legacy systems and spreadsheets with little and sometimes no control and visibility. In this situation, the capability to react quickly when accounting rules need to change is typically very difficult to achieve due to mandated and often heavy involvement of IT departments that typically support the legacy systems in the first place.

In FAH, the introduction of new rules and changes to the existing accounting rules can be achieved by business users themselves through the application's user interface. The "Subledger Accounting" functionality, which automatically creates accounting entries for transactions (both Fusion and non-Fusion) is not a new concept in Oracle Applications, and it existed, and still does, in Oracle E-Business Suite R12. However, the setup and configuration in Fusion Applications is simplified through a single user interface called "Journal Entry Rule Set," which defines how a journal entry is generated for a specific accounting event that occurs in the source system. It is true that some involvement from IT may still be required, especially when setting up transaction objects and such, but the role of technical IT departments and therefore dependency on them is considerably reduced. The accounting rules are migrated from development and test to production instance using the export function, which allows for a relatively simple transition from one environment to another.

Fusion Accounting Hub also provides drill-down and reporting features that allow you to link General Ledger account balances with individual transactions in subledgers that contributed to them. The importance of the drill-down functionality is evident when there is a requirement to reconcile GL balances, but GL itself doesn't have the detailed individual transactions that contributed to the balances posted to it. Fast identification of anomalies and outliers helps finance managers perform efficient control and reduces the risk of lengthy investigation when balances in FAH GL do not equate to transaction totals in corresponding subledgers.

Another important feature in FAH is the capability to configure and capture supporting references for the financial transactions. Supporting references keep additional information that pertains to the source system. This can occur on either the header or line level for the subledger journal entries. There is an option to maintain balances for the supporting references; for example, the trading department of the

ACME Bank may want to capture "Trade Type" and "Client" information and assign the corresponding two segments to a journal line. Balances are automatically generated for each combination of given accounts, trade type (for example, FOREX, ETF, Bonds) and client (bank's customers on whose behalf the bank executed trades). This is very handy when you want to reconcile accounting with source systems and report on dimensions that are not defined in the Chart of Accounts.

TIP
Think of supporting references as a tagging mechanism that marks journal entries with additional attributes to help link them back to the source system's entries.

Last but not least, we'd like to highlight the fact that most of the information is organized and presented through the use of dashboards such as the General Accounting Dashboard where GL accounts are analyzed in one place using native multidimensional reporting in real time, which is the result of incorporation of Hyperion tools and technologies into Fusion Applications. For example, the Account Monitor that is embedded into the General Accounting Dashboard allows users to set account threshold alerts, and when they are exceeded, they will pop up on the dashboard, and from the dashboard, we can perform analysis and drill-down into the individual transactions.

Key Technology Enablers

Oracle's middleware and database technologies used in Fusion Applications are covered in some detail in *Oracle Fusion Applications Development & Extensibility Handbook* (McGraw-Hill Education/Oracle Press, 2014). Here we are going to provide a brief summary of some of the key components of the technology stack used to build Fusion Accounting Hub and General Ledger.

The technical applications architecture that enables pivot and drill to any level of financial data is based on a best-of-breed relational (Oracle Database) and multidimensional Hyperion Essbase at the database or back-end tier. The core Subledger Accounting (SLA) data and processing model is based on E-Business Suite R12, while the concept of date-effective hierarchies is taken from PeopleSoft applications that allow multiple hierarchies with different dates to be used against the same data for analysis purposes. Hyperion Essbase provides real-time aggregation and interactive reporting capability through the Smart View tool. Also from Hyperion, FAH Allocation Manager borrows the use of Hyperion's Calculation Manager for mass allocations, even across multiple ledgers.

Relational OLTP and Multidimensional OLAP Technologies Working Together

During the General Ledger configuration, an Essbase cube is created when you create an instance of a Chart of Accounts and ledger. The end user doesn't need to do anything; this is all done behind the scenes, and the dimensions of the General Ledger cube are segments of the Chart of Accounts, calendar, ledger and ledger sets, currency, balance type, and currency type.

Every time a journal is posted, the GL cube, including aggregations, is updated in real time. The posting program ensures that balances in the Oracle relational table GL_BALANCES are kept in sync with what is in the Essbase cube. You may wonder what happens when a new segment value is added to the segment in the chart of accounts, which is recorded in the relational model as per the old E-Business Suite data model, and the answer is that the posting program will automatically launch a Chart of Accounts maintenance job to synchronize the missing values in the cube.

The whole posting process is conceptualized as a two-phase commit in which the program waits for the commit on the Essbase GL cube to be successful, and only after that, a transaction is committed in Oracle Database to update the relational GL_BALANCES table and set journal status to "posted." In case of failure, the transaction is rolled back and nothing gets posted.

Reporting Technology Enablers

Fusion Financials offer an extensive number of tools to meet various levels of reporting needs, from boardroom-ready financial and statutory reports all the way down to account monitoring with drill-down to individual transactions.

From a technology perspective, most of the reporting capabilities in Fusion Financials are coming from Hyperion and Oracle Business Intelligence Enterprise Edition (OBIEE) products. They are seamlessly integrated with the technology stack and form an integral part of it. The type of reporting and analytics tools you are going to find in Fusion Financials are Financial Reports that work off the Essbase GL balances cube and are built with Oracle Hyperion Financial Reporting Studio, Business Intelligence Publisher (BIP), Smart View for Excel-based slice-and-dice analysis of GL balances in Essbase cube, and Oracle Transactional Business Intelligence (OTBI) that allow real-time queries directly against Oracle Fusion product tables. OTBI is based on the Oracle Business Intelligence Enterprise Edition (Oracle BI EE) reporting platform, and it allows us to build our own reports and ad hoc queries using the OBIEE tool and subject areas delivered with Fusion Financials.

Fusion Middleware Core Components

Apart from Oracle Database Server and Oracle Hyperion Essbase, Oracle Fusion Middleware components provide the main infrastructure foundation to Fusion Applications and its product families like Fusion Financials. For example, Oracle

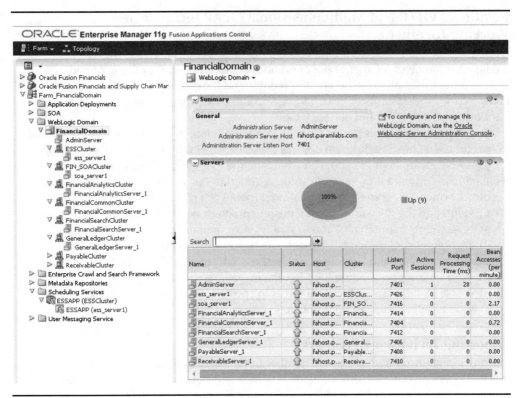

FIGURE 2-4. *Fusion Financials WebLogic Domain*

WebLogic Server is where applications and products are deployed, managed, and monitored. Figure 2-4 illustrates the structure of Fusion Financials domain (FinancialsDomain). In WebLogic Application Server terminology, the domains are logical groupings of WebLogic Server instances for administration and configuration purposes.

Readers with an E-Business Suite background will notice that some of the components like ess_server1 (Enterprise Service Scheduler server) and soa_server1 (SOA Server) that provide corresponding job execution time scheduling, similar to concurrent processing and workflow functionality in E-Business Suite, are bundled together with Financials Domain and are not shared with other application "pillars" like Human Capital Management (HCM) or Customer Relationship Management (CRM).

Summary

In this chapter we provided a very high-level overview of some of the key concepts relevant to Fusion General Ledger and Fusion Accounting Hub applications such as the difference between ledgers and subledgers, representation of Chart of Accounts in Oracle Applications, and a simple example of what kind of summary data like account balances is recorded in General Ledger. We also talked about some of the key benefits of Fusion Accounting Hub and highlighted its financial governance, integration, and reporting capabilities.

Fusion Applications are software components, after all, and we also briefly mentioned the role of some of the technology enablers like Hyperion Essbase, which aggregates GL balances and allows real-time reports and analytics to be run against that data.

Further chapters will provide concrete configuration and product setup based on the illustrative scenario outlined in Chapter 1.

CHAPTER
3

Implementation Project Plan Using Functional Setup Manager

The purpose of this chapter is to give you all essential information so that you can understand how the Functional Setup Manager (FSM) module can be used to plan, implement, track, report, and migrate implementation of Fusion applications. The FSM concepts discussed in this chapter are common for all Fusion-related applications, like Fusion Financials, Fusion Accounting Hub, Oracle Fusion Human Capital Management, Oracle Fusion Supply Chain Management, Oracle Fusion Project Portfolio Management, Oracle Fusion Customer Relationship Management, and Oracle Fusion Procurement. In Fusion, these applications are also known as *business solutions* or *offerings*, and readers can learn more about the functionality provided within each offering from the Getting Started page in FSM.

Functional Setup Manager

Oracle Functional Setup Manager (FSM) is a new module within Oracle Fusion that allows the project team to manage planning, configuration, implementation, deployment, and ongoing maintenance of Oracle Fusion Applications. FSM provides the following key advantages:

- **Self-service administration** FSM provides implementers with the Self-Service Portal to help identify the setup tasks based on project scope and also help to assign and track tasks by Business Users.

- **Centralized configuration for quick setup** Users familiar with earlier versions of Oracle E-Business Suite (11i, Release 12) will understand that FSM eliminates the need to switch between multiple modules for setup-related tasks and instead provides a single entry point to configure all Fusion Applications.

- **Comprehensive reporting** FSM has built-in reporting to track progress of the implementation tasks, and each task can be assigned to one or more task owners with start and end dates for completion of the task.

- **Pre-seeded and extensible setup task list** FSM has the ability to autogenerate setup tasks based on the business requirements, and it provides a streamlined approach to complete the setup tasks.

- **Export and import of setup data** FSM has a feature to migrate setup data from one instance to another instance, thus reducing the time and cost required to implement the system.

In this chapter, we will begin with explaining the FSM key concepts, such as Offerings, Options, and Features, that allow implementers to enable system functionality based on business requirements, followed by an explanation of the Functional Setup process. Next, we will look at the different roles and responsibilities defined within FSM, such as Project Managers, System Administrators, and Functional Users. Understanding these roles and responsibilities will be vital in order to align these roles to the Implementation Project team. Next, we will see how you can use the Setup And Maintenance work area to create an Implementation Project plan, which will generate a setup task list for configuring the Fusion General Ledger and Fusion Accounting Hub. We will also demonstrate how the Setup And Maintenance work area provides the facility to assign tasks to a project team and track progress. We will also see how we can easily migrate the setup data (also known as configuration packages in FSM terminology) across different instances such as Functional Prototype Workshop Instance, otherwise known as Conference Room Pilot (CRP), Development, Application Test, System Integration Test, User Acceptance Test (UAT), and Production within the Project Implementation lifecycle. At the end of this chapter, you will find additional useful information about the Financials Rapid Implementation task list for Cloud based implementation.

NOTE
Oracle Unified Method (OUM) Cloud Application Services Implementation Approach is Oracle's lightweight approach for Implementing applications running on a cloud infrastructure. It emphasizes an out-of-box approach and adaption of best practices inherent in the application products as a foundation element of the approach. OUM provides guidelines, templates, and a work breakdown structure for planning and executing the Fusion Implementations. Readers should note that this chapter only covers FSM and its related processes and doesn't cover the OUM implementation approach; however, certain activities in OUM will be performed using FSM. Also, readers should be aware that references to Implementation Project plan, its phase, processes, and related tasks mentioned are within the context of FSM only.

Setup And Maintenance Work Area

FSM is accessed through the Setup And Maintenance work area. Figure 3-1 shows the Setup And Maintenance work area and key links used during this phase of the implementation.

The steps to access the Setup And Maintenance area of FSM are as follows:

1. Access your Oracle Fusion Applications Home page by using the Universal Resource Locator (URL).

   The typical URL format would be https://<hostname>:<port>/homePage. Example: https://fahost:10643/homePage.

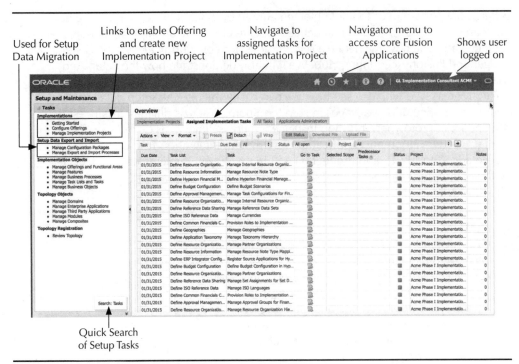

Used for Setup Data Migration — Links to enable Offering and create new Implementation Project — Navigate to assigned tasks for Implementation Project — Navigator menu to access core Fusion Applications — Shows user logged on

Quick Search of Setup Tasks

FIGURE 3-1. *The Setup And Maintenance area*

2. Sign in using the user account and password provided by system administrators. You will be prompted to reset the password if you are signing in to the Fusion Applications instance for the first time.

3. Access the Setup And Maintenance area as follows:

   a. Go to Navigator | More | Tools | Setup And Maintenance.

   b. On the Overview page, click the All Tasks tab.

   c. Search for the tasks by entering the name in the search field.

   d. In the search results, perform the task by clicking its Go To Task icon.

Key Concepts and Terminology Used in FSM

Figure 3-2 provides a graphic view of the key concepts and their relationships.

■ **Offerings** Fusion Offerings are application solution sets representing one or more business processes and subprocesses that are typically provisioned (installed) and implemented as a unit. They are primary drivers of the functional setup of Oracle Fusion Applications. Some examples of Offerings

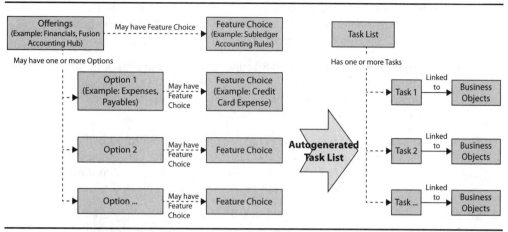

FIGURE 3-2. *FSM key concepts and their relationships*

are Financials, Financials Accounting Hub, Procurement, Sales, Marketing, and Workforce Management. If readers are familiar with older versions of Oracle E-Business Suite, Offerings can be considered logical groupings of different modules within the product family. For example, Financials Offerings includes modules like General Ledger, Accounts Payables, Fixed Assets, Accounts Receivables, Advanced Collections, and Internet Expenses. In Fusion, Offerings are modeled with respect to business process, which seems logical because Enterprise Resource Planning Software is implemented to meet the business process requirement rather than individual modules in silos.

A Fusion Offering may have one or more Options and/or Features:

■ **Options**   Each Fusion Offering in general includes a set of standard functionality and set of Optional Modules, which are called Options. These optional functionalities may not be relevant for all Fusion Applications implementations. For example, in addition to core Fusion General Ledger, Financials (Offering) provides Options like Payables, Expenses, Fixed Assets, Receivables, Collections, Intercompany, and so on.

■ **Features**   Features are optional or alternative business rules or processes within Options. For example, if you are implementing Fusion Expenses and require the ability to process Corporate Credits expenses for employees, then you can enable a feature to handle Corporate Cards within Expenses. This allows FSM to generate tasks related to setting up the Corporate Credit Cards functionality. Based on the feature, the user can be provided with one of the following selection choices:

■ **Yes/No**   A single check box is presented to allow the user to make a particular feature applicable or not applicable to an implementation.

- **Single Select** If a feature has multiple choices but only one is applicable, then multiple choices will be presented as a radio button. Users will be able to turn on only one of those choices.

- **Multiple Select** If a feature has multiple choices but one or more can be applicable to an implementation, then all the choices will be presented with a check box. Users will select all that applies by checking the appropriate check box or boxes.

- **Task List And Tasks** Tasks are individual setup steps performed within the Offerings, Options, and Features. The Task List is a logical grouping of tasks. As shown in Figure 3-1, Task List And Task will be auto generated during the Implementation project creation process based on selected offerings.

- **Business Objects** Business objects are a broader terminology used to represent setup data. They are a logical representation of real-world objects. Some of the examples are Ledgers, Business Units, Legal Entities, Taxes, Items, Orders, Opportunities, Campaign, Employees, and so on. Each task is associated with an underlying business object. For example, a Manage Legal Entity task will have a Legal Entity business object associated with it. This link is subsequently used for export and import of setup data from one application instance to another.

Functional Setup Manager Process Flow

FSM provides a well-structured setup process flow for implementing Oracle Fusion Applications. It provides six distinct processes or stages: Plan, Configure, Implement, Export/Import, Transact, and Maintain. Figure 3-3 shows how each of these Implementation processes or stages can be accessed within the Setup And Maintenance Work Area.

Plan

The Plan stage is the first stage of any Fusion Applications implementation. In this phase, we analyze the high-level requirements of the business and understand which offerings are required to meet the business needs. Typically, input for this stage would be requirements documents and future state business processes generated during the analysis phase of the overall project plan. The output of this phase would be finalization of the list of Offerings, Features, and Options to meet the requirements and business process. At this stage, we should also be able to identify both the interfaces that need to be built to integrate third-party systems with Fusion Applications and extensions that need to be developed to extend the product functionality.

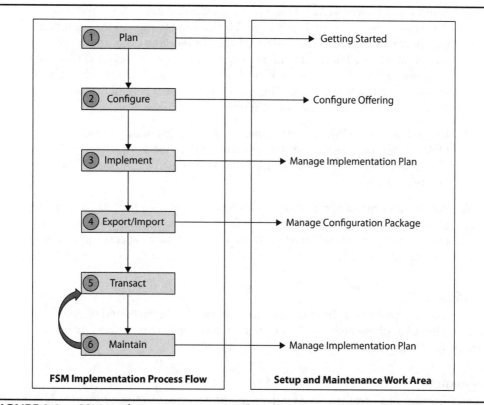

FIGURE 3-3. *FSM implementation process flow and Setup And Maintenance work area mapping*

Under each offering, there are certain pre packaged reports that provide further details about each offering. These reports can be accessed through the Getting Started link, and the following section provides introduction to these reports.

- **Offering Content Guide**   This document provides a list of business processes and product features covered as part of each offering. This is a good starting point for evaluating and understanding the capabilities of the Oracle Fusion Applications. It will help the users to finalize the offerings that need to be implemented.

- **Associated Features**   This report provides a listing of options and features for the offering. The report can be used for detailed application configuration and aid in making decisions about which features and options should be enabled.

- **Setup Task List And Tasks** This report provides a setup task list and tasks that need to be performed for Fusion Application configuration. The report also provides information about mandatory or required tasks and other conditional tasks that need to be performed based on the selected Offering, Features, and Options. We can identify the underlying business object used for each of the setup task lists. This report will be also helpful to understand the interdependency of different offerings.

- **Related Business Objects** This report provides a list of all Business Objects that the offering uses for functional setup and transactions tasks. This report will also help to identify what setup data need to be gathered by Business Users.

- **Related Enterprise Applications** This report provides a listing of enterprise applications that the offering requires for functional setup and transaction tasks. This report would be useful to understand how to access individual applications directly.

Configure

In this stage, we enable the Offerings and their associated features and options based on the plan phase analysis. This is more of a system-driven setup process to start the implementation.

Implement

In this stage, we first create the Implementation Project by selecting or including one or more offerings we have enabled in the Configure phase. FSM will automatically generate a comprehensive list of setup tasks based on the selected offerings and options. Users have additional control to add or remove tasks to/from the Implementation Project. Each task can be assigned to one or more Functional Users or Implementation Consultants (who are responsible for configuring the system as per the Business Requirement), and progress can be tracked against the due date and monitored with task status. The Go To Task link will provide access to individual setup tasks where setup data is entered.

Export and Import

FSM provides a facility to export and import setup data from one instance to another using configuration packages. A *configuration package* is the combined unit of an Implementation Project and its related setup data. A configuration package contains the Setup Import/Export Definition (list of setup tasks and their associated Logical Business Objects), as well as the Exported Setup data. At first when a configuration package is created, only the Setup Import/Export Definition is created. Once the configuration package is exported, appropriate setup data are added to the configuration package using the definition. Once a configuration package is exported, its setup export/import definition is locked and cannot be changed. FSM allows the ability to filter setup data to assist row-level migration in using Scope Parameter; however, it is enabled only for certain Logical Business Objects like Ledgers, Business Units, Legal Entities, and Subledger Applications.

Transact
This stage represents the production/Go Live phase where businesses start using the Fusion Application.

Maintain
This stage represents the Post-Production Support phase where ongoing maintenance of setup data is performed. Users can either query individual tasks to perform the setup change or create a separate Implementation Project. It is recommended that if the setup change is minor, like adding a list of values or changing a profile option, it can easily be accomplished by querying the individual task. However, if the tasks involve a larger scope and higher risk, like adding a new Tax Regime, rollout of new business, and so on, it is recommended to create a separate Implementation Project and add relevant setup tasks.

Users of Functional Setup Manager
Three categories or types of Application users will access the Setup And Maintenance area in FSM.

Implementation Project Managers
Implementation Project Managers are responsible for overall delivery of the Fusion Applications and making sure that the Oracle Fusion Applications are ready for transactions processing. Their responsibilities will include the following:

- Research and analyze which offerings need to be configured to meet the business requirement.

- Create an Implementation Project plan and generate setup tasks that need to be performed.

- Assign tasks to users who will perform the setup for resource allocation purposes.

- Closely monitor the progress of the tasks for purposes of time reporting, forecasting, and budgeting.

Implementation Consultants and Functional Users

Implementation Consultants are responsible for the initial configuration of Oracle Applications. They work alongside functional users to set up the system as per business requirements. Functional Users, known as Business Users, are Subject Matter Experts within each functional area/offering, and they also represent the various support organizations or functions within a company like Finance, Procurement, Sales, Human Resources, and so on. Together their responsibilities will include

- Configuring the initial Fusion Applications

- Gathering Business Requirements and entering the setup data

- Verifying that the system is working correctly for transaction processing as per business requirements

- Getting involved in a System Readiness program like Training the Business User Community or Knowledge Transfer for a Support Organization.

- Setting up data migration using FSM

System Administrator

System administrators are responsible for technical aspects of the Fusion Applications implementations. Their responsibilities include the following:

- Software installations and applying maintenance patches

- System configurations and registration of new Enterprise Applications

Seeded Roles within Fusion Applications

Oracle has seeded job roles that can be assigned to each type of Application users, as listed in Table 3-1. Please note that Chapter 7 on Security and Audit in Fusion Applications will explain in detail the concepts of different job roles and data roles. However, we will cover here the required job roles to start the implementation of Fusion Financials.

- **The Application Implementation Manager job role** allows you to configure Offerings, Options, and Features and assign resources to tasks. Additionally this job role provides access to manage and monitor Implementation Projects.

Business Application User Type	Seeded Job Role in Fusion Applications
Implementation Project Manager	Application Implementation Manager
Implementation Consultants and Functional Users	Application Implementation Consultant
System Administrators	Application Implementation Administrator IT Security Manager System Administrator

TABLE 3-1. *Seeded Job Roles for Business Application User Type*

■ **The Application Implementation Consultant job role** allows you to manage enterprise-wide Implementations. This job role inherits from all product-specific application administrators and entitles the necessary View All access to all secured objects. As a result, this job role has access to all setup tasks across all products. Optionally, create a data role for an implementation user who needs only the limited access of a product-specific Application Administrator by using the Create Data Role for Implementation Users. Then assign the resulting data role to the implementation user by using the Provision Roles to Implementation Users task.

Creating the ACME Bank Implementation Project

In this section, we will walk through the process and setup steps to create the ACME Bank implementation project.

Create Application Users

For segregation of duty and roles within the ACME Implementation Project, we will assume that there are three Implementation Application users created in the system, as shown in Table 3-2. Please refer to Appendix A to understand how Application Users can be created in the system.

NOTE
The Application user list provided here reflects how a typical implementation would be structured with different logins; however, for education purposes and to simplify the process, you can create a single Application user with the Application Implementation consultant job role to perform the setup tasks mentioned in this book.

#	Fusion Application User	Business Type User	Description
1	XXFA_IMPLEMENTATION_ MANAGER	Application Implementation Manager	Responsible for overall delivery of the project
2	XXFA_FIN_GL_ IMPLEMENTATION_ CONSULTANT	Application Implementation Consultant	Responsible for setting up Fusion Financials Core General Ledger
3	XXFA_FAH_ IMPLEMENTATION_ CONSULTANT	Application Implementation Consultant	Responsible for setting up Fusion Accounting Hub

TABLE 3-2. *ACME Bank Application User Logins*

Plan Phase: Analyze Requirement and Finalize Offerings

As part of the ACME Bank Finance Transformation Strategy, it has been decided that Oracle Fusion Applications will deliver the Centralized Financials System Platform to provide a foundation to address business process pain points and technical pain points (please refer to Table 1-1 in Chapter 1).

The Project team concluded that Core Financials (General Ledger) and Financials Accounting Hub Offerings need to be implemented as part of the Initial Phase 1 Project plan. The high-level rationales for the decision are listed in Table 3-3.

Configure Phase: Enable Offerings

In the Configure phase, we enable Fusion Financials and Fusion Accounting Hub Offerings for Implementation. Setup steps are as follows:

1. Log in as XXFA_IMPLEMENTATION_MANAGER (Implementation Project Manager) Application User.

2. Access the Setup And Maintenance area as follows:

    a. Go to Navigator | Tools | Setup And Maintenance.

    b. Click the Configure Offerings link.

3. Enable the Financials Offering And Associated feature.

    a. Make sure that the Provisioned check box column is Yes.

    b. Select Enable For Implementation For Financials.

Problem Area	Fusion Application Solution
Profitability by line of business	Make "Line of Business" part of the Chart of Accounts structure and use the Multi-Balancing Segment feature of Fusion Financials General Ledger to satisfy this requirement. Chapter 5 will discuss this in detail.
Cash Position	Implement Fusion Cash Management to manage Cash Forecasting and Cash Positioning. This module is out of scope for this book.
Manual processes to meet regulatory requirements and reputational risk	Use the Fusion Subledger Accounting Feature and Fusion General Ledger to account for transactions in different accounting methods (US GAAP, IFRS, UK GAAP) simultaneously to reduce manual processes and enhance data accuracy.
Risk of fraud	Use the RBAC (Role Based Access Control) Feature to restrict access. Chapter 7 will discuss Audit and Security in detail.
Expense and Cost Management	Implement Supplier Invoicing and Payments features to have better control over the supplier costs in Fusion. This module is out of scope for this book.
Lacking features and functionality and expensive IT support	Use cloud-based Oracle Fusion Applications to reduce IT maintenance costs and use best-in-class feature and functionality like Fusion Accounting Hub to integrate third-party applications with the required level of detail without compromising the reporting aspects. Chapter 9 will discuss how to implement Fusion Accounting Hub.

TABLE 3-3. *High-level Rationale for Fusion Application Solution*

    c. Click Select Feature Choice and select the following options:

        ■ Enterprise Structure Guide Flow: *Yes*
        Enables the Enterprise Structures Configurator, which is an interview-based tool that guides you through the process of setting up a basic enterprise structure. Based on your answers to questions about the enterprise, the tool creates a structure of divisions, legal entities, business units, and reference data sets that reflects your enterprise structure.

        ■ Governance, Risk And Compliance: *No*

- Local Installations Of Help: *Yes*

- Maintain Common Reference Objects: *Yes*

- Subledger Accounting Rules: *Maintain Subledger Accounting Application and Accounting Method*

- Application Toolkit Component Maintenance: *Yes*

   d. Click Save And Close.

4. Enable the Financials Accounting Hub Offering And Associated feature.

   a. Make sure that the Provisioned check box column is Yes.

   b. Select Enable For Implementation For Financials Accounting Hub.

   c. Click Select Feature Choice and select the following options:

- Governance, Risk And Compliance: *No*

- Legal Entity Assignments To Accounting Configuration: *No*

- Additional Accounting Representation In Primary Ledger: *Yes*

- Maintain Common Reference Objects: *Yes*

- Local Installations Of Help: *Yes*

- Secondary Ledger Requires Additional Accounting Representation: *No*

- Assign Balancing Segment Values To Legal Entities for Secondary Ledger: *No*

- Accounting Presentation Details: *Currency*

- Enterprise Structure Guided Flow: *Yes*

- Revisit Accounting Configurations: *Yes*

- Application Toolkit Component Maintenance: *Yes*

   d. Click Save And Close.

Figure 3-4 shows the Configure Offerings screen after these setup tasks have been performed.

Here are a few important points to consider while configuring Offerings:

- **Provisioned** Each offering has a separate column called Provisioned. The Provisioned column signifies that the Enterprise Application has been installed and is ready to be configured. Technically, it means registering the Enterprise Application with FSM. This Provisioned status should be set

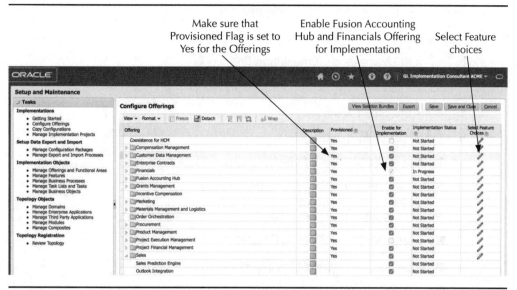

FIGURE 3-4.   *The Configure Offerings screen*

to Yes if you want to implement the particular Fusion Application offerings. FSM doesn't prevent users from configuring offerings that have not been provisioned; however, users will not be able to perform the tasks needed to enter the setup data for the offerings until the Enterprise Applications are provisioned and their locations are registered with FSM. FSM shows a warning message explaining the consequence when the user tries to configure an offering that is not provisioned.

■ **Revisit Offering Page**   FSM provides the ability to revisit the Offering page to enable options later. For example, in the ACME Implementation Project Plan, we have enabled only Core Financials Offerings and Fusion Accounting Hub Offerings. We have opted not to enable subledger options like Payables, Assets, Expenses, and so on, which are part of the Phase II rollout of ACME Finance Transformation. Once an offering has been enabled, it is available for all implementation projects created in the system.

Implement Phase: Create the Implementation Project

In the Implement phase, we create a new Implementation project for Fusion Financials Offering. Setup steps are as follows:

1. Log in as XXFA_IMPLEMENTATION_MANAGER (Implementation Project Manager) Application User.

2. Access the Setup And Maintenance area as follows:

    a. Go to Navigator | Tools | Setup And Maintenance.

    b. Click the Manage Implementation Projects link.

3. Under Manage Implementation Projects section

    a. Click the Create icon.

    b. Enter basic information

        ■ Name: *ACME Phase I Implementation Project*

        ■ Code: *XX_ACME_PHASEI_IMPL_PROJECT*

        ■ Description: *Implementation Project to manage Phase 1 Tasks*

        ■ Status: Not Started (Non-Editable)

        ■ Assigned To: *Defaults User Logged in*

        ■ Start Date: *Current Date*

        ■ End Date: *Current Date + 3 Months*

    c. Click Next.

    d. Under Select Offerings To Implement section, include the following offerings by selecting the check box:

        ■ Financials

    e. Click the Save And Open Project link.

The Implementation Project should have been successfully created with a hierarchy of setup task details as shown in Figure 3-5.

Here are a few important points to consider while creating the Implementation Project:

■ **Setup Task List** Autogenerated task lists are created based on the options and features enabled at the time of creating the Implementation Project. In the ACME Bank Implementation case, we haven't enabled any options like Assets, Expenses, Invoicing, Payments, and so on under Fusion Offerings. So the generated tasks will not have any setup tasks related to features of Supplier Invoicing, Payment, and so forth. However, if we intend to enable the option later, then we need to create a new Implementation Project to generate the tasks related to that newly selected option.

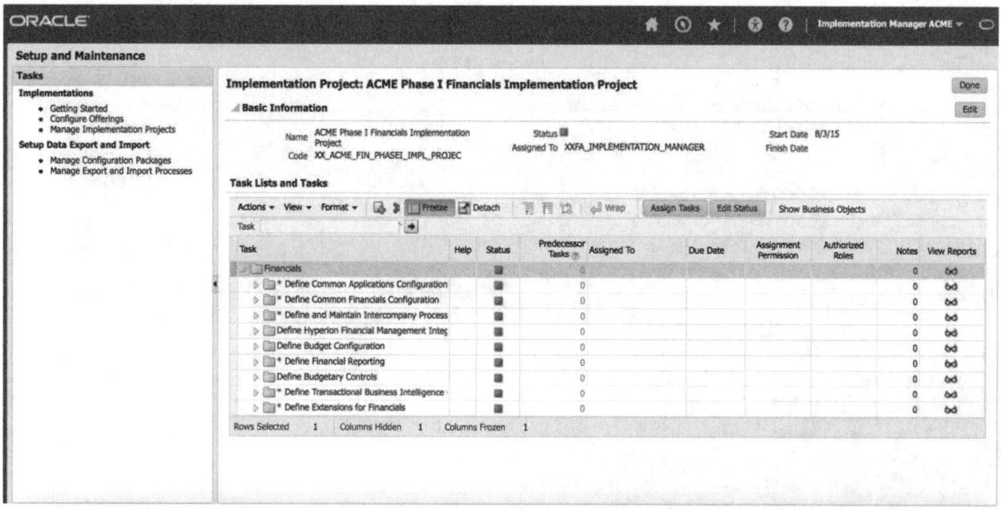

FIGURE 3-5.   *ACME Implementation Project with tasks*

- **Customizing the Implementation Task List**   Users can customize the autogenerated setup task list by adding or removing tasks based on the implementation needs of the business.

- **Assigning Tasks to Users**   Typically a Fusion Implementation Project would involve more than one Implementation Functional Consultant working on different areas of the solution. FSM allows individual tasks or groups of tasks assigned to task owners. The Project Management team will be able to use this task assignment for resource planning and track progress based on project completion date. Each task may have more than one task owner assigned.

In the case of the ACME Bank Implementation, we have created an Implementation User for Financials. The following steps will show how to assign the user to the tasks.

1. Log in as XXFA_IMPLEMENTATION_MANAGER.

2. Navigate to the Manage Implementation Projects link in FSM and click *ACME Phase I Implementation Project* link.

3. Assign all Financials Tasks to the Application User: **XXFA_GL_IMPLEMENTATION CONSULTANT** as shown in Figure 3-6.

Step 1: Select Multiple Tasks using the SHIFT key or Individual Tasks as required.

Step 2: Click Assign Tasks and click Add Icon To Select User.

Step 3: Search Application User and click Apply.

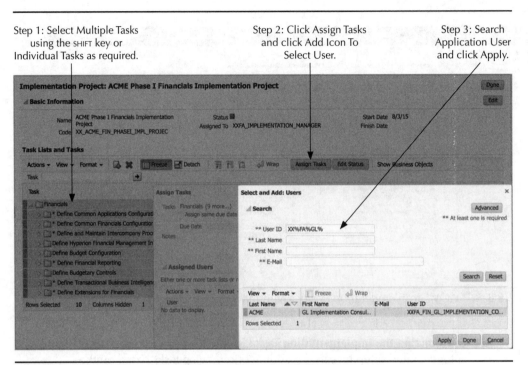

FIGURE 3-6. *Steps to assign tasks to the Application User*

■ **Tasks Status** The Task Owner will be able to periodically update the status of the tasks as progress is made on the setup. Some of the valid statuses are Not Started, In Progress, Completed, and Completed with Errors. FSM allows the user to add comments or notes whenever a status update is made on the task, and it also tracks the version history of the notes added, as shown in Figure 3-7. Status Of Task can be updated using the Edit Status button as shown in Figure 3-7.

■ **Implementation Project without Offering** FSM allows creation of an empty Implementation Project without selecting any offerings. This will be useful if users are using the Implementation Financials through the Rapid Implementation method (explained later in the chapter) or selecting some specific setup tasks for maintenance purposes like Maintenance Project. In both of these cases, the user should manually add the tasks that are required.

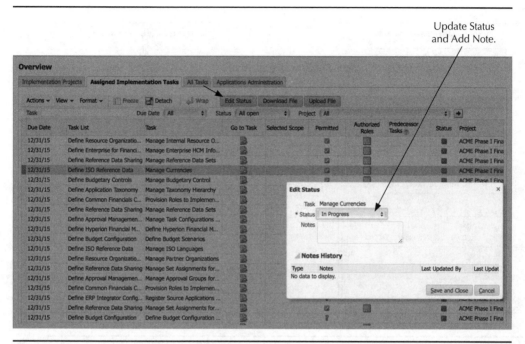

FIGURE 3-7. *Edit Status at task level*

■ **Create one Implementation Project per Offering** The current approach for the usage of FSM recommends creating one Implementation project per Offering for Export and Import of setup data. If an Implementation project is created with multiple offerings where shared business objects are used in multiple offerings, the import sequence defers based on the Offerings, which causes data issues and, as a result, application import fails.

Export and Import Processes of Setup Data

Every Implementation Project has a requirement to move setup data from one instance to another instance. For example, you may want to move the finalized configuration from User Acceptance Test (UAT) to Production Instance upon sign-off from Business Users, or set up a fresh or new instance like System Integration Test or Conversion Instance from the existing instance. FSM provides the ability to move setup data across the instances using Export and Import Setup data functionality. This feature greatly reduces the time to build a new environment and significantly reduces the overall costs of the project. This feature can be accessed from the Manage Configuration Packages page and the Manage Export And Import Processes page in FSM.

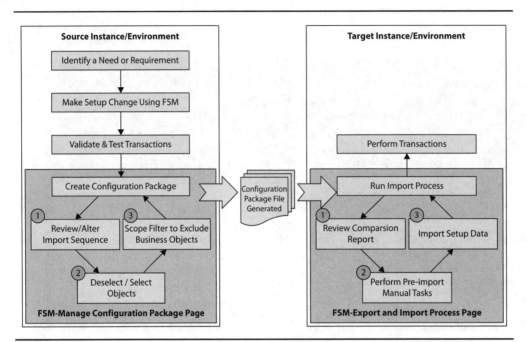

FIGURE 3-8. *High-level processes of Setup data Import and Export*

High-level Process of Setup Data Export and Import Functionality

Figure 3-8 shows the high-level processes of Import and Export Setup Data explained in this section. The process starts with identification of a requirement or need. This requirement can be a new Implementation Project (implementing a new offering in Fusion Application) or a Change Request Project (enhancement or modification to existing offering). The Implementation Consultant makes necessary changes to the setup and thoroughly validates and tests the setup using transactions. Once the setup is verified and validated, the setup is now ready to be moved from Source Instance to Target Instance. The next step is to create a configuration package.

Create a Configuration Package

A configuration package is an Export/Import definition file that contains tasks to be included along with the Business Objects in the export process. A configuration package provides two options for Export:

- Export Task List Only
- Export Both Task List and Setup Data (Business Objects)

If a configuration package is created with the Export Task List Only option, only the task list from the selected Implementation Project will be migrated but no setup data will be migrated.

Here are the steps to create a configuration package:

NOTE
The example Implementation Project ACME FIN Project provided in the following example is a mock project created specifically for this exercise.

1. Click Create Configuration Package under the Setup And Maintenance area.

2. Enter basic information to select the Implementation Project To Export as shown in Figure 3-9 and click Next.

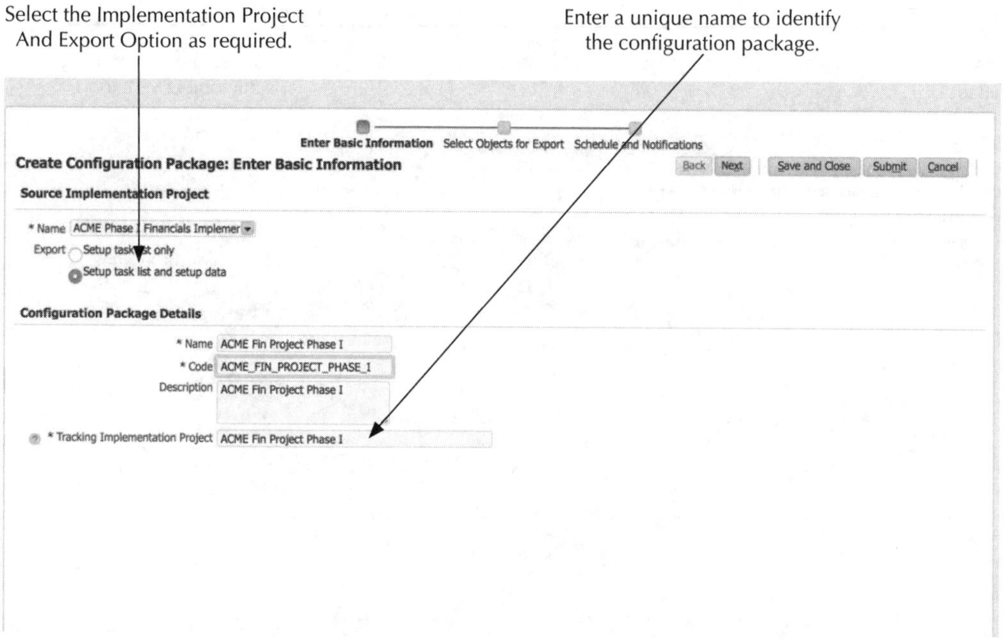

Select the Implementation Project And Export Option as required.

Enter a unique name to identify the configuration package.

Enter Basic Information Select Objects for Export Schedule and Notifications

Create Configuration Package: Enter Basic Information   Back Next   Save and Close   Submit   Cancel

Source Implementation Project

* Name ACME Phase I Financials Implemer ▼
Export ○ Setup task list only
       ⦿ Setup task list and setup data

Configuration Package Details

* Name ACME Fin Project Phase I
* Code ACME_FIN_PROJECT_PHASE_1
Description ACME Fin Project Phase I

⊚ * Tracking Implementation Project ACME Fin Project Phase I

FIGURE 3-9. *Create Configuration Package: Enter Basic Information screen*

3. On the Select Objects For Export page, the user can perform the following actions as shown in Figure 3-10 on the Select Objects For Export page:

- **Review/Alter Import Sequence** The user can accept or alter the import sequence of Objects selected. While altering the sequence, the user needs to make sure that dependencies are already loaded correctly before this object is imported; otherwise, the import process will fail.

- **Deselect/Select Objects** The user can deselect or select tasks that are not required for import in the Target Instance using the Enabled check box under the Export Column as shown in Figure 3-10.

- **Scope Filter to Exclude Business Objects** The user can selectively add which Business Objects need to be imported. Figure 3-10 shows how we can selectively add certain Legal Entities to be imported to the Target Instance by filtering on the Scope. By default, all Business Objects associated with the Implementation Project will be exported.

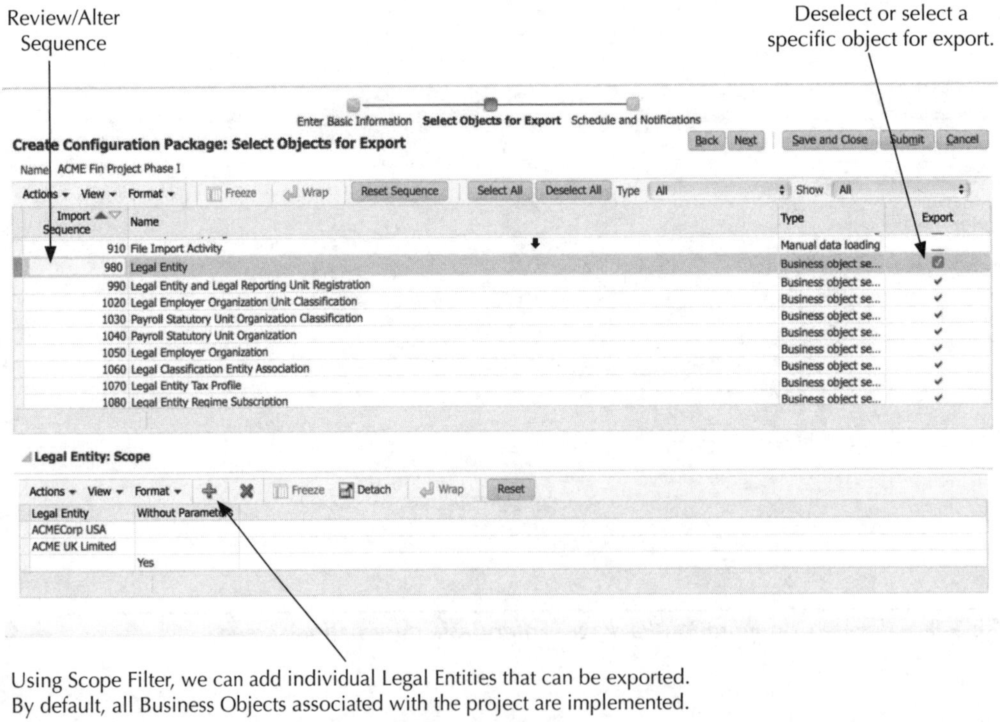

Using Scope Filter, we can add individual Legal Entities that can be exported.
By default, all Business Objects associated with the project are implemented.

FIGURE 3-10. *Create Configuration Package: Select Objects For Export page*

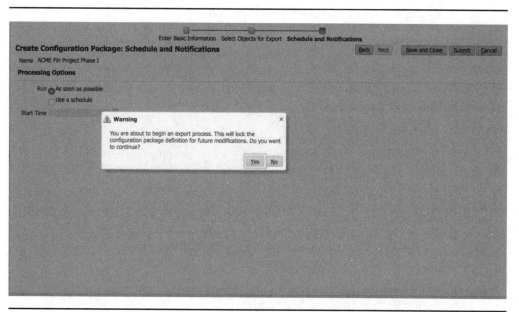

FIGURE 3-11.   *Create Configuration Package: Submit screen*

4. Click Next and then click the Submit button. You will receive a warning message as shown in Figure 3-11 stating that the configuration package definition will be locked for further modifications. Click Yes to proceed to create a configuration package.

5. Once the Export and Import process program runs successfully, the user can download the configuration package that will be moved to the Target Instance using the Download link against the Configuration package.

Compare and Import Configuration Package in Target Instance

FSM provides a comparison feature on the Manage Export and Import Process page. Using this feature, Implementation consultants can identify the discrepancies in setup data between two different configuration packages or two versions of the same configuration package. To compare two versions of same configuration package, simply export the setup data for the same configuration package a second time (which will create a second version).

The steps to compare processes are as follows:

1. Navigate to Export And Import Page under Setup And Maintenance Area.

2. Click the Compare button; the Comparison process page opens.

3. Create a new comparison using the Create icon.

4. In the Compare Window, select both Source 1 and Source 2 configuration package information and provide the process name.

5. Click Submit and monitor the comparison process.

6. Once it completes, review the comparison report.

The comparison report provides a summary of setup data discrepancies per business object and a user can click links provided to get details of the discrepancies. The discrepancy can be one of the following types:

- **In Both with Mismatch:** Indicates how many records exist in both sources but have some differences.

- **Only in Source 1:** Indicates how many records exist only in the first source and don't exist in the second source.

- **Only in Source 2:** Indicates how many records exist only in the second source and don't exist in the first source.

Using this report, the Implementation user can take the next action to see which configuration package to import or what modification needs to be performed in the environment.

The next step is to import the configuration package in the Target Instance. Steps to perform the Import process are as follows:

1. Log in to the Target Instance with an Application user login that has an Implementation Consultant Job role.

2. Navigate to the Manage Configuration Page under the Setup And Maintenance Area.

3. Click the Upload button.

4. Select the location of the Configuration file and click the Get Details button.

5. Click Submit. This process will load the Configuration package successfully.

6. Select the Configuration package and click the Import Setup data button and follow the instructions to import the setup data into the Target Instance.

Points to Consider

Here are a few important points to note while exporting and importing setup data:

- **Fusion Release Level**   One of the prerequisites for this feature to work properly is to ensure that the Source and Target environments are in the same Fusion release level.

- **Implementation Project**   As discussed earlier in the chapter, it is recommended that Implementation Projects be created one per Offering so that they are self-sufficent, which will reduce the dependencies during the Export and Import process.

- **Command-Line Script**   FSM also provides an option to use a command-line script to move setup data from the source environment to the target environment.

- **Tasks Eligible for Export**   Irrespective of the Tasks status, all tasks within the configuration package will be exported unless the user explicitly excludes them during the configuration package creation.

- **Seeded Business Objects**   FSM doesn't export/import Seeded Business Objects created as part of the Fusion installation. Only user-created Business Objects are exported and imported across.

- **Invalid Setup Data**   If you have any invalid test setup data Source Instance, it is recommended to end date those setup data (1/1/1951) before export to ensure that an invalid setup is not active in the production environment.

Financials Rapid Implementation Configuration

As we have seen earlier, the standard Financials Offerings task list consists of both Mandatory/Critical tasks and Optional tasks. In order to minimize the time required to complete the key setups and quickly enable Oracle Fusion Financials for day-to-day use, Oracle provides a Financials Rapid Implementation task list to help users focus only on critical or minimum setup tasks to rapidly deploy Fusion Applications. This method of implementation is really useful for cloud-based implementation (in the software-as-a-service model) to deliver projects with lower costs and a reduced time frame.

Here is the list of rapid implementation configuration options available for Fusion Financials Applications:

- Define Accounting Entry Configuration for Rapid Implementation

- Define Common Financials Configuration for Rapid Implementation

- Define ERP Integrator Configuration for Rapid Implementation

- Define Enterprise Structures Configuration for Rapid Implementation

- Define Expenses Configuration for Rapid Implementation

- Define Financial Reporting Center Configuration for Rapid Implementation

- Define Financials Configuration for Rapid Implementation

- Define Financials Security Configuration for Rapid Implementation

- Define Fixed Assets Configuration for Rapid Implementation

- Define Fusion Accounting Hub Configuration for Rapid Implementation

- Define Invoicing and Payments Configuration for Rapid Implementation

- Define Ledger Configuration for Rapid Implementation

- Define Receivables Configuration for Rapid Implementation

- Define Taxes for Rapid Implementation

Some of the rapid implementation tasks include spreadsheet templates that can be used to quickly load setup data and eliminate manual data entry. Spreadsheet templates can be downloaded from the FSM task list and all setup data can be loaded using those templates quickly and easily. Hence it is recommended that Implementers assess available spreadsheet templates to leverage them.

Examples of rapid implementation spreadsheets are

- Create Chart of Accounts, Ledgers, Legal Entities and Business Units

- Create Cross-Validation Rules

- Create Account Combinations in Bulk

- Create Segment Value Security Rules

- Create Sequencing Configuration

- Create Banks, Branches and Accounts

- Create Fixed Assets Configuration

Create the Financials Rapid Implementation Project
A Rapid Implementation Project task list can be created from the Manage Implementation Projects page in the Setup And Maintenance work area.

The following steps provide details of creating a Rapid Implementation project for Financials.

1. Navigate to the Manage Implementation Projects link under the Setup And Maintenance work area.

2. Click the Create icon.

3. On the Create Implementation Project page, enter information as follows:

   ■ Name: *Financials Rapid Implementation project*

   ■ Code: *XX_FIN_RAPID_IMPL_PROJECT*

   ■ Description: *Financials Rapid Implementation Project*

4. On the Implementation Project page, click Add in the Task List And Tasks Table.

5. In the Select And Add: Task List And Tasks dialog box, enter **%Rapid Implementation%** in the Name field. Click Search.

6. Select the Define Financials Configuration For Rapid Implementation row.

7. Click the Done button.

Here are a few important points to note while using Financials Rapid Implementation Configuration:

■ **Adding tasks manually**   Even though the Financials Rapid Implementation project comes with pre-seeded tasks, the user can add tasks to the project from the Standard Offering task list as well.

■ **Spreadsheet Template**   To identify these templates, Implementers can search on "spreadsheet" within the All Tasks tab in the Functional Setup Manager.

Summary

In this chapter we have provided a high-level overview of the Functional Setup Manager module and briefed the reader on key concepts and terminology used within the Fusion Application implementation. We have also seen how the Functional Setup Manager Process flow is structured, and we have also reviewed the different types of Application Users who will access the Setup And Maintenance area. We have created an ACME Implementation Project to include Fusion Financials and generated a comprehensive task list. Finally, we looked at how to export and import configuration packages across different instances.

In the next few chapters, we will dive deep into the setup details of each task to implement the selected offerings.

CHAPTER
4

Enterprise Structure
for Financials

I n this chapter we look at how a company or corporation can be represented in Enterprise Structure for Financials within Fusion Applications. Enterprise Structure is a broader terminology used to represent common elements within Human Capital Management (HCM) and Fusions Financials like Enterprise itself, Legal Entities, and so on, and there are other specific elements within Fusion Financials like Financials Reporting Structures (Chart of Accounts, Calendar & Currency) and Ledgers.

This chapter has two major sections. The first section will introduce the concepts of Enterprise Structure and help you understand the relationship between the elements that make up Enterprise Structure. We will also explain the significance of each of the elements so readers can apply what they've learned to their own implementation. The second section will guide users to apply these concepts to configuring the Enterprise Structure for ACME Bank.

Overview of Enterprise Structure

Every enterprise has three fundamental business perspective structures: Legal, Managerial, and Functional Axis. These perspectives provide the basis for the company's operational and legal reporting. The simplest way to understand this Enterprise Structure is to start with investigating how the company is structured in the real world, both legally, which provides insight into where the company is registered, where they are filing their financial returns, to whom they are paying their taxes, and so on, and operationally (management and functional structure), which provides insight into how they operate and how their internal organization is structured to serve their customers and deliver the company's strategic vision. In the next few sections, we will explain what these structures mean in detail and how this will influence the implementation decision of Fusion Financials.

Legal Structure A legal structure is a group of legal entities operating across various business and functional organizations. Legal entities can own and trade assets and employ people in the jurisdiction in which they are registered. In Fusion, legal structure is implemented using Legal Entities and Enterprise.

Management Structure A management structure can include Line of Business, Divisions, Subdivisions, Cost Centers, or Strategic Business Units. Management structure provides segregation of business within an enterprise by their strategic objectives and allows the enterprise to measure their results. In Fusion, Management Structure is implemented using Divisions and Business Units.

Functional Structure A functional structure is basically a functional organization that is structured around people and their competencies. Sales, Marketing, Procurement, Finance, and so on are some components of the functional organization. In Fusion, functional structure is implemented using Departments and usually flagged as a Cost Center Segment or Label in Chart of Accounts Setup.

High-Level Components of Enterprise Structure

Enterprise Structures are basic building blocks for implementing Fusion Applications. In the next few sections, we will introduce each component.

Enterprise

Enterprise is an umbrella entity for the entire implementation of the company and usually represents the parent legal entity or group company that controls all the subsidiary or legal entities underneath. Business Units, Departments, and Legal Entities are created within this Enterprise.

Legal Entities

As per Oracle Fusion Applications Financials Implementation Guide documentation, a *Legal Entity* is a recognized party with rights and responsibilities given by legislation. Legal entities have the right to own property, the right to trade, the responsibility to repay debt, and the responsibility to account for themselves to regulators, taxation authorities, and owners according to rules specified in the relevant legislation.

In Fusion, we can capture all aspects associated with a legal entity or company using different configuration elements as explained in the following list:

■ **Legal Address**   A company needs a physical address for correspondence with external entities like tax agencies, customers, and suppliers, and so on. Companies flag a primary address as a legal address to register with a legal authority where they conduct their business. In Fusion, a legal address needs to be defined first before we create a legal entity.

■ **Legal Reporting Unit**   A company needs to report their Financials position and comply with local statutory reporting. For example, U.S. companies need to pay corporation tax or company income tax on the earnings and report the financial figures to the Internal Revenue Service (IRS). In Fusion, we can capture this reporting need as a Legal Reporting Unit. Oracle automatically creates a Legal Reporting Unit for each legal entity with the same name as the Legal Entity.

■ **Legal Registration**   As part of the process of a company coming to existence in the world, the first activity would be to register the company name with the legal authority or legal authorities in the country or local region where it operates. As part of the registration process, companies are provided a unique registration number. This information can be captured as part of Legal Registration associated with the Legal Entity. Oracle automatically creates a Legal Registration based on the registration information provided at the time of creating the Legal Entity. Registration information can be used in financial statements and legal reports.

■ **Legal Payroll Unit** A company would have employees and therefore would be flagged as legal employers using a Legal Payroll Unit. Legal Payroll Units are associated with Legal Entities and used in Oracle Fusion Human Capital Management (HCM) Applications. This is optional in the case of Fusion Financials–only implementation, as is the case here for ACME Bank.

Legal Jurisdictions and Authorities

Apart from the configuration elements discussed earlier, two other important configuration elements associated with a Legal Entity are legal jurisdiction and authority.

Jurisdiction generally refers to a geographic area, such as county, state, and federal, within which legal authorities (also known as government agencies or legal bodies) may properly exercise their powers or legislation. Legal authorities have the power to make laws, collect fees, and impose taxes. They also administer whether legal entities operating under their legal jurisdiction comply with their laws or legislation. For example, in the United States, the IRS is a legal body or government agency responsible for tax collection and tax law enforcement. In the United Kingdom, HM Revenue and Customs (HMRC) is a government agency responsible for enforcing U.K. Transaction Tax Law (that is, value-added tax). In these examples, U.S. income tax law and U.K. transaction tax law are called *legal jurisdictions*, and IRS and HMRC are called *legal authorities*.

There are three types of jurisdictions:

■ **Identifying jurisdictions** An identifying jurisdiction provides the legitimacy for a company to conduct business in a country or region, and it is the first jurisdiction to be registered.

■ **Income tax jurisdiction** An income tax jurisdiction imposes taxes on the income generated by the business.

■ **Transaction tax jurisdiction** A transaction tax jurisdiction imposes taxes on the customers' and suppliers' transactions.

In Fusion Financials, you can create Legal Entities and associate them with legal jurisdictions and legal authority. Legal authority and legal jurisdictions support the registration of multiple Legal Entities.

Depending on the country or area in which the company operates, the same legal authority may be responsible for multiple jurisdictions. For example, HM Revenue and Customs is the United Kingdom's tax and customs authority responsible for both income tax jurisdictions (corporation tax) and transaction tax jurisdictions (value-added tax). Oracle Fusion supports defining multiple jurisdictions using the same legal authority.

NOTE
Oracle Fusion Tax and Oracle Fusion Payroll uses Legal Authority and Legal Jurisdictions. Oracle Fusion Tax is internally used in seeded subledgers like Oracle Fusion Payables and Oracle Fusion Receivables for tax calculations. Since we are not implementing Fusion Tax, this feature will not be relevant in the context of this book.

Financials Reporting Structures

Financials Reporting Structures includes Chart of Accounts structure, Calendar, and Currency, which are used to define the ledger. Financials Reporting Structure will be covered in the next chapter.

How to Create Enterprise Structure

There are two methods to create Enterprise Structure in Fusion. They are

- Using Enterprise Structure Configurator

- Using a manual method

Using Enterprise Structure Configurator

The Enterprise Structure Configurator (ECS) is an interview-based tool that guides the user through the process of configuring the organizational structure. The key benefit of using ECS is that business users will be able to preview their resulting enterprise structure and, if required, create multiple scenarios to finalize a configuration to load into Fusion.

High-level steps using Enterprise Structure Configurator would be as follows:

Step 1: Establish Enterprise Structure: Implementers or Business Users can answer the questions about the enterprise, and the tool will create a structure of Divisions, Legal Entities, Business Units, and reference data sets that reflects the Enterprise Structure.

Step 2: Establish Job and Position Structure: Once the Enterprise Structure is established, the tool will also guide the user through the process to determine the recommended approach for HR Work structure to use (either Jobs or combinations of Jobs and Positions) based on the primary industry of the implementation company.

NOTE
A Job represents duties people perform within an enterprise, and Position represents a specific instance of a job. For example, Job would be "Accountant," whereas Position would be "Payroll Accountant."

Oracle Fusion supports capturing additional attributes to provide more details about the individual Job or Position. For example, Job can have an attribute called Job Type to represent "Consultant," "Manager," and "Senior Manager" roles within a company and can have another attribute called Job Level to represent different skill set levels within the Job type like Level 1, Level 2, Level 3, and so on. Fusion uses descriptive flexfields to capture additional information attributes. These attributes can be global, that is, enterprise level or context specific within a specific business unit as well.

Step 3: Review Configuration: Once the Job and Position structures are established, the tool allows reviewing the configuration and amending as required. At this stage, a technical summary report is generated, which shows a list of Legislative Data Groups (LDGs) created automatically and a resulting Organization Hierarchy. Legislative Data Groups are created one per country in which the company operates, and this is a way to partition payroll and related data in HCM. You can have more than one Legislative Data Group for a single country, but you should have at least one. LDGs are assigned to the Payroll Statutory Unit of the Legal Entity.

Step 4: Load Configuration: Once you are satisfied with the final Enterprise Structure configuration, you can load the configuration into Fusion.

Figure 4-1 illustrates the process of configuring an enterprise using the Enterprise Structure Configurator. This method is really useful when implementing Fusion HCM as part of Oracle Fusion Applications to define the initial configuration of the Enterprise Structure.

Using the Manual Method
If Fusion HCM is not implemented as part of the Oracle Fusion Applications, implementers can use this manual method to create Enterprise Structure elements that are only required for Fusion Financials. In this method, a Seeded Setup Enterprise name is modified to reflect the enterprise, and other elements of the Enterprise Structure are manually created as illustrated in the process flow shown in Figure 4-2.

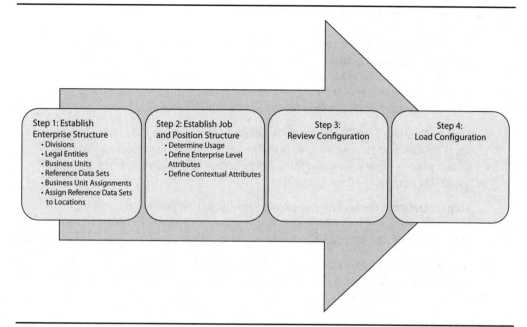

FIGURE 4-1. *The process flow for the Enterprise Configurator*

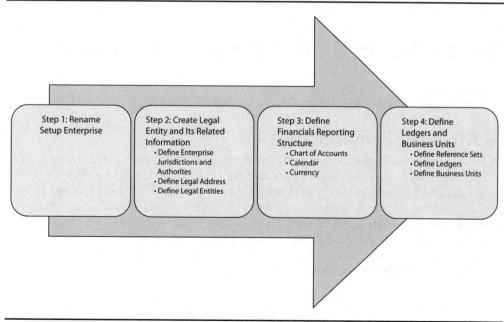

FIGURE 4-2. *The process flow for the manual method*

High-level steps using the manual method would be as follows:

Step 1: Rename Setup Enterprise: Fusion Applications comes with Seeded Enterprise, which can be renamed to reflect the actual enterprise or company. In Fusion, we can have only one enterprise per instance, so it is recommended that the enterprise name reflect the group company or parent company or corporation name for which the Fusion instance is configured.

Step 2: Create a Legal Entity and Its Related Information: Here we create legal entities and related information like legal jurisdictions and authorities, which make up the entity structure. This chapter will focus on Steps 1 and 2 using this manual method in detail.

Step 3: Define a Financials Reporting Structure: Financials Reporting Structure refers to Chart of Accounts, Calendar, and Currency. We will look at these topics in detail in Chapter 5.

Step 4: Define Ledgers and Business Units: After the Chart of Accounts has been configured, we can define Ledgers and Business Units. We will cover this topic in Chapter 6.

ACME Bank will be implemented using this manual method because Fusion HCM is not implemented as part of this Phase I Implementation. Still, some of the shared features of Fusion HCM, like Legal Entities, Departments, and Employees, will be used.

Define ACME Bank Enterprise Structure

In this section we will provide requirements for the ACME Bank Enterprise Structure and provide details of how this can be modeled using Oracle Fusion Applications. We will also provide detailed steps for defining Enterprise and Legal Entities.

ACME Bank Requirements

ACME Bank is a multinational bank that operates in several countries including the United States (U.S.), Latin America, Japan, and the United Kingdom (U.K.). ACME Bank has purchased an Oracle Fusion Enterprise Resource Planning (ERP) software package and as part of a Finance Transformation Project, has decided to implement Oracle Fusion Financials (General Ledger and Fusion Accounting Hub) for U.K. and U.S. operations as part of a Phase I rollout. The following list describes the key requirements that would need to be considered while designing the enterprise structure of ACME Bank in Oracle Fusion.

Requirement 4.1: ACME Bank is a publicly listed company and requires the ability to produce consolidated quarterly and yearly financial statements for shareholders. ACME Corporation has complex consolidation requirements, as it needs to aggregate balances across different legal entities operating in different currencies. Latin America and Japan have their own ERP system to meet their localized statutory reporting and tax compliance. However, it is expected that consolidation should happen in a centralized location using the global Chart of Account structure that would be recommended as part of this implementation.

Requirement 4.2: In addition to this group-level reporting, ACME Corporation needs to provide financial reporting at the Balance Sheet level and Profit and Loss (revenue and expenses) level at both the Legal Entity level and Line of Business level (Insurance, Banking, Finance, Investment) at which it operates. Figure 4-3 shows a diagram of the Legal Entity structure and Line of Business for U.S. and U.K. operations.

Requirement 4.3: Legal Entity level reporting satisfies local regulatory requirements. For example, ACME UK Limited needs to prepare, audit, and disclose accounts to U.K. income tax authorities.

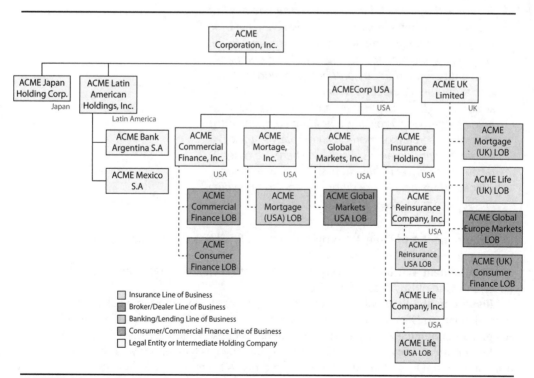

FIGURE 4-3. *ACME Bank Legal Entities and Line of Business structure*

Requirement 4.4: The Line of Business (LOB) level reporting requirement is driven partially by management strategy to provide more autonomy to the line of business management with respect to their own cash position and to make them accountable for their profit and loss. Another requirement is that ACME Corporation needs to provide detailed reporting for their line of business in their quarterly and annual financial statements for their shareholders.

Requirement 4.5: ACME Insurance Holding Company is an intermediate company, which holds balances of both ACME Reinsurance Company, Inc., and ACME Life Company, Inc. One of the major challenges the ACME Insurance Holding Company currently faces in their reporting is the inability to identify their risk exposure per location. This reporting is required to satisfy regulatory requirements, and the current manual process delays the final submission of accounts for the ACME Group. The ACME Corporation CFO is very keen to get this report delivered with minimum manual intervention and is looking to the implementation team for their recommendation.

NOTE
To model the ACME Bank company structure as close to a real company scenario as possible, we have used the terms "holding company" and "subsidiary" in this chapter. For the reader's benefit, a holding company is an entity formed to buy and hold a majority of stocks of other companies, whereas a subsidiary is a business whose majority of stock is owned by a holding company. Typically, a holding company must control 50 percent or more of a company's stock before it's considered a subsidiary. There are other differences between them in terms of how they are structured financially, operationally, and so on, which are beyond the scope of this book.

Requirement 4.6: Table 4-1 provides details of ACME US Operations: Legal Entity and Line of Business information.

Requirement 4.7: Table 4-2 provides details of ACME UK Operations: Legal Entity and Line of Business information.

Requirement 4.8: ACME US operating companies all have the same calendar year—January to December. US operating companies need to report in US Generally Accepted Accounting Principles (GAAP) standards consolidated at ACME Corp USA.

Requirement 4.9: ACME UK Operating Company has a calendar year that runs from January to December. ACME UK Limited needs to report in US Generally Accepted Accounting Principles (GAAP) standards to the parent company and UK Statements of Standard Accounting Practice and Financial Reporting Standards for local regulatory reporting needs.

Company/Legal Entity Name	Line of Business	Subsidiary/Holding Company of	Additional Comments
ACMECorp USA		ACME Corporation, Inc.	Parent Company of US Operations
ACME Commercial Finance Inc	Consumer/ Commercial Finance	ACMECorp USA	Deals with loans for business
ACME Mortgage Inc	Banking/Lending	ACMECorp USA	Deals with loans for properties
ACME Global Markets Inc	Broker/Dealer	ACMECorp USA	Deals with trading of financial instruments
ACME Insurance Holding	Insurance	ACMECorp USA	Holding company for insurance line of business
ACME Reinsurance Company Inc	Insurance	ACME Insurance Holding	Deals with undertaking risk from other insurance company products. Also known as "insurance for insurers"
ACME Life Company Inc	Insurance	ACME Insurance Holding	Deals with life insurance line of business

TABLE 4-1. *ACME US Operations: Legal Entity and Line of Business Information*

Company/Legal Entity Name	Line of Business	Subsidiary Of	Additional Comments
ACME UK Limited	Consumer/Commercial Finance, Banking/ Lending, Insurance, Broker/Dealer	ACME Corporation, Inc.	Parent company of UK operations

TABLE 4-2. *ACME UK Operations: Legal Entity and Line of Business Information*

Requirement 4.10: ACME US and UK have all administrative, account payables, procurement, and human resources functions performed at their corporate headquarters. Any proposed solution should be able to meet their Shared Service Center requirement.

Requirement 4.11: ACME Corporate management requires reports showing total organizational performance with drill-down capability to the supporting details.

Requirement 4.12: All companies require a monthly calendar with one adjustment period at the end of the year.

Requirement 4.13: All U.K. general and administrative costs are processed at the U.K. headquarters.

Requirement 4.14: All U.S. general and administrative costs are processed at the U.S. corporate headquarters.

Global Enterprise Structure for ACME Bank

Table 4-3 provides details of the proposed Global Enterprise Structure Model for ACME Bank.

Proposed Structure	Reason	Corresponding Requirement ID
Create an enterprise called "ACME Bank"	ACME Bank is the parent company for all the entities and all results are consolidated at that level.	4.1
Create a Global Chart of Accounts (COA) Structure called "ACME Global COA"	Global COA will provide the benefits of easier consolidation and comparison of financial results across different countries with minimum effort.	4.1
Create a separate Insurance COA Structure called "ACME Insurance COA" with a segment called Risk Location	The U.S. insurance business has a unique requirement to satisfy regulatory reporting around risk location, which is not required for any other business operated in other countries.	4.1, 4.5
	Note: It is not required to create a separate COA for this requirement; rather, we can add one additional segment in the Global COA to meet this requirement. The only drawback of using Global COA is that this segment of risk location is only used for a specific business within the United States. So having this segment across all businesses will confuse the user base. Also, we have taken this approach deliberately to demonstrate the consolidation feature of Fusion for this company. However, we recommend using a single Global COA structure as a guiding principle as much as possible.	
Create a Chart of Accounts structure with two Balancing Segments (Primary and Secondary) for Company and Line of Business.	This feature provides Trial Balance at both Company and Line of Business level. **Note:** Chapter 5 will provide more details about this functionality.	4.2, 4.3, 4.4
Create a 13-Period Calendar (Jan to Feb Monthly Calendar with one adjustment period at the end of the year)	Because the reporting calendar period is common across all countries, one calendar would be sufficient and one adjustment period will allow for year-end adjustment for balance reclassification as per Legal Reporting requirements.	4.8, 4.9, 4.12

TABLE 4-3. *ACME Bank Requirements Mapping (Continued)*

Proposed Structure	Reason	Corresponding Requirement ID
Create three ledgers: ■ ACME US Ledger ■ ACME US Insurance Ledger ■ ACME UK Ledger	*ACME US Ledger* is created for US Operations and to account transactions as per US GAAP Accounting rules. *ACME US Insurance Ledger* is specifically created to satisfy the Insurance Business Regulatory requirement. *ACME UK Ledger* is created for UK Operations and to account transactions as per UK GAAP Accounting rules. **Note:** Chapter 6 will provide more details about how to define ledgers.	4.6, 4.7, 4.8, 4.9
Overhead costs will be booked in a Centralized Cost Center and will be distributed across different business as per predefined allocation rules.	Businesses normally use a central department to accumulate overhead costs, which will be redistributed later based on the usage or certain predefined criteria. Allocation of overhead costs can be handled using the Calculation Manager feature. **Note:** Allocation rules will be covered as part of Chapter 11.	4.13, 4.14
Create one Business Unit for US Operations and one Business Unit for UK Operations to handle administrative functions like Accounts Payables, Procurement, and so on	Creating a Business Unit for each of the UK and US Operations will allow the company to process administrative costs correctly in the respective ledgers.	4.10
ACME UK ledger will use ACME Global COA with Jan – Dec (13 Period) Calendar and Functional GBP Currency. This Ledger will represent UK Operations and it will have an additional Secondary Ledger for US GAAP Reporting.	UK ledger should satisfy both Local and Global Reporting requirements. **Note:** We have decided to create a Secondary Ledger for UK Ledger instead of Report Currency for the following reasons: Firstly, the Secondary Ledger allows us to have a US GAAP Accounting representation which is different from Primary Ledger UK GAAP Accounting representation. This Secondary Ledger book allows us to create adjustment entries and rebook journals in the US GAAP representation with better audit and traceability. Secondly (purely from the standpoint of concept coverage in this book), it is a way to demonstrate to readers how to create Secondary Ledgers in the system. Readers will learn more about Secondary Ledger concept in Chapter 6.	4.9

TABLE 4-3.   *ACME Bank Requirements Mapping*

The proposed structure of the Ledger and Legal Entity will be as shown in Figure 4-4.

NOTE
All the setup steps performed in this chapter will be using the ACME GL Implementation Consultant login (XXFA_FIN_GL_IMPLEMENTATION_CONSULTANT Application User), which we created earlier in Appendix A. We will define the ACME Bank Enterprise Structure in Fusion Applications.

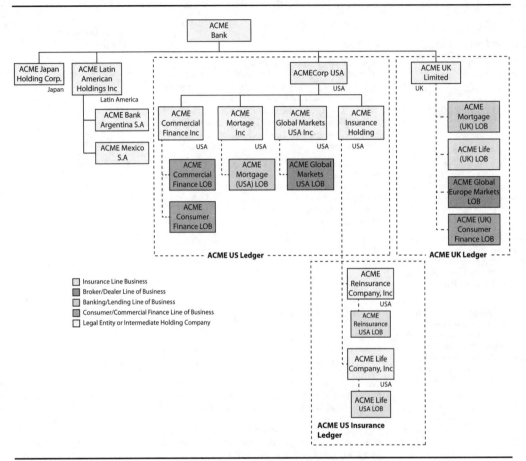

FIGURE 4-4. *Proposed ACME Bank ledger structure with Legal Entities*

In the next few sections, we will cover how to define Enterprise Structure for ACME Bank in Fusion Applications with detailed steps. Table 4-4 shows the high-level steps that will be performed.

NOTE
In the following example, readers will learn how to create a US Legal Entity called "ACMECorp USA" successfully. Readers are encouraged to create other Legal Entities in the United States and United Kingdom for ACME Bank, using these detailed steps as an example. Also we are covering only how to define the Enterprise itself, Legal Entity, and its related setup in this chapter. The Financials Reporting Structure will be covered in the next chapter.

	Configuration Step	**Setup Data**
Step 1	Define Enterprise	ACME Bank
Step 2	Define Legal Jurisdictions and Authorities	U.S. Income Tax Law Jurisdiction and Internal Revenue Service Legal Authority
Step 3	Define Legal Address	900 ACME Parkway Redwood Shores, CA 94065 United States
Step 4	Define Legal Entity	ACMECorp USA
Step 5	Define Legal Registration (Optional)	Review autocreated Legal Registration
Step 6	Define Legal Reporting Unit (Optional)	Review autocreated Legal Reporting Unit

TABLE 4-4. *High-Level Steps to Define ACME Bank Enterprise Structure*

Define Enterprise

Oracle Fusion Applications installations come with a default Setup Enterprise. The following steps provide details of updating the Setup Enterprise:

1. Access the Setup And Maintenance area as follows: Go to Navigator | More... | Tools | Setup And Maintenance.

2. Click the Manage Implementation Projects link.

3. Click the ACME Phase I Implementation Project link.

4. Navigate to Manage Enterprise HCM Information Task under the Define Enterprise For Financials task list and select Go To Task.

5. Click Edit | Correct In Enterprise: Set up the Enterprise page as shown in Figure 4-5.

6. Edit the Name field under the Enterprise Description section from "Setup Enterprise" to "ACME Bank Enterprise."

7. Select Submit.

Since Fusion HCM is out of scope for this implementation, default values for the other fields in the Setup Enterprise page like Worker Number Generation, Workday Information, and so on remain the same.

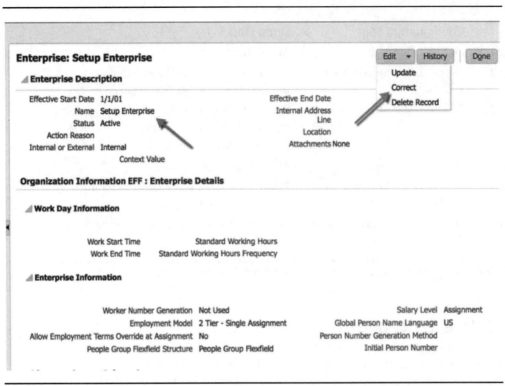

FIGURE 4-5. *Changing the "Setup Enterprise" Name to ACME Bank Enterprise*

Now that the enterprise has been created successfully, we can proceed to create the rest of the ACME Enterprise Structure.

Define Legal Jurisdictions and Authorities

The next step is to create the Legal Jurisdictions and Legal Authorities.

Create Legal Jurisdictions

Oracle Fusion comes with seeded/predefined Legal Jurisdictions. To review existing jurisdictions, take the following steps:

1. Navigate to the Manage Legal Jurisdictions page from the Setup And Maintenance work area by querying on the Manage Legal Jurisdictions task and selecting Go To Task.

2. Under Manage Legal Jurisdictions, select the Territory value and click the Search button as shown in Figure 4-6.

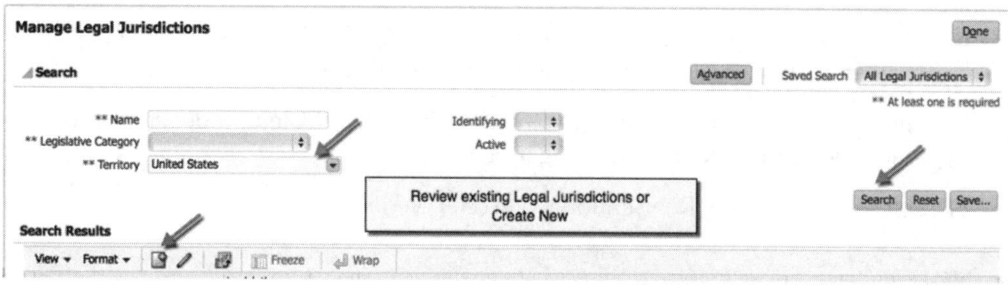

FIGURE 4-6. *Search seeded Legal Jurisdictions*

For this ACME Bank definition, we will use a Seeded Legal Jurisdiction called "United States Income Tax" as shown in Figure 4-7.

Alternatively, create a new Legal Jurisdiction for the United States territory by following these steps:

1. Navigate to the Manage Legal Jurisdictions page from the Setup And Maintenance work area by querying on the Manage Legal Jurisdictions task and selecting Go To Task.

2. Select Create.

3. Enter a unique name, for example, **United States Income Tax**.

4. Select United States for the Territory field.

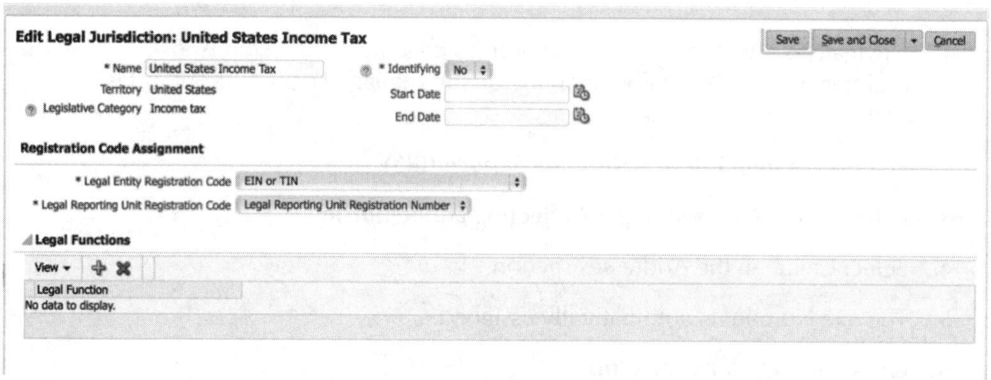

FIGURE 4-7. *United States Income Tax Legal Jurisdiction*

5. Select Income Tax in the Legislative Category field.

6. Under Identifying, select Yes. Identifying indicates the first jurisdiction a legal entity must register with to do business in a country.

7. Enter a Start Date if desired. You can also add an End Date to indicate a date when the jurisdiction may no longer be used.

8. Select a Legal Entity Registration Code, EIN or TIN.

 NOTE
A Taxpayer Identification Number (TIN) is an identification number used by the Internal Revenue Service (IRS) in the administration of U.S. tax laws. An Employer Identification Number (EIN) is also known as a federal tax identification number in the United States, and is used to identify a business entity.

9. Select Legal Reporting Unit Registration Number in the Legal Reporting Unit Registration Code field.

10. Optionally, enter one or more Legal Functions.

11. Select Save And Close.

Repeat the preceding steps for other Legal Jurisdictions.

Create Legal Authorities

Create Legal Authorities for the United States territory by following these steps:

1. Navigate to the Manage Legal Authorities page from the Setup And Maintenance work area by querying on the Manage Legal Authorities task and selecting Go To Task.

2. Enter the Name: **Internal Revenue Service (IRS)**.

3. Enter the Tax Authority Type: **Collecting and Reporting.**

4. Select Create in the Addresses section.

5. The Site Number is automatically assigned.

6. Optionally, enter a Mail Stop.

7. Select United States in the Country field.

8. Enter Address details as shown:

    Address Line 1: Department of Treasury
    City: Ogden
    State: UT

9. The From Date defaults to today's date. Update if necessary.

10. Optionally, enter a To Date to indicate the last day the address can be used.

 NOTE
You can optionally enter Address Purpose details.

11. Select Add Row.

12. Select Purpose.

13. The Purpose From date will default to today's date.

14. Optionally, enter a Purpose To date.

15. Select OK.

16. Click on the Create icon under Legislative Categories.

17. Select Income Tax as shown in Figure 4-8.

18. Select Save And Close.

Repeat the preceding steps for other Legal Authorities.

Create Legal Authority	Save Save and Close ▾ Cancel

* Name   US Internal Revenue Service (IRS)
* Tax Authority Type   Collecting and reporting ▾

Addresses

Actions ▾ View ▾ Format ▾ ▢ ▣ ✎ ▾ ⊲ Wrap						
Primary	Current Status	Address	Purpose	Contact Preferences	Site Number	Time Zone
▶	⬆	*Department of Treasury,OGDEN, UT 84201			124005	
Columns Hidden 2					Address date range : Current	

Legislative Categories

View ▾   ✛ ✖

Legislative Category ⊛	
Income tax ▾	Enter Legal Authority Name, Tax Authority Type, Address, and Legislative Categories as shown

FIGURE 4-8.   *The Create Legal Authority screen*

Define Legal Address

A Legal Address should be created first before a Legal Entity can be created. To create a legal address for ACMECorp USA Legal Entity, take the following steps:

1. Navigate to the Manage Legal Address page from the Setup And Maintenance work area by querying on the Manage Legal Address task and selecting Go To Task.

2. Select Create.

3. Select United States in the Country field.

4. Enter Address Line 1, **900 ACME Parkway**.

5. Optionally enter Address Line 2.

6. Enter **Redwood Shores** for the city.

7. Enter **CA** in the State field.

8. Enter or select Zip Code of **94065**.

9. Optionally enter US Pacific Time in the Time Zone field.

10. The Location Create screen will look as shown in Figure 4-9.

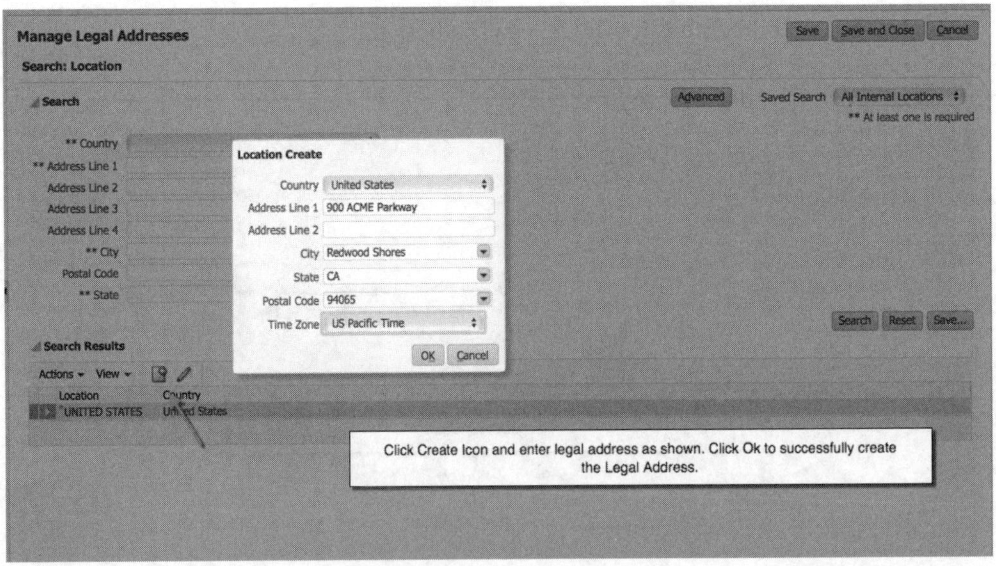

FIGURE 4-9. *The Create Legal Address screen*

11. Select OK.

12. Select Save And Close.

The Legal Address will be created successfully.
Repeat the same steps, creating other US Legal Addresses and UK Legal Addresses.

Create Legal Entities, Legal Registrations, and Legal Reporting Units

In this section, we will look at setup steps to Create Legal Entity, Legal Registration, and Legal Reporting Units.

Create Legal Entity

Create a Legal Entity named "ACMECorp USA" by following these steps:

1. Navigate to the ACME Phase I implementation project that contains the Define Legal Entities task list from the Setup And Maintenance work area.

2. Click Go To Task for the Define Legal Entities task list within the implementation project.

   The following message appears:

   You must first select a scope value to perform the task.

   - Select and add an existing scope value to the implementation project.
   - Create a new scope value and then add it to the implementation project.

3. Select Create New as shown in Figure 4-10 and click the Apply And Go To Task button.

4. From the Manage Legal Entities page, select Create.

5. Accept the default Country, United States.

6. Enter **ACMECorp USA** in the Name field.

7. Enter **US0001** in the Legal Entity Identifier field.

8. Optionally, enter a Start Date. When the Start Date is blank, the Legal Entity is effective from the creation date.

9. Optionally, enter an End Date.

10. Optionally, if the Legal Entity should be registered to report payroll tax and social security insurance, select the Payroll Statutory Unit check box.

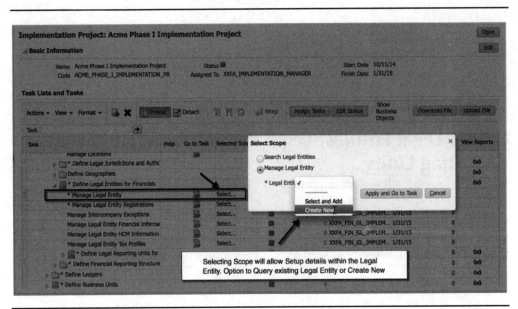

FIGURE 4-10. *Select the scope of the new Legal Entity.*

11. Optionally, if the Legal Entity has employees, select the Legal Employer check box.

12. Optionally, if this Legal Entity is not a payroll statutory unit, select an existing payroll statutory unit to report payroll tax and social security insurance on behalf of this Legal Entity.

    Enter the Registration Information.

13. Accept the default Identifying Jurisdiction: United States Income Tax.

14. Search for and select a Legal Address: 900 ACME Parkway, Redwood Shores, CA 94065.

NOTE
The Legal Address must have been entered previously using the Manage Legal Address task.

15. Select OK.

16. Optionally enter a Place of Registration.

17. Enter the EIN or TIN.

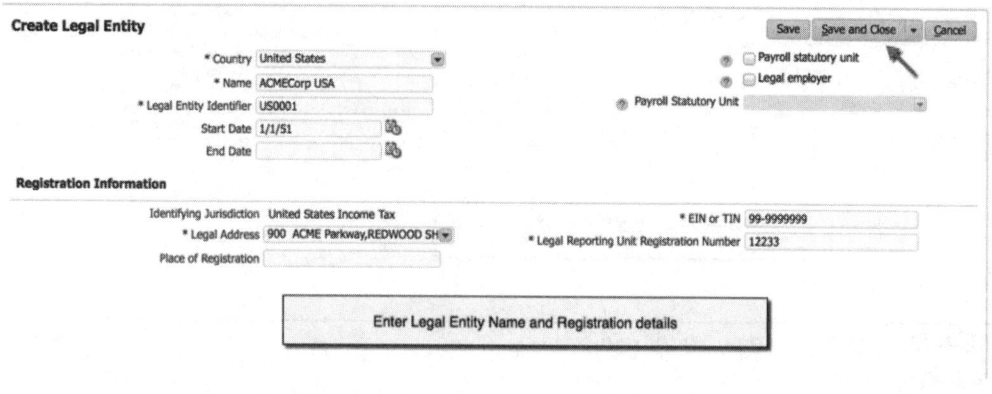

Create Legal Entity

* Country United States
* Name ACMECorp USA
* Legal Entity Identifier US0001
  Start Date 1/1/51
  End Date

☐ Payroll statutory unit
☐ Legal employer
Payroll Statutory Unit

Save | Save and Close ▾ | Cancel

Registration Information

Identifying Jurisdiction United States Income Tax
* Legal Address 900 ACME Parkway,REDWOOD SH ▾
  Place of Registration

* EIN or TIN 99-9999999
* Legal Reporting Unit Registration Number 12233

Enter Legal Entity Name and Registration details

FIGURE 4-11. *The Create Legal Entity page*

18. Enter the Legal Reporting Unit Registration Number as shown in Figure 4-11.

19. Select Save And Close to navigate back to the Manage Legal Entities page.

20. Select Done to return to the implementation project.

Create Legal Entity Registrations

A legal entity registration with the same name as that of the Legal Entity will be created by default. To verify this, take the following the steps:

1. Navigate to the ACME Phase I implementation project from the Setup And Maintenance work area. Verify that the parent Legal Entity scope value is set correctly; in this case, "ACMECorp USA."

2. Expand the Define Legal Entities task list within the implementation project.

3. Click Go To Task for Manage Legal Entity Registrations.

4. Verify that the Legal Registration was created as shown in Figure 4-12.

Legal Reporting Unit

When a Legal Entity is created, a Legal Reporting Unit with the same name as that of the entity is also automatically created. To create more Legal Reporting Units or modify the settings, follow these steps:

1. Navigate to the ACME Phase I implementation project from the Setup And Maintenance work area.

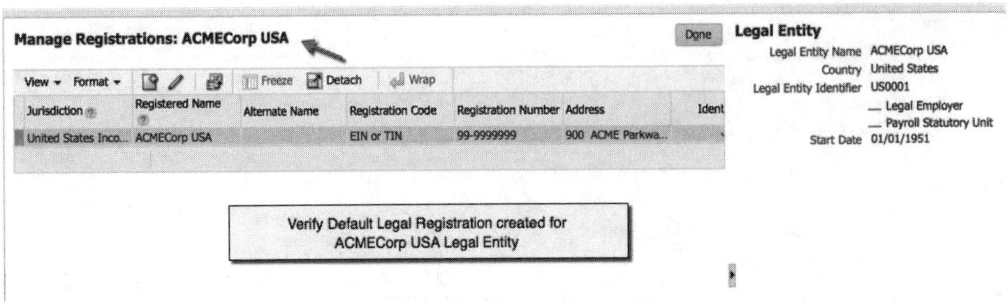

FIGURE 4-12. *Verifying Legal Entity registration*

2. Select Go To Task for the Define Legal Entities task list within the implementation project.

3. Click Manage Legal Reporting Unit Task.

4. Select the scope as shown in Figure 4-13.

   4a. Select Legal Entity: ACMECorp USA
   4b. Select Legal Reporting Unit: Select And Add
   4c. Click Apply And Go To Task.

5. The Select And Add: Legal Reporting Unit window will open as shown in Figure 4-14.

6. Select the Legal Reporting Unit ACMECorp USA and click Save And Close.

7. The Edit Legal Reporting Unit page opens as shown in Figure 4-15.

8. Review the information.

9. Click Save And Close.

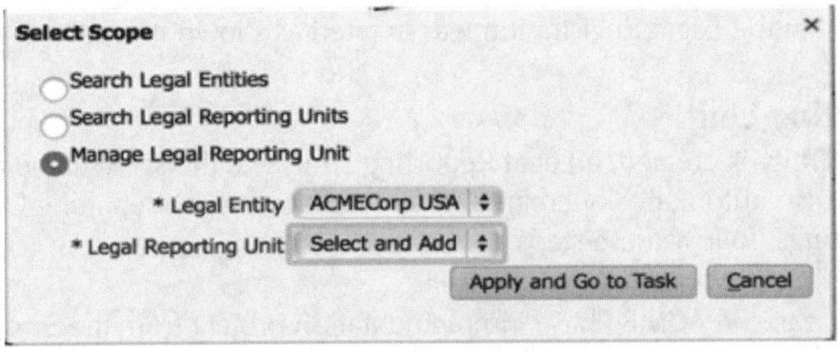

FIGURE 4-13. *Select the scope for the Legal Reporting Unit.*

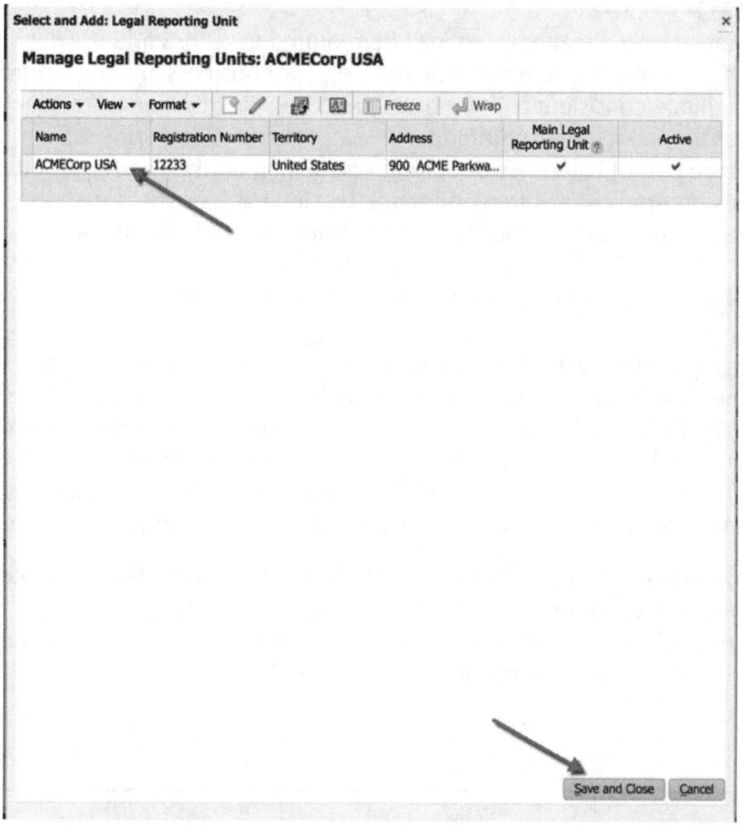

FIGURE 4-14. *The Select And Add: Legal Reporting Unit window*

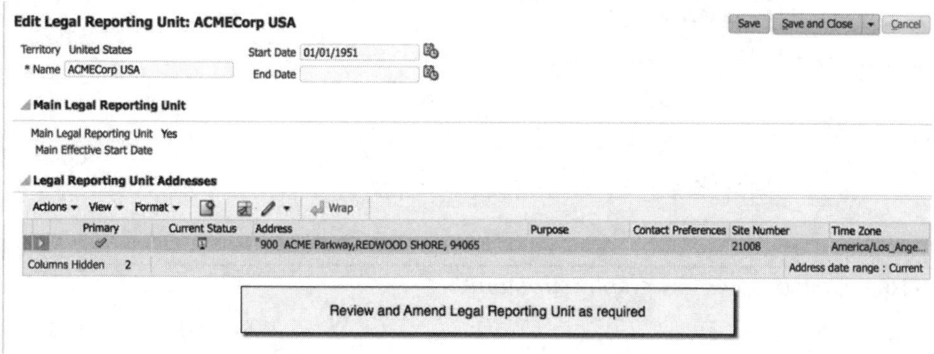

FIGURE 4-15. *The Edit Legal Reporting Unit page*

Geographies

In Fusion Financials Applications, we may be required to record address details of Legal Entity, Customers, Suppliers, Employees, etc., for business and legal purposes. In order to facilitate consistent capture of valid address details (like the correct postal address format) in the user interface, we can define Geographies. Geographies are part of Enterprise Structure, and setting up the correct structure is critical for Fusion Applications to work correctly. Geographies structure and data are shared across all applications, and it allows real-time validation of the address. Geographies structure is also used in Fusion E-Tax for tax calculations.

Geographies consists of three interdependent components:

- **Geography structure** The Geography structure needs to be defined one per country. Each Geography structure is made of Geography types, and each Geography type will be hierarchically related to the Geography structure in terms of levels. For example, for United States Country, Geography types would be State, County, City, and Post Code, and using the Geography structure, we can define how the levels are related, as shown in Figure 4-16.

- **Geography hierarchy** The Geography hierarchy enables you to create values for each of the Geography types and link them hierarchically. Figure 4-17 shows how United States is linked to different States and States are linked to County using Geography hierarchies.

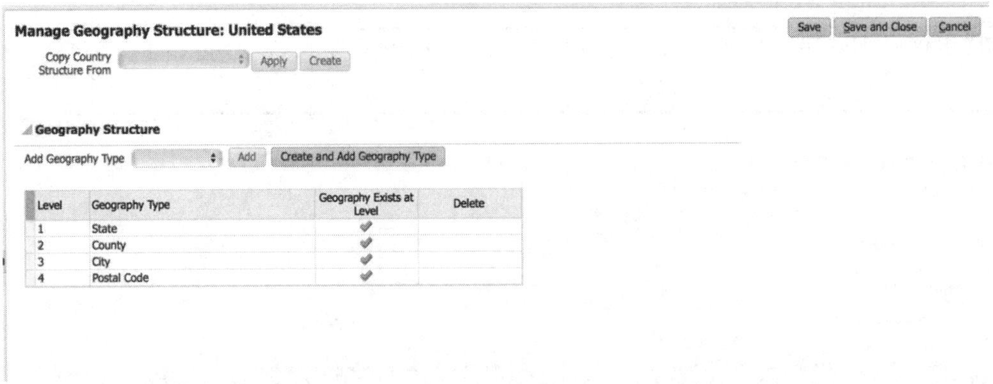

Manage Geography Structure: United States

Copy Country Structure From [ ] Apply   Create

⊿ **Geography Structure**

Add Geography Type [ ] Add   Create and Add Geography Type

Level	Geography Type	Geography Exists at Level	Delete
1	State	✓	
2	County	✓	
3	City	✓	
4	Postal Code	✓	

FIGURE 4-16. *United States Geography structure*

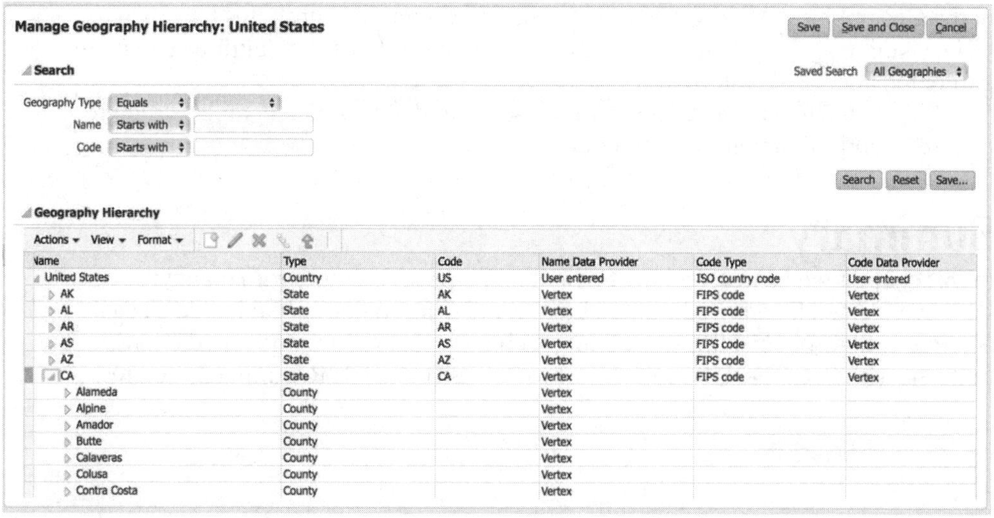

FIGURE 4-17. *United States Geography hierarchy*

■ **Geography validation** Geography Validation allows linking address style formats with the Geography hierarchy defined for the country earlier. Each of the Geography types can be mapped to address attributes and can be enabled for Geography or Tax validation as shown in Figure 4-18. Additionally, it is possible to specify whether the Geography type needs to be enabled for a list of values, thereby reducing the data entry errors.

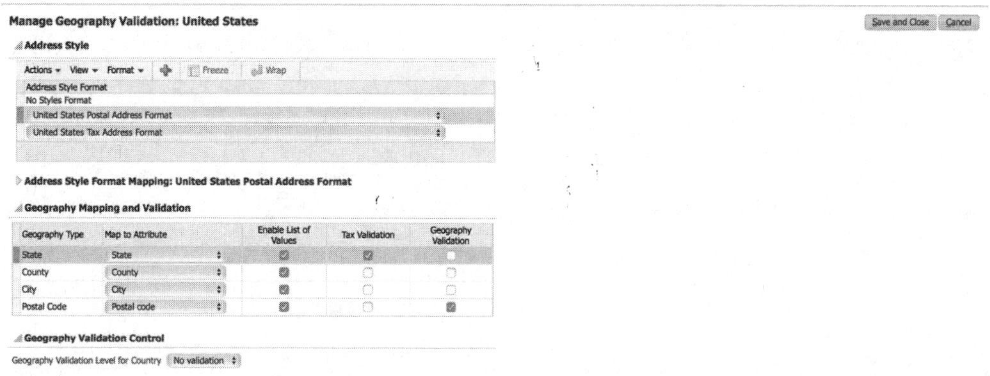

FIGURE 4-18. *United States Geography validation*

In addition to Geography validation, users can define Address Cleansing for each of the Geographies. Address Cleansing validates Geography attributes like State, County, and Post Code that we discussed earlier and Address line attributes that are part of the address style format.

Using the Manage Geographies Task, users can define the Geography structure, hierarchy, and validation for each country.

Summary

In this chapter we have seen how to create Enterprise Structure for Financials. We have created Enterprise Structures for ACME Corporation, Legal Entities, Legal Address, and associated the Legal Entity with Legal Authorities and Jurisdictions. In the next chapter, we will look at how to define Financials Reporting Structures.

CHAPTER
5

Financials Reporting Structure: Chart of Accounts Structures, Calendars, and Currencies

Continuing from the previous chapter, which described the financial enterprise structures of our example ACME Corporation and outlined the high-level business reporting requirements, we are now going to delve further into Fusion Financials techniques and methods that will help us to meet those requirements. More specifically, this chapter will cover the creation of charts of accounts structures, charts of accounts instances, calendars, and currencies as prerequisites to the creation and implementation of ledgers in Fusion Financials. Collectively, we also refer to these structures as Financials Reporting Structures.

In Oracle Applications documentation and literature, the combination of chart of accounts, calendar, and currency is often referred as the "three Cs," and the term "chart of accounts" is often abbreviated as CoA, which is a convention we are going to use frequently from now on. The concept of CoA is arguably the most important enterprise structure along with legal entities, ledgers, accounting configurations, and the concept of business units. For that reason, most of this chapter will be dedicated to CoA structures and instances. Calendars and currencies are equally required when setting up a ledger in Fusion Financials; however, they are configuration elements that are fairly easy and straightforward to understand.

Through examples using our ACME Corporation and ACME Bank use cases, we'll learn how to set up and organize CoA structures and instances, and how to set up calendars and currencies in the system. Whenever possible, we will provide recommendations and good practices in addition to introducing concepts such as CoA structure and CoA instance.

Let's start this chapter by providing the intuition behind the Fusion Financials CoA concept, as well as the motivation for such a product design approach.

Introduction to the Chart of Accounts Structure Concept

In Chapter 2, we highlighted the role that ledgers play in Fusion Financials. We described how business transaction data is recorded in ledgers and subledgers using different types of accounts, and we also stated that the list of all accounts made available for recording of transactions grouped by account type is called the chart of accounts (CoA). In Chapter 2 we also provided an example of accounting transactions using an Accounts Receivables (AR) use case to introduce some very basic accounting concepts. We now have an outline of ACME Corporation organizations, and we are in a position to provide a more representative use case and example from the banking industry, which is used throughout the book.

We start our exploration of the intuition behind the CoA structure concept by introducing a new accounting use case that is applicable to the ACME Global Markets, Inc., legal entity and the ACME Global Markets USA LOB (line of business) as shown in Chapter 4 in Figure 4-1.

An Example: Securities Trading Accounting Events Use Case

This use case covers a securities trading scenario through our ACME Global Markets legal entity (company). In a nutshell, *securities* are financial instruments that are bought and sold on the financial markets. ACME Global Markets' trading division trades stocks on a short-term basis with the intent to buy and sell for short-term profit. Such investments can be held on the bank's books for a few days, weeks, or even bought and sold within the same day. ACME Global Markets doesn't short-sell stocks (also known as *short selling*) in the open market. All securities in this use case are considered trading securities for accounting purposes.

The securities that ACME Global Markets trades are considered highly liquid and are classified on the balance sheet as current assets. The changes in value of the stocks are calculated and recorded as the operating income, which is sometimes referred to as Earnings Before Interest and Taxes and is part of the income statement (profit and loss, or P&L, statement).

The following business events apply:

- Stock (shares) purchase

- Dividends receipt (if any)

- Stock sale (for profit or loss)

- Stock price (fair value) change at the end of an accounting period

In Figure 5-1 we show these four events and transaction flow using "T account" representation describing the use case where a trader buys 10 shares of Oracle stock at $10, keeps it for a while until Oracle Corporation declares a $0.50 cash dividend for each share, and decides to sell the shares on the stock exchange.

Chart of Accounts and Multiple Segment Chart of Accounts Structure

As mentioned in Chapter 2, in double-entry accounting systems, every transaction has two effects known as Debit (Dr) and Credit (Cr), and for every Dr entry there is going to be an equal Cr entry that will be posted into a ledger. The entries are posted against accounts, which in our use case are Trading Stock, Cash, Dividend Receivable, Dividend Income, and Realized Gain accounts. These accounts are referred to as *natural accounts* and they are usually associated with numbers. For example, the accounts that belong to the Assets type can have a range of 1000-1099 associated with it, and under this range we can further subdivide it into 1000-1009 for Cash and 1010-1019 for Receivables. The cash accounts range can further be subdivided

Event 1: Trader buys 10 shares of Oracle stock priced at $10.00

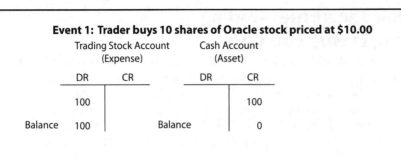

	Trading Stock Account (Expense)			Cash Account (Asset)	
	DR	CR		DR	CR
	100				100
Balance	100		Balance		0

Event 2: Oracle declares $0.50 cash dividend for each share

	Dividend Receivable (Asset)			Dividend Income (Revenue)	
	DR	CR		DR	CR
	5				5
Balance	5		Balance		5

Event 3: ACME Bank receives cash dividend

	Cash Account (Asset)			Dividend Receivable (Asset)	
	DR	CR		DR	CR
	5				5
Balance	5		Balance		5

Event 4: Trader sells 10 Oracle shares at $12.00 market price

	Realized Gain Account (Revenue)			Trading Stock Account (Expense)			Cash Account (Asset)	
	DR	CR		DR	CR		DR	CR
		5			5		120	
Balance		5	Balance		5	Balance	125	

FIGURE 5-1. *Use-case example of securities trading accounting transactions*

into account 1001 for Regular Cash, account 1002 for Payroll Cash, account 1003 for Petty Cash, and so forth.

Single-Segment Chart of Accounts

This is just an arbitrary example, but the point is that the list of all accounts in use by accountants or the system is referred to as the chart of accounts. From an accounting perspective, there is nothing to stop us from recoding securities trading transactions and entering journal entries manually in a simple spreadsheet, using account numbers like 1001, 5002 for trading expense, 1003 for dividend receivable account, and so forth, as illustrated in Figure 5-2.

The example in Figure 5-2 shows transactions generated to record the trader's actions of buying Oracle stock and business events related to Oracle Corporation's dividend declaration, which has a direct impact on ACME Global Markets' books as soon as the dividend is announced. In an enterprise like ACME Corporation, which has trading lines of business in many countries spread across multiple legal entities, it would be really difficult to meet the reporting requirements such as those listed in Chapter 4 without having a flexible mechanism of being able to add an arbitrary number of data elements capable of capturing additional information on the transaction level.

Multiple-Segment Chart of Accounts

In simple terms, a single-segment chart of accounts that consists only of a list of natural accounts is not going to help us in answering questions like: "What is the total dollar value of stocks that ACME Corporation held in all legal entities across the globe for the month of April in 2014?" This is because we are not capturing legal entity information on a journal-line level, and to meet those reporting requirements, we would need to provide alternative processes, such as manual spreadsheet merging and the like.

This brings us to the idea of using a multiple-segment chart of accounts, which is a concept inherited and borrowed from Oracle E-Business Suite. The idea is

Journal Line Number	Journal Line Description	Debit Amount	Credit Amount	Natural Account	Date
1	BUY ORCL@10.00	100		5002	10-Apr-14
2	BUY ORCL@10.00		100	1001	10-Apr-14
3	DIVI DECLARED ORCL	5		1003	28-Now-14
4	DIVI DECLARED ORCL		5	5002	28-Nov-14
				Single-Segment CoA	

FIGURE 5-2. *Example journal lines using a single-segment chart of accounts*

Journal Line Number	Journal Line Description	Debit Amount	Credit Amount	Natural Account	Company	LOB	Date
1	BUY ORCL@10.00	100		5002	ACME US MKT	TRADING	10-Apr-14
2	BUY ORCL@10.00		100	1001	ACME US MKT	TRADING	10-Apr-14
3	DIVI DECLARED ORCL	5		1003	ACME US MKT	TRADING	28-Now-14
4	DIVI DECLARED ORCL		5	5002	ACME US MKT	TRADING	28-Nov-14
5	BUY IBM@100.00	1000		5002	ACME US MKT	TRADING	11-Apr-14
6	BUY IBM@100.00		1000	1001	ACME US MKT	TRADING	11-Apr-14
7	DIVI DECLARED IBM	50		1003	ACME US MKT	TRADING	13-Dec-14
8	DIVI DECLARED IBM		50	5002	ACME US MKT	TRADING	13-Dec-14
				Multiple-Segment CoA			

FIGURE 5-3. *Example journal lines using a multiple-segment chart of accounts*

illustrated in Figure 5-3, which shows additional data elements being captured on a journal-entry level: Company and LOB (line of business).

These additional data elements captured at the source allow us to answer more complex questions in our reports, including one we asked in the previous section. Most readers will also recognize them as dimensions, and in fact, all segments that make up a multiple-segment CoA are dimensions in Fusion Financials Reporting Business Intelligence (BI) tools.

We can go on and add another segment called "Ticker," for example, to capture stock exchange ticker information such as ORCL and IBM. This would enable us to further slice and dice our data in relation to individual stocks that we own or owned in the past.

Intuitively, it implies that we need to take into consideration what in our organization makes sense from a transactional reporting and analytics perspective, and it is the concrete business reporting requirements that should drive the structure and granularity of the data we capture in General Ledger through a multiple-segment CoA structure in Fusion Financials. To state the obvious, we cannot report against data that has not been captured; therefore, having an appropriate CoA structure is one of the key considerations when planning Fusion Financials implementation. On the other hand, capturing too much data, or even data that is not required by the business, is going to slow down both the system performance and data entry into the system (manual or automated).

Core Fusion CoA Structures, Instances, and Other CoA Components

We demonstrated in previous sections that in Oracle Fusion Financials the concept of the chart of accounts is based on the CoA structure, which defines key CoA attributes that we also think of as reporting dimensions. As previously mentioned, this product design approach is borrowed from Oracle E-Business Suite, but in

Fusion Financials the product design introduces a new component: a chart of accounts instance or CoA instance for short. To be able to understand the difference between structure and instances, we need to have a very basic understanding of other CoA building blocks such as value sets, account hierarchies, and others that Oracle Applications implementation consultants collectively often refer to as just a chart of accounts or CoA.

CoA Building Blocks Overview

Each CoA structure attribute is also known as a CoA segment. If we look back at Figure 5-3, the business transactions require concrete values such as account numbers and company code to be recorded in each journal entry. In Fusion Financials we associate value sets with each segment, which are merely a container for concrete segment values such as 1001, 1003, and so on for account segment and ACME US MKT and ACME UK MKT for company segments in our previous example. Value sets also provide a validation and formation mechanism during data capture, for example, when the end user is entering data through the user interface in the browser. Security can be applied at the value-set level by enforcing security rules along with cross-validation rules, which determine what segment values can be combined with other values across the segments in the CoA.

The unique combination of segment values such as "5002.ACME US MKT .TRADING" is called *account combination*. In Oracle Fusion Financials, this is how the accounts are uniquely identified. The "." (dot) character in this example is used as a segment delimiter, but implementers can also use the "-" (hyphen) or other symbols as delimiters.

Another important concept specific to Oracle Fusion is the concept of segment labels. Segment labels enable us to mark some segments in the CoA structure with special tags or qualifiers. The purpose of doing this is to enable and assign special meaning and functionality to those segments. The list of segment labels as shown in Table 5-1 is documented in multiple places in Oracle product documentation.

For example, if we mark the "Company" segment depicted in Figure 5-3 in Fusion CoA as "Primary Balancing," we are indicating to the system that all entered journals must balance by the "Company" segment value.

 NOTE
For readers without an accounting background who are wondering what balancing actually means in this context, please refer to Chapter 2 where we covered the very basics of accounting concepts, including journal balancing.

Segment Label	Usage
Primary balancing segment label	Validates and enforces that all journals are balanced in accounting terms for each primary balancing segment value. (Required)
Second balancing segment label	Validates and enforces that all journals are balanced in accounting terms by a combination of balancing segment values. In practice you would use it if balancing is required below the legal entity level. This is an optional label.
Third balancing segment label	Validates and enforces that all journals are balanced in accounting terms by a combination of balancing segment values. In practice you would use it if balancing is required below the legal entity level. This is an optional label.
Intercompany segment label	This label is used for intercompany balancing. Although optional, it is recommended to enable it for new CoA implementations.
Cost center segment	By assigning this label to an appropriate segment, we can group natural accounts by cost centers to track expenses, for example. Similar to the intercompany segment, it is recommended to enable it for new CoA implementations. Although it is optional, certain Fusion Financials products, such as the Assets module, mandate for this segment to be enabled.
Natural account segment label	The segment marked with this label denotes a natural account that can be an asset, liability, expense, revenue, or owners equity. (Required)
Management segment label	Must not be used in current releases. This is reserved for future Fusion Financials releases.

TABLE 5-1. *CoA Segment Labels*

From a functional perspective, having a balancing segment label assigned to a segment allows the user to create balance sheets and trial balances by individual balancing segment values representing legal entities or companies, for example.

Additionally, implementation consultants can optionally create account hierarchies to identify management, company, or geographical relationships between value sets to summarize general ledger balances vertically. There are many other uses for hierarchies in Fusion Applications, such as in CoA mappings and cross-validation rules, but from a financial reporting perspective, account hierarchies are used in GL balance cubes in true OLAP (Online Analytical Processing) fashion. In this scenario, the dimension is organized in a hierarchical parent-child set of elements, where the parent balance is typically a sum of child balances. In Fusion Applications, a CoA segment can have multiple hierarchies, which in turn can have multiple versions, allowing you to analyze the same data using different hierarchies.

CoA Structure Versus CoA Instance

Every Fusion Financials implementation must have at least one chart of accounts structure. But what about the CoA instances? It turns out that there should also be at least one CoA instance too, and it is the instances that we work with when operating the system after the implementation. CoA instances inherit all the elements and attributes of the CoA structure, and we can create as many as we like to meet our requirements. An obvious use case is to, for example, have a global CoA with value sets controlled by each country to meet their local reporting and organization structure requirements. One of the benefits of this approach is consistent interpretation of revenue and costs elements across the whole enterprise.

Figure 5-4 shows an example of a simple CoA structure consisting of three segments with default value sets attached to each segment. This could be global or any other CoA structure for that matter, and it is the instances of this structure that are customized to meet specific reporting and/or transactional requirements by attaching and assigning specific value sets and account hierarchies (dashed boxes). Additionally, each instance can control the dynamic account creation feature by switching it on and off.

NOTE
The concept of CoA structures and instances is somewhat related to an object-oriented paradigm. We can think of the CoA structure as a template or blueprint, whereas instances are the actual run-time realizations of structures that we work with. CoA instances receive or inherit the properties of CoA structures. However, in a CoA instance, we can indicate what is different from the CoA structure without having to create a new structure each time. This approach promotes reuse and a better governance process related to Fusion Financials implementations.

In the next sections we will proceed with practical considerations for our example ACME Corporation CoA implementation.

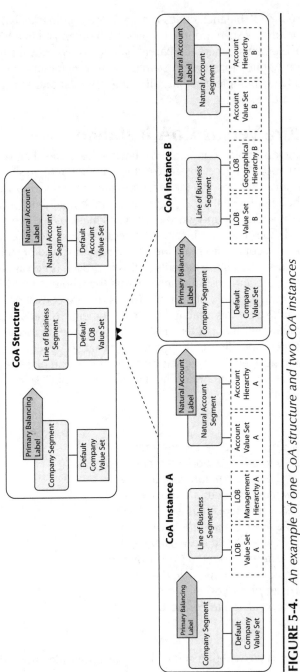

FIGURE 5-4. An example of one CoA structure and two CoA instances

An Example: Key CoA Design Decisions

The decisions around CoA design and General Ledger strategy are probably the most important design decisions that impact Fusion Financials implementation, as well as wider enterprise information, data, and application architectures.

The CoA structure must be designed carefully to meet current business requirements, but must also take into consideration future growth and expansion by, for example, inclusion of "spare" segments. The granularity of data detail that we intend to record in General Ledger depends on how we want to use it: financial control purposes, reporting, or both. If the primary focus is on financial control, then the CoA structure usually will have fewer segments, which results in something known as "thin" General Ledger. On the other hand, business requirements that stress financial reporting usually yield a CoA structure with many segments to allow capturing a finer level of transaction detail.

The design of the CoA structure usually starts with business analysis of regulatory, statutory, and management requirements. There are many aspects of the business that can be tracked, like companies, legal entities, lines of business, cost centers, regions and countries, departments, products, projects, and so forth. However, we also need to take into consideration non-functional requirements, such as how the performance of the system is impacted by capturing transaction detail otherwise available in subledgers; for example, availability of non–Oracle Fusion reporting tools, existing data warehouse and reporting strategy, and so on.

ACME Chart of Account Design Considerations

Let us recall that our example ACME Corporation operates across several regions in the United States, Latin America, Japan, and the United Kingdom. Its core activities are typical for the financial services industry and include retail banking, wealth management, international markets, and insurance. As outlined in Chapter 4, there are two primary types of reports we need to cater for:

- **Legal entity–level reporting**   Required to satisfy regulatory requirements. Also, on the ACME group level, ACME Corporation needs to aggregate balances across all legal entities to produce quarterly and yearly financial statement reports.

- **Line-of-business–level reporting**   Required to satisfy the corporation's management requirements and corporate strategy; in particular, to increase line-of-business management efficiency and accountability for profit and loss.

Additionally, the ACME Insurance Holding company in the United States holds balances for both the ACME Reinsurance Company, Inc., and ACME Life Company, Inc. ACME Insurance Holding Company is required to identify their risk exposure per location. It is a regulatory requirement, which is dealt with by a manual process at the current time.

ACME Global CoA Structure

After analyzing the ACME Corporation business as a whole, reporting requirements, and non-functional requirements such as volume and type of transactions, it was proposed that the ACME Global Chart of Accounts (Global CoA) should consist of six segments, as shown in Table 5-2.

Figure 5-5 shows the structure of the ACME Global CoA.

Segment Name	Segment Label	Description
Company	Primary Balancing	<ul><li>Company segment represents ACME legal reporting line.</li><li>Flagging Company segment as "Balancing" segment will provide Trial Balance (Profit & Loss and Balance Sheet) at Company segment level.</li><li>Each legal entity within ACME will be presented as a balancing segment value or company code within this segment. For example, ACME UK PLC will be a legal entity and will be presented by a unique company code "20," whereas ACME US Inc. will be assigned company code "10."</li><li>Sometimes company codes can be created without linking to any real legal entity. These are called GL-only company codes or quasi-companies as they can't be used in a subledger. An example would be adjustment entities or an elimination company for consolidation and reporting purposes.</li></ul>
Line of Business	Secondary Balancing	<ul><li>The Line of Business segment represents the ACME Divisional or Stream and Business reporting line. Flagging this segment with a "Secondary Balancing" label will provide trial balance (Profit & Loss and Balance Sheet) at this level in addition to the "Company" segment.</li><li>Because ACME Corporation is a global company with diversified interests, as part of its quarterly and annual reporting, it needs to provide its investors with detailed reporting of its stream and/or divisions' performance. This allows investors more insight about the company's earnings and balance sheet representing the health of the company on a line-of-business level. It will allow investors to compare the ACME Corporation's performance to an equivalent company in their particular sector or line of business. Flagging the "Line of Business" segment as "Secondary Balancing" would provide this level of reporting.</li><li>It also allows ACME Corporation's management team within each division or stream to be run as a separate company with more responsibility and accountability.</li></ul>

TABLE 5-2. *ACME Global CoA Structure (Continued)*

Segment Name	Segment Label	Description
Cost centre	Cost Centre	Cost Centres represent the destination of an expense in ACME Corporation.
Account	Natural Account	Determines the account type: asset, liability, expense, revenue, or equity.
Intercompany	Intercompany	Assigns the segment to be used in intercompany balancing functionality.
Spare		ACME Corporation may use this segment in the future.

TABLE 5-2.   *ACME Global CoA Structure*

ACME Reporting Hierarchies and Roll-Ups

Hierarchies allow us to summarize and view the same accounting data from different perspectives. As shown in Figure 5-5, ACME will have separate segments (dimensions) for legal entities ("Company" segment) and lines of business ("Line of Business" segment) to which we plan to attach corresponding entity and management hierarchies, which are shown in Figures 5-6 and 5-7, respectively. (In Figure 5-6, we showed the Latin America region for illustration purposes only. Recall that in Chapter 4 we excluded Latin America from our example implementation project.)

TIP
When designing a CoA, use numeric codes for child values such as company codes (for example, 01, 02, 21, and so on). Use letters for parent values such as "US" and "UK" to make it easier to tell apart one level in the hierarchy from another when designing and looking at reports.

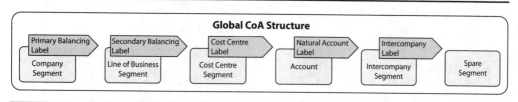

FIGURE 5-5.   *ACME Global CoA structure segments*

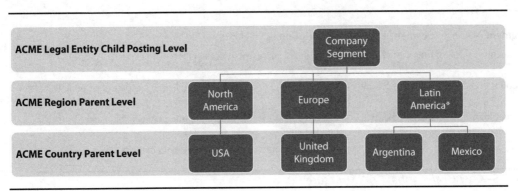

FIGURE 5-6. *Legal Entity reporting hierarchy*

The ACME Corporation reporting hierarchy that hangs off the "Lines of Business" segment is shown in Figure 5-7.

An example of how hierarchies get created is covered later in the book; for now let's make a note that account hierarchies in Fusion Applications are extensively used, and some examples are Cross-validation rules, Revaluations and Chart of Accounts mappings, and in Financial Reporting in allocations, smart views, and so forth.

NOTE
There could be multiple hierarchies for each segment for different purposes. Also, as per Oracle Support Note: 1980180.1, if you have value set values that do not participate in a hierarchy tree and those values are associated with transactions, then you have to create a dummy tree to include those nodes; otherwise, these particular value set values will not appear in Business Intelligence (BI).

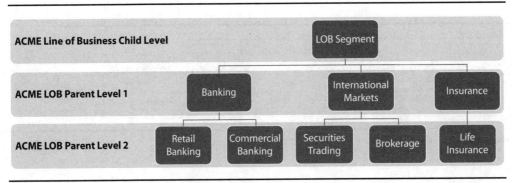

FIGURE 5-7. *Line of Business reporting hierarchy*

ACME Insurance CoA Structure

As mentioned in Chapter 4, one of ACME Insurance Holding Company's major challenges in their statutory and regulatory reporting is identification of their risk exposure per location. For that reason a separate ACME Insurance CoA structure will be created, which will have all of the segments from Global CoA plus one additional segment called "Location." It is believed that adding the "Location" dimension will increase reporting productivity, as well as improved governance, around statutory and regulatory reporting requirements specific to ACME Corporation's insurance business.

With that in mind we'll now proceed to show the practical steps involving the CoA structure and instances creation in Fusion Applications.

An Example: ACME Chart of Accounts Implementation Steps

In our demonstration we are going to use "GL Implementation Consultant ACME" (user id XXFA_FIN_GL_IMPLEMENTATION_CONSULTANT). This implementation user has already been assigned relevant tasks, which can be verified in Functional Setup Manager as shown in Figure 5-8.

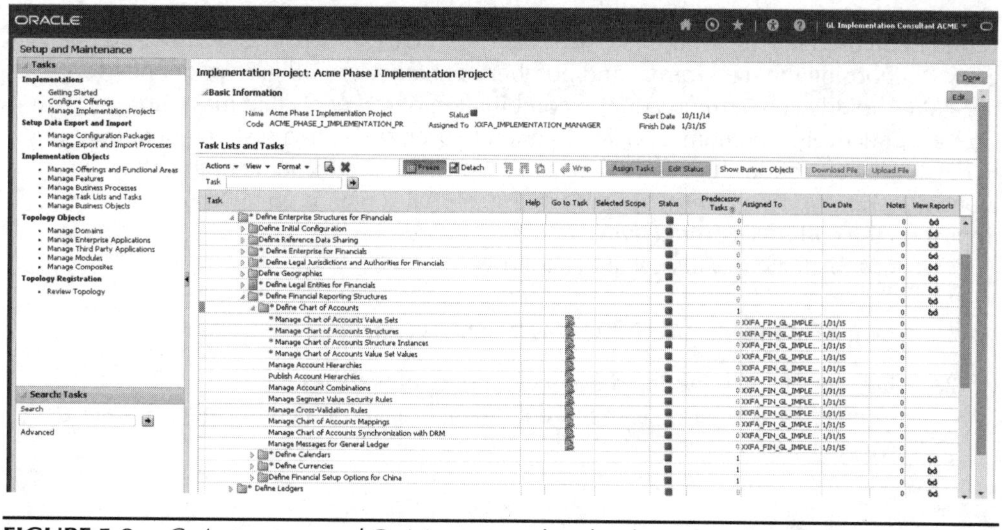

FIGURE 5-8. *CoA structure and CoA instance-related tasks assigned to implementation user*

As you can see, the configuration tasks are listed in the Define Financial Reporting Structures section and the process can be summarized as follows:

■ Create empty value sets with no values (required step).

■ Define CoA structures (required step).

■ Create CoA instances (required step).

■ Create value set values and assign attributes to them if required (required step).

■ Define and publish account hierarchies (optional step).

■ Define segment value security rules (optional step).

■ Define cross-validation rules (optional step).

In the following sections we are going to describe the required steps, as well as the key actions that need to be performed in the system when configuring CoA structures and instances.

Create ACME Value Sets

Value sets determine the types and format of data values such as character, number, or date. We can also define the validation of values by, for example, forcing a list of values to be used in CoA segments. Needless to say, careful consideration should be given in choosing the right format and number of characters or digits we define here. We should keep in mind that the combination of segments that make up a CoA are effectively a combination key frequently used by human system operators in day-to-day operations; therefore, having to type in a complicated combination of alphanumeric characters for an account in the journal screen is going to have an impact on the end user's productivity.

The steps to create a value set are as follows:

1. Navigate to the Manage Value Sets task from Functional Setup Manager.

2. Click the Create button and populate the input fields as per Table 5-3. For example, for company segment, enter details as illustrated in Figure 5-9 and save your work.

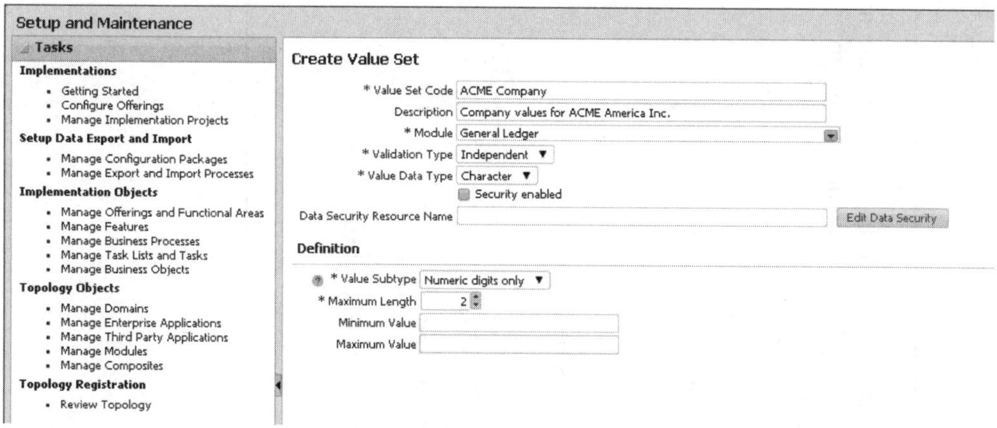

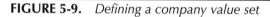

FIGURE 5-9.   *Defining a company value set*

TIP

If you want to define and create hierarchies from the values that belong to a value set, use the Independent validation type. Most implementations use the Character data type and the Independent validation type, and we also recommend that you start the design considerations using that format and validation combination.

Table 5-3 lists value sets we created in our example ACME Corporation implementation. Note that we specified a maximum of only two digits for the "Company" segment, which means that we can handle only up to 100 legal entities or companies in our ACME enterprise.

We have created all value sets that we can use as defaults in CoA instances, as shown in Figure 5-10.

Value Set Code	Description	Module	Validation Type	Value Data Type	Security Enabled	Value Set Subtype	Maximum Length
ACME Account	Natural Account Values	General Ledger	Independent	Character	Unchecked	Text	5
ACME Company	Company values for ACME America, Inc.	General Ledger	Independent	Character	Unchecked	Text	2
ACME Cost Centre	ACME Cost Centre	General Ledger	Independent	Character	Unchecked	Text	4
ACME Intercompany	ACME Intercompany	General Ledger	Independent	Character	Unchecked	Text	2
ACME Line of Business	ACME Line of Business	General Ledger	Independent	Character	Unchecked	Text	4
ACME Spare	Values for Spare segment	General Ledger	Independent	Character	Unchecked	Text	5

TABLE 5-3.   *List of ACME Corporation Value Sets*

Manage Value Sets					Save	Save and Close	Cancel

⊿Search

```
** Value Set Code   ACME%
** Validation Type          ▼
** Value Data Type          ▼
** Module                                      ⊠
```

** At least one is required

Search   Reset

Search Results

Actions ▾   View ▾   Format ▾   📄 ✏ ✖   ▥ Freeze   ▦ Detach   ◧ Wrap | Manage Values |

Value Set Code	Protected	Description	Module	Validation Type	Value Data Type
ACME Account		Natural Account Values	General Ledger	Independent	Character
ACME Company	—	Company values for ACME America Inc.	General Ledger	Independent	Character
ACME Cost Centre	—	ACME Cost Centre	General Ledger	Independent	Character
ACME Intercompany	—	ACME Intercompany	General Ledger	Independent	Character
ACME Line of Business	—	ACME Line of Business	General Ledger	Independent	Character
ACME Spare		Values for spare segment	General Ledger	Independent	Character

FIGURE 5-10. *Default ACME value sets*

NOTE
Although Figure 5-10 shows the value set for ACME Intercompany, it is not used in our example implementation. As we will see later, ACME Global CoA uses Company Value Set for the Intercompany segment in our example. Also, as per the Oracle Fusion Financials Implementation Guide, value sets for a chart of accounts must use the Value Data Type of Character. The Value Subtype is, in most implementations, set to Text, as a combination of these two settings support values that are both numbers and characters, which are typical in natural account segment values.

Define ACME CoA Structures

The definition of the CoA structure is one of the key activities in General Ledger implementation where we define the number of CoA segments, their sequence of appearance, segment names and prompts (labels) that appear on user interface screens, and segment labels and default value sets that can be overwritten when creating CoA instances.

As discussed earlier in this chapter, our example implementation has a requirement to define two CoA structures:

■ ACME Global CoA Structure, consisting of six segments: Company, Line of Business, Cost Centre, Account, Intercompany, and Spare.

■ ACME Insurance Structure, which is the same as the ACME Global CoA structure with the addition of a Location segment to deal with special reporting requirements that are specific to ACME Corporation's insurance business.

In this section we'll provide the steps required to create CoA structures in Fusion Financials using ACME Global CoA as an example.

Logged in as the ACME GL Implementation user, we navigate to the Manage Chart Of Accounts Structures screen by querying this task in Functional Setup Manager. As mentioned earlier, this task is assigned to us already, and there are various navigation paths to reach the screen, as shown in Figure 5-11.

Once the Manage Key Flexfield Structures screen is open, we click the Create button to define our ACME Global CoA structure as shown in Figure 5-12.

In the Create Key Flexfield Structure screen, we enter the following values:

Name: **ACME Global COA Structure**
Description: **ACME Global COA Structure**
Delimiter: **. (dot character)**
Enabled: **Checked**

After clicking the Save button (not shown in Figure 5-12), we can proceed to add segments to our Global CoA by clicking the Create button in the Segments region on

1. Go to the Manage Chart Of Accounts Structures screen and click Go To Task.

2. Enter **General Ledger** in the Module field and click the Search button.

04:57:05 27/10/2014

Manage Chart of Accounts Structures   Done

⊿**Search**

Key Flexfield Code
Key Flexfield Name
Module General Ledger   Search Reset

Search Results

Actions ▾ View ▾ Format ▾ ▥ Freeze ▥ Detach ▥ Wrap | Manage Structures | Manage Structure Instances | Deploy Flexfield |

| Application | Key Flexfield Name | Key Flexfield Code | Module | Entity Usages | Deployment Status |
| General Ledger | Accounting Flexfield | GL# | General Ledger | | |

3. Select the General Ledger application and click the Manage Structures button.

FIGURE 5-11. *Selecting the General Ledger application on the Manage Chart Of Accounts Structures screen*

1. In the Manage Key Flexfield Structures task, click the Create button to open the Create Key Flexfield Structure screen.

2. In the Create Key Flexfield Structure screen, enter the following values:
Structure Code: ACME_GLOBAL_COA_STRUCT

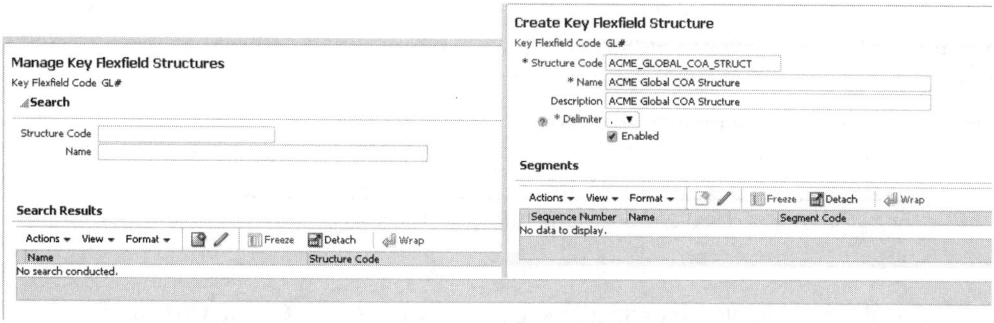

FIGURE 5-12. *Creating a CoA structure in Fusion Financials*

the screen, which opens Create Key Flexfield Segment screen to define accounting flexfield segments like it is illustrated in Figure 5-13.

In Table 5-4 we list the main attributes and their values that we use in our ACME Corporation implementation. Note that in our example the Intercompany segment has ACME Company assigned as its default value set.

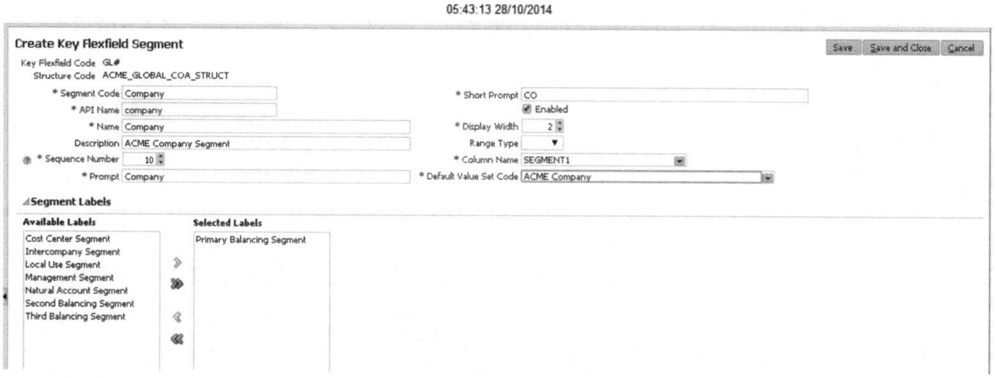

FIGURE 5-13. *Defining an Accounting Flexfield company segment*

Segment Code	Sequence Number	Selected Labels	Column Name	Default Value Set Code
Company	1	Primary Balancing Segment	SEGMENT1	ACME Company
LOB	2	Second Primary Segment	SEGMENT2	ACME Line of Business
COSTCENTRE	3	Cost Centre Segment	SEGMENT3	ACME Cost Centre
ACCOUNT	4	Natural Account Segment	SEGMENT4	ACME Account
Intercompany	5	Intercompany Segment	SEGMENT5	ACME Company
Spare	6	(none)	SEGMENT6	ACME Spare

TABLE 5-4. *Accounting Key Flexfield Segment Attribute Values*

Once all the segments are defined, we can query the ACME Global CoA, and the refreshed screen should show all of the segments as illustrated in Figure 5-14.

We can now proceed with the creation of the ACME CoA instance based on the structure that we have just created.

Define ACME CoA Instances

For ACME Corporation we are going to have only two instances of the CoA that correspond to CoA structures we mentioned in the previous section. Again, for demonstration purposes we are going to cover the creation of only one ACME Global CoA instance.

In Functional Setup Manager we navigate to the Manage Chart Of Accounts Structure Instances task and query key flexfields for the General Ledger module. Clicking Manage Structure Instances will open the Manage Key Flexfield Structure

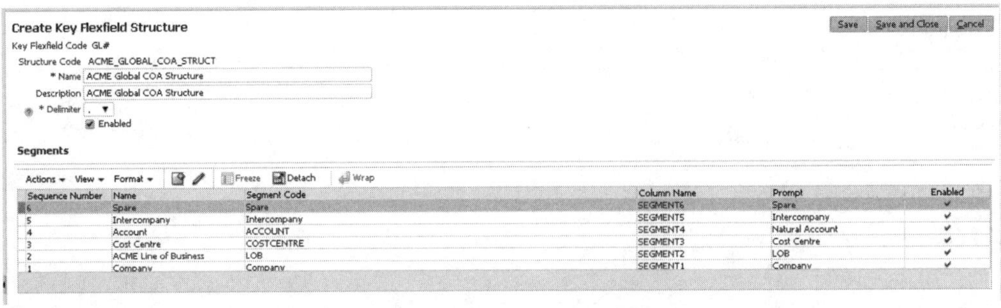

FIGURE 5-14. *List of segments assigned to ACME Global CoA structure*

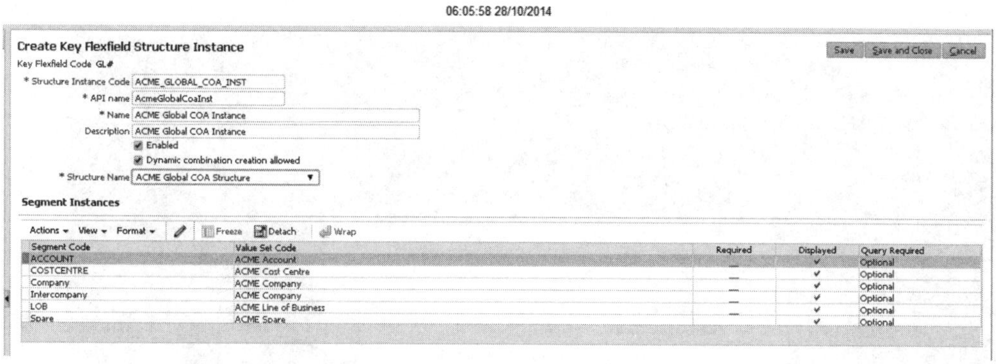

06:05:58 28/10/2014

Create Key Flexfield Structure Instance

Key Flexfield Code GL#

		Save	Save and Close	Cancel

* Structure Instance Code ACME_GLOBAL_COA_INST

* API name AcmeGlobalCoaInst

* Name ACME Global COA Instance

Description ACME Global COA Instance

☑ Enabled

☑ Dynamic combination creation allowed

* Structure Name ACME Global COA Structure ▼

Segment Instances

Actions ▼ View ▼ Format ▼ ✎ ▓ Freeze ▓ Detach ▓ Wrap

Segment Code	Value Set Code	Required	Displayed	Query Required
ACCOUNT	ACME Account	—	✔	Optional
COSTCENTRE	ACME Cost Centre	—	✔	Optional
Company	ACME Company	—	✔	Optional
Intercompany	ACME Company	—	✔	Optional
LOB	ACME Line of Business	—	✔	Optional
Spare	ACME Spare	—	✔	Optional

FIGURE 5-15. *Defining an ACME Global CoA instance*

instance screen, where we click the Create button to create our ACME Global COA Instance as shown in Figure 5-15.

NOTE
For each CoA instance, account balances are kept in a separate GL Essbase cube, and this needs to be taken into consideration when defining CoA and General Ledger strategies.

Deploying an Accounting Flexfield

The next step is to deploy the CoA instance we've just created.

In Functional Setup Manager, we navigate to the Manage Chart Of Accounts Structure Instances task and query key flexfields for the General Ledger module. If everything is defined correctly, clicking the Deploy Flexfield button should result in successful Accounting Flexfield deployment as shown in Figure 5-16.

Create ACME Value Set Values

ACME headquarters provided the implementation consultants with the list of legal entities (companies), and it was agreed to use entity identifiers as listed in Table 5-5.

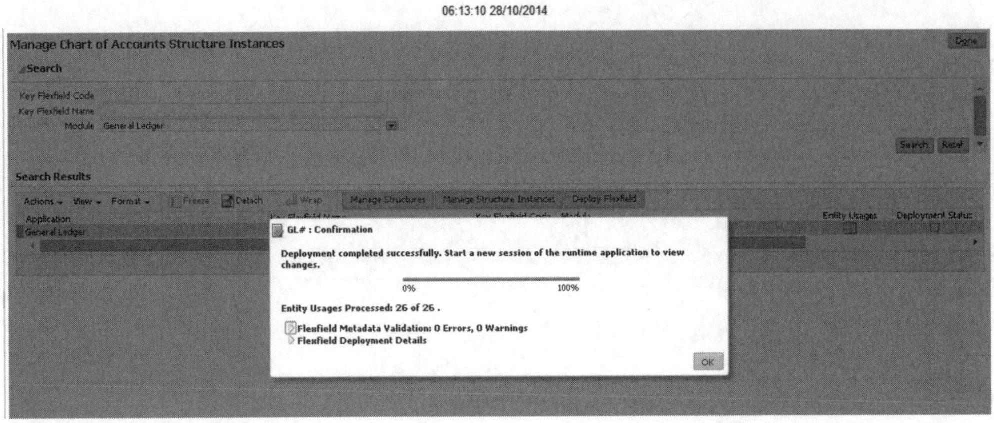

FIGURE 5-16. *Confirmation of successful Accounting Flexfield deployment*

To create value set values, we navigate to the Manage Chart Of Accounts Value Sets page and click the Manage Values button to enter values for each segment. Figure 5-17 shows the Create Value screen where we defined the Value "01" for ACME Bank legal entity (company).

Legal Entity	Legal Entity Identifier
ACME Bank	01
ACME Corp USA	10
ACME Commercial Finance, Inc.	11
ACME Mortgage, Inc.	12
ACME Global Markets, Inc.	13
ACME Insurance Holding	14
ACME Reinsurance Company, Inc.	15
ACME Life Company, Inc.	16
ACME UK Limited	20

TABLE 5-5. *List of ACME Legal Entities*

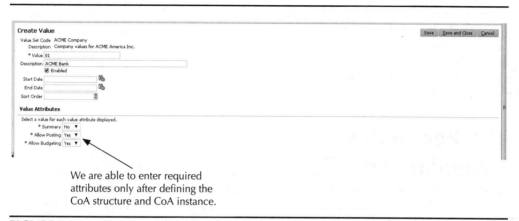

We are able to enter required
attributes only after defining the
CoA structure and CoA instance.

FIGURE 5-17. *Creating ACME Company value set values*

It is important to note that when creating a new CoA with new value sets, we
should create an empty value set definition with no values associated with it and
use it like a placeholder until we define our CoA structure and instance. This will
allow Fusion Financials to derive the appropriate value set value attributes in the
Create Value screen. Figure 5-18 shows an example of ACME Account value set
values, which have attributes relevant to the natural account segment functionality

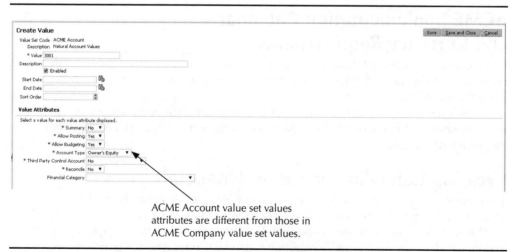

ACME Account value set values
attributes are different from those in
ACME Company value set values.

FIGURE 5-18. *ACME Account value set values attributes*

in our CoA. This is achieved by marking the CoA structure segment as Natural Account as mentioned in previous sections.

NOTE
The Sort Order attribute is not used when defining CoA structures and instances.

The Remaining Cs: Calendars and Currencies

Finally, we are going to mention a few words about the role of Calendars and Currencies, which are often referred to as the three C's along with Chart of Accounts in the world of Oracle Applications.

Accounting calendars enable business transactions to be recorded in accounting periods. Unlike calendar years we use in everyday life, the accounting years can run in arbitrary periods. They can start at any month, say in April rather than January, for example, which requires a system like Fusion Financials to provide flexible options to control the calendar definition. In addition to accounting calendars, we can create transaction calendars, which are used to track both the business and non-business days to calculate average balances should we need to do so.

Likewise, Fusion Financials comes with a predefined set of currencies that we can use to record the business transactions. Of course, there is also an option to create new currencies, and for both seeded and user-created currencies, we can maintain daily exchange rates between currencies.

ACME Implementation Calendar and Currency Requirements

In our example implementation we are going to assume an accounting calendar that coincides with the normal calendar year that runs from January to December with one adjusting period.

As for currencies, we will assume that General Ledger will be multicurrency with balances held in the original currency and translated to functional and reported currencies where required.

Creating Calendars in Fusion Financials

The process of creating accounting calendars in Fusion Applications is much improved and simplified in comparison to E-Business Suite releases.

We navigate to the Manage Accounting Calendars task and click the Create button, which opens the Create Accounting Calendar screen where we specify

1. Define calendar options, including the adjusting period frequency.

2. Define period details by accepting or amending the system-generated individual periods.

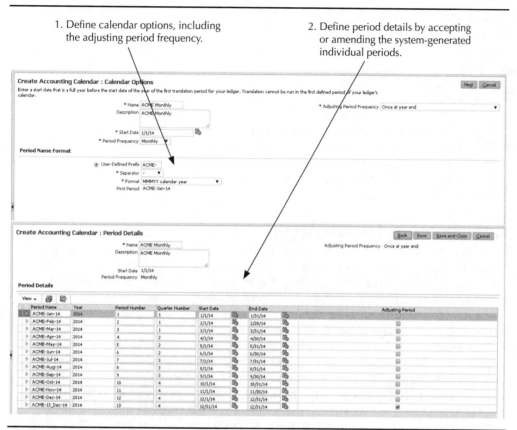

FIGURE 5-19. *ACME monthly accounting calendar*

options and populate calendar attributes and parameters as prompted on the page. The process consists of two steps as illustrated in Figure 5-19:

- **Create Accounting Calendar Options** We call our calendar ACME Monthly and initially it consists of 12 monthly periods that run from January to December 2014 plus an adjustment period at each year end. All periods are prefixed with "ACME."

- **Create Accounting Calendar Period Details** The period details are automatically generated for the most frequently used type of calendar frequencies (one year), which is the case with ACME Monthly calendar, although there is an option to change the system-generated periods should we wish to do so.

Of course, we can create multiple calendars and assign them to different ledgers if that is required by our ledger strategy.

TIP
We suggest that you carefully select the start period for a calendar. The reason for this is that when the first period is opened in General Ledger, the periods before cannot be opened. Also, functional currency translation of balances into another currency cannot be run in the first period due to the mechanism of opening balances being derived from the ending balance of the previous period.

Currencies in Fusion Applications

In addition to the chart of accounts and calendars, in Fusion Financials, as in many other ERP systems, currencies play an important role in a variety of business processes. As we shall see in succeeding chapters, when defining ledgers, we also define and assign currencies to them. Such currency is also called a *ledger functional currency*, which is the designated currency for group reporting, for example, U.S. dollars for ACME Corporation.

However, transactions that take place in everyday life, such as expenses incurred in a currency different than the one of the General Ledger, often require some kind of "accounting treatment." The currency that is used in ledger journals is called an *entered currency* (transaction currency), and the system needs a mechanism of translating between the two when deriving balances if the entered currency is also a foreign currency. In Fusion Financials, the balances are maintained in both the functional (ledger) and non-functional (foreign) currencies.

The processes that involve currencies are documented in Oracle Fusion Applications Financial Control and Reporting, Accounting Transactions, Tax Transactions, and Reporting Guide. Table 5-6 provides a summary for reference.

Process Name	Description
Revaluation	Adjusts foreign balances to allow for currency fluctuations between the functional and foreign currency. Performed on the account balances level.
Translation	Converts functional currency balances to foreign currency balances, usually to generate reports in a more stable currency.
Conversion	Transaction level of conversion performed on the fly to the functional ledger currency.

TABLE 5-6. *Currency-related business processes in Fusion General Ledger*

We assign conversion rate types to currency exchange rates to convert foreign currency journal amounts like British pound sterling into ledger functional currency like U.S. dollars. Functional currencies are automatically calculated based on daily exchange data that we provide during the conversion process.

NOTE
When defining a ledger, which we will go through in the next chapter, Fusion provides a feature to enable the Suspense check box in the Specifying Options page to handle automatic imbalances during posting. You can specify a Rounding Account attribute (field) and Entered Currency Balancing Account attribute (field) to balance a standard, reversal, or intercompany journal entries.

Cross-Validation Rules

The cross-validation rules ensure clean data is entered into journals during posting. These rules prevent specific combinations of segment values to be posted into account code combinations. For example, you may wish to prevent posting a journal into a consumer loan account for an insurance company. Such validations are logical because in this case an insurance company will not be giving consumer loans.

Cross-validation rules can be entered using a task named Manage Cross-Validation Rules task. In your implementation project this task is available within Define Common Applications Configuration For Financials | Define Enterprise Structures For Financials | Define Financial Reporting Structures | Define Chart Of Accounts, as shown in Figure 5-20.

In this example, go to the Cross-Validation Rules task and click the plus icon. Give your cross-validation rule a name, for example, "Disallow insurance company from giving consumer loans." Provide error message text that the system will show when journals are created with criteria that meet the filter conditions defined.

There are two filter conditions to be defined when creating cross-validation rules. First is the condition filter as shown in Figure 5-21. The condition here dictates that the system will evaluate this rule only for company 15, that is, Insurance Company.

Next you define the validation filter in which you state that account cannot be 42910, which represents a short-term consumer loan account. This is achieved by entering a validation filter with account does not equal 42910, as shown in Figure 5-22. Finally you can click the Enabled check box to activate this rule.

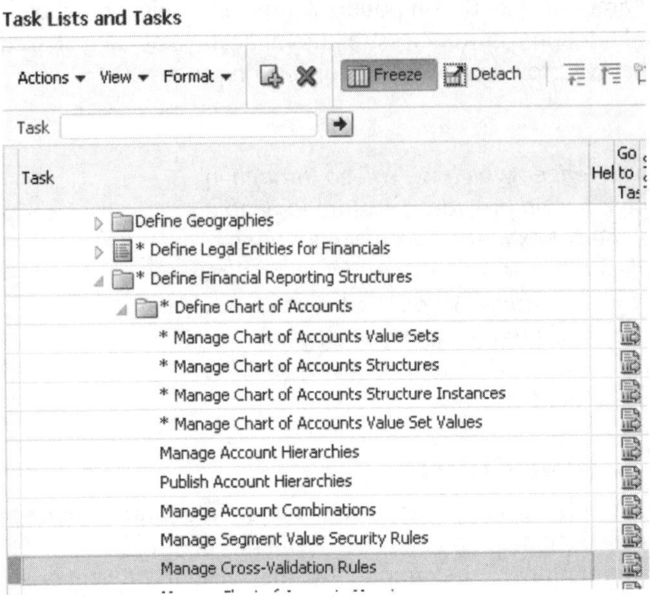

FIGURE 5-20. *Manage Cross-Validation Rules task*

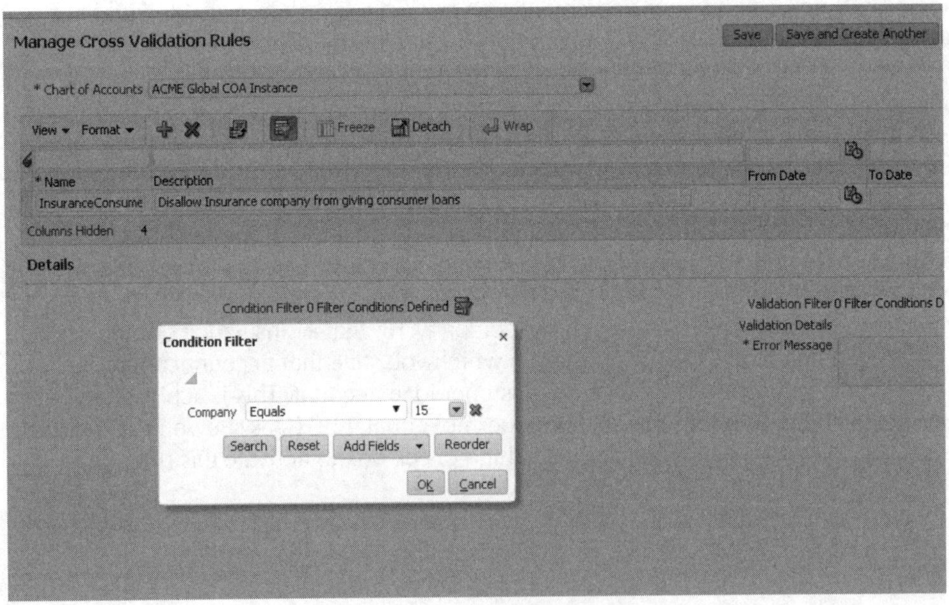

FIGURE 5-21. *Add condition filter to cross-validation rule*

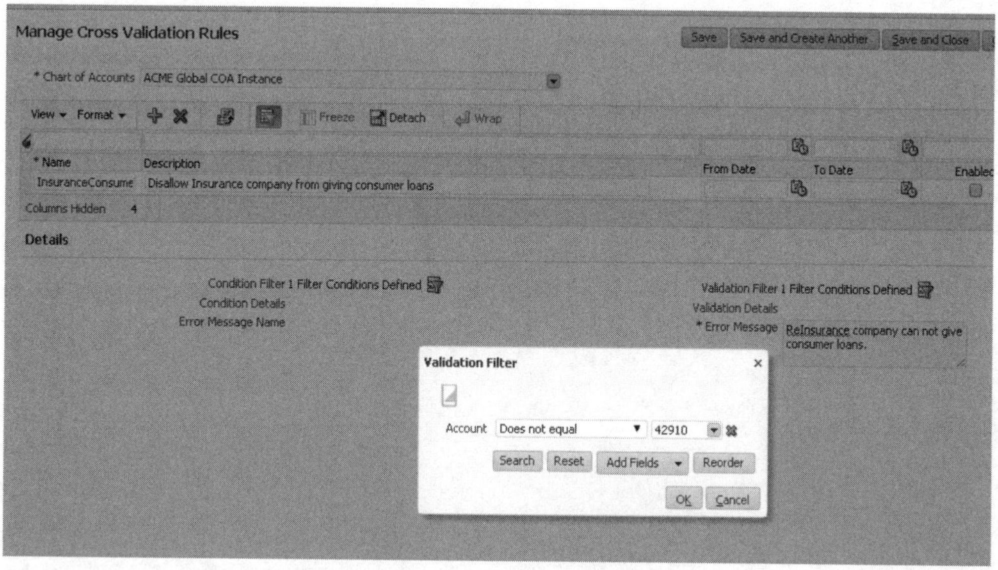

FIGURE 5-22.   *Add validation filter to cross-validation rule*

Summary

In this chapter we introduced the concepts of chart of accounts, calendar, and currencies in Fusion Financials. We also provided concrete examples using the ACME Corporation fictional company to demonstrate how these key structures are configured.

The chapters that follow will provide further detail on how to use these components to set up a ledger in Fusion Financials, how to enable security, and much more.

CHAPTER
6

Implement Ledgers and
Business Unit

In this chapter, we will introduce readers to the Ledgers and Business Unit concept in Enterprise Structure. A *ledger* is a principal book or computer file for recording and totaling transactions by account, with debits and credits in separate columns and an "opening" and "closing" balance for each account. A Business Unit is an organization in Enterprise Structure that processes transactions on behalf of one or more Legal Entities. Business Units are associated with Subledgers like Accounts Payable, Accounts Receivables, Procurement, and so on, where actual business transactions like Customer Invoicing, Customer Payments, Supplier Invoices, and Supplier Payments are processed.

In the previous chapter, we explained Financials Reporting Structures for Enterprise, namely Chart of Accounts, Currency, and Calendar. Financials Reporting Structures are fundamental building blocks for creating ledgers. In the first part of this chapter, we will understand how Financial Reporting Structures can be used to define ledgers and will introduce different types of ledgers that can be used to meet the statutory and management reporting requirements. We will also provide a high-level overview of how Enterprise Structure components and Financial Reporting Structures are associated and linked to enable the functioning of Fusion Financials General Ledger application. We will also explain the key decisions that influence creating a new Business Unit and how master data or reference data like supplier payment terms and customer payment terms can be shared across Business Units using reference data sets. In the second part of the chapter, we will apply our knowledge to create an ACME Ledgers structure and ACME Business Unit. At the end of the chapter, we will look at Intercompany Accounting processing options, which enable business activity among more than one Legal Entity within the Enterprise.

Ledgers

A Ledger is a combination of Currency, Accounting Calendar, Chart of Accounts, and Accounting Method as illustrated in Figure 6-1. The Ledger records transactional balances using this combination in the system. See a specific example shown in Figure 6-2.

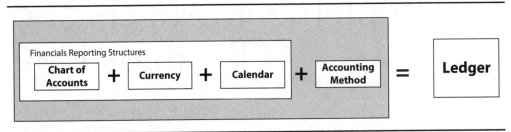

FIGURE 6-1. *The Ledger concept*

FIGURE 6-2. *An example Ledger created for a U.S.-based company*

Types of Ledgers

Fusion General Ledger provides three types of ledgers to be defined in the system. They are Primary, Secondary, and Reporting Currency. A Primary Ledger can be linked to one or more Secondary Ledgers, and Reporting Currency can be linked to one or more ledgers, either Primary or Secondary. The conceptual diagram in Figure 6-3 shows the types of ledgers and their relationships.

Primary Ledger

The Primary Ledger is the main record book of accounting information, and it is mandatory that every implementation has at least one Primary Ledger. The Primary Ledger is closely associated with Subledger transactions to provide context and accounting for the transactions. The Primary Ledger is uniquely identified using the following Financials Structure:

- Chart of Accounts

- Currency

- Accounting Calendar

- Accounting methods, that is, US GAAP Accounting, UK GAAP Accounting, Standard Accrual, Cash Based Accounting, or create Custom Subledger Accounting Method (SLAM).

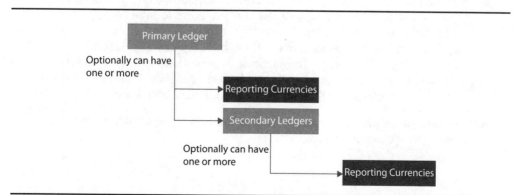

FIGURE 6-3. *Ledger types and their relationships*

Secondary Ledger

The Secondary Ledger is optional and always linked to the Primary Ledger. A Secondary Ledger is usually created for the purpose of tracking alternative accounting and provides the ability to report the balances in more than one way. The most important feature of the Secondary Ledger is that it allows defining a Chart of Accounts structure that is different from the Primary Ledger, in addition to having a different Currency, Accounting Calendar, and Accounting Method. This means that the Primary Ledger can have a COA structure with additional segments to satisfy local reporting needs, and the Secondary Ledger can mimic the COA structure of the group. This kind of Secondary Ledger setup allows for easy consolidation for group reporting with the level of data conversion required.

The Secondary Ledger provides four types of data conversion levels or processing options:

- **Balances level** Only balances are transferred from the Primary Ledger to the Secondary Ledger level. This is the least costly data conversion option, and balances are usually transferred as part of a period end process when the ledger balances are up to date in the Primary Ledger. Because only balances are transferred across to the Secondary Ledger, there is no drill-down to see details of journal entries or Subledger transaction details. The user has to run the Transfer Balances program to move balances from the Primary to Secondary Ledger.

- **Journal level** Only General Ledger Journals are transferred from the Primary Ledger to Secondary Ledger level. This transfer is performed as part of the General Ledger Posting Program. Whenever a journal is posted in the Primary Ledger, the same journal is replicated in the Secondary Ledger as part of the posting process for the journal sources and categories that are set up for this behavior.

- **Subledger level** This is the most expensive method of data conversion in terms of data storage, as both Journals and Subledger Journal entries are replicated in both Primary and Secondary Ledgers. Subledger Accounting Application (SLA) creates journal entries in both Primary and Secondary Journals using the Subledger Transactions, and the Posting program creates journal entries for all other transactions, including manual journal entries that do not integrate with the Subledger Accounting Application.

- **Adjustment-only level** Only adjustment journals are replicated from the Primary to Secondary Ledger.

NOTE
It is usually recommended that implementers choose the least costly level of data conversion for processing options, this being either the Balance or Adjustment data conversion level. However, in cases where countries have a history of a high inflationary economy and fluctuating exchange rates, it is recommended that implementers consider using the Subledger or Journal level data conversion.

TIP
As a best practice, before creating a Secondary Ledger, implementers should validate whether the same alternative accounting requirement can be met using the Reporting Currency Feature, where balances are stored in one additional currency apart from Primary Currency or one-time translation of balances from one Source Currency (Primary Ledger Currency) to Target Currency.

The Chart of Accounts mapping feature provides the ability to map accounts or entire account segments from one chart of accounts to another. A chart of accounts mapping is required if the Secondary Ledger uses a different chart of accounts structure than the Primary Ledger and the data conversion option is set to Balance or Journal in the Secondary Ledger. We will look at the Chart of Acounts mapping feature in detail later in the chapter.

Reporting Currencies

The Reporting Currency feature provides additional currency representation for a Primary or Secondary Ledger with different data conversion options to meet the accounting requirement.

Because it is closely attached to a source ledger (either Primary or Secondary), it will share the same Chart of Accounts, Calendar, and Accounting Method. However, it can have its own Currency and Processing Option for data conversion.

Reporting Currency provides three types of data conversation or processing options:

- **Balance level**   Only balances are transferred from the Source Ledger to the Target Currency.

- **Journal level** General Ledger Journals are transferred from the Source Ledger to the Target Currency.

- **Subledger level** This is the most expensive method of data conversion in terms of data storage, as both Journals and Subledger Transactions are replicated in both the Source Ledger and Reporting Currency.

Accounting Configuration

Using the Accounting Configuration definition task, implementers can define ledgers (Primary, Secondary, and Reporting Currency) and deploy the ledger definitions to a Fusion instance for booking transactions.

To navigate to the Define Accounting Configurations setup page, take the following steps:

1. Log in to Oracle Fusion Applications.

2. Click Navigator.

3. Navigate to the Tools | Setup And Maintenance link.

4. Search for the task Accounting Configuration, and the Define Accounting Configurations setup page will appear as shown in Figure 6-4.

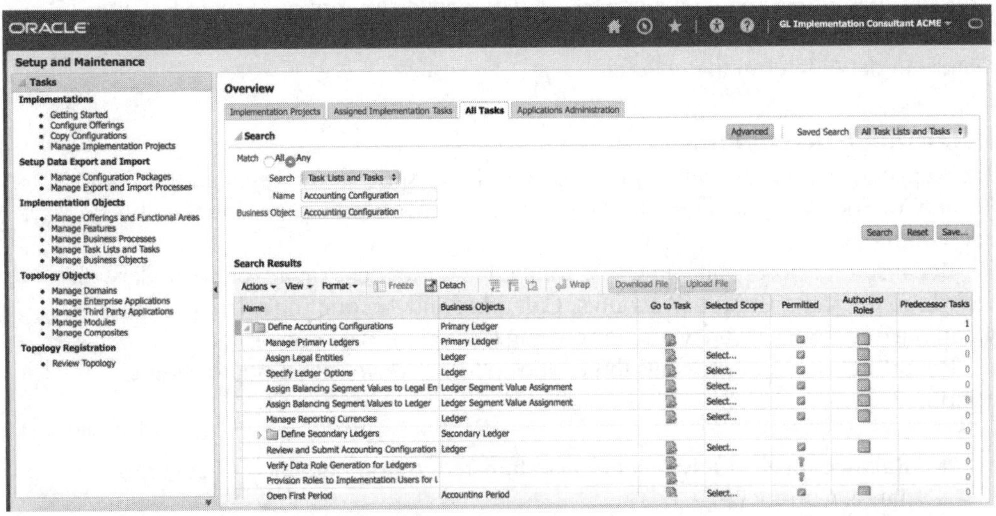

FIGURE 6-4. *The Define Accounting Configurations setup page*

Assigning Legal Entities and Balancing Segments to Ledgers

Legal Entities are assigned to the Primary Ledger to reflect where the entities operate and the legal reporting requirements that need to be satisfied. Balancing Segment Values (BSVs), part of the Chart of Accounts structure assigned to Legal Entities, will help to identify Legal Entities during transaction processing and reporting for both regulatory and tax authorities. If implementers don't assign any balancing segments to Legal Entities, all BSVs will be available for transaction processing. Alternatively, if there are BSVs that are not used at the Subledger level, these can be assigned directly to the Ledger level. These BSVs assigned only at the Ledger level usually represent nonlegal entity transactions like elimination companies or adjustment companies for consolidation and reporting purposes. Sometimes dormant companies are usually attached at the Ledger level rather than the Legal Entity level. However, the recommended approach is to assign BSVs to Legal Entities and assign only those BSVs to the Ledger level that are not assigned to Legal Entities. One point that implementers should understand with regard to assigning BSVs to Legal Entities: Subledgers don't have any method to restrict which BSVs can be used against a Legal Entity Transaction. For example, say Company number 01 BSV value is assigned to Legal Entity 1 at Ledger level and, while creating a transaction in Subledgers, User can select Legal Entity 1 in the transaction header level; however, at the Account distribution level, they can select company code 2 BSV value belonging to Legal entity 2. So, Oracle Fusion doesn't restrict the BSV usage against the Legal Entity in Subledgers. The transaction data entry process should ensure that correct BSV and its associated Legal Entity are selected.

Business Units

A Business Unit is basically an organization that processes business transactions on behalf of one or more Legal Entities. Each Business Unit performs certain business functions for the Legal Entities. Business Units are associated with Subledger modules like Accounts Payables, Accounts Receivables, Collections, Employee Expenses, Order Management, Procurement, and so on.

Table 6-1 shows a list of Business Functions available at the Business Unit level (as per Oracle Fusion Applications version 11.1.8.0 / Release 8).

The notion of a Business Unit is similar to the Operating Unit in earlier versions of Oracle E-Business Suite like Releases 12 and 11i. Each Business Unit is associated with a Primary Ledger and Default Legal Entity.

NOTE
There is no direct relationship between Business Unit and a legal entity. The mapping is indirectly inferred from the Primary Ledger assigned to the Business Unit and its associated Legal Entities.

Business Function Name

Billing and Revenue Management

Collections Management

Customer Contract Management

Customer Payments

Expense Managements

Incentive Compensation

Marketing

Material Management

Order Capture

Payables Invoicing

Payables Payment

Procurement

Procurement Contracts Management

Project Accounting

Receiving

Requisitioning

Revenue Compliance and Accounting

Sales

Service Request Management

TABLE 6-1. *List of Business Functions That Can Be Assigned to a Business Unit*

Implementation Considerations

Depending on the implementation requirement, you can associate a Single Business Unit to a Single Ledger or a Multiple Business Units to a Single Ledger. Reducing the number of Business Units will reduce the maintenance and implementation costs. Business Units can be used for the following:

- **Partition Transactions** Business Transactions created in a particular Business Unit are stored separately from transactions processed in other Business Units.

- **Secure Transaction** Oracle Fusion Financials controls data access at the Business Unit level for Subledgers, so it is easier to secure business transaction data access at the Business Unit level. You can assign data roles associated with a Business Unit to secure access to the particular Business Unit.

■   **Reference Data Sharing**   Reference data sets allow the same master data to be shared across multiple Business Units in order to reduce setup effort.

TIP
Organizations implementing Shared Service Centre for business functions like Finance, Procurement, and so on, can leverage Fusion functionality to allow data access to multiple Business Units.

Reference Data Sets and Sharing Methods

Reference data sets are groupings of Reference Objects, which allow sharing those reference data sets across different Business Units. Reference objects are typically master data used for setup, like Payment Terms, AR Transaction Types, Memo Lines, and so on. Since reference data sets can be shared across different Business Units, it reduces the setup effort. Each Business Unit has a default reference set assigned. Implementers have an option to override the default set individually for each reference object. For example, a Business Unit can have its own payment terms by overriding at the Payment Terms Reference Object level.

Understand the Big Picture: Enterprise, Ledgers, Legal Entities, Business Units and Their Association

In this section, we will understand how different components within the Enterprise Structure and Financial Reporting Structure fits together to facilitate entering business transactions and journals in Fusion Subledger Applications and Fusion General Ledger, respectively.

Enterprise provides overall context for the implementation of Fusion Applications in which all other setup components like Legal Entities, Ledgers, and Business Units are created, as shown in Figure 6-5. Normally we create one enterprise for a customer implementation.

Legal Entities represent different companies that operate within the customer organization. Legal Entities engage in business transactions like Sales Invoices, Purchase Orders, Receipts, Purchase Invoices, Payments, and Receipts, and these transactions are performed within a Business Unit. These business transactions are then accounted against BSVs or Company Numbers in Fusion Applications, which allows you to track assets, liabilities, expenses, and revenues and ultimately to prepare financial statements like a Balance Sheet, Income statements, and Cash flow statements. BSVs are linked to Legal Entities, which are in turn attached to a Ledger so that all business transactions are accounted within the Ledger. BSVs or Company Numbers are usually represented in a Chart of Accounts structure as a Primary Balancing Segment value, as shown in Figure 6-5.

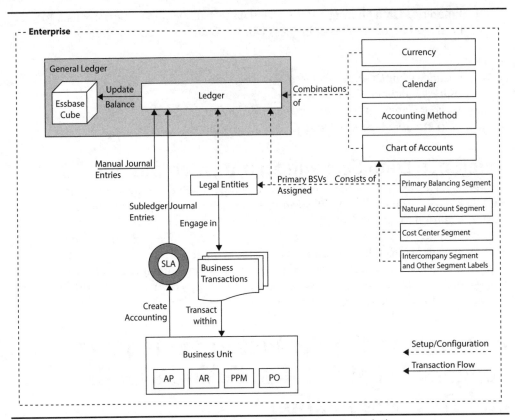

FIGURE 6-5. *Enterprise and Financial Reporting Structure associations*

A Ledger provides the accounting representation like US GAAP or UK GAAP for legal reporting purposes. A Ledger is formed using a combination of Currency, Calendar, Accounting Method, and Chart of Accounts instance. The Chart of Accounts instance consists of segments and values, and each segment will have segment qualifiers or labels like Primary Balancing Segment, Cost Center Segment, Natural Account Segment, etc. for correct functioning of the application. Primary Balancing Segment values are attached to Legal Entities; however, it is also common practice to assign the Primary Balancing Segment value to the Ledger level in case of Adjustment Companies or Elimination Companies, which are not real companies. Chapter 10 will provide more information on the need for Elimination Companies.

Business transactions are processed within the Business Unit, and it is possible to have more than one Legal Entity or BSVs transact within a Business Unit. Fusion the supports the Shared Service Center model (SSC) where a processing clerk is able to process transactions for more than one Business Unit using a single user interface. The Business Unit supports various business functions as seen in an earlier section. For illustration purposes, in Figure 6-5, we show only four business functions within the Business Unit like Accounts Payable (AP), Accounts Receivables (AR), Purchasing (PO), and Project Portfolio Management (PPM). The Reference data set helps to share setup data across different Business Units.

The Create Accounting program part of Subledger Accounting application (SLA) will create Subledger Journal entries using the transaction details. These Subledger Journal entries are then transferred to General Ledger and Posted. Subledger Accounting application uses Subledger Accounting Method definition (SLAM) and Journal entry rule set assignments to account for the transaction in correct accounting representation.

Successful posting of Journals and Subledger Journal entries will affect balances in the Ledger, and those balances are automatically updated in Essbase cube. Fusion reporting tools like Smart View and Financial Reporting Center use Essbase cube balances for providing real-time analysis of legal entities' balances.

Define ACME Ledgers and Business Units

As per the proposed ACME Ledger structure in Chapter 4, we will create the following three Primary Ledgers in Fusion Financials:

- ACME US Ledger

- ACME US Insurance Ledger

- ACME UK Ledger

In addition, we will create a Business Unit called "ACME US Business Unit" and attach it to ACME US Ledger. Because ACME UK Ledger would be based on UK GAAP accounting principles, we will create a Secondary Ledger to represent US GAAP principles for ACME Bank group legal reporting purposes and data conversion or processing option will be set at the Journal level.

Define Ledgers

In the next few sections, we will cover how to define Ledgers for ACME Bank with detailed steps. Table 6-2 shows the high-level configuration tasks that will be performed.

	High-Level Configuration Tasks in FSM	Description
Step 1	Manage Primary Ledgers (Mandatory)	Specify Ledger Name, Chart of Accounts, Accounting Calendar, Currency, and Accounting Method.
Step 2	Specify Ledger Options for Primary Ledger (Mandatory)	Specify Ledger Controls, like number of future open periods, Retained Earnings account, Journal Approval features, Document Sequence for Journals, and so on.
Step 3	Assign Legal Entities (Optional)	Specific Legal entities that can transact within the Ledger.
Step 4	Assign Balancing Segments to Legal Entities (Optional)	Assign company values to each of the Legal entities assigned in the preceding step.
Step 5	Assign Balancing Segments to Ledgers (Optional)	Assign nonlegal entity company values like adjustments and eliminations, balancing segment values to the ledger.
Step 6	Define Secondary Ledger Using Manage Secondary Ledger task (Mandatory)	Specify Secondary Ledger Name, Chart of Accounts, Accounting Calendar, Currency, Accounting Method and Conversion Level.
Step 7	Specify Ledger Options for Secondary Ledger (Mandatory)	Specify Ledger Controls like number of future open periods, Retained Earnings account, Journal Approval features, Document Sequence for Journals, and so on.
Step 8	Complete Primary to Secondary Ledger Mapping (Mandatory)	Specify the rules to use for Conversion of Primary to Secondary Ledger.
Step 9	Review and Submit Accounting Configuration (Mandatory)	Create Ledgers in Fusion GL.
Step 10	Open First Period	Open first period to transact journals and transactions in the General Ledger.

TABLE 6-2. *High-Level Steps to Create Ledgers*

Define Primary Ledgers

Create Primary Ledgers for ACME Bank using the following steps:

1. Access the Setup And Maintenance area.

2. Navigate to the Define Accounting Configuration task list.

3. Open Manage Primary Ledgers and click the Go To Task icon.

4. Click the Create icon.

5. Enter the following values as shown in Figure 6-6 and as per Table 6-3.

6. Click the Save And Edit Task List icon.

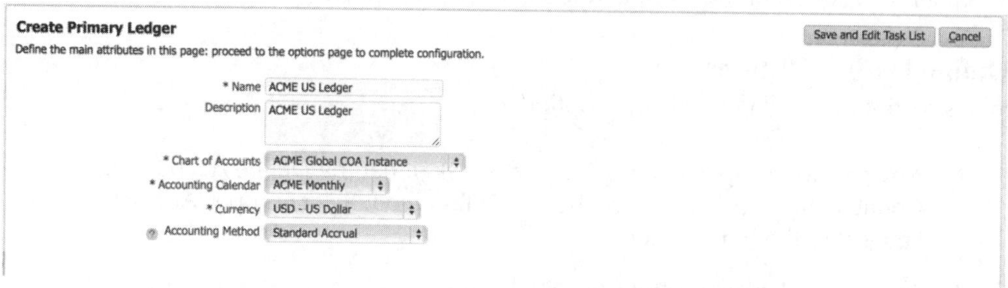

FIGURE 6-6.   *Creating the ACME US Ledger Primary Ledger*

Field Name	Value
Name	ACME US Ledger
Description	ACME US Ledger
Chart of Accounts	ACME Global COA Instance
Accounting Calendar	ACME Monthly
Currency	USD
Accounting Method	Standard Accrual

TABLE 6-3.   *Primary Ledger Field Values for Creating ACME US Ledger*

Field Name	Value
Name	ACME US Insurance Ledger
Description	ACME US Insurance Ledger
Chart of Accounts	ACME Insurance COA Instance
Accounting Calendar	ACME Monthly
Currency	USD
Accounting Method	Standard Accrual

TABLE 6-4. *Primary Ledger Field Values for Creating the ACME US Insurance Ledger*

Create the ACME US Insurance Ledger and ACME UK Ledger using the information provided in Table 6-4 and Table 6-5, respectively.

Define Ledger Options
In this section, we will define Ledger options.

1. Navigate to the Specify Ledger Options task under the Define Accounting Configurations task list. Click the Go To Task icon. Select scope "ACME US Ledger" as the Primary Ledger.

2. The Specify Ledger Options page will open.

Field Name	Value
Name	ACME UK Ledger
Description	ACME UK Ledger
Chart of Accounts	ACME Global COA Instance
Accounting Calendar	ACME Monthly
Currency	GBP
Accounting Method	Standard Accrual

TABLE 6-5. *Primary Ledger Field Values for Creating the ACME UK Ledger*

Field Name	Value
Ledger Name	AMCE US Ledger
First Opened period	ACME-Jan-14
Number of Future Enterable Periods	1
Journal Language	American English
Retained Earnings	10.401.1000.35040.00.00000

TABLE 6-6. *Specify Ledger Options for the ACME US Ledger*

3. Enter the information for mandatory fields as shown in Table 6-6 under the Accounting Calendar, Subledger Accounting, and Period Close sections as shown in Figure 6-7.

4. Click the Save And Close button.

5. Repeat the preceding steps to specify the Ledger options for ACME Insurance Ledger and ACME UK Ledger as per Table 6-7 and Table 6-8, respectively.

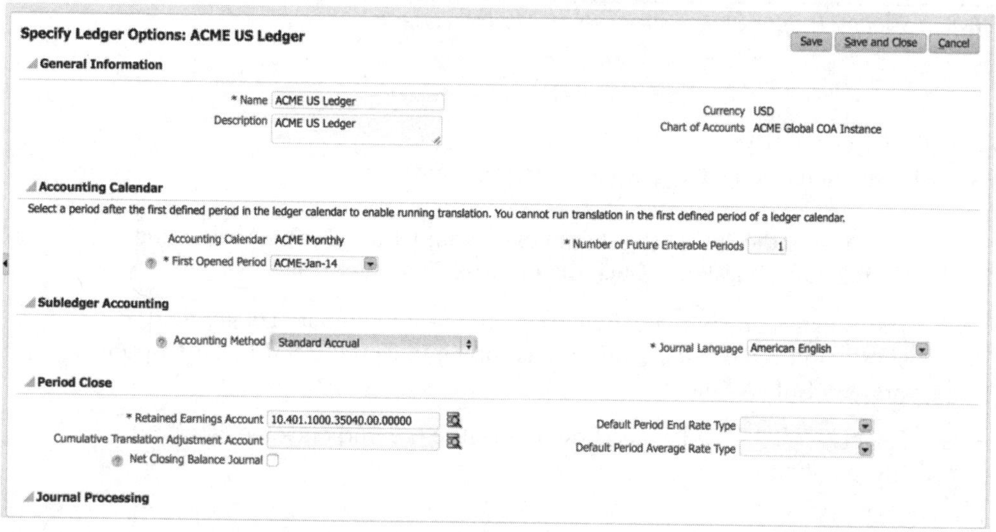

FIGURE 6-7. *The Specify Ledger Options page*

Field Name	Value
Ledger Name	ACME Insurance Ledger
First Opened period	ACME-Jan-14
Number of Future Enterable Period	1
Journal Language	American English
Retained Earnings	15.101.1000.35040.00.000.00000

TABLE 6-7. *Specify Ledger Options for ACME Insurance Ledger*

Field Name	Value
Ledger Name	ACME UK Ledger
First Opened period	ACME-Jan-14
Number of Future Enterable Period	1
Journal Language	American English
Retained Earnings	20.103.1000.35040.00.00000

TABLE 6-8. *Specify Ledger Options for the ACME UK Ledger*

Assign Legal Entities

Assign Legal Entities to Ledgers using the following steps:

1. Navigate to the Assign Legal Entities task under the Define Accounting Configurations task list. Click the Go To Task icon.

2. The Select Scope window will open, and for the Primary Ledger field, choose the value Select And Add as shown in Figure 6-8. Click the Apply And Go To Task button.

3. Select ACME US Ledger as shown in Figure 6-9 and click the Save and Close button.

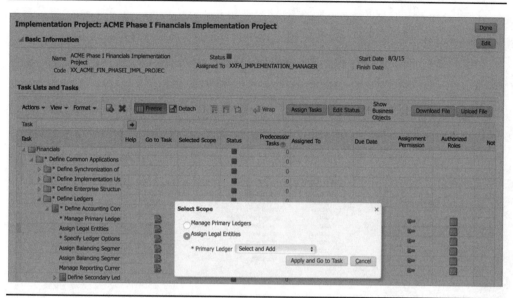

FIGURE 6-8. *Assign Legal Entities task selection*

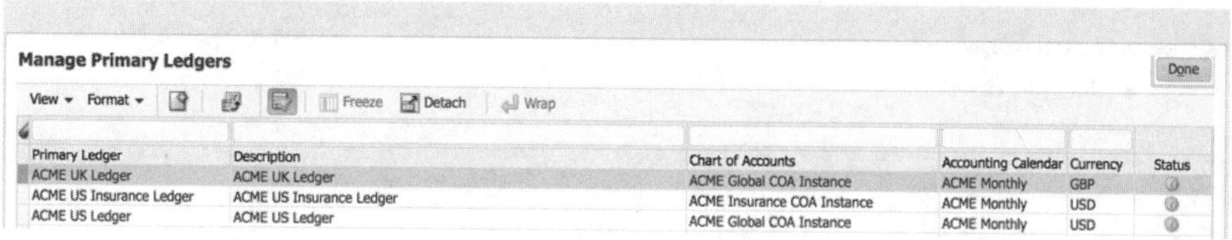

Manage Primary Ledgers

Primary Ledger	Description	Chart of Accounts	Accounting Calendar	Currency	Status
ACME UK Ledger	ACME UK Ledger	ACME Global COA Instance	ACME Monthly	GBP	
ACME US Insurance Ledger	ACME US Insurance Ledger	ACME Insurance COA Instance	ACME Monthly	USD	
ACME US Ledger	ACME US Ledger	ACME Global COA Instance	ACME Monthly	USD	

FIGURE 6-9. *ACME US Ledger Primary Ledger selection*

4. When the Assign Legal Entities page opens, click the Create icon. Under Legal Entity, search for ACMECorp USA and select the same. Click Apply and then click Done as shown in Figure 6-10.

5. The Legal Entity will be successfully added as shown in Figure 6-11.

6. Repeat the preceding steps to assign other Legal Entities to ledgers as per Table 6-9.

7. Click the Save And Close button.

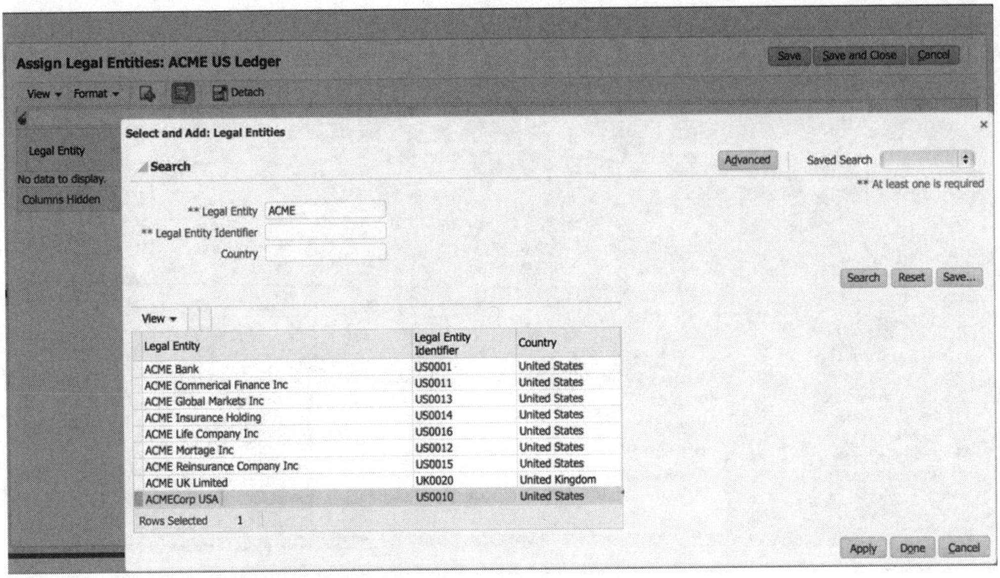

FIGURE 6-10. *The Assign Legal Entities page*

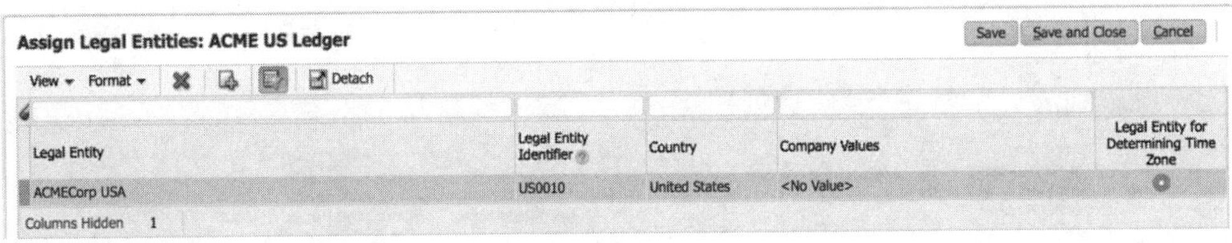

FIGURE 6-11. *The ACMECorp USA Legal Entity has been added to the ACME US Ledger.*

Ledger Name	Legal Entities
ACME US Ledger	ACMECorp USA
	ACME Commercial Finance Inc
	ACME Mortgage Inc
	ACME Global Markets Inc
	ACME Insurance Holding
ACME US Insurance Ledger	ACME Reinsurance Company Inc
	ACME Life Company Inc
ACME UK Ledger	ACME UK Limited

TABLE 6-9. *List of Entities to Be Assigned to Ledgers*

Assign Balancing Segments to Legal Entities

In the previous step, we have successfully added Legal Entities to the Ledger. We will now link the primary balancing segments values of the Chart of Accounts to Legal Entities by following these steps:

1. Navigate to the Assign Balancing Segment Values To Legal Entities task under the Define Accounting Configurations task list. Click Go To Task. Select the Scope ACME US Ledger. The Assign Balancing Segment Values To Legal Entities page will open.

2. Click the Create icon and assign a company value to Legal Entity ACMECorp USA as shown in Figure 6-12.

3. Repeat the preceding steps to assign the remaining company values to the ledgers as per Table 6-10. Figure 6-13 shows the resulting ACME US Ledger configuration after adding the remaining balancing segment values to the Ledger.

Assign Balancing Segments to Ledgers

Optionally, you can assign non–Legal Entity balancing segment values directly to the Ledger by following these steps:

1. Navigate to the Assign Balancing Segment Value To Ledger task. Click Go To Task.

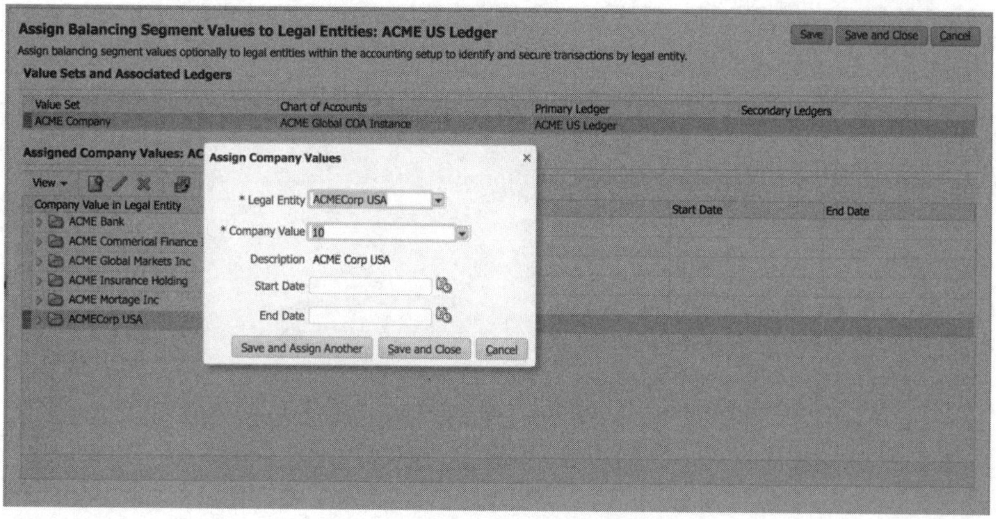

FIGURE 6-12. *Assigning company values to the Legal Entity*

Primary Ledger	Secondary Ledgers	Legal Entity	Company Value	Description
ACME US Ledger		ACME Bank	01	ACME Bank
		ACME Corp USA	10	ACME Corp USA
		ACME Commercial Finance Inc	11	ACME Commercial Finance Inc
		ACME Mortgage Inc	12	ACME Mortgage Inc
		ACME Global Markets Inc	13	ACME Global Markets Inc
		ACME Insurance Holding	14	ACME Insurance Holding
ACME US Insurance Ledger		ACME Reinsurance Company, Inc	15	ACME Reinsurance Company Inc
		ACME Life Company, Inc	16	ACME Life Company Inc
ACME UK Ledger	ACME UK - Secondary Ledger	ACME UK Limited	20	ACME UK Limited

TABLE 6-10. *List of Company Values to Be Assigned to Legal Entities*

2. Select the scope of the Ledger and add company values.

3. Optionally enter a start date.

4. Click the Save And Close button.

Create a Secondary Ledger

Create a Secondary Ledger for the ACME UK Ledger by following these steps:

1. Navigate to the Define Accounting Configuration task list.

2. Open Manage Secondary Ledgers and click Go To Task.

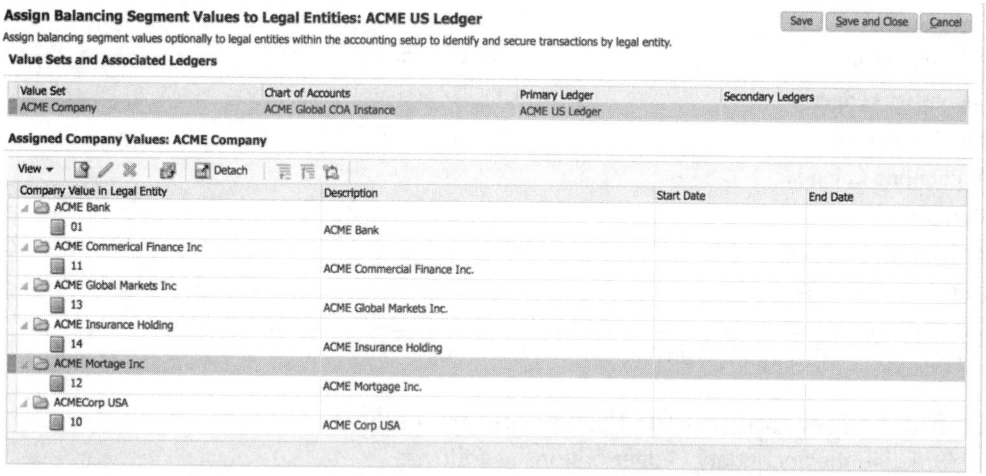

FIGURE 6-13. *ACME US Ledger after assigning all company values*

3. Select ACME UK Ledger as the scope and click the Create icon.

4. Create a Secondary Ledger as shown in Figure 6-14 using the information in Table 6-11. Readers may note that we have left the Accounting Method blank for the Secondary Ledger because the Accounting method field is not required to be set when the Data conversion level is set to Journal. It is implicitly understood that ACME UK Secondary level has been created to satisfy US GAAP Accounting for Group Reporting so all journals posted should comply with US GAAP accounting requirements.

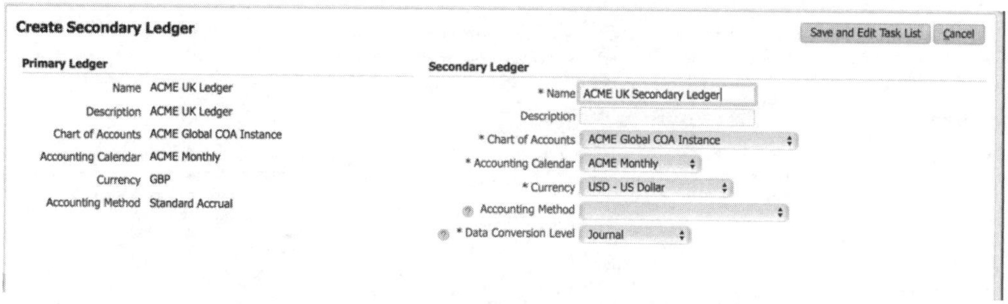

FIGURE 6-14. *The Create Secondary Ledger page for ACME UK Ledger*

Field Name	Value
Primary Ledger	ACME UK Ledger
Secondary Ledger	ACME UK Secondary Ledger
Chart of Accounts	ACME Global COA Instance
Accounting Calendar	ACME Monthly
Currency	USD
Accounting Method	*leave blank*
Data Conversion Level	Journal

TABLE 6-11. *Create Secondary Ledger ACME UK – Secondary*

Define Ledger Options for the Secondary Ledger

Now define the Secondary Ledger options as follows:

1. Navigate to the Specify Ledger Options task under Define Secondary Ledgers. Click the Go To Task icon. Select ACME UK Ledger as the Primary Ledger and ACME UK Secondary Ledger.

2. The Specify Ledger Options page will open. Enter mandatory fields as shown in Figure 6-15.

3. Click the Save And Close button.

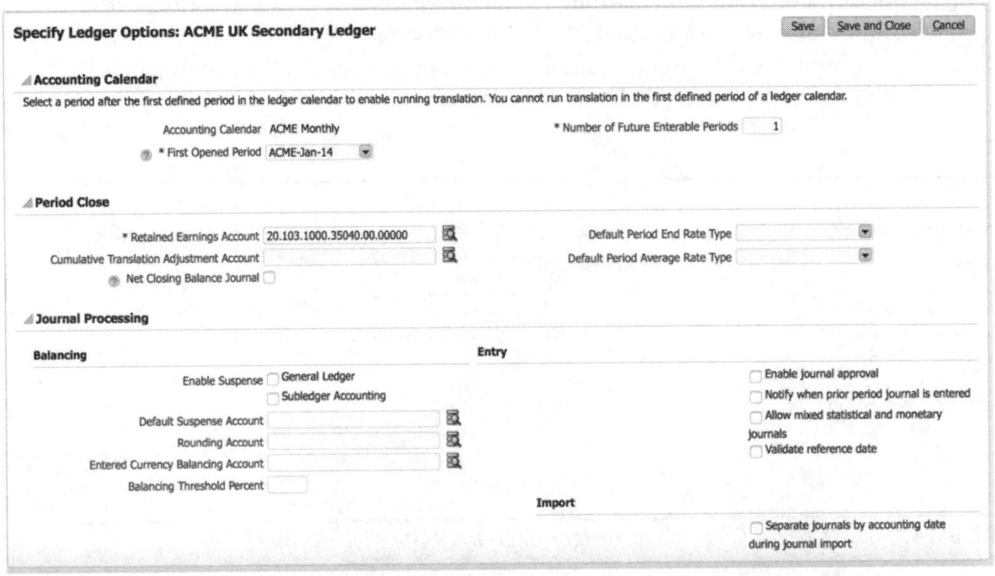

FIGURE 6-15. *Specify Ledger Options for the Secondary Ledger*

Complete Primary to Secondary Ledger Mapping

Create ACME UK Ledger to Secondary Ledger mapping information by following these steps:

1. Navigate to the Complete Primary To Secondary Mapping task and click Go To Task.

2. Enter Primary to Secondary mapping information as shown in Figure 6-16.

Now we have successfully created the ACME Primary Ledgers and associated ACME UK Ledger to the Secondary Ledger for consolidation purposes. Readers would have noticed that we haven't created the Chart of Accounting mapping definition to map Primary to Secondary COAs. The reason is that we are using the same COA for both Primary and Secondary, and if no Chart of Accounts mapping is defined, the posting program will use the Primary Ledger's original code combinations while replicating journals in the Secondary Ledger.

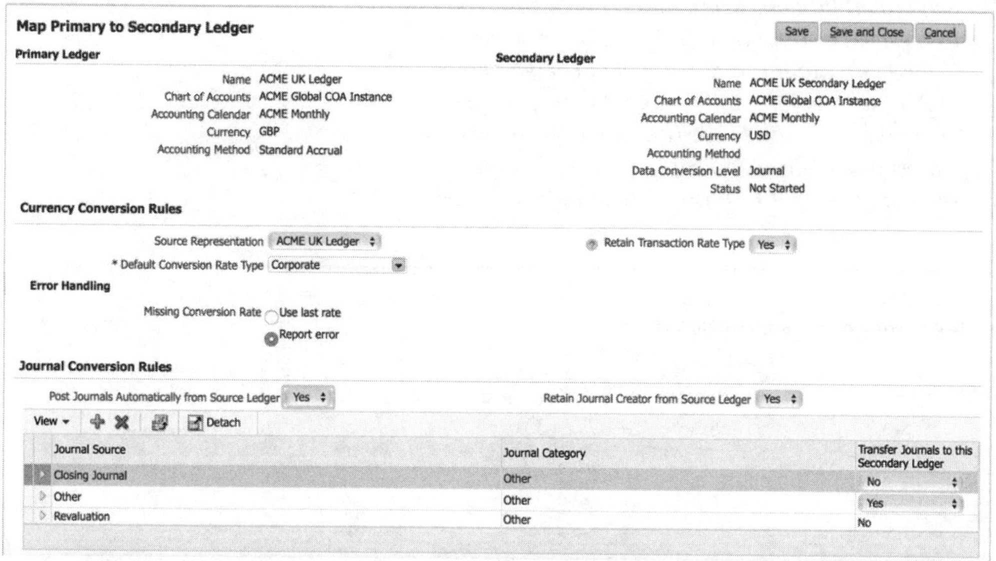

FIGURE 6-16. *Complete Primary to Secondary mapping.*

Review and Submit Accounting Configuration

The final steps in the Ledger configuration are to review and submit the accounting configuration.

1. Navigate to the Review And Submit Accounting Configuration task. Click the Go To Task icon. Select ACME US Ledger as the scope.

2. The Review And Submit Accounting Configuration page will provide an overview of all the Legal Entities and Ledger configuration as shown in Figure 6-17.

3. Click the Submit button.

4. You will receive a confirmation message of the Complete Accounting Configuration process submission as shown in Figure 6-18. Ensure that all of the submitted programs complete successfully.

NOTE
You can view the submitted process via Tools | Scheduled Processes link under Navigator. The Complete Accounting Configuration process will invoke two other processes called Load Chart of Accounts Values and Create Balances Cubes as shown in Figure 6-19. The Create Balances Cubes process is responsible for creating the multidimensional Essbase cube of the GL ledger.

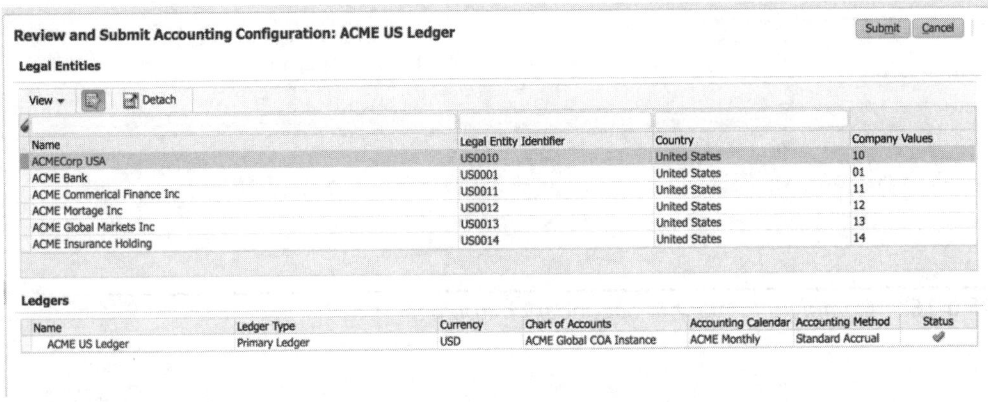

Review and Submit Accounting Configuration: ACME US Ledger   Submit   Cancel

Legal Entities

View ▾   🔲   📄 Detach

Name	Legal Entity Identifier	Country	Company Values
ACMECorp USA	US0010	United States	10
ACME Bank	US0001	United States	01
ACME Commerical Finance Inc	US0011	United States	11
ACME Mortage Inc	US0012	United States	12
ACME Global Markets Inc	US0013	United States	13
ACME Insurance Holding	US0014	United States	14

Ledgers

Name	Ledger Type	Currency	Chart of Accounts	Accounting Calendar	Accounting Method	Status
ACME US Ledger	Primary Ledger	USD	ACME Global COA Instance	ACME Monthly	Standard Accrual	✓

FIGURE 6-17. *ACME US Ledger Review and Submit Accounting Configuration page*

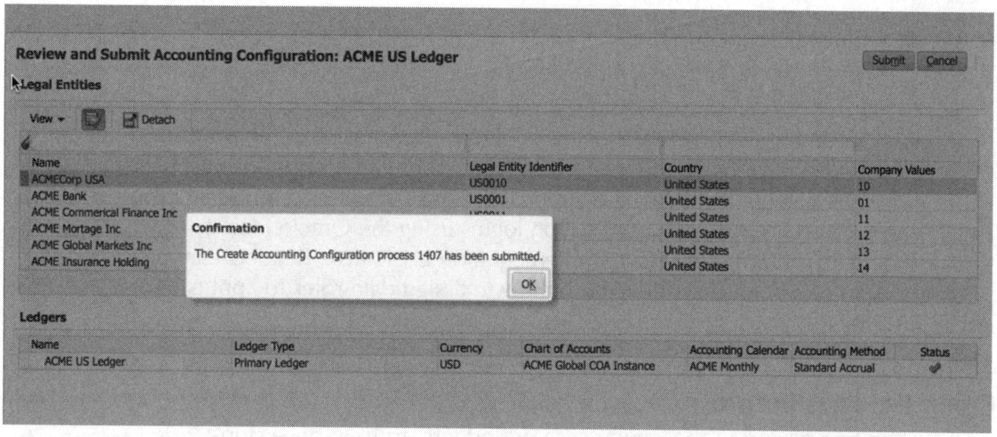

Review and Submit Accounting Configuration: ACME US Ledger   Submit Cancel

▶Legal Entities

View ▾ [icon] Detach

Name	Legal Entity Identifier	Country	Company Values
ACMECorp USA	US0010	United States	10
ACME Bank	US0001	United States	01
ACME Commerical Finance Inc		United States	11
ACME Mortage Inc		United States	12
ACME Global Markets Inc		United States	13
ACME Insurance Holding		United States	14

Confirmation

The Create Accounting Configuration process 1407 has been submitted.

OK

Ledgers

Name	Ledger Type	Currency	Chart of Accounts	Accounting Calendar	Accounting Method	Status
ACME US Ledger	Primary Ledger	USD	ACME Global COA Instance	ACME Monthly	Standard Accrual	✔

FIGURE 6-18. *Create Accounting Configuration process confirmation message*

5. Repeat the preceding steps for the other two Ledgers: ACME UK Ledger and ACME Insurance Ledger.

NOTE
Fusion automatically creates data roles for the ledgers successfully created. The data role display name is created as a concatenation of the following seeded external role names and Ledger name:

■ Financial Analyst

■ Controller

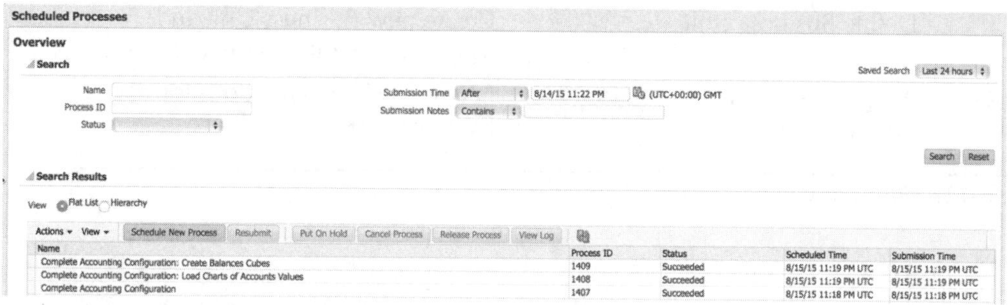

Scheduled Processes

Overview

◢ **Search**   Saved Search Last 24 hours ▾

Name [   ]   Submission Time After ▾ 8/14/15 11:22 PM (UTC+00:00) GMT
Process ID [   ]   Submission Notes Contains ▾ [   ]
Status [   ] ▾

Search Reset

◢ **Search Results**

View ◉ Flat List ○ Hierarchy

Actions ▾ View ▾ Schedule New Process Resubmit Put On Hold Cancel Process Release Process View Log [icon]

Name	Process ID	Status	Scheduled Time	Submission Time
Complete Accounting Configuration: Create Balances Cubes	1409	Succeeded	8/15/15 11:19 PM UTC	8/15/15 11:19 PM UTC
Complete Accounting Configuration: Load Charts of Accounts Values	1408	Succeeded	8/15/15 11:19 PM UTC	8/15/15 11:19 PM UTC
Complete Accounting Configuration	1407	Succeeded	8/15/15 11:18 PM UTC	8/15/15 11:18 PM UTC

FIGURE 6-19. *The Create Accounting Configuration process*

- Chief Financial Officer
- General Accountant
- General Accounting Manager

Each data role provides various levels of restricted access to certain functionality within Fusion General Ledger and aimed at different types of business users who can potentially access the application. Business Users can be provisioned the GL data roles to their application logins using the Oracle Identify Manager login URL or from the Create Implementation Users task. Readers can refer to Appendix A for detailed steps of how to assign data roles to application user logins.

Open the First Period

To open the first period of the newly created ledgers, follow these steps.

1. Navigate to the Open First Period task and click the Go To Task icon.

2. On the Submission page, Select the Ledger ACME US Ledger and the period to open.

3. Click the Submit button to launch the Open General Ledger Periods Program.

4. Repeat the process for other Ledgers as well.

Define a Business Unit

In the next few sections, we will cover how to define a Business Unit for ACME US Ledger. Table 6-12 shows the high-level steps that will be performed.

	Configuration Step	Description
Step 1	Define Business Unit	Create new Business Unit and associate default reference data set.
Step 2	Assign Business Functions to Business Unit	Enable Business Functions for Business Unit

TABLE 6-12. *Steps to Create Business Units*

Field Name	Value
Name	ACME US Business Unit
Manager	Optionally enter a value
Active	Yes
Location	
Default Set	ACME US BU Set

TABLE 6-13. *Create Business Unit Values*

Create Business Unit

Create a Business Unit for ACME US Business Unit by following these steps:

1. Navigate to the Define Business Unit task list.

2. Open Manage Business Unit and click Go To Task.

3. Click the Create icon.

4. Enter the following values in Table 6-13, as shown in Figure 6-20, which shows the Create Business Unit screen.

5. Click the Save button.

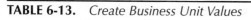

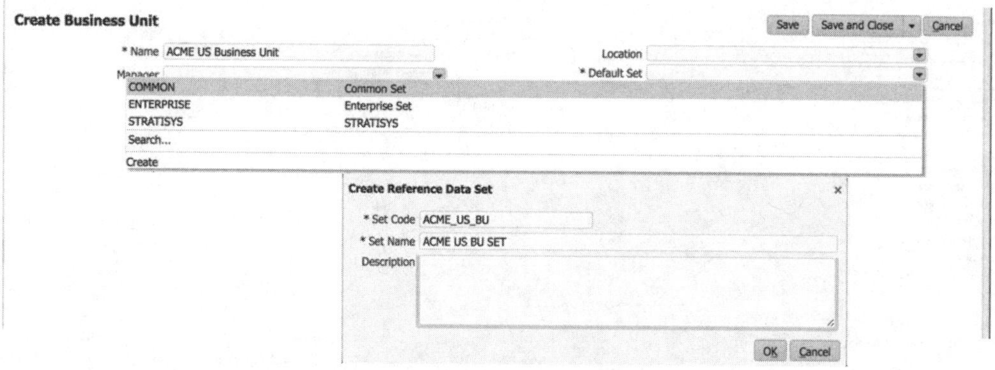

FIGURE 6-20. *Creating the ACME US Business Unit*

Assign Business Function to Business Unit

Assigning a Business Function is performed in ACME US Business Unit by following these steps:

1. Navigate to the Define Business Unit task list.

2. Open Assign Business Unit Functions and click Go To Task. Select ACME US Business Unit for the scope.

3. Assign Business Functions, Primary Ledger, and Default Legal Entity as shown in Figure 6-21. In the example scenario, we have enabled Accounts Payables and Expenses Management related functions only. Now we can proceed to implement the related subledger setups.

NOTE
Readers should note that even though we have created a Business Unit, it is not yet ready for entering transactions, as we need to perform additional setups specific to the Business Function enabled. These additional steps are part of the task list of the specific Business Function implementation. Once those setup tasks are completed, we can generate data roles and assign the same to the Applications user for business operations.

Assign Business Functions: ACME US Business Unit
Save   Save and Close   ▼   Cancel

Business Unit Functions

Select all business functions that this business unit will perform.

View ▼   Format ▼   ☐ Freeze   ⊲ Wrap

Name	Enabled
Billing and Revenue Management	☐
Collections Management	☐
Customer Contract Management	☐
Customer Payments	☐
Expense Management	☑
Incentive Compensation	☐
Materials Management	☐
Payables Invoicing	☑
Payables Payment	☑
Procurement	☐
Procurement Contract Management	☐
Project Accounting	☐
Receiving	☐
Requisitioning	☐
Revenue Compliance and Accounting	☐
Sales	☐
Service Request Management	☐
Columns Hidden 1	

Financial Reporting

Select the primary ledger and default legal entity for the business function you chose so that financial transactions can be generated.

* Primary Ledger   ACME US Ledger   ▼

* Default Legal Entity   ACMECorp USA   ▼

FIGURE 6-21.   *The Assign Business Functions screen*

Chart of Accounts Mapping Feature

The Chart of Accounts Mapping feature provides the ability to define mapping information from a source COA to a target COA to allow posting balances and journal entries using alternative COA representation. This mapping definition is used for the following scenarios:

- Balance Transfer Program for transferring General Ledger balances (Balance level) from Primary Ledger to Secondary Ledger.

- Balance Transfer Program for transferring General Ledger balances (Balance level) across different (unrelated) Ledgers, also called Cross-Ledgers. A good example for this case is the transfer of consolidation data from Subsidiary Ledger to Parent Ledger as part of consolidation using Global Consolidation System.

- Posting Program in propagating General Ledger journal entries (Journal Level) from the Primary Ledger to the Chart of Accounts used by the Secondary Ledger.

Navigation for Chart of Accounts Mapping setup is as follows:

1. Navigate to the Setup And Maintenance work area.

2. Click on Search Tasks.

3. Enter Chart of Accounts Mappings and click Go.

4. The Chart Of Accounts Mapping window opens. Figure 6-22 shows an example **Chart of Accounts Mapping** setup screen.

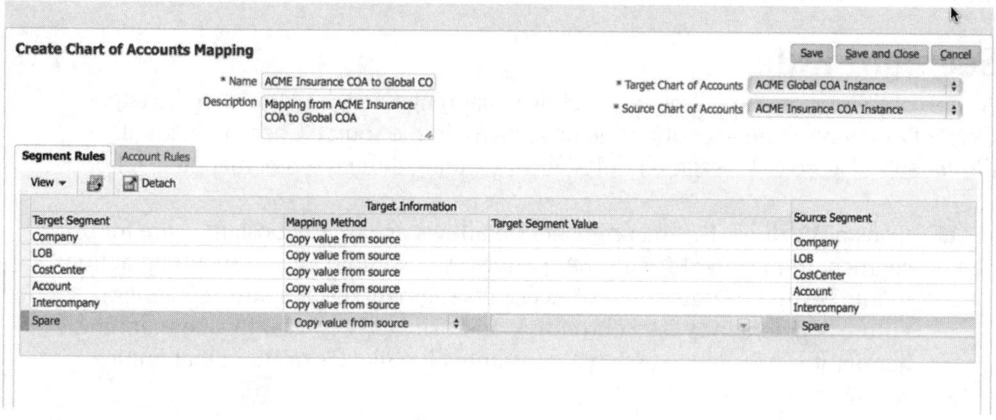

FIGURE 6-22. *Example Chart of Accounts Mapping setup screen*

NOTE
In Chapter 10, we will look at an example of how to use the Chart of Accounts Mapping feature to consolidate balances in the Cross-Ledger scenario.

User can define Chart of Accounts mapping based any one of the following rule types:

- Segment Rule

- Account Rule

- Combination of both Segment and Account Rule

NOTE
Readers would have learned in Chapter 5 that the COA is made up of a number of segments and each segment consists of individual account values or segment values that can represent either a Parent (where journal posting is not allowed) or Child (where journal posting is allowed) value. Since mapping rules types are based on Segment and Account values that are fundamental blocks for the COA, it provides greater flexibility for the implementers to accomplish any kind of complex source COA to target COA mapping.

Figure 6-23 illustrates different mapping actions that you can create on each of the Segment and Account Rule types. We shall look at each of the rules in detail in the next few sections.

Segment Rule

As the name implies, the segment rule allows mapping to each segment of the target Chart of Accounts to an account value or segment in the source Chart of Accounts. As illustrated in Figure 6-21, segment rules allow creating three types of mapping actions:

- **Constant Value** This mapping action allows assigning constant value for a segment in the target Chart of Accounts. An example for this mapping action would be that a target Chart of Accounts segment has a Spare Segment or Future Segment (not used currently), and using this constant value mapping action, it is possible to assign a constant value like 0's or 9's in that Future Segment.

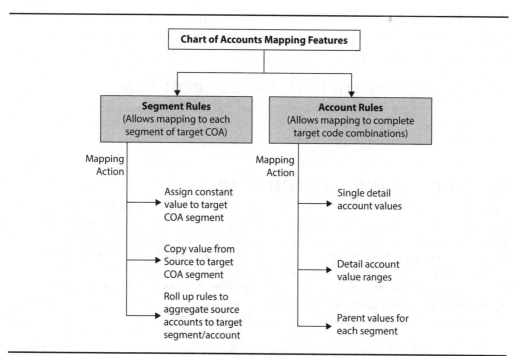

FIGURE 6-23.   *Chart of Accounts mapping rule types and mapping actions*

■ **Copy Value**   This mapping action simply copies the Source Segment value to the Target Segment. In order for the mapping function to work correctly, the Source and Target Segment should use identical values in their Segment value sets.

■ **Rollup Rule**   This mapping action allows mapping of a group of values from a Source Segment to a Target Segment or account. Additionally, it can leverage the date-effective Hierarchy version information to dynamically pick all the child values for a given parent during posting or transfer the program to get the aggregated value into the Target Segment or account. The accounting date on the journal is used to select the correct Hierarchy version. It also allows mapping of specific detailed values from a Source Segment to a specific detailed value in the Target Segment.

Account Rule

The account rule would allow defining mapping from one or more Source Account Code Combinations to Target Account Code Combinations and hence account rule provides much more granular-level mapping. Account rule uses Source Account filters, which provide greater flexibility to map each the segment of the source COA to Target Account code combinations.

Overlap of Account Rule and Segment Rule

If a system determines that both the segment rule and account rule are applicable for a given scenario, the account rule will supersede the segment rule to derive the correct Target Segment value or account.

Intercompany Accounting

Any posting to the Ledger should always balance at the Balancing Segment level. For example, if the Chart of Accounts structure is defined to have a balancing segment at the Primary and Secondary levels, any journal entry posted to the Ledger should be balanced at both the primary and secondary Segment level; that is, the sum of debits and credits at both primary and secondary Segments should total to zero.

Let us take an example to illustrate what happens when an imbalance occurs at the Balancing Segment level during Ledger posting.

Consider a COA structure as follows with three segments:

■ Company (Primary Balancing Label enabled)

■ Account (Natural Account Label enabled)

■ Intercompany (Intercompany Segment Label enabled)

Assume that we are posting journal entries for intercompany transactions in General Ledger between the two Legal Entities 01 and 02 as per Table 6-14 for recharge of services provided.

In this case, the system would expect that the debit and credit should be balanced at the Company level. In almost all implementations, we would have transactions or journals booked across different companies or divisions within the same enterprise for several reasons. For example, one line of business (Central

Original accounting entry				
Company	Account	Intercompany	Debit	Credit
01	3000 (Expenses)		100	
02	4000 (Revenue)			100

TABLE 6-14. *Example Intercompany Accounting Entry*

Finance or Procurement Shared Service Center) within a large enterprise would provide services to other lines of business under different companies, and a need arises to raise Intercompany Invoicing for booking revenue and expenses correctly against each company's books. Another example would be that sometimes companies do operate as a separate entity within an enterprise to satisfy any country-specific legislation or for tax purposes.

Fusion Financials allows us to handle these kinds of scenarios in two different ways:

- **Suspense Account**   This feature is enabled at the ledger setup where any imbalance in the journal is posted into a suspense account. The logic behind this to make sure that the finance team will later move the balances from these suspense accounts to the correct intercompany posting.

NOTE
Enabling this suspense account feature is not a common practice in Oracle ERP implementations. However, some companies use suspense accounts to capture issues and exceptions rather than dealing within standard accounting transactions.

- **Intercompany Rules**   This feature generates automatic intercompany journals based on the intercompany rules defined in the system.

If intercompany rules are defined in the system, as in the preceding example, the final posted journals will be as shown in Table 6-15. The system can identify these imbalance journals during posting and generate correct intercompany payables and intercompany receivables accounting entries so that the journal entries are balanced.

Original accounting entry				
Company	**Account**	**Intercompany**	**Debit**	**Credit**
01	3000 (Expenses)		100	
02	4000 (Revenue)			100
Automatic intercompany journal lines to balance the accounting entries				
01	2000 (Intercompany Payable)	**02**		100
02	1000 (Intercompany Receivable)	**01**	100	

TABLE 6-15.   *Example Final Intercompany Accounting Entry Using Intercompany Rules*

As you can see, the journals are balanced at the Company level and Intercompany Segment is automatically populated, which helps to track the trading partner.

Few points to note on the Intercompany Accounting feature:

■ The Intercompany Accounting feature is set up at the Enterprise level to ensure consistent creation of intercompany balancing journals across legal entities within an Enterprise. It also supports business activity between more than one or more legal entities within the Enterprise.

■ Enabling the intercompany segment qualifier within the COA structure will allow trading partners to be populated automatically based on the Primary Balancing Segment value. It is recommended that Intercompany segment values have the same valueset values as the Primary Balancing Segment values to ensure this feature works properly. Readers should note that the Intercompany Accounting feature will work even without the Intercompany segment qualifier in the COA structure; however, using the intercompany segment qualifier will greatly reduce the manual elimination entries required during consolidation and eliminates the intercompany differences.

■ The Define and Maintain Intercompany Processing Rules Configuration task list in the Setup and Maintenance work area contains all relevant setup tasks for this Intercompany Accounting feature.

Types of Intercompany Processing Options

Fusion provides two types of intercompany processing options to meet business requirements regarding intercompany accounting.

■ Intercompany Balancing

■ Manual Intercompany Transaction Processing

Intercompany Balancing

This feature will ensure that all journals and subledger journal entries are balanced at the Primary Balancing Segment (mandatory), Secondary Balancing Segment (optional), and Third Balancing Segment Values (optional). Using the intercompany payable account and intercompany receivable account in Intercompany Balancing rules ensures that the debits and credits are equal per the Legal Entity or Management reporting entity to get a balance sheet reporting. Balancing intercompany journals are generated during the posting of journals in General Ledger and during the create accounting process for subledger journal entries in Subledger Ledger Application.

Setup tasks relevant for this processing option are as follows:

1. **Assign Balancing Segment Value to Legal Entity and Ledger**   This task is part of the Ledger setup as seen earlier in this chapter. This ensures that the Primary Balancing Segment Value linked to the Legal Entity can be used in intercompany balancing rule configuration.

2. **Enable Ledger Option**   This task is also part of Ledger setup. This task ensures that the Ledger is enabled for intercompany processing.

3. **Manage Intercompany Balancing rules**   This task is part of the Intercompany Accounting feature.

   This setup consists of intercompany balance rules defined at the following levels:

   - Primary Balancing Segment rules (lowest level)

   - Legal Entity rules

   - Ledger rules

   - Chart of Account rules

   Figure 6-23 shows the Manage Intercompany Balancing Rules setup page with separate tabs for each of the balancing rules. Each of these rules has

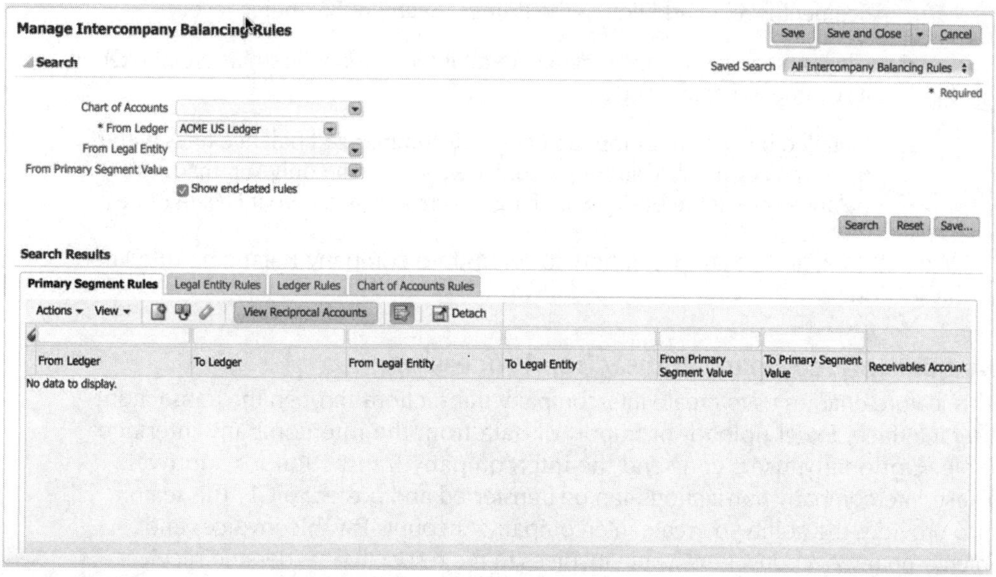

FIGURE 6-23.   *Manage Intercompany Balancing Rules page*

journal source, journal category, and transaction type fields to further narrow down the default Intercompany Payable and Intercompany Receivable account to use.

The intercompany process will look for the intercompany balance rule at the lowest level and work up the order from Primary Balancing Segment rules to Legal Entity rules to Ledger rules to Chart of Accounts rules. If the process encounters more than one rule within a balancing rule level, say the Primary Balancing Segment rule, then it will use the following order to select the balancing rule to apply for the accounting entry:

- Specific journal source and specific journal category and transaction type are used to derive the appropriate rule for balancing.

- Specific journal source and all other journal category or all other transaction type.

- All other journal sources and specific journal category and all other transaction type.

- All other journal source and all journal category and all other transaction type.

4. **Manage Intercompany Balancing option** This task is part of the Intercompany Accounting feature. This task needs to be implemented if one or more of the following requirements need to be satisfied:

- The business needs to balance journals at the Second and Third Balancing Segment level in addition to the Primary Segment Balancing level.

- Clearing company balancing where all intercompany journals are booked in a separate company code.

- Detailed balance lines instead of default summarized balance lines within the same Legal Entity are required. However, Fusion only summarizes balance lines if the business activity occurs across different Legal Entities.

We will look at an example of how to set up Intercompany Balancing rule later in the section.

Manual Intercompany Transaction Processing

This feature enables us to create intercompany transactions through the transaction user interface, Excel upload, or import of data from the intercompany interface table. Optionally, users can send the intercompany transaction for approval. These intercompany transactions can be transferred and posted to GL. This feature also provides the ability to create intercompany Accounts Payable invoices and intercompany Accounts Receivable invoices in the respective sender and receiver organization or Business Unit to meet statutory requirements. Suppliers and customer assignment setups allow simplified creation of intercompany invoice generation. This intercompany transaction processing setup is leveraged within Fusion Project Portfolio Management and Inventory for processing intercompany transactions. This feature also supports a separate Intercompany calendar so that open and close periods can be independent of the General Ledger accounting close period. Implementers have the choice to use one corporate currency for intercompany transaction processing, thereby eliminating foreign exchange rate fluctuations. Default provider and receiver distributions accounts are set up in Subledger Accounting's Transaction Account rules.

Setup tasks relevant for these processing options are as follows:

1. Set Invoicing Required Option at Legal Entity Level.

2. Define Business Unit and Its Related Setup.

3. Setup Intercompany Transaction configuration.

   a. Manage Transaction Types.

   b. Manage Intercompany System Options.

   c. Manage Intercompany Period status.

   d. Manage Intercompany Organizations.

   e. Manage Intercompany Customer and Supplier Assignments.

   f. Manage Intercompany Receivables Assignments.

4. Subledger Accounting–Transaction Account Rules.

5. Intercompany Transaction Approval Setup.

Intercompany Balancing Rule Setup Example
In this section, we will look at how to set up a simple Legal Entity Balancing Rule between two Legal Entities within a same Ledger. Let us assume that the ACME Corp USA Legal Entity and ACME Commercial Finance Inc Legal Entity within ACME US Ledger engage in business activity, and as a result, any accounting entries between these Legal Entities need to be balanced automatically.

Setup
Step 1: Enable Ledger Options

1. Navigate to the Enable Ledger Options Task for ACME US Ledger.

2. Check Enable Intercompany Accounting to allow intercompany balancing as shown in Figure 6-24.

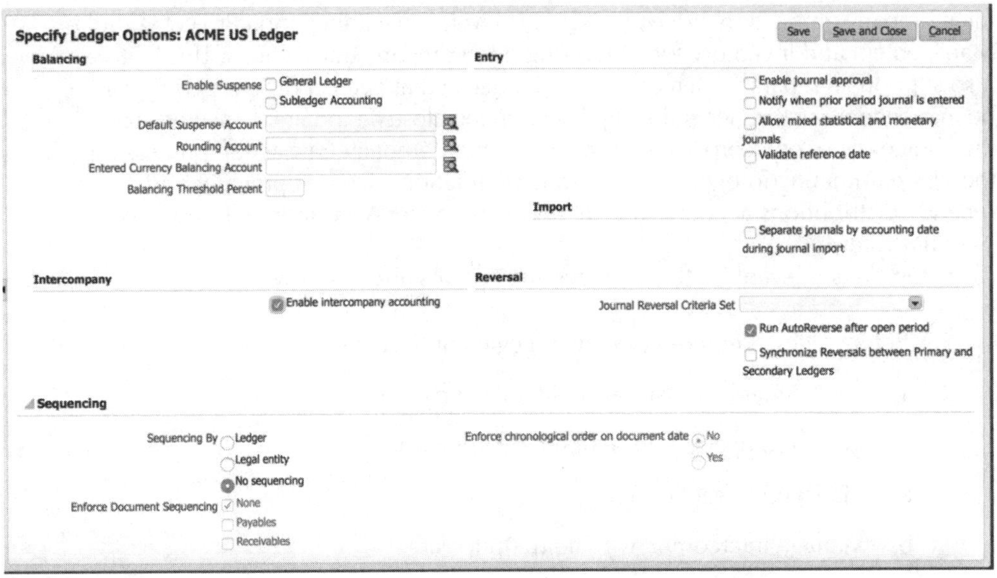

FIGURE 6-24. *Enable Intercompany Accounting for ACME US Ledger*

Step 2: Intercompany Balancing Rules

1. Navigate to the Manage Intercompany Balancing Rules task under the Define And Maintain Intercompany Processing Rules Configuration Tasks List.

2. Create Legal Entity level balancing rules as shown in Figure 6-25.

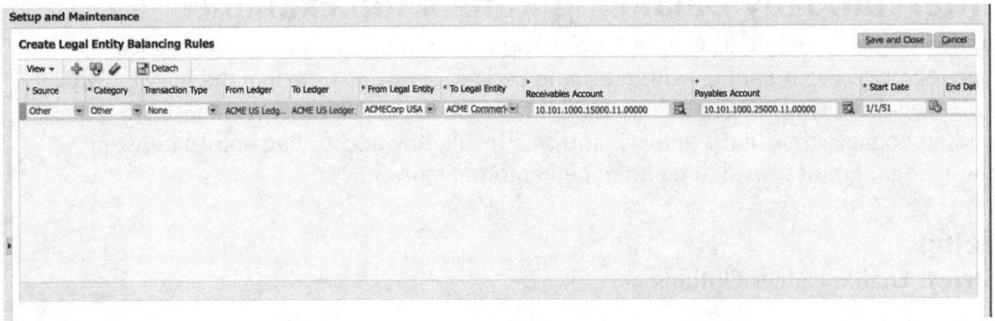

FIGURE 6-25. *Create Legal Entity Balancing rules between ACME Corp Bank and ACME Commercial Finance Inc.*

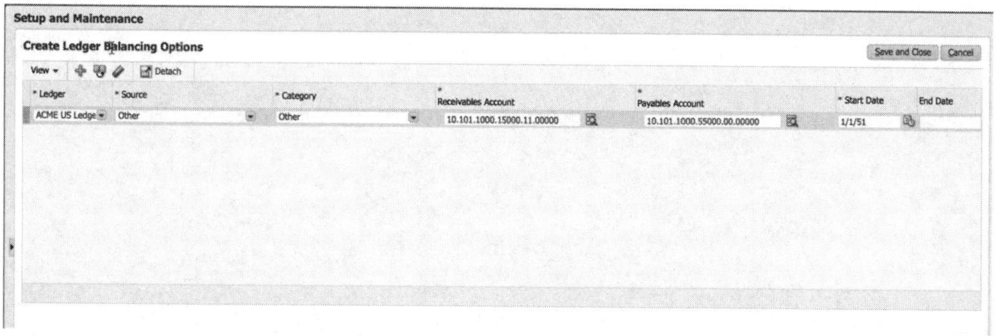

FIGURE 6-26. *Create Ledger Balancing Option for ACME US Ledger*

Step 3: Define Ledger Balancing Options

1. Navigate to the Define Ledger Balancing Options task under the Define and Maintain Intercompany Processing Rules Configuration Tasks List.

2. Create the Ledger Balancing Option for ACME US Ledger as shown in Figure 6-26.

Now we should be able to create journal entries between ACME Corp Bank and ACME Commercial Finance Inc, and during posting, automatic journal lines will be generated. Chapter 8 provides details of how to enter manual journal entries in General Ledger.

Summary

In this chapter we have explained the concept of the Ledger and the different types of Ledgers that can be defined in Fusion General Ledger. We have also introduced the concepts of Business Unit, reference data sets and intercompany accounting processing options. We have also created ACME Bank Ledgers and Business Units and looked at Intercompany Accounting options. In the next chapter, we will concentrate on how to secure access to Ledger data.

CHAPTER
7

Security and Audit in
Fusion Applications

The purpose of this chapter is to ensure that you can understand and work on the key security aspects in Oracle Fusion Applications across various features within this application suite. Every business application has a basic need to secure its resources and its data. Oracle Fusion Applications is no exception to those requirements. At a very high level there are two key components in any security model. These are authentication and authorization. Authentication means that the application ensures that a person accessing a protected resource has been validated for their username and password. The objective of authentication is to verify that the user is actually who they say they are. Once Fusion Applications identifies the user through authentication, then authorization is the basis for limits on what the user can do. For example, the authorization layer settings in Fusion General Ledger govern questions like these:

- Is the user authorized to access the Journal Entry screen?

- Should the user's activity in the Journal Entry screen be restricted to a set of ledgers or balancing segment values in the Chart of Accounts?

- Should the user be allowed to enter the journals and also to post the journals?

In this chapter, we will begin with giving an overview of the security model, followed by an explanation of how usernames, passwords, and their access are validated. The key emphasis, however, will be on authorization and data access in Authorization Policy Manager (APM). APM is the security layer that governs the screens, web services, and other components that the users can access and what data they can view or modify. We will see how the data security has been implemented in some of the key modules within Fusion Applications, taking examples in Oracle Fusion General Ledger in the context of ACME Bank.

Business Requirements

The ACME Corporation wants to ensure that accountants can access journals and balances related to the ledgers that they maintain. There is also a need to segregate the data visible by primary balancing segment values and lines of business. The line-of-business security will allow business owners to track the activities in their business streams. In order to implement these business requirements, it is important that we fully understand the security architecture of Oracle Fusion Applications.

Security Overview in Oracle Fusion Applications

Fusion Applications security is based on Role Based Access Control. The security layer in the product allows the system to assess who does what. The security layer ensures that you can only do what is appropriate for your job assignment.

The product comes out of the box with a predefined list of roles and permissions. This predefined configuration is also known as *reference implementation,* which provides over a hundred jobs. These jobs very closely match the actual jobs that people are hired to perform in enterprises.

Fusion Applications security is powered by Oracle Fusion Middleware; that is, the security capability is a part of the Fusion Middleware solution. Unlike Oracle EBS, Siebel, and PeopleSoft, the security layer is totally externalized from the modules and offerings. It also implies that in Fusion Applications, you configure your security rules in only one place across all the offerings, and they get referred to in various places in the business logic across all tools and technologies in the Fusion Applications stack. In other words, the product provides one way of securing access and data in a central place.

In a traditional ERP system, security administrators have to manage users and give appropriate access, and it is very common to have constant complaints about password management and integration between governance, risk, and compliance, making sure that we are compliant with all appropriate regulations that exist within an enterprise. Fusion Applications security not only reduces the risks but also the administrative costs that result in increased productivity. The security layer in Fusion Applications applies across all the tools in the product. For example, the security defined on General Ledger Balancing segment values will apply equally in user interfaces, Business Intelligence reports, analytics in Essbase cubes, and integrations.

Fusion Applications also introduces self-service provisioning and automated on-boarding so that the administrator doesn't have to constantly work on user access, password provisioning, and so on. It allows staff to work on value-added activities such as defining the security policies for their enterprise.

The reference implementation provides transparency because the product externalizes security policies and puts them into an area where auditors can get a 360-degree view of access policies across the entire application. Fusion Applications also makes it easy to review and approve the access of individuals who are accessing the product.

Comparison of Security Model to Other Oracle ERP Products

In Fusion Applications, there is a job role such as General Accountant, which is probably equivalent to the top-level menu within E-Business Suite and also within

Peoplesoft. The job role gives you the list of functions that should be available to an accountant in Oracle Fusion General Ledger. The next level down is the data role in Fusion Applications. A data role gives access to certain functions, but it also gives access to a set of data. So if you are a General Accountant for ACME UK Insurance, then you should be able to see the journals of ACME UK Insurance Ledger, but you should not be able to view the journals of ACME US Insurance Ledger.

Fusion Applications allows you to create a role hierarchy. This is just a grouping of privileges that you want to share between different jobs; for example, you might want to share a set of duties that are common to both General Accountant and an Intercompany Accountant, because both will need the ability to report on their chart of account balances.

The next level down is the duty role. The duty roles are mapped to the job roles. On a job board you will typically see a list of duties that will be performed by a job. For example, a General Accountant will manage journal entry, budget entry, and currency administration. In Oracle Fusion Applications, each of these activities are captured as duty roles. The reference implementation makes sure that each duty role can be verified as appropriate lines on a job description in various job portals.

The next level down is the level of privilege; for example, managing journals can involve various entitlements such as entering journals by spreadsheet or entering journals from screen or importing journals or deleting journals, and so on. In other words, deleting a journal is a task in the real world and corresponds to a privilege in Oracle Fusion Applications. These privileges are assigned to the duty roles. In the E-Business Suite, it is a Form Function, and in PeopleSoft, it is a Permission List.

The final level of security is the reference to the Permission levels in the source code of various toolsets in Oracle Fusion Applications. The development team locks access to executables that are the real pages or buttons and so on, or things such as Excel spreadsheets or web services within Fusion.

For readers with an Oracle E-Business background, Table 7-1 explains the analogy between the various security layers of Oracle E-Business and Fusion Applications.

Fusion Applications	Oracle E-Business Suite
Data role	Responsibility
Job role	Top-Level Menu
Duty role	Submenu
Privilege	Form Function
Permission	Executable

TABLE 7-1. *Fusion Applications and Oracle E-Business Security Layers*

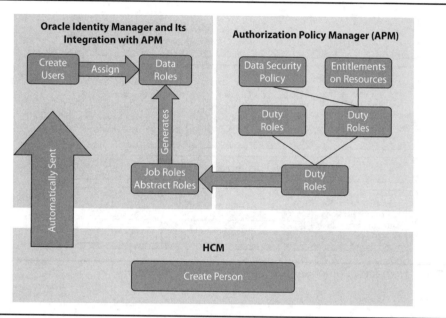

FIGURE 7-1. *Security objects in Fusion Applications*

Figure 7-1 shows a diagram of the relationship between various components used in Oracle Fusion Applications security. The details for each component are explained in subsequent sections of this chapter. As you can see, the provisioning process begins with creation of the person in Fusion HCM (Human Capital Management).

Architecture Components in Oracle Fusion Applications Security

Figure 7-2 shows the high-level components in Fusion Applications security. The actual technical stack has further Oracle components; however, the components listed in this figure will give you an idea of the architecture of Fusion Applications security. Even though some of these components may sound technical in nature, from our experience it is important that you understand these layers at a high level. During the implementation project, be it on-premise or cloud-based, you will be using most of these architectural components even when working in a Functional Configuration role.

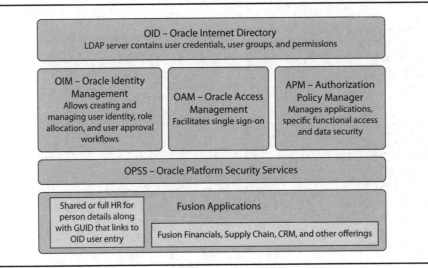

FIGURE 7-2. *High-level components in Fusion Applications security*

Oracle Internet Directory

At the very back end of the security layers is an Oracle tool named OID (Oracle Internet Directory), where the user credentials are stored along with the user groups, permissions, and various other user login–related attributes. When you install Oracle Fusion Applications, a tool called ODSM (Oracle Directory Services Manager) gets installed as well, and it has a URL similar to http://hostname:port/odsm. ODSM allows you to interrogate the OID contents from a browser. Any kind of role that is created in Fusion Applications gets registered as a group within OID. The users that have access to that role get registered as the members of those groups in OID. Even though Fusion Applications provides user-friendly screens to create users, roles, permissions, and so on, behind the scenes, these get registered into OID's LDAP-based repository. For SaaS customers, you will almost never get access to this repository, but on-premise customers will find this useful for troubleshooting.

Oracle Identity Manager

Oracle Fusion Applications also comes installed with OIM (Oracle Identity Manager). OIM allows a company to manage its users and their access to various roles centrally from a web console. Corporations implementing Fusion Applications on-premise have an option to leverage the Identity Management Suite installed as a part of Fusion Applications as an enterprise-wide system. This approach has some benefits such as out-of-the-box integration with Fusion Human Resources to manage leaver and joiner processes in order to allow automatic allocation and revocation of roles.

Further possibilities include leveraging OIM's integration with SOA (Service Oriented Architecture) within Fusion Middleware to facilitate various self-service–based user management approval processes and to streamline integration with the security card system of the corporation, integrating with canteen card facilities, staff gym membership, and so on, as applicable, subject to licensing costs verified with Oracle for the usage of the platform beyond Fusion Applications.

Authorization Policy Manager (APM)

Oracle Authorization Policy Manager is a web-based console for Oracle Entitlements Server (OES) with some additional capabilities for data security in Fusion Applications. As an implementer, this is the area where you will spend most of your hours in configuring security to match the business needs. APM is a fine-grained authorization product that defines policies that allow organizations to control security at a granular level. For example, coarse-grained security might allow or disallow a user from accessing a screen, whereas fine-grained security can allow or disallow users seeing specific buttons and might hide or show a field or make a field read-only and conditionally control data-related operations. At a very high level, APM has the components listed in the following sections.

Resource Types in APM

Every artifact such as a user interface screen or workflow process or Enterprise Scheduler Service or web service is associated with a resource type. APM allows you to define the possible actions that can be performed on each registered resource.

Resources in APM

Think of resource definition as registering a Fusion Applications artifact that is to be protected for access. For example, when defining a resource, you will capture the web service name or the path of the screen. A resource points to an actual physical deployed code that delivers a piece of functionality.

Entitlements in APM

After you register the resource in APM, next you define entitlements for that resource. These entitlements are also known as *privileges* in Fusion Applications. Here you can bundle a group of resources and specify the actions that are allowed on each such resource within the privilege. This bundling of resources along with the permissible actions allowed on them is called an *entitlement*. For example, a resource of type Journal Entry screen can have an action named Create Journals. When that entitlement is granted to a user via a role, then that user will be allowed to perform the specified actions on the resource as defined in the entitlement definition.

Duty Roles in APM

Using APM, you can create duty roles. Oracle Fusion Applications comes seeded with a long list of duty roles in the reference implementation. A duty role gives a representation of the features in the product that can be controlled for their access. For example, the Journal Entry role and Journal Posting role can be two separate duty roles. An organization may want a single individual to be disallowed from performing both the functions of entry and posting on the journal, even though both the actions can be performed from the same journal entry screen. To handle this scenario, the Oracle Fusion Applications product team would create one duty role for each of these activities. Duty roles are also referred to as *application roles* because these are specific to an application. For example, a duty role that allows creation of new employee records has to belong to the HCM (Human Capital Management) application and cannot belong to the Financials suite in Fusion Applications.

Authorization Policy in APM

Next you define an Authorization policy in APM. When defining the Authorization policy, you specify which duty roles can perform what actions on which set of resources. You do so by attaching one or more resources to a duty role within the Authorization policy definition. There are two ways to attach a resource to a duty role. You can either attach a resource directly to the duty role, or you can attach an entitlement to the duty role.

Oracle Platform Security Services

OPSS is the short name for Oracle Platform Security Services. You can think of OPSS as a decision engine that resides between the Oracle Fusion Applications code and the security repository. Each request made by the application is sent via OPSS to Oracle Identity Management; therefore, it is the central integration point between the application logic and the security layer. OPSS also has an auditing feature to log which user requested access to which resource and at what timestamp. This enables the Fusion Applications product to capture an audit of user interactions. As an implementer, you will never interact with the OPSS layer directly, unless you are a developer for an on-premise implementation.

Role Based Access Control (RBAC)

RBAC restricts access to the system based on the role of the user within the organization. Of course, the desired roles have to be granted to the user in the first place. RBAC in Fusion Applications defines "who can do what on which set of data." In Fusion Applications the security based on RBAC has been implemented using a common framework across all its applications.

The terminology behind the various types of roles can be confusing. Therefore, for simplicity in this chapter, we will classify the roles into two types, that is, external roles and application roles. These roles can have further subclassifications as explained in Table 7-2.

Role Type	Also Known As	Comments
Job roles	Enterprise roles	These roles get mapped to one or more duty roles, because a person who takes on a job in a company is meant to perform several duties. The name of this role has the suffix _JOB. Some examples are Account Payables Manager Job, General Ledger Accounting Manager Job, and so on.
Abstract roles	Enterprise roles	These roles are associated with a user, irrespective of the job they perform within an organization. Therefore, abstract roles are at a higher level, spanning various jobs, and hence the name abstract. Examples are Employee role, Temporary Staff role, and so on. An organization might decide to autoprovision an Expense Entry Duty role to all the employees, and likewise may decide to autoprovision a Timesheet Entry Duty role to all the contract workers.
External roles	Enterprise roles	Job roles and Abstract roles are also called external roles as these are defined in Oracle Identity Manager, which is external to APM.
Duty roles	Application roles	These are the granular duties performed by the jobs. Examples are GL Journal Entry Duty, GL Journal Approval Duty, GL Journal Posting Duty, and so on. The name of this role has the suffix _DUTY. The duty role provides access to screens, reports, and dashboards via privileges and provides access to data behind the screens using data security.
Data roles	External roles	You can think of these roles as data wrappers around the job and abstract roles. If a job role is a loaf of bread, then a data role is a slice of that loaf. A data role is a filter condition applied to the database resources that the job or abstract roles have access to via their underlying duty roles. The data roles inherit from the job roles or abstract roles. For example, a job role may allow access to the Journal Inquiry screen, but the data role will allow access to the data in certain ledgers via that screen.

TABLE 7-2. *Types of Roles in Fusion Applications*

Both application roles and job roles categorize the users into different groups. The job roles are categorized as per the company's organization structure, whereas application roles are driven by the capabilities within the product. For example, if Fusion Applications were not to have a feature for Journal Posting, then there would be no point in defining an application role named "Journal Posting Duty." Therefore, application roles also reflect the application features. Someone on the Oracle design team recognized the need that the Fusion Applications product must have a Journal Posting feature that can be potentially separated from the Journal Entry feature; therefore, they created these as two different duty roles.

Role Hierarchy

Both the external roles and the application roles support nesting via hierarchies. The hierarchical concept of roles is explained using Figure 7-3. As is evident from the example in this figure, the policies applied to the roles at a higher level are automatically inherited by the roles at a lower level. In other words, the policies added to the child roles are applied in addition to the policies for the parent roles.

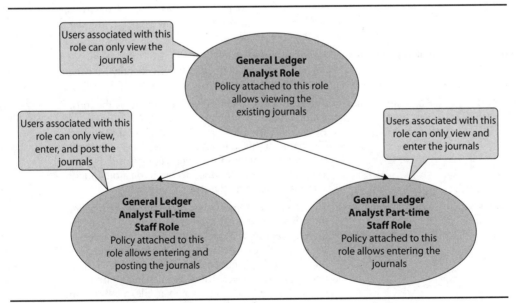

FIGURE 7-3. *Role hierarchy in Fusion Applications*

Authentication in Fusion Applications

In order to appreciate the authentication approach implemented in Fusion Applications, it is important to highlight how the security works in traditional applications. In old-school enterprise software, the authentication process is local to the application itself, and in those systems, it is not possible to integrate authentication with a central corporate authentication system. Local authentication means that the user logins and their passwords are stored within the application tables itself instead of being stored in a centralized corporate repository. In the real world, staff can potentially be using dozens of applications across the enterprise. This has become even more widespread with cloud-based products being introduced into the enterprises.

Companies these days use a variety of systems in their enterprises. Some of these systems are hosted within the company data center, whereas other systems could be hosted in the cloud. In order to keep the user experience seamless, it is advantageous to have the same username/password across various applications. Fusion Applications makes centralized authentication a possibility because it delivers an out-of-the-box integration with Oracle Internet Directory and Oracle Identity Management.

Technically it is possible to use the on-premise Fusion Applications security platform for centralized corporate authentication, subject to your licensing agreement with Oracle. Alternatively, it is also possible to configure Fusion Applications to be authenticated from an existing centralized LDAP server such as Microsoft's Active Directory, IBM's Tivoli Directory Server, and so on. For example, every morning the staff walks into their workplace and logs in to their Windows terminal. Their username and password authentication occurs against an LDAP repository. Likewise, it is possible to configure Oracle Fusion Applications as well to authenticate against the same repository.

Typically, Human Capital Management (HCM) systems are the starting point for registering new staff into the organization. Therefore, you will find that the creation of employee records in HCM usually triggers the creation of new user records in Fusion Applications. In order to facilitate the use cases where users have to be automatically created from the HCM records, Oracle Identity Management has a feature that allows organizations to define their username construction logic. For example, some organizations will create a username called TSMITH for Mr. Tom Smith, whereas in other organizations they might want to automatically create a username of SMITHT. If the usernames are automatically generated, then the password, too, can be automatically generated by the system. Again, Oracle Identity Management allows implementers to write their own initial password creation logic.

Authorization in Fusion Applications

Permission to access a resource is called authorization. Authorization ensures that the user only has access to resources they have been specifically granted access to. These grants are also known as privileges or entitlements. These grants are defined in APM. APM is based on another Oracle Product named Oracle Entitlement Server (OES). In

Fusion Applications, an authorization check is a combination of function and data security. It must be noted that the data security feature is not a part of Oracle Entitlement Server. The Fusion Applications team added the data security feature to OES under the umbrella of APM.

Function security ensures that a user can access only those resources for which they have been granted permissions. The data security controls access to the data. The authorization checks can either be enforced via APM or explicitly implemented by a developer either declaratively or programmatically.

Function security decides which user can perform which set of actions on which set of resources. A grant provides a role (or user) access for a permission set (or individual resource). The permission set is a grouping of related permissions required to complete a task. For example, the permissions to access a page and all related task flows may be grouped together into a permission set such that they can be granted together instead of granting each separately. This grouping of permissions is also known as entitlements.

Data Security

Data security defines "who can do what action on which set of data." From this definition, "which set of data" can be enforced by appending a filter condition via a SQL WHERE clause.

APM User Interface

APM has a URL similar to https://host:port/apm. Figure 7-4 shows the key components of APM. As mentioned previously, the APM product is based on Oracle Entitlement Server. The Fusion Applications team, however, added a data security feature to OES. As shown in Figure 7-4, you can search for artifacts defined in APM by searching in the left-hand pane. When searching for components in the left-hand pane, it is important that you first select the application, because the policies defined in this area are application-specific policies segregated by HCM, FSCM, CRM, and so on. Application FSCM contains the Financials and Supply Chain Management artifacts. This includes component offerings such as Fusion Accounting Hub, Fusion Payables, Fusion Receivables, and so on. HCM is the Human Capital Management application, and CRM is the Customer Relationship Management application.

Exploring the APM Contents on the Public Website

Security reference implementation is the definition of authorization roles and policies that get delivered out of the box by Oracle Fusion Applications. Besides the APM, you can also browse the contents of reference implementation in https://fusionappsoer.oracle.com/oer/index.jsp. When you navigate to that URL, you will be asked to log in to your Oracle account first, and then you can select the guest

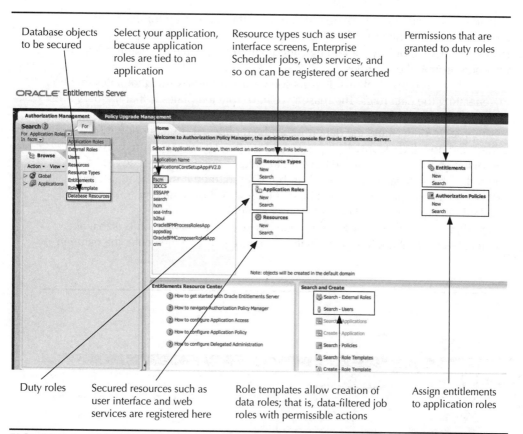

Database objects to be secured

Select your application, because application roles are tied to an application

Resource types such as user interface screens, Enterprise Scheduler jobs, web services, and so on can be registered or searched

Permissions that are granted to duty roles

Duty roles

Secured resources such as user interface and web services are registered here

Role templates allow creation of data roles; that is, data-filtered job roles with permissible actions

Assign entitlements to application roles

FIGURE 7-4.   *APM home page that allows you to secure artifacts in Fusion Applications*

option. Under Search Criteria Type, select Role. In the Logical Business Area field, select All Fusion Apps: Logical Business Area. Click the Search button and then select Fusion Accounting Hub or any other desired offering you want to explore. Under the Documentation tab, open Security Reference Manual.

How Does Oracle Secure Database Resources in Fusion Applications?

The data security policy is to secure the data in Fusion Applications. For example, if you are given access to the General Ledger Accounting Manager job role, you will still not be able to view or enter any journals or balances unless you have access to the ledger via the data security policy. In other words, with the job roles you may be able to see the screens but not operate on the data. The reason for this is that the function security is different than the data security. The data security is implemented in Fusion Applications by something called *data roles*, which are nothing but the wrappers around the job roles.

Oracle Fusion Applications delivers some out-of-the-box role templates that help in generating the data roles. The reason we have role templates is that the data roles always have a dependency on a job role.

In order to understand the data roles and templates, it is first important to understand how the security is implemented on the database resources. At the very end of the chain, it is a database table that contains the data that needs to be secured. If this database object needs to be secured, then it must be registered in APM by a Fusion Applications developer. Figure 7-5 shows the registration of the standard Oracle table GL_LEDGERS as an example.

In APM, as shown in Figure 7-5, to search on existing database objects that are secured, select Database Resources in the left-hand pane and then enter the name in

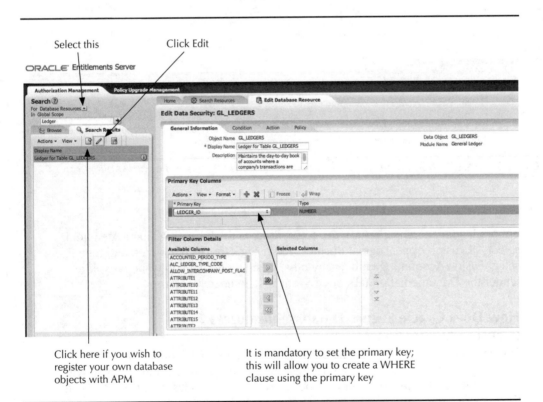

FIGURE 7-5. *Registered database resource in APM*

the Search field and click the right arrow. Next, click the Edit icon to browse the database resource in APM. You will notice that it is mandatory to register the primary key of the database resource in APM. Functional consultants can always rely on Fusion Application developers in their team to implement these data roles. Implementers working on SaaS can seek help from Oracle Support with these data roles.

To create a set of WHERE clauses, a Fusion Applications developer can click the Condition tab as shown in Figure 7-6. Conditions are responsible for returning a set of rows at run time, and these conditions are known as instance sets. When the data roles are assigned to a user, then these conditions are applied at run time when the corresponding database resource is accessed via the applicable duty role in the application.

Once the data is accessible, Fusion Applications then allows implementers to define the permissible actions. Actions can be insert, update, or delete. However, the product development team may define further actions on certain database resources. The Policy tab on the database resource is where job, action, and

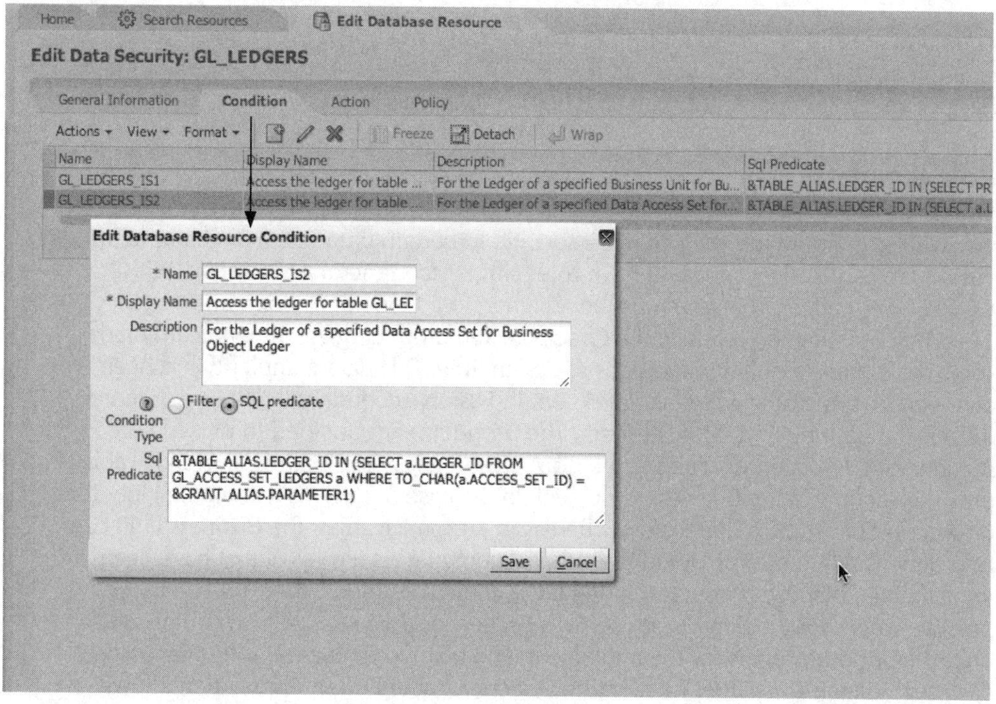

FIGURE 7-6. *The conditions can be defined as SQL predicates.*

| | Home | 🗋 **Edit Database Resource** ✕ |

Edit Data Security: GL_LEDGERS

| General Information | Condition | Action | **Policy** |

| Actions ▾ | View ▾ | Format ▾ | 🗋 ✎ ✖ | 🔲 Freeze | 🖼 Detach | ↵ Wrap |

Policy	Role	Actions	Condition
Grant on Ledger	FUSION_APPS_SETUP_ESS_...	Report Oracle Fusion General Ledg...	All Values
Financial Extrac...	FUN_FIN_OBIA_ETL_DUTY	Report Oracle Fusion General Ledg...	All Values
	GL_GENERAL_ACCOUNTANT...	Report Oracle Fusion General Ledger	Access the ledger for table GL_LEDGERS for gl - for
	GL_GENERAL_ACCOUNTING...	Report Oracle Fusion General Ledger	Access the ledger for table GL_LEDGERS for gl - for
	GL_FINANCIAL_ANALYST_JO...	Report Oracle Fusion General Ledger	Access the ledger for table GL_LEDGERS for gl - for
	GL_CONTROLLER_JOB_MA0...	Report Oracle Fusion General Ledger	Access the ledger for table GL_LEDGERS for gl - for
	GL_CHIEF_FINANCIAL_OFFI...	Report Oracle Fusion General Ledger	Access the ledger for table GL_LEDGERS for gl - for
	GL_GENERAL_ACCOUNTANT...	Report Oracle Fusion General Ledger	Access the ledger for table GL_LEDGERS for gl - for
	GL_FINANCIAL_ANALYST_JO...	Report Oracle Fusion General Ledger	Access the ledger for table GL_LEDGERS for gl - for
	GL_CONTROLLER_JOB_MA0...	Report Oracle Fusion General Ledger	Access the ledger for table GL_LEDGERS for gl - for

FIGURE 7-7.   *Policies that secure the data in Fusion Applications*

condition are stitched together for the data security, as shown in Figure 7-7. For example, in the Policy tab, you can define that the General Ledger Controller job has permission to update journals that belong to ACMECorp USA.

Role Templates

During the implementation project, when it comes to granting roles to the users, you will be granting job roles that are specific to certain data sets. For example, in Fusion General Ledger, you will have roles similar to General Accountant ACME_ CORP_USA_Ledger. This role must be assigned to a General Accountant.

When building the product, the Oracle Fusion product development team made some basic data granularity decisions at design time. This data granularity has been achieved by something called a *dimension*. In Fusion Accounting Hub, one or more ledgers can belong to a GL access set. The product team decided to provide data security for GL-related job roles at the GL Access Set levels. Similarly, Fusion Payables provides security at the Business Unit level. In the case of Fusion Accounting Hub, the GL Access Set can be a dimension, whereas in Fusion Payables, the Business Unit can be a dimension. It must be noted that other security layers also exist that have been implemented in those products. During large implementations, there will be many possible values for the dimensions such as Ledgers or Business Units. It can become quite a laborious process for the implementation team to define job roles manually for each such dimension value. To ease this process, Oracle Fusion Application allows automatic generation of data roles that are wrappers around the job roles. This is achieved by means of a role template.

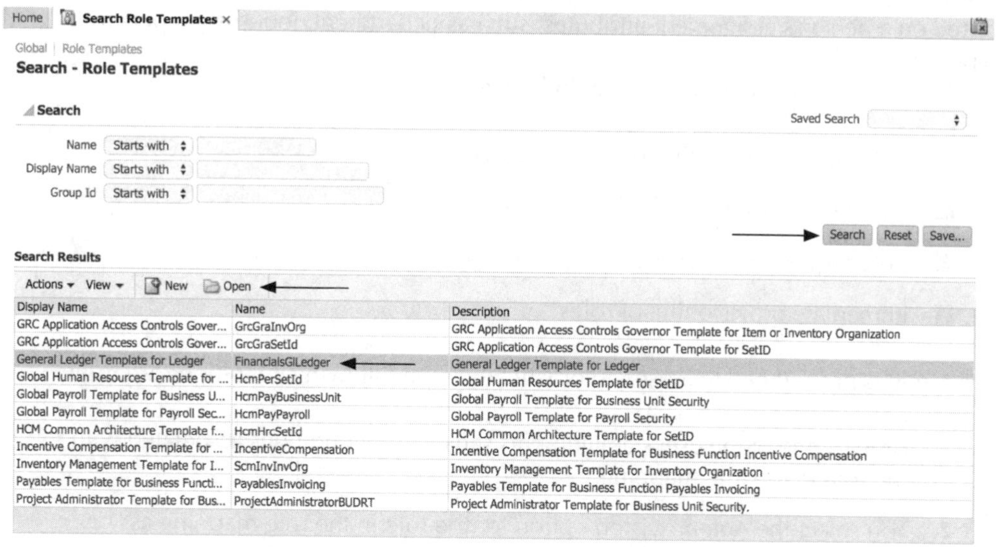

FIGURE 7-8.   *Role templates*

Figure 7-8 shows some of the role templates that exist out of the box in the product. APM allows you to define your own role templates as well, which is useful when you are developing custom modules and wish to leverage the security model framework delivered by Fusion Applications.

These role templates come predefined with some components. These components can be extended, or new role templates can be created in APM by the project implementation team to secure the data in custom applications that you are developing.

At design time, each Fusion Application team decides the applicable dimensions for a set of job roles. For example, the Fusion Accounting Hub team decided that the accountant's access to journals should be controlled by GL Access Sets, which in turn is based on GL Ledgers or primary balancing segment values.

Joiners, Movers, and Leavers

Oracle Fusion HCM provides a functionality that allows roles to be provisioned automatically to the users when certain conditions are met. This feature is available even for the Fusion Financials customers using the HCM in shared mode. This feature allows roles to be allocated to the users automatically based on certain attributes in their person definition. To implement this feature, you need to define a mapping between the role and a set of conditions. The conditions can be defined based on a person's assignment attributes, such as department, job, system person type, and so on.

The role mapping can support the following:

- Automatic provisioning of roles to users

- Manual provisioning of roles to users

- Role requests from users

- Immediate provisioning of roles

A role is provisioned to a user automatically if the following conditions are true:

1. At least one of the user's assignments satisfies all conditions associated with the role in the role mapping.

2. You select the Autoprovision option for the role in the role mapping as shown in Figure 7-9.

For example, you may want to automatically assign the Expense Management ACME US Corp role to employees who have the position of Manager in the ACME

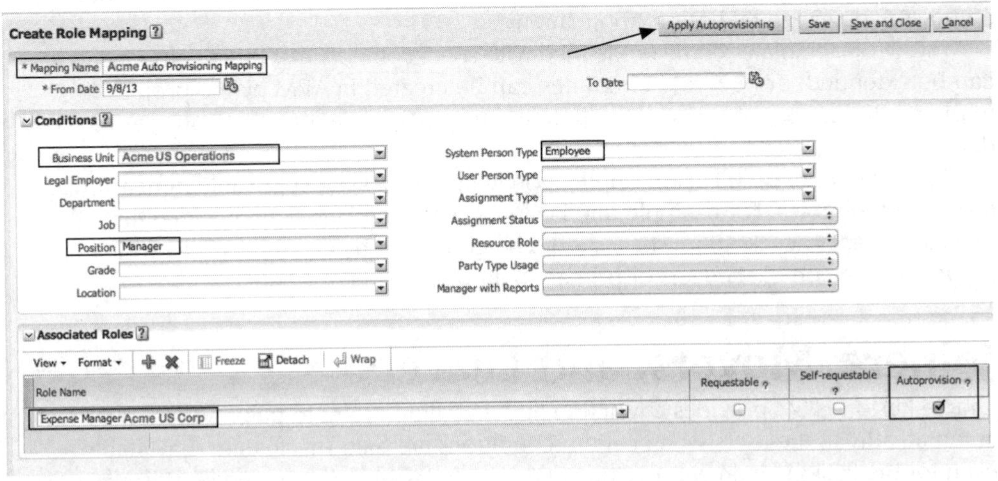

FIGURE 7-9. *Automatically assigning the Expense Manager role to all Employee Managers*

US Operations business unit. Automatic role provisioning occurs as soon as the user is confirmed to satisfy the role-mapping conditions, which can be when the user's assignment is either created or updated. The provisioning process also removes automatically provisioned roles from users who no longer satisfy the role-mapping conditions. Therefore, in this example, if the person is no longer a manager, then the Expense Manager role will be automatically removed.

The automatic provisioning of roles to users may be rejected if it violates segregation-of-duties rules. Segregation of duties is a functionality that can help prevent fraudulent activities by preventing the provision of an invalid combination of roles to a user.

System Auditing

Auditing in Oracle Fusion Applications is in compliance with SOX, PCI, HIPAA, and other industry standards. This mitigates any security risk to an enterprise. This auditing framework is also applicable to custom extensions developed in Oracle Fusion Applications.

Using the audit feature, you can search what a specific user did on a specific date or over a date range. Or you can search by a business object to see who changed something on a set of tables. Within these business objects, the important attributes are preselected by the Oracle Product development team for auditing.

Even the direct update to databases via Web Services and batch update processes can be captured by the auditing feature in Fusion Applications. The key components audited in Oracle Fusion Applications are

- System configuration changes
- Security access changes
- Business data changed by the user

During implementation you can decide the level of auditing that you wish to use. You may decide to cut down on the volume of data being captured during auditing. Some examples of auditing are

- Who approved
- Who made changes to security rules
- Login attempts, both successful and failed logins
- Who performed data migration
- Customizations

Broadly speaking, there are two types of audits: audit of data changes and audit of events. Fusion Applications Business Objects capture audit of data changes using shadow tables. This approach is similar to Oracle EBS. However, the Fusion Middleware product also audits events such as authentication, successful login, and so on to a central audit table when those events have occurred. The reporting user interface can retrieve data from shadow tables and from common audit tables of Fusion Middleware.

The reporting of the audit history is shown in a single user interface for both data changes and events being audited.

Configuring System Audit Policies

Fusion Applications contains a user interface named Manage Policies. This is where you configure your audit policies. As shown in Figure 7-10, you can audit the business objects such as expense reports, value sets, and so on. For a user to be able to configure audit policies, they must have the Application Administrator job role.

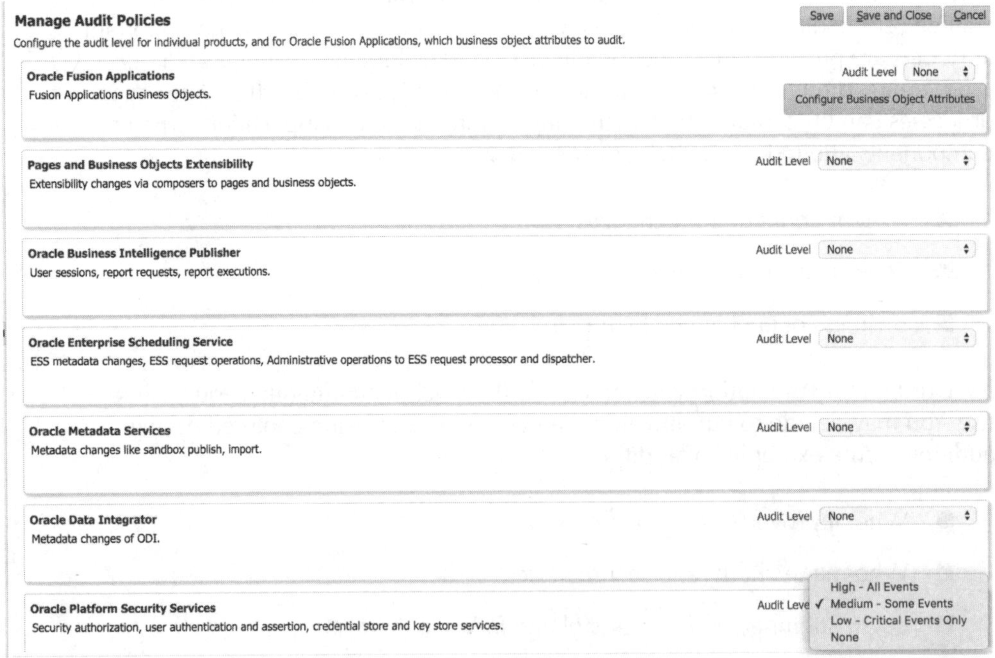

FIGURE 7-10. *Managing auditing policies in Fusion Applications*

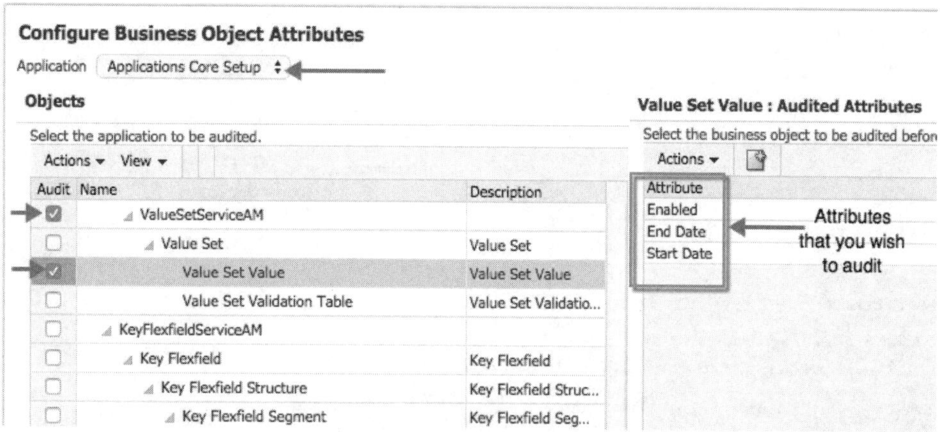

FIGURE 7-11. *Changing Audit value set values*

Within Oracle Platform Security Services, you can audit at a high or medium or low level. When you set this level to low, then only the critical events will be captured.

Figure 7-11 shows how you can enable the audit to track the changes to values in the value set values. This figure shows that Oracle Fusion Application presents to you a variety of predefined business objects on which auditing can be enabled. The product gives you further flexibility in auditing a selected set of attributes in the business objects. For example, Figure 7-11 shows how you can enable auditing for changes to value set values when either the Enabled flag or the End Date or the Start Date were to change.

Reporting on System Audit Policies

In order to see the audit data, you must have a job role named Internal Auditor allocated to the user. Figure 7-12 shows the Audit Reports user interface. To access this screen, click the Navigator menu and select the menu item Audit Reports.

Using this search screen, auditors or administrators can see the changes made to the business objects and any audit captured in Fusion Middleware products used by Fusion Applications. For example, it is very common to audit which role was assigned to which user by whom and when.

In order to audit the business objects such as database tables, the implementers can easily build reports using BI Publisher straight from the browser to report data in shadow tables.

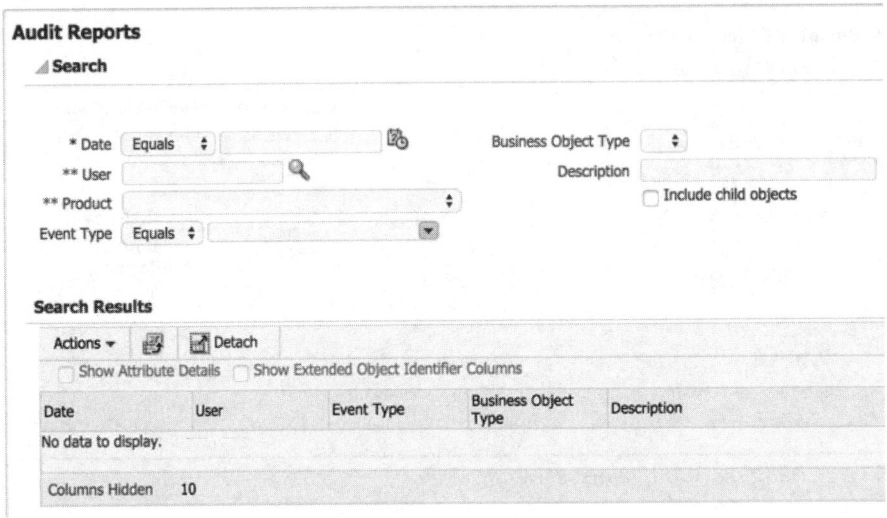

FIGURE 7-12. *Audit Search user interface*

Implementing the Business Requirements

The business requirement is to create three users, with the access shown in Table 7-3. These examples assume that the user FAADMIN will already exist in the system and will have access to all the ledgers and balancing segment values via Data Access Sets for every ledger being assigned to this user. This user will also have access to OIM and APM via the IT Security Manager role. In order to create a system administrator user, visit the link http://goo.gl/8fwa9e.

Username	Ledger Accessible	Primary Balancing Accessible	Line Of Business Accessible
ACMEUS01	ACME US Ledger	All Company Segment values are accessible	All Line Of Business values are accessible
ACMEUS02	ACME US Ledger	Only the Company Segment value 12, that is, ACME Mortgage Inc, is accessible	All Line Of Business values are accessible
ACMEUS03	ACME US Insurance Ledger	Only the Company Segment value 12, that is, ACME Mortgage Inc, is accessible	Only the Line Of Business segment value of 202, that is, ACME Commercial Finance (USA) LOB, is accessible

TABLE 7-3. *Business Requirements for ACME US Insurance Users*

A data access set in Fusion General Ledger allows autocreation of data roles for access to Ledgers and Primary Balancing segment values. In the following exercises, we will see how the data access set controls the access to Ledger and Balancing segment values.

Create User ACMEUS01 and Related Roles

Log in as a FAADMIN user, and click Setup And Maintenance. In the left-hand pane click Manage Implementation Projects. Click on the project titled ACME Phase I Implementation Project. Expand the project task tree for Financials | Define Common Applications Configuration For Financials | Define Security For Financials | Define Data Security For Financials | Manage Data Access Sets. Click Go To Tasks. Here you will find that a data access set named ACME US Ledger already exists. This data access set is created by default for every single ledger automatically by the system, as shown in Figure 7-13.

Next, click Search: Tasks and search for Role Template and click Search using the right-arrow icon. Click the Manage Role Templates task in the search window. Click Search Role Template and search using Display Name General%Ledger%. Click Open | Generate Roles. You will notice that Data roles with the following display names have been generated:

- General Accounting Manager ACME US Ledger

- Financial Analyst ACME US Ledger

- Controller ACME US Ledger

- Chief Financial Officer ACME US Ledger

- General Accountant ACME US Ledger

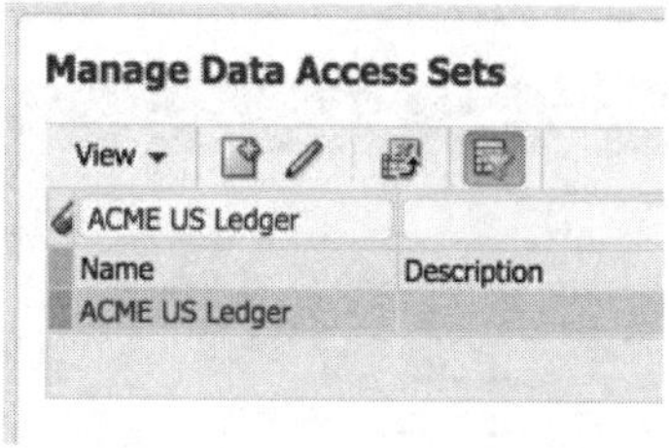

FIGURE 7-13. *The default access set created for every ledger*

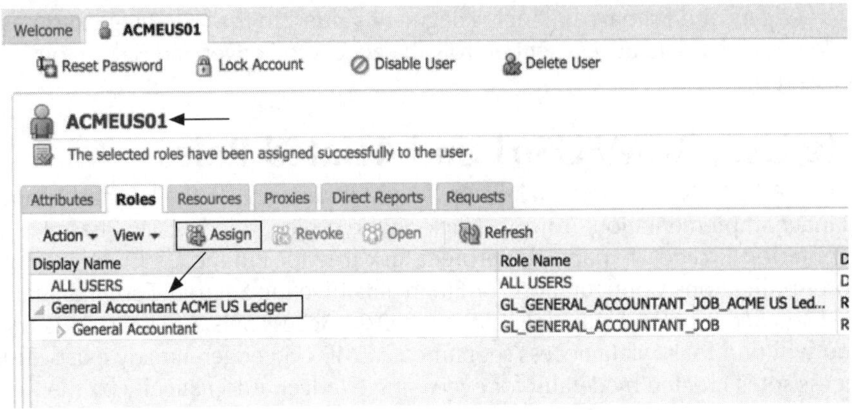

FIGURE 7-14. *Assigning a data role for ACME US Ledger's default data access set*

Navigate to Oracle Identity Manager using a URL similar to http://host:port/oim. Click Administration in the top-right corner and click Create User. Create a user with the following details:

Last Name: ACMEUS01
User Login: ACMEUS01
Organization: Xellerate Users
User Type: Other
Password: Welcome1

Click Save and assign the roles as highlighted in Figure 7-14.

Log in to Fusion Applications as user ACMEUS01 and reset your password as prompted. Click the Navigator icon as shown in Figure 7-15, and then click Journals under General Accounting.

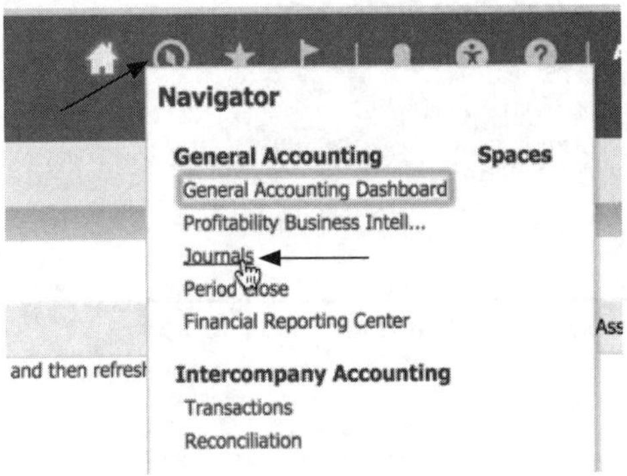

FIGURE 7-15. *Journal Entry screen*

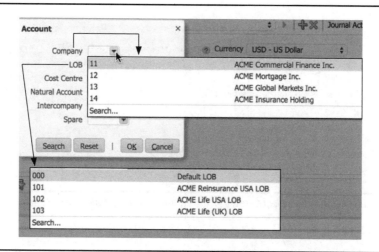

FIGURE 7-16. *The default ledger access set does not restrict the list of values in the account segment.*

After logging in, create a Journal batch, followed by a Journal Header with the category Manual, and add a code combination to the journal lines. As shown in Figure 7-16, you will be able to select all the values in the Company and Line of Business segment. This is so because for this user, there is no data security defined for the Company segment, which is the Primary Balancing segment.

Create User ACMEUS02 and Related Roles

In this example, we will create a user that will have access to just one value in the company segment. Log in as a FAADMIN user, and navigate to Manage Data Access Sets as was explained in the prior example. Click the + icon to create a new data set, with the following details:

> **Name:** ACME US Mortgage Data Access
> **Chart of Accounts:** ACME Global COA Instance
> **Accounting Calendar:** ACME Monthly
> **Access Set Type:** Primary Balancing Segment Value
> In the Access Set Assignments region, click the plus sign (+).
> **Ledger:** ACME US Ledger
> **All Values:** Uncheck this check box.
> **Specific Values:** Single Value
> **Segment Value:** 12

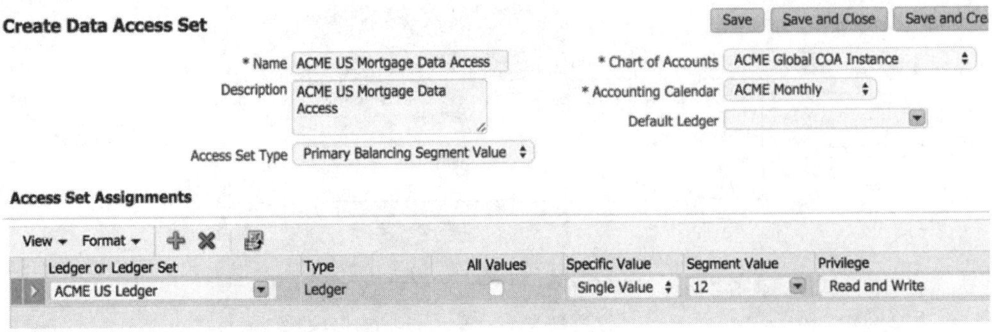

FIGURE 7-17. *The data access set created for a specific primary balancing segment value*

Save the data access set as shown in Figure 7-17, and you will see a confirmation message that the corresponding data roles are being generated. Click OK.

Navigate to Oracle Identity Manager and create a user as shown:

Last Name: ACMEUS02
User Login: ACMEUS02
Organization: Xellerate Users
User Type: Other
Password: Welcome1

Click Save and assign the role as highlighted in Figure 7-18.

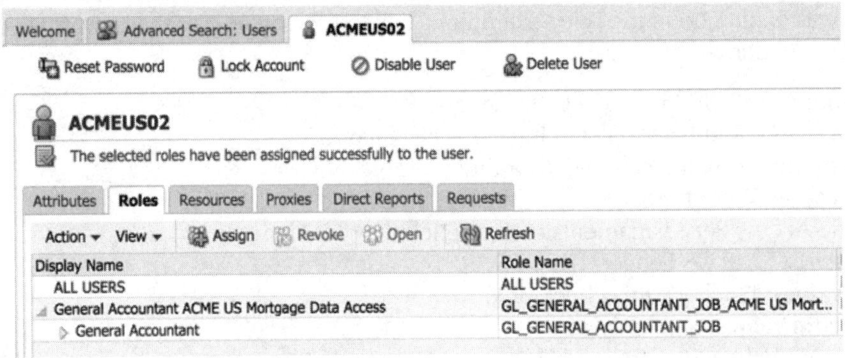

FIGURE 7-18. *Assigning a data role for the Mortgage Company Segment value*

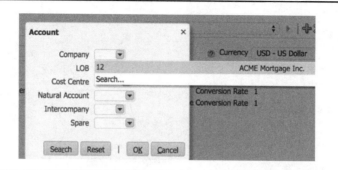

FIGURE 7-19. *The data access set can restrict values in the Primary Balancing segment.*

Log in to Fusion Applications as user ACMEUS02, and reset your password as prompted. After logging in, create a Journal batch, followed by a Journal Header with the category Manual, and add a code combination to the journal lines. As shown in Figure 7-19, you will be able to select a value of 12 in the Company segment.

Create User ACMEUS03 and Their Roles

In this example, we will create a user that will have access to just one value in the company segment and one value in the Line of Business segment. The high-level steps for this exercise are listed in Table 7-4.

Step	Reason
Create an abstract role XX_ACME_LOB_ABSTRACT	This abstract role will be the underlying basis for a data role that gets assigned to ACMEUS03.
Create a role template XX_ACME_LOB_R_TEMPLATE	This role template will generate data roles for Line of Business. One data role will be generated for each Line of Business value. The data role then gets assigned to the users.
Secure value set named ACME Line of Business	Securing the value set tells Fusion Applications that there are filter conditions to be applied on the segment using the value set.
Create Data Security Resource named XX_ACME_LOB_SECURITY	The data security resource name is where filter conditions are defined. These filter conditions are then assigned to the data role. The data role is assigned to the user. It must be noted that the data role in this case is a dummy data role, because the security model does not allow a data security resource to be assigned directly to the user.

TABLE 7-4. *Steps to Create Value Set Security*

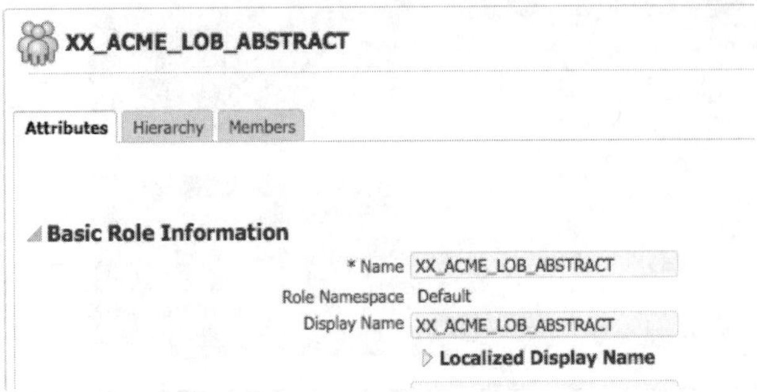

FIGURE 7-20. *Create an abstract role to allow data roles to be generated for value set values.*

Create Abstract Role

Log in to Oracle Identity Manager, and click Administration; then click Create Role. Provide both the name and display name as XX_ACME_LOB_ABSTRACT as shown in Figure 7-20 and save.

Create Role Template

The role template allows the data roles to be generated. In this case, we will create a role template for the Line of Business value set so that one data role can be generated for each Line of Business value.

Navigate to APM, and click Create Role Template. Provide the name XX_ACME_ LOB_R_TEMPLATE and the display name as ACME Line Of Business Role Template. Click the External Roles tab, and attach the abstract role as shown in Figure 7-21.

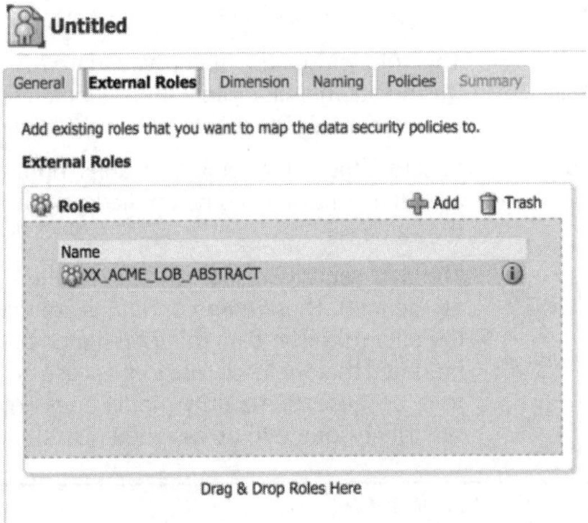

FIGURE 7-21. *Attach the abstract role to a role template.*

Click the Dimension tab, and enter the SQL statement shown. In your implementations, you will give an appropriate name for your value set.

```
select flex_value_set_id, flex_value from fusion.fnd_flex_values_vl
where flex_value_set_id =
(
select flex_value_set_id from fusion.FND_FLEX_VALUE_SETS
where flex_value_set_name like 'ACME Line of Business'
)
```

Click Preview, and you will be able to see all the Line of Business codes defined as shown in Figure 7-22.

Click the Naming tab, and provide a naming convention for the role templates to be generated. In this case, we will be concatenating ROLE_CODE with "-"

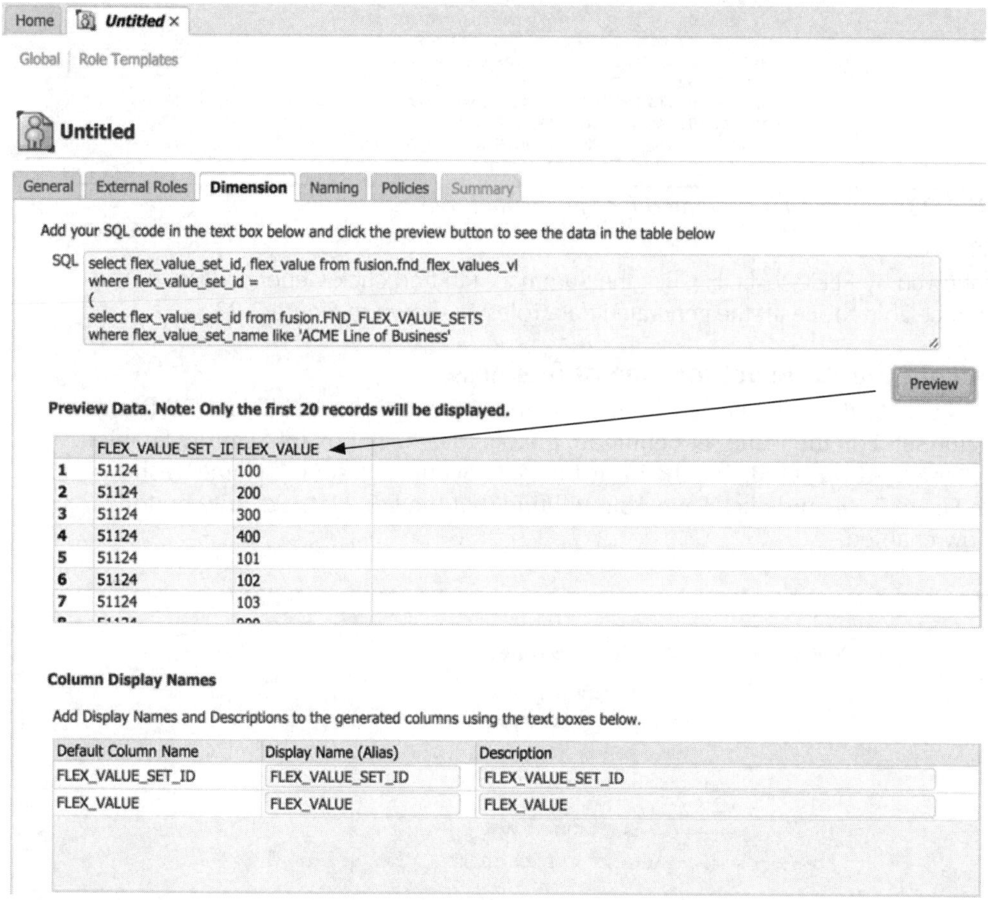

FIGURE 7-22. *Dimension for role template*

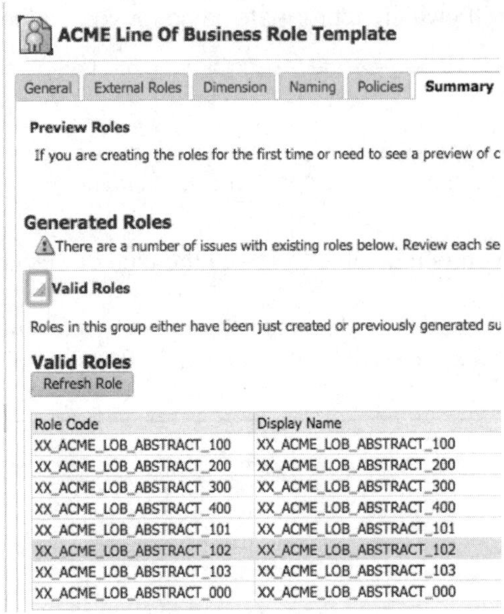

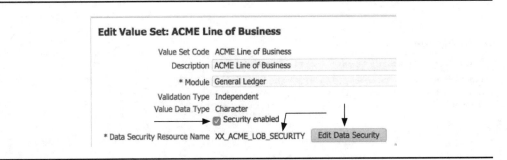

FIGURE 7-23. *Data roles generated for the abstract role*

followed by FLEX_VALUE. Click the Summary tab and click Generated Roles. You will be able to see all the generated data roles as shown in Figure 7-23.

Secure the Value Set for Line of Business

Navigate to the task Manage Value Sets, and search for the ACME Line Of Business value set. Edit the value set definition, enable the check box for Security Enabled, enter **XX_ACME_LOB_SECURITY** as the Data Security Resource Name as shown in Figure 7-24, and click Save. You will find that the Edit Data Security button is now enabled.

FIGURE 7-24. *Enabling value set security*

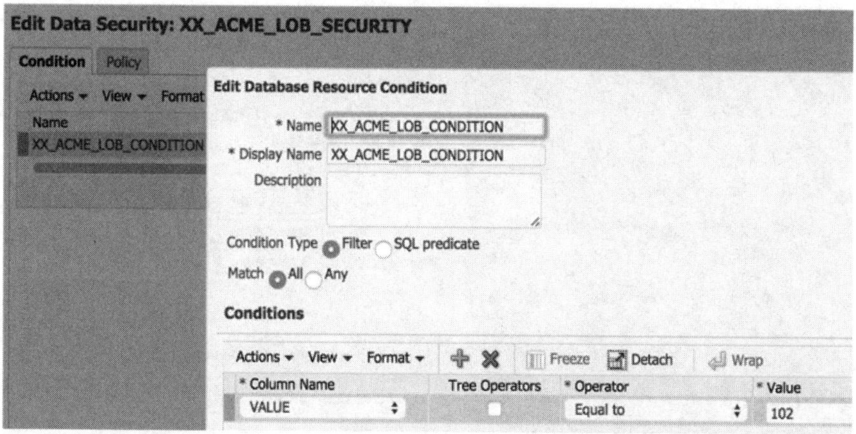

FIGURE 7-25. *Value set filter for value set security*

Click the Edit Data Security button. We need to capture the filter condition to secure the value set value in the Edit Data Security window. Create a new condition for the database resource and add a condition for value 102, as shown in Figure 7-25. Check the Oracle support website for the list of operators that are eligible for the Oracle Fusion General Ledger module. If the Tree Operators check box is enabled, you can select descendants and siblings of any node in the value set hierarchy.

Click the Policy tab, and this is where you will associate the data role to the condition as shown in Figure 7-26.

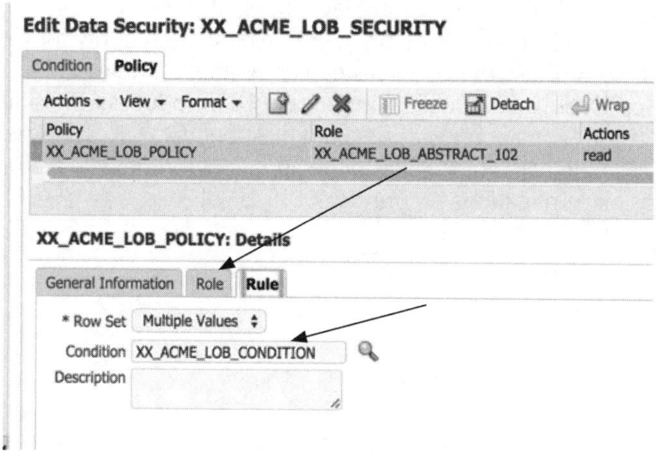

FIGURE 7-26. *Associate the generated data role to the filter condition.*

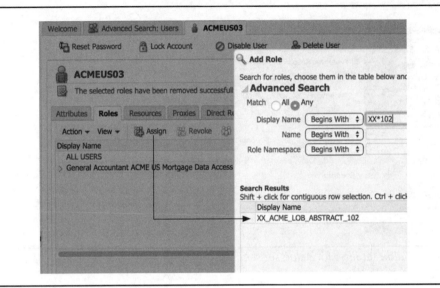

FIGURE 7-27. *Assign the data role for Line of Business 102 to the user.*

Finally, you can navigate back to OIM and create user ACMEUS03 and assign roles to this user as shown in Figure 7-27. By doing so, for this user, the application will filter on the Line of Business 102 value.

Summary

In this chapter we have explained the architecture of security in Oracle Fusion Applications. We saw how the application layer integrates with the Oracle Identity Manager. The guided examples will help you implement the security for Oracle Fusion General Ledger. These examples have been written on Release 11.1.8 of Oracle Fusion Applications. Oracle Fusion Release 10 introduces a simplified reference model for Fusion Security, as detailed in Appendix A. Readers working on Fusion Release 10 or higher should refer to the appendix for the new features introduced in Fusion Applications security.

CHAPTER
8

Journals and Budgets

I n this chapter we will understand how to record balances in ledgers using various methods. We will provide details of how users can configure journal approval for a ledger so that business can validate the correctness of the journal entries before posting. We will also understand how budget data can be captured in ledgers, which can be used for variance reporting.

Journals

Journals are accounting entries recorded in the accounting system, usually in a double-entry bookkeeping method by debiting one or more accounts and crediting another one or more accounts with the same total amount. In Fusion General Ledger, the journals are posted against a specific ledger, commonly referred to as Journal Entry. Journal Entry usually contains the date of the transaction, the Debit and Credit amounts, details of the account (Chart of Account segments) to which the balance is booked, and a description or explanation of the transaction. Journal entries can be reversed after posting if required.

Types of Journals

In Fusion General Ledger, we can enter two types of journals:

- **Actual journals** These journal entries can be entered in Primary Ledger, Secondary Ledger, or both as required to update the balances of the ledger. It should have both the Debit side and the Credit side of entries and should be always balanced as per the Balancing Segment Option (Primary, Secondary, Third) setup at the Chart of Accounts instance level.

- **Statistical journals** These journals are a one-sided entry (either Debit or Credit) used to capture certain non-currency-based transaction information called STAT Currency against natural accounts. These natural accounts are internally associated with Statistical Unit of Measure, which provides the type of information captured in the Statistical Journal. These kinds of journals are predominantly used for reporting and Cost/Overhead allocation purposes. For example, we could capture a headcount of each department as a statistical journal entry so that overhead rental costs for Office Building can be reallocated to all departments based on the number of employees working in each department.

Overview of Journal Capture Methods

Oracle Fusion allows four different methods to capture journal details. Figure 8-1 shows the different methods to capture journals and process flow to update balances in Essbase Cube. Each of these methods is explained in detail in the following sections.

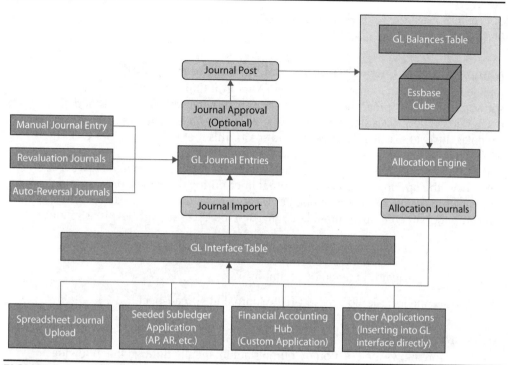

FIGURE 8-1. *Capture Journals: high-level overview*

Manual Journal Entry Through the Journal Entry Screen

In this method, Journal entries are entered directly in General Ledger through the standard Journal Entry screen. This method of entry is normally used in cases of error corrections, reclassifying account balances based on certain legal or operational accounting requirements, adjustment entries, and so on. Because data entry is manual and time-consuming, this method is prone to human error. As a result, most companies would like to have better control over the quality of manual journal entries entered into the system and prefer to enable Journal Approval for these kind of journals.

Navigation to the Journal Entry screen is as follows:

1. Log in to Oracle Fusion Applications.

2. Go to Navigator | General Accounting.

3. Navigate to Task | Journals | Create Journal.

NOTE
The Data Access set dictates which ledger user has access to enter the journals.

Manual Journal Entry Through Excel Spreadsheet Upload

Oracle Fusion allows journal entry through Microsoft Office Excel spreadsheet software. The Excel spreadsheet method not only provides an easy means of data entry, but also leverages standard spreadsheet functionalities, such as macros, formulas, links to existing documents, and so on. This method is useful for entering ad hoc journals as well as recurring journals. Journals are entered in the spreadsheet and loaded into Oracle Fusion using the GL Interface table as shown in Figure 8-1. Users have the option to validate the journal lines during the Import process and can initiate a Post process, which updates balances as well.

Navigation to enter the Journal Entry through the Excel spreadsheet is as follows:

1. Log in to Oracle Fusion Applications.

2. Go to Navigator | General Accounting.

3. Navigate to Task | Journals | Create Journal In Spreadsheet.

Automatic Journals

Oracle Fusion allows the creation of journals automatically through the following methods:

- **Allocation journals** Allocation journals are generated by the Allocation Engine using Allocation Rules and Rulesets in Oracle Fusion Calculation Manager. We will discuss in detail how this type of journal is created in Chapter 11.

- **Reversal journals generated through Define Journal reversal criteria sets** Reversal journals are used for automatic reversal of journal entries that match the criteria defined. The AutoReversal program triggers creation of these journals, and it can be run manually or scheduled.

- **Revaluation journals** Revaluation journals are generated as part of the revaluation process to account for unrealized gains and losses on currency exchange fluctuations. The revaluation program triggers creation of these journals, and it can be run manually or scheduled. The revaluation process is discussed in detail as part of Chapter 12.

■ **Use the Balances Transfer process for generic cross-ledger balance transfers** These journals are generated when balances are transferred from source ledger to target ledger using Chart of Accounts mapping information between the ledgers. These journals are used for consolidation or group reporting requirements needs. We will discuss this in detail in Chapter 10.

Importing Journals

This type of journal contributes to the bulk of the journals created in the General Ledger and can be imported in the following ways:

■ **Seeded Subledger Applications (part of Oracle Fusion Applications)** Oracle Fusion Applications comes with seeded Subledger Applications like Accounts Payables, Accounts Receivables, Fixed Assets, Procurement, Project Billing, Project Costing, and so on where business-related transactions are processed, like Supplier Invoicing, Payments, Customer Invoicing, Receipting, Asset Capitalization, Depreciation, Project Billing, Project Revenue Recognition, Project Expenditure, and so on. All these business-related transactions are accounted for in the respective Subledger Applications, and then the Create Accounting program is run, which will generate the necessary subledger journal entries. These subledger journal entries are imported through the GL Interface table and later posted either automatically or manually.

■ **Financial Accounting Hub (FAH)** Oracle FAH supports the creation of custom applications to integrate accounting data from a third-party system. We will explain the FAH concepts and creation of custom applications in detail in the next chapter.

■ **Inserting journals directly into the GL Journal Interface table** Oracle provides the option to insert journal entries directly into the GL Journal Interface table. This method is commonly used in implementations for conversion of a large volume of GL balances programmatically as a one-time activity to reduce manual intervention. More information about file based journal data import can be found in Oracle Fusion Application Enterprise Repository accessible at the URL https://fusionappsoer.oracle.com/.

Journal Entry Structure

In this section, we will understand the key components of Journal Entry. Journal Entry consists of Batch, Journal, and Lines as shown in Figure 8-2.

Batch

A Journal Batch is a logical grouping of journals identified using a unique batch name. It can contain journals from multiple ledgers as long as all the ledgers within the batch share the same Accounting Calendar and Chart of Accounts.

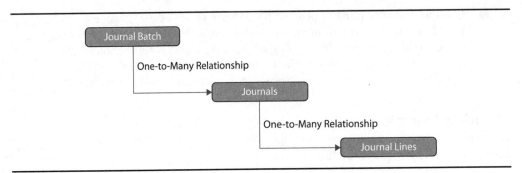

FIGURE 8-2. *Journal Entry structure*

Some of the key fields in Journal Batch are

- **Journal Batch** The user can provide the Journal Batch name to uniquely identify the record later. If no value is provided in the field, the system will automatically generate a batch name.

- **Description** Optional field to enter a description of the Journal Batch.

- **Accounting Period** The GL period in which the journals will be posted.

- **Journal Source** Indicates the source of the journal creation and automatically defaults based on the journal source. For example, "Manual" refers to journals entered through the Manual Journal Entry method, and "Allocations" source refers to journals created through the Allocation process, and so on.

- **Approval Status** Indicates various statuses within the journal approval process. Some of the valid status are Not Required, Approved, Rejected, In Progress, and so on.

- **Attachment** The user can attach supporting documents to the Journal Batch.

Journals
A Journal is created for a Ledger with currency details. Some of the key fields in a Journal entry are

- **Journal** The user can provide the Journal name to uniquely identify the record later. If no value is provided in the field, the system will automatically generate a Batch name.

- **Description** Optional field to enter a description of the Journal.

- **Ledger** Specify the ledger of the Journal.

■ **Accounting Date**   The accounting date indicates the GL Period for which the journal will be posted, and accounting balances will be affected for that period after the posting process is successful.

■ **Currency**   Specify the currency of the Journal.

■ **Conversion Rate Date, Rate Type, and Conversion Rate**   If the journal entry is in a foreign currency, specify the currency conversion details in these fields. This information will allow the foreign currency amount to be converted into either Functional Currency or Ledger Currency.

■ **Journal Category**   "Category" indicates the type of journal being posted; for example, "Allocations" in the case of allocation journals and "Payments" in the case of supplier payments, and so on.

■ **Control Total**   Optional field to capture a control total for data entry validation.

Lines

A journal may contain a number of lines. Each line contains a GL Account string or code combination along with the amount details entered in the Credit or Debit column. Figure 8-3 shows an example screenshot of a Journal Entry with all key components.

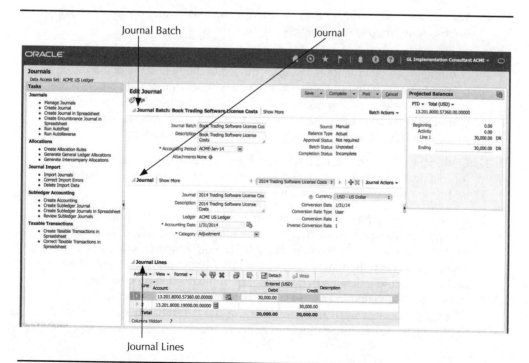

FIGURE 8-3.   *Sample Edit Journal screen with key components*

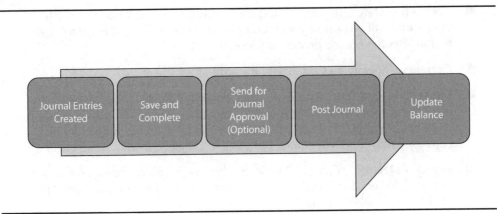

FIGURE 8-4. *The journal processing cycle*

Journal Processing Cycle

Let us try to understand what happens during a typical journal processing cycle while entering manual journal entries in the Create Journal screen. The steps in this process are shown in Figure 8-4.

1. User creates the journal entries by entering mandatory and optional fields at the Batch, Journal, and Line levels.

2. User has the option to save the journal for later rework or make it "Complete" so that the journal can be moved to the next stage of the process. During either of these actions, you will be prompted to enter all the mandatory fields, and the system will also check whether the Account Code combinations used at the journal-line level violate any cross-validation rules, which prevents invalid code combinations in the system.

3. Optionally the journal can be sent for approval based on the setup. If the journal doesn't require approval, the Approval status on the Journal batch will be automatically set to "Not Required."

4. Once the journal has been approved, it will be automatically posted. Posting can happen only in "Open" accounting periods. Journals cannot be posted in a "Closed" or "Future Enterable" period; however, you can enter journals and keep them in "Complete" status without initiating the posting process in future enterable periods. As part of the posting process, ledger balances are updated in Essbase Cube. Fusion calculates Period To Date (PTD), Quarter To Date (QTD), and Year To Date (YTD) balances based on the balances stored in each Chart of Account segment code combination.

Create Journals for ACME Bank

Now that we have looked at the concepts around journals, let us go through the step-by-step process of booking the Actual and Statistical journals in the system using the Journal Entry screen.

Business Requirements

The ACME Global Markets USA line of business has five departments that are also separate cost centers:

■ Central Trading (Cost Center 8000)

■ Fixed Income Trading (Cost Center 8100)

■ Foreign Exchange Trading (Cost Center 8200)

■ Commodities Trading (Cost Center 8300)

■ Equity Trading (Cost Center 8400)

All trading departments use the same software platform for their trading activities, and management decided to divide the license fee cost based on the number of employees in each department. To meet that requirement, the Finance department created the following natural accounts: 57360 (Expense Related to Trading Software License), 79000 (Trading Software Licenses), and 19000 (Cash Account).

Account 79000 is defined as a statistical account to hold the department headcount.

Finance department accountants need to book the actual journals in the system to record the costs of the licenses, as shown in Table 8-1.

Line	Account	Entered Debit	Credit	Description
1	13.201.8000.57360.00.00000	300,000.00		License costs booked to Central Trading
2	13.201.8000.19000.00.00000		300,000.00	Cash paid via bank

TABLE 8-1. *Record License Costs to Central Trading*

In this case, the license cost will be booked initially to the Central Trading Department, which will act as a central pool for all the costs incurred by the trading floor. Later, we will use the Allocation feature in Chapter 11 to re-allocate costs to respective departments.

NOTE
Normally these kinds of transactions will be recorded in the Fusion Accounts Payable Subledger as Supplier Invoices and payment will be made from the company bank account. For purposes of simplicity, we have assumed that the Finance department will book the manual journal in the system.

Finance department accountants need to book the license used in each department as a statistical journal for re-allocation of costs, as shown in Table 8-2. This chapter will only emphasis on how to enter both actual and statistical journal entries in General Ledger. Readers will understand how to allocate costs using Calculation manager using this same example in Chapter 11.

Line	Account	Entered Debit	Credit	Description
1	13.201.8100.79000.00.00000	10		Licenses used in Fixed Income Trading Department
2	13.201.8200.79000.00.00000	20		Licenses used in Foreign Exchange Trading Department
3	13.201.8300.79000.00.00000	30		Licenses used in Commodities Trading Department
4	13.201.8400.79000.00.00000	40		Licenses used in Equity Trading Department

Note: The Central Trading Department (8000) doesn't have any licenses issued for its department as it merely acts as a cost collection center in this case. Also, readers should have noted that statistical journals have only debit entries and no credit entries in this case to record license usage, as these journals are one-sided entries.

TABLE 8-2. *Record License Usage for Each Department*

Create Actual Journals Through the Manual Journal Entry Form

In this section, we will look at how to record license costs to the Central Trading department as shown in Table 8-1.

Create Journal Through the Journal Entry Form

Follow these steps to post actual journals in the system:

1. Go to Navigator | General Accounting.

2. Navigate to Task | Journals | Create Journal.

3. Enter Journal Batch information:

   - **Journal Batch:** Book Trading Software License Costs

   - **Account Period:** Jan-14 (as per current open period)

4. Enter journal information:

   - **Journal:** 2014 Trading Software License Costs

   - **Ledger:** ACME US Ledger

   - **Currency:** USD – US Dollar

   - **Account date:** 01/31/2014 (default)

   - **Category:** Adjustment

NOTE
If you are entering information into a journal denominated in a foreign currency other than ledger currency, then you need to enter the exchange rate for the currency conversion. Most companies do have a corporate exchange rate loaded for each of the foreign currencies used in the Fusion system. Usually these rates are loaded from the external feed as a "Corporate" conversion rate type.

5. Enter Journal Line information as shown in Table 8-1, Record License Costs to Central Trading. Now the Create Journal page will be as shown in Figure 8-5.

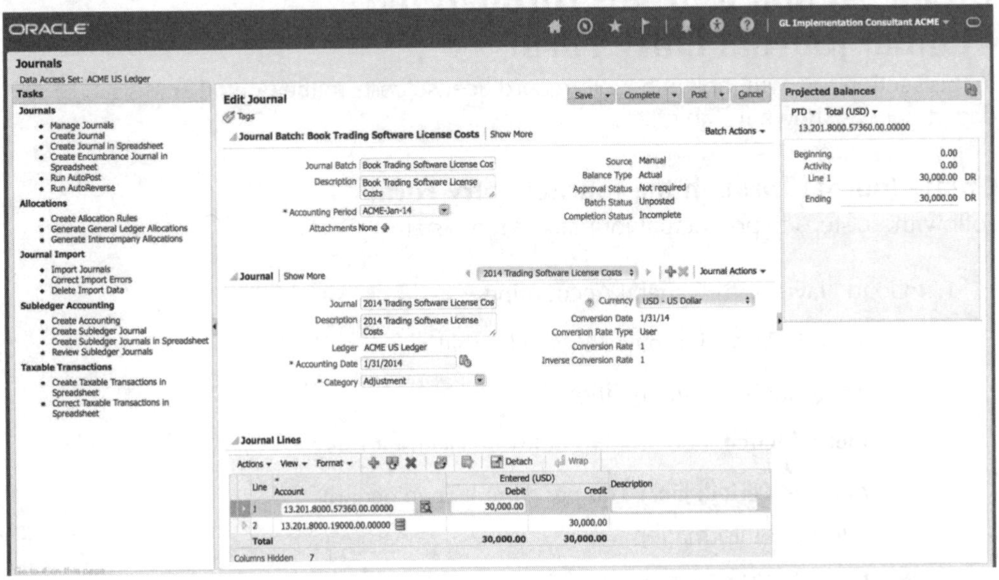

FIGURE 8-5. *Create Journal page after entering trading costs*

NOTE
In Figure 8-5, readers would have noticed a Projected Balances pane in the Create Journal page. This feature allows the user to view the impact of a general ledger adjustment on the current balance of an account before completing the transaction.

6. Click the Save button and then the Complete button to validate the information entered.

7. Click the Post button, and you will receive a confirmation message that the posting program has been submitted as shown in Figure 8-6.

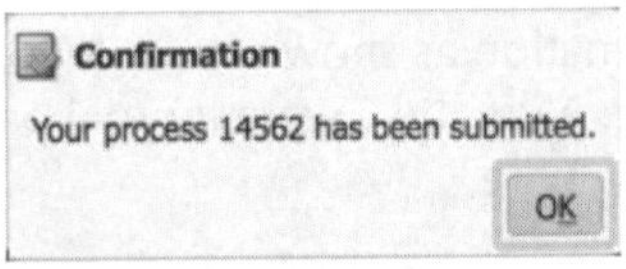

FIGURE 8-6. *Confirmation message for posting*

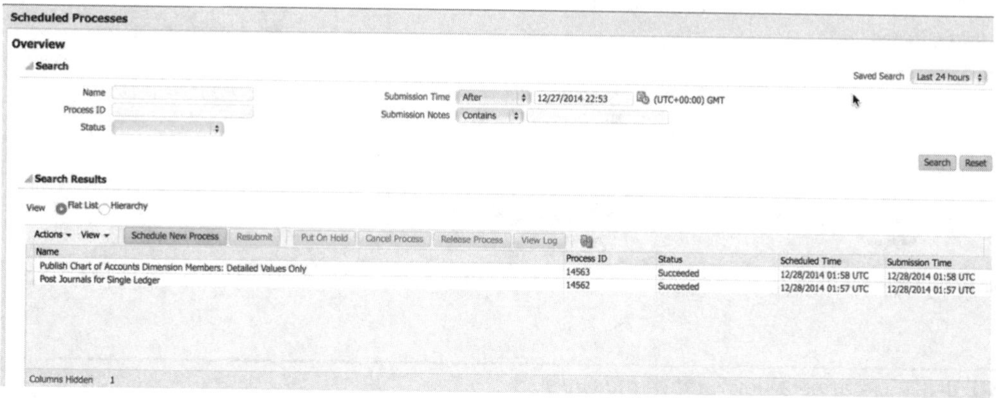

FIGURE 8-7. *Posting process for the journal*

8. From the Scheduled Processes form, we can review the status of Post Journals for Single Ledger program submitted as shown in Figure 8-7. Additionally, the journal posting program can invoke a child process called Publish Chart Of Accounts Dimension Members: Detailed Values Only when new or changed segment values do not exist in the GL balances cube during posting.

Create Statistical Journals

In this section, we will look at how to record license usage for each department as shown in Table 8-2. Note that Fusion General Ledger allows maintaining statistical as well as monetary balances in an account.

Manage Statistical Units of Measure

Before entering a statistical journal for an account, we should first create a statistical unit of measure (UOM) and associate the UOM to the account. The following steps provide details of how to accomplish this task:

1. Go to Navigator | Setup And Maintenance.

2. Navigate to Search Tasks. Search for the Manage Units Of Measure task.

3. Create a new UOM for License as shown in Figure 8-8 and click Save.

4. Navigate to Search Tasks. Search for the Manage Statistical Units Of Measure task.

5. Associate the new UOM license to Account 79000 as shown in Figure 8-9 and click Save. Make sure to select the Chart of Accounts as ACME Global COA Instance before entering the account and unit of measure.

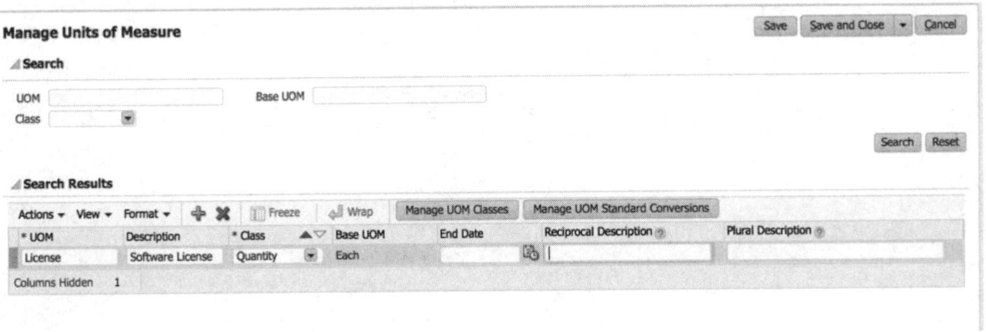

FIGURE 8-8. *Creating a new unit of measure*

Create a Statistical Journal

Take the following steps to post statistical journals in the system:

1. Go to Navigator | General Accounting.

2. Navigate to Task | Journals | Create Journal.

3. Enter journal batch information:

   ■ **Journal Batch:** Book Trading Software License Usage for Jan-2014

   ■ **Account Period:** Jan-14

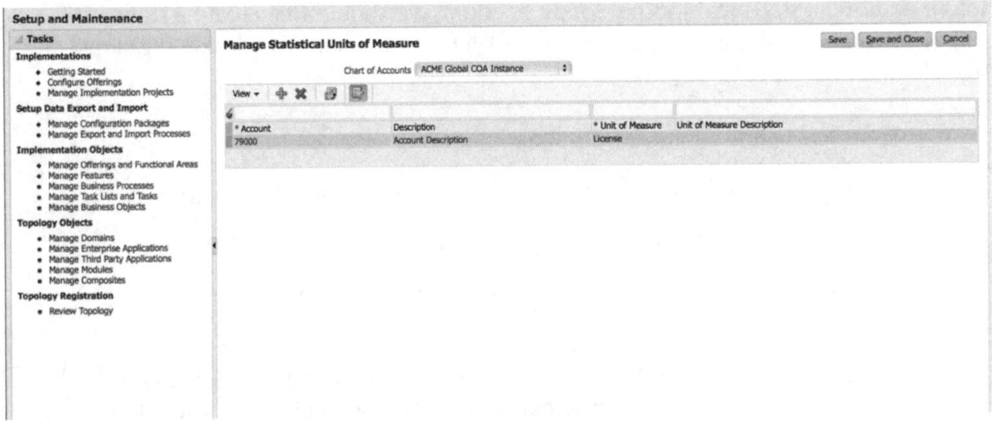

FIGURE 8-9. *Associating a unit of measure with an account*

4. Enter journal information:

- **Journal:** Number of Licenses used in Jan-14
- **Ledger:** ACME US Ledger
- **Currency:** STAT – Statistical
- **Account date:** 01/31/2014 (default)
- **Category:** Adjustment

NOTE
Posting statistical journals requires the currency to be always selected to STAT- Statistical with the exception of mixed journals, which allows posting in a single journal both statistical and monetary balances.

5. Enter journal line information as shown in Table 8-2. Now the Create Journal page will appear as shown in Figure 8-10.

6. Click the Save button and then the Complete button to validate the information entered.

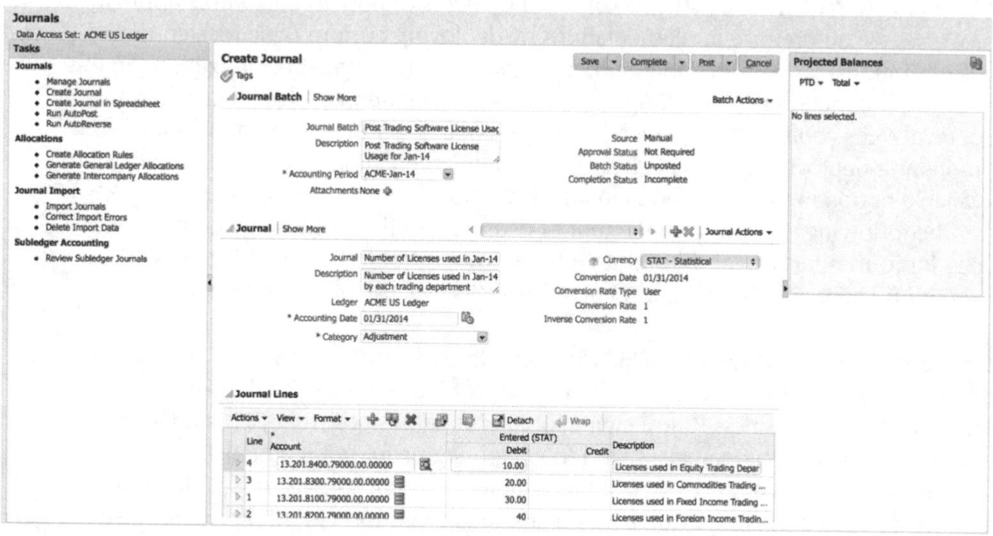

FIGURE 8-10. *Statistical journal created for booking license usage for different departments*

7. Click the Post button, and you will receive a confirmation message that the journal posting program has been submitted. From the Scheduled Processes form, we can review the Succeeded status of the Post Journals for Single Ledger program.

Journal Approvals

The journal approval feature allows organizations to review the journal before it gets posted to the ledger. This feature enables organizations to have better control over what journal entries can be posted and reject any journals that don't satisfy accounting requirements.

Technical Enablers

Although the technical architecture that underpins Fusion Applications is beyond the scope of this book, it is worth mentioning that Fusion Applications leverage technology components of Oracle SOA Suite and Oracle BPM Suite for approvals. In the current releases, we note the prevalent use of the Oracle BPEL (Business Process Execution Language) component for approvals, which is also the case in the General Ledger application.

The options on how to configure approvals in Fusion Applications General Ledger depend on the type of implementation and application deployment: cloud or on-premise. Our previous title, *Oracle Fusion Applications Development and Extensibility Handbook* (Oracle Press, 2014), explains the details of how to customize approval processes for on-premise implementations by deploying custom code (design-time customizations), as well as configuring approval rules (run-time customization). In this book we'll concentrate on setting up approvals for General Ledger journals via approval rules configuration, which is the approach that works for both the cloud and on-premise deployments and also carries less implementation risk, and currently is an available option in Oracle Fusion Financials Cloud.

The following sections provide a brief overview of the technology components used for journal approval, like Oracle SOA Suite, Oracle Business Process Execution Language (BPEL), and Oracle Business Process Management (BPM).

Oracle SOA Suite and Oracle BPEL   The Oracle SOA Suite consists of a number of components and service engines, including BPEL engine for BPEL process implementations, Business Rules engine for executing business rules, Human Workflow engine for managing human tasks, and Mediator engine for service mediation.

Put in very simple terms, we can assemble the components of Oracle SOA such as BPEL and Business Rules into a single application called SOA composite. The SOA composite that executes the GL Journal Approval process is called *FinGlJrnlEntriesApprovalComposite*.

For on-premise implementations, this composite can be exported and modified as explained in *Oracle Fusion Applications Development and Extensibility Handbook*. However, the level of allowed customizations varies between the releases, and implementation consultants need to be aware of the risks associated with introducing potentially intrusive design-time customizations.

In the Oracle Fusion Financials Cloud, this type of customization is not allowed at the current time, and approvals customization is performed via configuration. Approval Management Extensions of the Oracle SOA suite (also known as AMX) enables to define complex task routing rules for business documents like Expense Reports, Invoices and Journals. AMX integrates with Oracle Fusion Human Capital Management to derive the supervisory and position hierarchy based approvers.

Oracle Business Process Management (Oracle BPM)   In current releases of Fusion Financials, the role of Oracle BPM technology components primarily revolves around the BPM Worklist application, which is a web-based application that allows users to access tasks assigned to them and perform actions based on their roles in the approval process. Business process owners and system integrators use BPM Worklist to configure and manage approval rules, and within the BPM component, List Builders are used to generate approvers.

The Fusion Middleware Modeling and Implementation Guide for Oracle BPM describes product documentation following approval list builders typically found in Fusion Applications:

- **Approval Groups**   Includes predefined approver groups in the approver list. Approval groups can be static or dynamic.

- **Job Level**   Ascends the supervisory hierarchy, starting at a given approver and continuing until an approver with a sufficient job level is found.

- **Position**   Ascends the position hierarchy, starting at a given approver's position and continuing until a position with a sufficient job level is found.

- **Supervisory**   Ascends the primary supervisory hierarchy, starting at the requester or at a given approver, and generates a chain that has a fixed number of approvers in it.

- **Names and Expressions**   Enables you to construct a list using static names or names coming from XPath expressions.

- **Management Chain**   Enables you to construct a list based on management relationships in the corresponding user directory.

- **Rule-based**   Enables you to model rules that return different list-builder types based on different conditions. For example, if you model a supervisory list builder with rules, the rule can return only the supervisory list builder. If you model a rule-based list builder, the rule can return different list-builder types.

NOTE
Supervisory- and position-level hierarchies are defined through Human Capital Management (HCM) configuration.

Oracle BPM tasks allow business process owners to configure approval rules and control how the approval workflow works. Each task under the task configuration represents an underlying SOA composite, which needs to be tailored to satisfy the business process requirement. For GL Journal Approvals, we need to edit FinGlJournalApproval.

NOTE
In addition to the example provided in this chapter, Oracle Support article: Need Task Name To Customize Journal Approval Rule (Doc ID 1988087.1) *explains how to access the BPM Worklist to edit FinGlJournalApproval in Release 11.1.8.0.0. As mentioned in the note, this approach works for both the Oracle Cloud and on-premise implementations.*

ACME Bank Journal Approval

This section will provide configuration steps for ACME Bank journal approval.

ACME Bank Approval Requirements   The CFO would like to have all manual journal entries posted for the ACME US Ledger reviewed and approved by the finance controller. However, the CFO would like to have other journal sources, from subledgers like Accounts Payables, Accounts Receivables including Fusion Accounting hub to be posted without any workflow intervention.

NOTE
In a real-world scenario, the journal approval requirements would be much more complex, involving several levels or tiers of approval based on the amount or department to which the journal creator belongs and sometimes based on Human Capital Management (HCM) setup of employee hierarchies and employee job or position or both. We have kept this exercise simple, as most often, new Fusion Application installations will not have any HCM configuration to support any kind of complex approvals and second, it is easier for readers to understand the concept with a simple static approval group.

ACME Bank Journal Approval Setup   Perform the following instructions to enable the journal approval for the ACME US ledger.

Step 1: Enable Journal Approval for the Ledger

To enable journal approval for the ACME US Ledger, follow these steps:

1. Go to Navigator | Setup And Maintenance. Go to Implementation Project.

2. Navigate to Task | Define Ledgers | Define Accounting Configurations | Specify Ledger Options.

3. Make sure that the scope of the task is set to ACME US Ledger.

4. Click Go To Task.

5. Specify Ledger. The Options page will open.

6. Check the Enable Journal Approval check box for the ledger.

Step 2: Enable Journal Approval for Journal Source

To enable approval for the manual journal source, follow these steps:

1. Go to Navigator | Setup And Maintenance. Go to Implementation Project.

2. Navigate to Search: Task.

3. Search for and open the Manage Journal Sources task.

4. Check the Require Journal Approval check box for Manual Source.

Step 3: Disable Default Supervisor Journal Approval Rule Set

The user access the BPM Worklist running on Financials WebLogic Domain to disable the default rule set. Oracle BPM provides the BPM Worklist application, which allows system administrators, implementation consultants, business analysts, and others to administer, configure, and customize approval and non-approval business rules. A user needs to be assigned an appropriate role such as Financial Application Administrator (FUN_FINANCIAL_APPLICATION_ADMINISTRATOR) to be able to access the BPM Worklist application. The task customization is performed from the Task Configuration tab in the BPM Worklist application.

There are various ways to access the BPM Worklist application:

■ The user can access the BPM Worklist directly by logging on to http(s)://:\<FinancialsDomain_Host |/:\<FinancialsDomain_Port |/integration /worklistapp and navigating to it by clicking the Administration link and the Task Configuration tab.

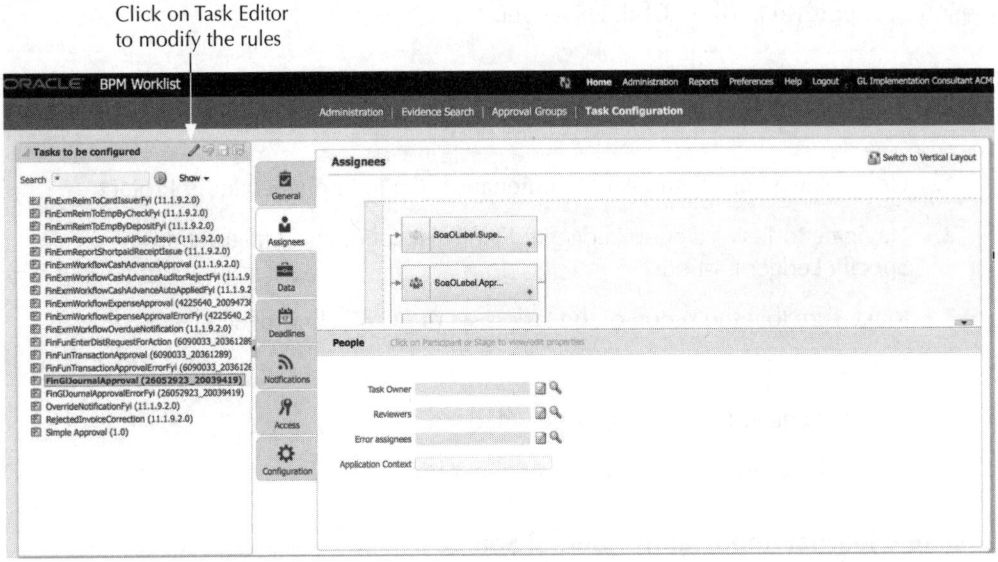

Click on Task Editor
to modify the rules

FIGURE 8-11. *Customizing a task in the BPM Worklist application*

■ Alternatively, in FSM, search for and open the Manage Task Configurations For Financials task. In the Task Configuration tab, select the FinGlJournalApproval task and click the Assignees subtab as shown in Figure 8-11.

To make changes to tasks, click the Edit Task icon to enter the editing mode as shown in Figure 8-11.

Supervisory_JournalApprovalRuleSet is configured out of the box, and if your Fusion Applications instance HR Supervisory Hierarchy is not configured, an attempt to run an approval task will result in an error. Therefore, we are going to disable it by selecting the Ignore Participant check box under the Advanced tab of SupervisoryJournalApprover assignees as shown in Figure 8-12.

The detailed navigation steps are as follows:

1. Under Task Configuration, click the FinGlJournalApproval task. Click Edit Task Icon and enter Edit mode.

2. Click Assignees.

3. Click SoaOLabel.SupervisoryJournalApprover.

4. Click the Advanced tab under the SoaOLabel.SupervisoryJournalApprover section.

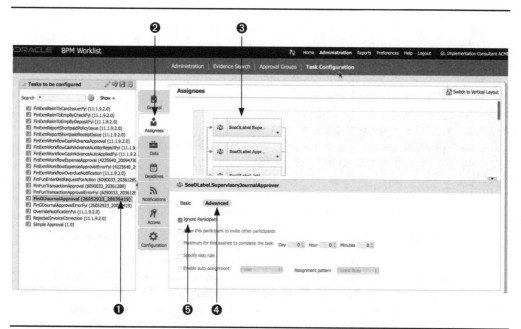

FIGURE 8-12. *Disabling the Supervisory Journal Approval rule set*

5. Check the Ignore Participant check box.

6. Make sure to click Save Changes.

7. Click Commit Task icon.

8. Optionally, enter comments and click OK.

9. An information window will open with the following confirmation:

    TaskEditor Data Saved Successfully

    TaskEditor Data Commited Successfully

NOTE
In some cases we have noticed that this change doesn't disable the Supervisory Journal Approval rule set. Another method to disable this rule set is create a dummy business rule called IgnoreJournalApprovalParticipantRule with the following condition under Supervisory_ JournalApprovalRuleSet:

If 1 is 1
Then
Call IgnoreParticipant
Edit Arguments
Name: Rulename Type: String Value: "IgnoreJournalApprovalParticipantRule"
Name: Lists Type: Lists Value: "Lists"

Step 4: Create a Static Approval Group

Using the Approval Groups tab in the BPM Worklist application, a user can create a static approval group as shown in Figure 8-13.

The detailed steps to create a static approval group are as follows:

1. Go to BPM Worklist | Approval Groups tab.

2. Click the Create Static Approval group called XxGlStatic_ApprovalGroup.

3. Click the plus (+) icon to add approval group members. In this example, we have used xx_gl_approver application user, which was specifically created for this demo. You can refer to Appendix A, which provides steps to create an application user in the system. This user xx_gl_approver will act as a finance controller to approve the manual journals created in the ACME US Ledger.

4. Click the Save button.

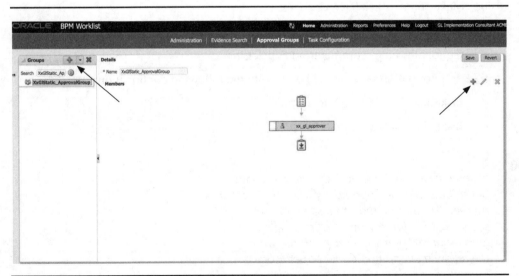

FIGURE 8-13. *Creating a static approval group*

Our static approval group that we called XxGlStatic_ApprovalGroup is very simple and it consists of only one member user called xx_gl_approver. This is hardly a requirement you will find in real-life implementations, but we are merely demonstrating the principles here.

Step 5: Assigning the Static Approval Group to the Approval Group List Rule Set

The detailed steps to assign a newly created approval group to the Approval Group rule set are as follows:

1. Under Task Configuration, click the FinGlJournalApproval task.

2. Click Edit Task Icon and enter Edit mode.

3. Click Assignees.

4. Navigate to SoaOLabel.ApprovalGroupJournalApprover and click Go To Rule.

5. Under Rule Sets, select ApprovalGroup_JournalApprovalRuleSet. Delete the existing IgnoreJournalApprovalParticipantRule as shown in Figure 8-14.

6. Add a new business rule called Require Approval From Finance Controller as shown in Figure 8-15.

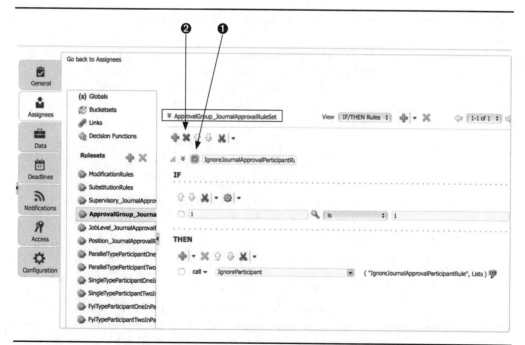

FIGURE 8-14. *Delete the existing IgnoreJournalApprovalParticipantRule rule.*

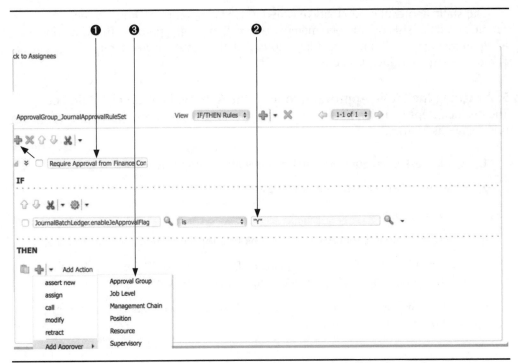

FIGURE 8-15. *Adding a new business rule for finance controller approval.*

Notice that we have also set a business rule test inside the Require Approval from Finance Controller rule to evaluate at run time if JournalBatchLedger .enableJeApprovalFlag is set to a value of "Y" (you need to surround the letter Y with double quotes as shown in Figure 8-15). In the Add Action drop-down list, select Approval Group, also as shown in Figure 8-15.

7. Under the THEN section, configure the rule as shown in Figure 8-16. Select the XxGlStatic_ApprovalGroup approval group, created as per the previous step. Click the Save icon to save the changes while editing.

8. We need to commit the changes by clicking the Commit Task button, which is situated to the right of the Save button, after which the following pop-up message will be displayed:

"The Rules defined for the list builders of this task are saved successfully

The Rules defined for the list builders of this task are committed successfully"

Now we can proceed to test whether the changes we introduced have produced the desired effect; for example, we are expecting the xx_gl_approver user to be assigned an approval task after successfully submitting a journal batch for approval.

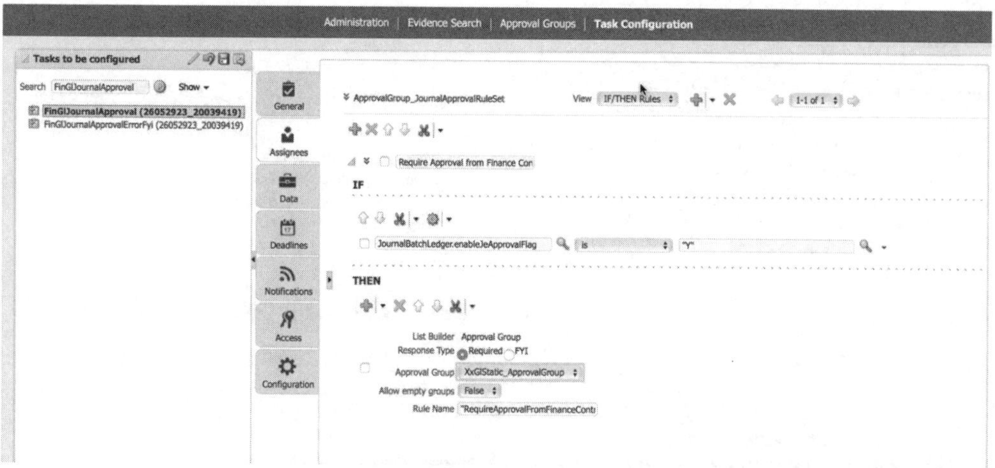

FIGURE 8-16.   *Adding a static approval group to the business rule*

Step 6: Submitting a Journal Batch for Approval and Verifying the Approval Rule Changes

In this step we log in to Fusion Applications as a user who has access to the Create Journal screen from, say, the General Accounting Dashboard. In our case, that is the XXFA_FIN_GL_IMPLEMENTATION_CONSULTANT user, and we enter the journal batch as demonstrated in the preceding section, "Create Actual Journals Through the Manual Journal Entry Form."

Before posting the journal batch named Approval Test 001 in Figure 8-17, we first need to complete it by clicking the Complete button and then post the journal by clicking the Post button, which results in the following pop-up message being displayed:

"The journal requires approval before it can be posted, and has been forwarded to the approver."

If we now log in as the xx_gl_approver user, we should see in the home page application a notification informing us about the pending task that needs to be carried out, as illustrated in Figure 8-18. Clicking the Journal Batch Journal Approval Test 01 for the GL Implementation Consultant ACME link in the Worklist region application will open a task page, which will allow us to review the journal batch details before approving or rejecting it (as shown in Figure 8-19). Once approved, the journal will be posted automatically, and the creator of the journal (in this case XXFA_FIN_GL_IMPLEMENTATION_CONSULTANT) will receive a notification in the worklist showing that the journal has been approved successfully.

In real-life implementations, we would probably be asked to build custom rules for every combination of ledger entered amount, approval level, and other attributes that can be derived from journal data, like how to test for the maximum journal line amount by adding it to the existing rule set as illustrated in Figure 8-20.

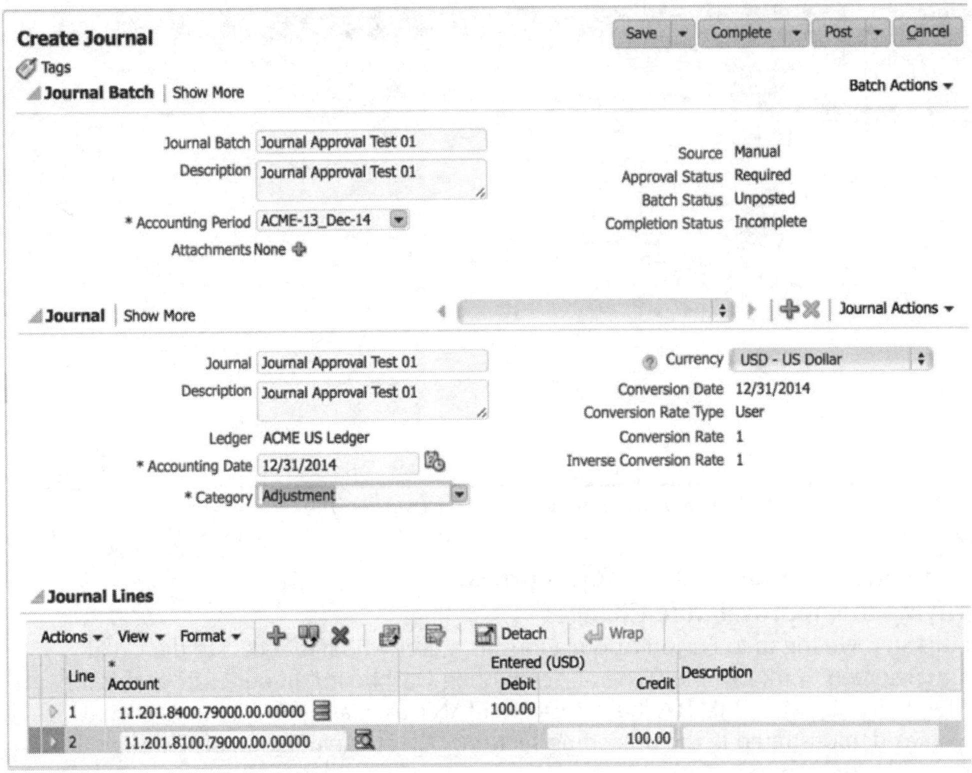

FIGURE 8-17. *Creating a sample journal for approval*

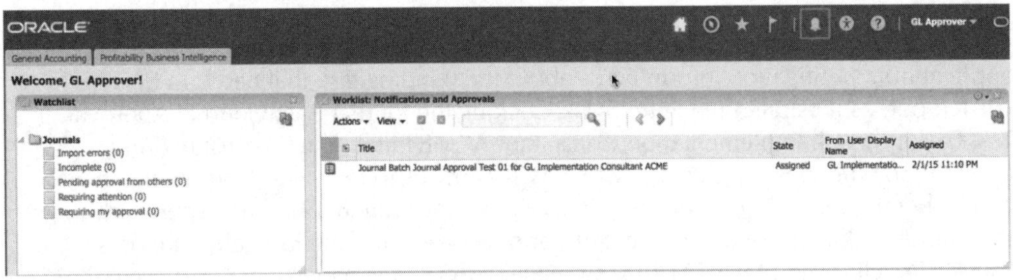

FIGURE 8-18. *The approver as defined in the custom approval group is assigned an approval task.*

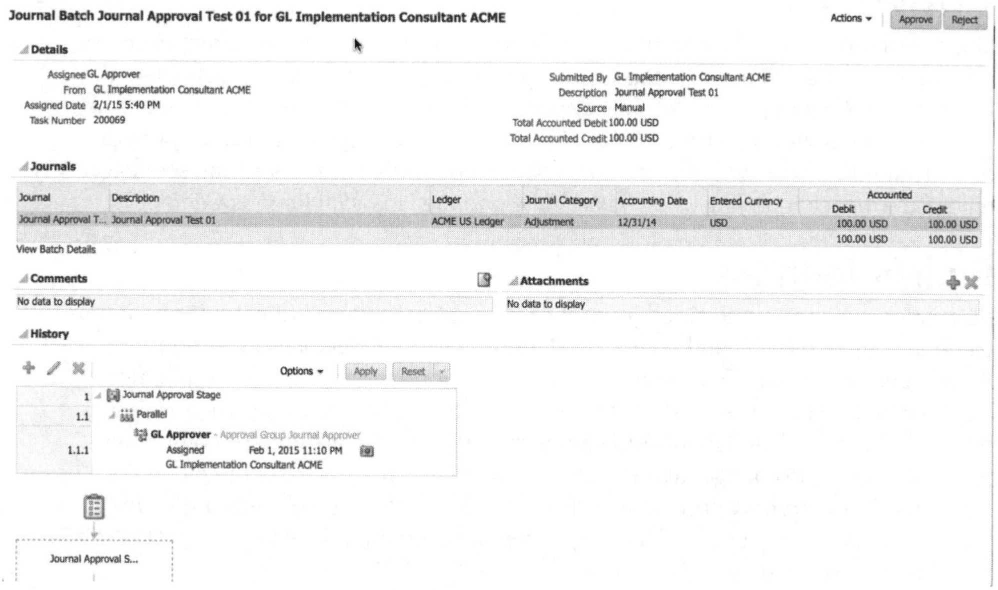

FIGURE 8-19. *Journal Batch approval task in the BPM Worklist application*

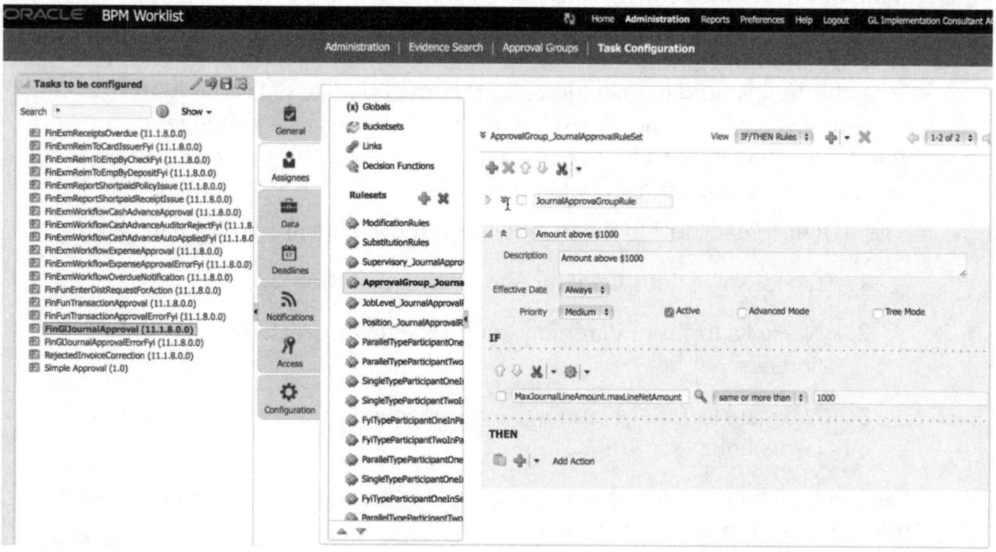

FIGURE 8-20. *Adding rule tests and conditions*

Budgets

Finance planning is a key component for companies to manage and drive business performance. Oracle Fusion supports finance planning using the Budgets functionality. Even though Oracle Fusion doesn't support workflow capabilities for budgeting like the Oracle Hyperion Enterprise Financial Planning Suite product, it does provide basic features to load the budgets into Essbase Cube so that businesses can see real-time performance reporting using Smart View and the Financial Reports Center.

Budget Journals

Budget Journals are a one-sided journal entry used to capture budget information in General Ledger, which can be later used for actual vs. budget variance reporting. Budget figures are usually entered on a monthly or quarterly basis for a specific legal entity, line of business, department, and account combination. The level of detail in which budget data is uploaded varies widely across different companies. Some businesses do budget at a detailed individual, natural account level, while others tend to keep budgeting at a fairly higher level. Budget amounts are stored only in GL Balances Cube and are not stored in relational tables like GL_BALANCES as in the case of Actuals.

Overview of Budget Capture Methods

Oracle Fusion supports many different ways to load budgets efficiently and quickly based on the business requirement as shown in Figure 8-21:

■ **ADF Desktop Integrator Tool** Otherwise known as the ADFdi spreadsheet tool, this tool is used to enter, load, and correct budget data. The ADFdi spreadsheet tool uses the GL_BUDGET_INTERFACE table to budget data into the GL Balances Cube as shown in Figure 8-21. This tool can also be used to correct budget data in Interface tables.

The ADFdi spreadsheet tool can be accessed using the following navigation:

1. Go to Navigator | General Accounting Dashboard.

2. Navigate to Task | Planning And Budgeting | Create Budgets In Spreadsheet link.

3. Navigate to Task | Planning And Budgeting | Correct Budget Import Errors link.

Later in the chapter we will see how to upload budgets for ACME Bank using the ADF Desktop Integrator tool.

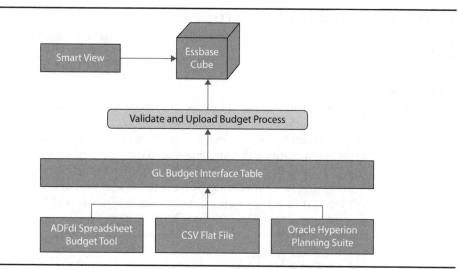

FIGURE 8-21.   *Overview of different budget capture methods*

- **CSV flat file**   Budget data can be imported as a comma-separated values (CSV) file. This method is used when businesses want to import budget data from third-party planning applications. Budget data is exported from external planning applications in a predefined CSV flat-file format. Using the Enterprise Scheduler Service Process "General Ledger Validate and Load Budgets," users can load the budget data in Fusion General Ledger. Customers in Oracle Cloud can use External Data Integration Services to load data into the GL Budget Interface Table from external sources. This integration service provides templates to structure, format, and generate the data file according to the requirements of the target application tables (in this case, for GL_BUDGET_INTERFACE Table). More information about this service can be found in Oracle Fusion Application Enterprise Repository, accessible at the URL https://fusionappsoer.oracle.com/.

- **Smart View**   Smart View is an Excel-based analysis tool and is directly integrated to Fusion General Ledger Balances Essbase Cube in real time. Using Smart View, we can load budget balances directly into Balances Cube.

- **Oracle Hyperion Planning Suite Integration**   Oracle Hyperion Planning Suite (Fusion Edition) is a web-based budgeting and planning application used for Enterprise Performance Management. Oracle Fusion Applications provides integration to write back budget data from Oracle Hyperion Planning Suite through Oracle Financial Data Quality Management ERP Integrator Adapter.

ACME Budget Creation Process

In this section, we will understand how to set up and load budget data as per ACME Bank requirements.

Business Requirements

The ACME Corp USA would like to load budgets and forecasted figures as part of their financial planning process into Fusion General Ledger. Currently the Finance department collates all the budget and forecasts figures from the operations. They use an Excel spreadsheet to consolidate the figures, and it is quite difficult for them to run reporting from the same excel spreadsheet data. The Finance department currently does the budgeting twice a year (at the start of the year and mid-year for a revised budget). Also they do a rolling forecast every quarter. They would like to load all the budget and forecast information into Oracle Fusion General Ledger so that they can do the reporting directly from Smart View or Financial Reports Center.

Create Budget Scenarios

Based on the business requirements described in the preceding paragraph, we could conclude that the Finance department would require the following six types of budgets/scenarios in the system:

- Original Budget - Current Year Budget (loaded during the start of the year)
- Revised Budget – Revised Budget (loaded mid-year)
- Forecast Q1 - Forecast figure for Current Year Quarter 1
- Forecast Q2 - Forecast figure for Current Year Quarter 2
- Forecast Q3 - Forecast figure for Current Year Quarter 3
- Forecast Q4 - Forecast figure for Current Year Quarter 4

To define budget scenarios, follow these steps:

1. Go to Navigator | Setup And Maintenance. Click Implementation Project.

2. Navigate to Task | Define Budget Configuration | Define Budget Scenarios.

3. The Define Budget Scenarios form opens.

4. Select the Accounting Scenario value set and click Manage Values.

5. Enter the value for the value set in the Value box as shown in Figure 8-22 and click Save.

6. Repeat step 6 to enter other types of budget scenarios in the Accounting Scenario value set.

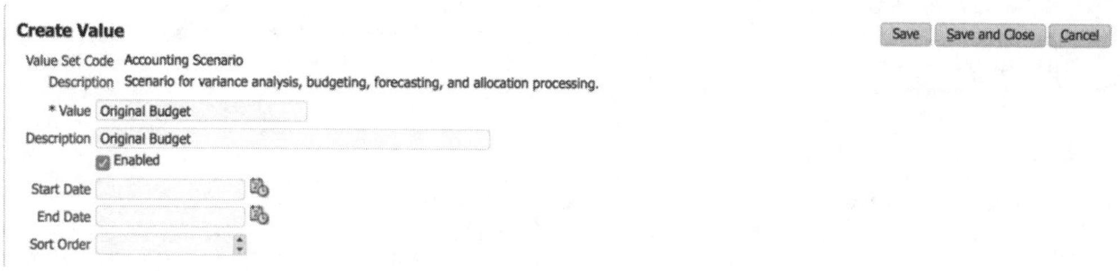

Create Value

Value Set Code Accounting Scenario
   Description Scenario for variance analysis, budgeting, forecasting, and allocation processing.
   * Value Original Budget
Description Original Budget
   ☑ Enabled
Start Date
End Date
Sort Order

Save   Save and Close   Cancel

FIGURE 8-22.   *Create new budget scenario*

Create Budget Data Through a Spreadsheet

To enter budgets through a spreadsheet, follow these steps:

1. Go to Navigator | General Accounting.

2. Navigate to Task | Planning And Budgets In Spreadsheet | Create Budgets In Spreadsheet.

In case the budget load fails during the import process, the user can correct this using the Correct Budget Import Errors link. Navigation for this step is as follows:

1. Go to Navigator | General Accounting.

2. Navigate to Task Planning And Budgets In Spreadsheet | Correct Budget Import Errors.

Budget Data Security

Organizations would like to restrict their budget data access based on roles. For example, the finance controller would need access to all budget versions, whereas the general accounting manager would need access to only the original and revised budgets. Oracle allows us to secure budget data access using the Segment value security of the Accounting Scenario value set.

To enable segment security for a budget, follow these steps:

1. Go to Navigator | Setup And Maintenance. Click Implementation Project.

2. Navigate to Task | Define Budget Configuration | Define Budget Scenarios. The Define Budget Scenarios form opens.

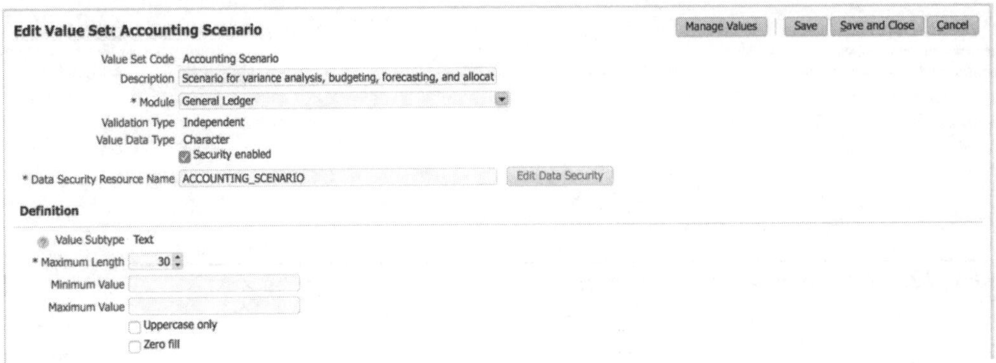

FIGURE 8-23. *Enable data security for the Scenario value set*

3. Select the Accounting Scenario value set and click the Edit icon.

4. Check Security Enabled.

5. Enter the data security resource name, if not populated: ACCOUNTING_ SCENARIO as shown in Figure 8-23.

6. Click Edit Data Security to set up the data policies. To publish the budget data security policies to the cube, run the job Publish Chart of Accounts Dimension Members and Hierarchies.

Please note that we will not go further into details of data policy creation and assignment to roles since we will cover segment security in detail as part of Chapter 7.

Summary

In this chapter we have seen how to create actual and statistical journals in General Ledger. We have also introduced the journal approval concept and provided an example of how to configure the system for approval using a static approval group. We have also understood different methods to load budgets and how to secure budget data. In the next chapter, we will look in detail at how to configure Fusion Accounting Hub to bring in journals from external applications.

CHAPTER
9

Oracle Fusion
Accounting Hub

Oracle Fusion Accounting Hub (FAH) is used for accounting transformation, which is a process to convert events into journal entries. The accounting transformation involves a diverse set of source systems and applications ranging from investment banking, core banking systems, premium and claim management systems for insurance, asset management, retail, healthcare, telecoms, and so on. For a large organization, you will find that each of these source systems may sometimes have its own local accounting engine. This can cause duplication of accounting rules across various different systems. The cost of making changes to accounting rules across many systems is usually very high. Oracle Fusion Accounting Hub allows organizations to define their accounting rules in a single place.

Oracle Fusion Accounting Hub Overview

The typical source systems in an enterprise come from various different vendors ranging from different time periods when those platforms were developed. These legacy systems also have diversified processes of accounting transformation with very little centralized governance. The manual adjustments are usually made in spreadsheets or are isolated in each source system with limited audit capabilities. In many cases, these changes are not visible to the governance and accounting teams, and therefore, when something changes in the source systems, it is hard to know who made the changes or why. The Oracle Fusion Accounting Hub provides a configurable and auditable rule-based accounting engine that can be used to create accounting for these systems. These accounting systems can be generated for multiple reporting bases such as US GAAP, UK GAAP, IFRS, AIFRS, and other reporting standards.

Fusion Accounting Hub provides easy-to-use screens for configuring the accounting rules in one central place within the organization. The accounting generated from Fusion Accounting Hub is natively integrated with Fusion General Ledger for reporting at the Chart of Account level. But sometimes organizations require operational reporting, which requires dimensions that are more granular than Chart of Account segments. To facilitate this, Oracle Fusion Accounting Hub allows you to track balances at the sub-Chart of Accounts level, also known as supporting references. For example, an insurance company might want to know their liabilities at the insurance product level, or an investment bank may wish to know their exposure to counterparty. FAH allows you to define supporting references that are the Chart of Accounts equivalent but at subledger level. This allows tracking the balances at a much finer grain than Chart of Accounts.

Components of Fusion Accounting Hub

In prior releases of Oracle ERP, for example, in Oracle EBS R12 version, the term "Financial Accounting Hub" used the same engine as that of Subledger Accounting R12. When implemented in Financial Services, it is called the Financial Accounting Hub. The results from Financial Accounting Hub would then be posted into another Oracle General Ledger module in R12.

In Fusion Applications, Oracle has dropped the term Financial Accounting Hub and instead it is now called Fusion Accounting Hub, but it is also sometimes referred to as Fusion Financial Accounting Hub. The term Fusion Accounting Hub is more generic in nature, and can be implemented for any type of industry, not just financial services. Fusion Accounting Hub now is the overarching umbrella above and over Oracle Fusion General Ledger. In this chapter every reference to FAH indicates Fusion Accounting Hub, as opposed to R12's Financial Accounting Hub. Figure 9-1 shows the key components of Fusion Accounting Hub. The various components of Fusion Accounting Hub are described in the following sections.

Oracle Fusion Accounting Transformation Engine

The accounting rules engine in FAH provides an accounting transformation engine for the source transactions. It allows you to create journal entries and transfers reference information from diverse systems into Oracle General Ledger. The accounting transformation engine is also referred to as Fusion Subledger Accounting Engine.

Oracle Fusion General Ledger (GL)

Fusion GL provides journal entry import and creation, real-time balances from Essbase Cubes, accounting controls and data security, and period close functionality. Fusion GL also contains intercompany balancing, an allocation manager for the definition of allocation rules using complex formulas, automatic generation of allocation journals, enhanced journal approval, and year-end process management.

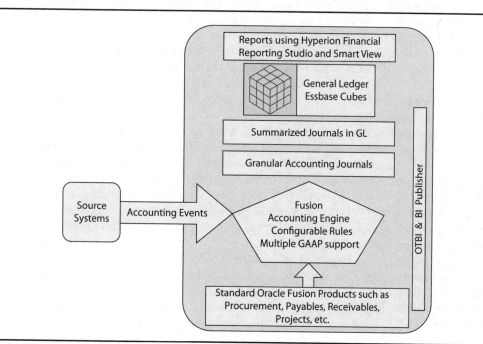

FIGURE 9-1. *Fusion Accounting Hub components*

Oracle Fusion Financial Reporting

Oracle Fusion Accounting Hub leverages the Hyperion Financial Reporting Studio for analytic reporting on the Chart of Accounts. Further, it has BI Publisher technology to generate reports in various formats. In addition to BI Publisher, the Oracle Business Intelligence Enterprise Edition (OBIEE) comes pre-integrated with Fusion Applications, and FAH provides various out-of-the-box ad hoc reports using Oracle Transactional Business Intelligence (OTBI).

Approach for Fusion Accounting Hub Implementation

To implement Fusion Accounting Hub, it is important to understand the underlying transactional data that must be accounted for. The rules defined in FAH generate the journal entries for the transactions from external source systems. In other words, the Oracle Fusion Accounting Hub provides a solution to convert transactional data into accounting journal entries.

After the analysis of the source system transactions, the integration into Fusion Accounting Hub begins by first defining and building the transaction object, which is a database representation of the source transactions. Next, we define journal rules to generate journal entries that consume those transactions. The implementation starts with a thorough analysis of the transactional system that must be integrated with the Oracle Fusion Accounting Hub. Therefore, it is of utmost importance to invest time in identification of the transactions that must be accounted for and the activities in the lifecycle of those transactions.

For example, in a mortgage management system, a bank can issue both fixed interest rate loans and variable rate loans. The lifecycle of each type of loan is different. There are different kinds of activities and events that occur during the lifecycle of these mortgages. For each type of mortgage loan, the implementers can identify the list of possible events and then decide with accountants the subset of events that have an accounting implication.

When working in Fusion implementations, it is very common to hear of the use of event-based terminology in Oracle Fusion Accounting Hub. Any activity in the source system that requires accounting can be classified as an accounting event. Event Class represents the classification of the transaction. For example, a Loan Type of Fixed Rate or Variable Rate is an event class. The Event Type represents the type of activity against the event class. For example, payment of a due amount is an event type. From experience, you will learn that the granularity of Event Class definition can vary from one implementation to another.

Accounting Rules are defined at the combination of Event Class and Event Type levels. For example, accounting for late payments and on-time scheduled payments will have a different accounting behavior in Fusion General Ledger. Typically, the accounting will be different for these so that a financial analyst can see from the GL Balances the late payments or the accrued payments by each period.

Minimal Data Requirement

To create accounting entries, you will always need Currency Code, Amount, and Accounting Date besides the Chart of Accounts. However, you will find that typically an organization will also have requirements to report on additional attributes such as Loan Broker, Loan Rate, and Number of Years for which the mortgage is fixed. These pieces of information are typically nice to have for operational Business Intelligence, but are not required for accounting and therefore can be captured via something known as supporting references.

Therefore, the bare minimum data required for accounting generation are accounting date, transaction currency, transaction amount, accounting amount, or currency conversion rate. Sometimes your accounting requirements can be complex, in which case you need more information than the minimal attributes. In fact, it is very common that you will need to handle additional transactional attributes to derive the GL code combination. To derive the account combination for a journal line, either the source system will send the account codes in the transaction feed, or you will derive the account codes from the transaction attributes. For example, a late payment will be accounted to Account Code 243933, whereas the scheduled payment will be accounted to 244600. When the source system sends account codes in the transaction feed to FAH, this is known as *pass-through accounting*.

As an implementer, it will be your responsibility to ask various questions to the business users, such as

1. What is the additional information they wish to see on the journal line besides the code combination?

2. Where should this additional information be displayed? In the journal line description or a dedicated field or in the reporting layer only?

3. What should be the description of the journal at the header level and at the line level?

4. How would you like to classify the journal entries in various groupings?

For example, in the case of mortgages, it is common that the business users will demand to see the following in the journal line:

■ Bank branch name issuing the mortgage

■ Mortgage number

■ Interest rate

■ Customer number/name

The source system transactions are typically sent to Oracle Fusion Accounting Hub on a daily basis, with the accounting processes running every night. However, in some cases the business users might want to see the information almost in real time in Fusion General Ledger. Both these requirements can be met, but as an implementer, it is your responsibility to ask these questions of the business users.

The granularity of the journal lines in Fusion Accounting Hub can be the same as that in the source system, or it can be at a summarized level. The business needs will most often dictate the granularity requirements. You may find that some banks will want only the bank branch name to be captured in the journal line so that source transactions are summarized before being accounted. This will increase the processing speed in Fusion General Ledger, and storage requirements will be kept to a minimum. Even though disk space is considered to be cheap these days, the high volume of data produced by large organizations can lead to expensive annual storage costs, considering the costs of high-performing enterprise storage. Therefore, size considerations must be considered during the implementation phase.

Typical FAH Implementation Steps

The typical implementation steps are listed in the following sections.

Register Tables and Capture Accounting Event Data for Source Transactions   Register tables and views for multiple data sources. These tables will receive the source system transactions that are meant to be accounted for by applying the accounting rules.

Create Accounting Rules   Configure rules for various reporting bases such as US GAAP, UK GAAP, IFRS, AIFRS, and so on.

Generate Accounting Engine Technical Events   Call the FAH technical APIs to raise technical events. These events reside in a table named XLA_EVENTS. One event will correspond to one journal per reporting basis in Fusion Accounting Hub.

Transfer and Post   Create accounting by running Oracle Fusion account creation processes and transfer and post those accounting entries to Fusion General Ledger. It must be noted that journals are created in two places: first in Fusion Subledger Accounting, and then in Fusion General Ledger. The GL posting then updates the GL Chart of Account cubes in Essbase.

Report and Analyze   Microsoft Excel-based Smart View technology can be used to interrogate the Essbase cubes. Further, users can build ad hoc financial reports using Hyperion Financial Studio, which reads the data from Essbase cubes. Additional reporting is possible using OTBI, and that is explained in Chapter 13.

System Implementation Steps in FAH

Implementing FAH is a mixture of technical and configuration work. Table 9-1 segregates the nature of the work for each key step in the implementation of FAH.

Implementation Step	Nature of Work	Comments
Stage data for accounting	Programmer	A technical specialist is required to source the data and make it available for consumption by FAH.
Raise technical events	Programmer	A technical specialist writes a program to execute the accounting event registration APIs. These are PL/SQL APIs used to generate technical events in the queue for processing.
Configure accounting rules	Analyst	A system analyst or functional consultant will configure these rules. A technical specialist with sound knowledge of accounting principles can also carry out the same exercise.
Process accounting events to create journals	System-scheduled process or end-user initiated or event driven	These enterprise scheduler jobs can be scheduled to run, or the end user can submit them, or they can be initiated via API.

TABLE 9-1.   *Nature of Work for FAH Implementation*

Stage Data to Be Accounted

The data to be accounted is received in custom tables. Technical specialists in the implementation teams create these tables. It is a common practice to make the table designs and their structures agree. In almost every implementation a common data model is created to receive these transactions into staging. The high-level steps are listed in Table 9-2.

Object Type	Owner	Further Grants To
Staging tables	Custom schema	FUSION & FUSION_RUNTIME
PL/SQL package for technical events	FUSION	
Database views on staging table	FUSION	FUSION_RUNTIME

TABLE 9-2.   *Technical Objects Created to Support FAH Accounting Rules*

Configure Accounting Rules

The purpose of the accounting rules is to build the journal lines. The high-level steps for accounting rule configuration are listed in Table 9-3.

Configuration Step	Purpose	Mandatory/ Optional
Subledger application	It is a common practice to create one application for each source system. Some implementations register the source application for each line of business. But there is no fixed rule for deciding on the number of applications. Much depends on the landscape and commonality across the different systems being integrated.	Mandatory
Process category	You define process categories to segregate different events as per processing needs. For example, you may wish to generate run accounting for core banking events only at night. In such a case, you define a processing category for all the retail banking events. In most cases, you will define just one process category for each subledger application.	Mandatory
Event Class	The simplest way to define an event class is to create an event class for each staging table. Think of an event class as an object on which various types of business events take place. For example, a retail loan is an event class, and event types such as loan initiation, loan period extension, or loan termination can take place on the loan object.	Mandatory
Event Type	Event type identifies the nature of the operation that takes place on an event class. For example, loan termination is an event type that must be accounted for.	Mandatory
Transaction Object	Transaction object is created for an event class. The transaction object references the database table used for staging the source system transaction.	Mandatory

TABLE 9-3. *Configuration Steps in Fusion Accounting Hub (Continued)*

Configuration Step	Purpose	Mandatory/ Optional
Accounting Attributes	An accounting attribute is a mapping between the database table column and the journal attribute. For example, a database column named CURR_ CODE can be mapped to the journal line currency. Another example is that a column named LINE_ AMOUNT or TRADE_AMOUNT could be mapped to journal line amount.	Mandatory
Account Rule	The Manage Account Rule screen allows you to define rules for account code combination derivation. For example, your rules to derive values for the Entity segment or the Cost Centre segment are configured in the Account Rule screen.	Mandatory
Journal Header Description	This is where you configure the rules to construct the journal header description. This step is optional.	Optional
Journal Line Description	This is where you configure the rules to construct the journal line description. This step is optional as well.	Optional
Journal Line Rule	It is the configuration in Journal Line Rule that decides whether the journal line will be a credit or a debit entry.	Mandatory
Supporting References	Supporting references are used for capturing additional information related to the source transaction. This can be captured either at the journal header or line level. You also have the option to maintain balances at the supporting reference level.	Optional
Journal Entry Rule Set	This is where the account rule, journal line rule, description rules, and supporting references are combined for a complete journal creation.	Mandatory
Accounting Method	The accounting method is attached to the ledger. You will attach the event class, event type, and rule set combination to the accounting method.	Mandatory

TABLE 9-3.   *Configuration Steps in Fusion Accounting Hub*

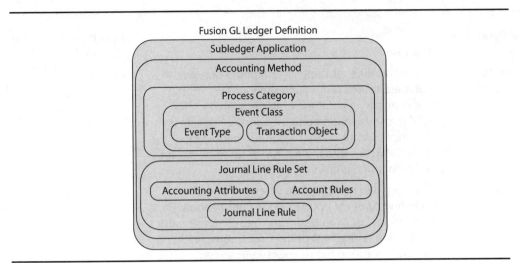

FIGURE 9-2. *Mandatory components of Oracle FAH*

Figure 9-2 explains all the mandatory components used for configuration of Oracle FAH.

As seen in Figure 9-2, it is the accounting method that gets attached to the ledger. You will create an accounting method for each reporting basis such as UK GAAP, US GAAP, or IFRS. Effectively, this allows your UK ledger to contain UK accounting behavior and your US ledger to contain US GAAP accounting behavior.

Raise Technical Events

The technical specialist must write a PL/SQL routine to execute the API named xla_events_pub_pkg.create_event. This will place the accounting event in the pending queue to be processed.

Process Accounting Events to Create Journals

You need to run a Create Accounting process to create journals. This process applies the accounting rules to the technical events and produces the journals that can be posted to Oracle General Ledger.

Steps to Implement Business Requirements for ACME

All insurance companies have an asset management division. The money collected from premiums gets invested into various investment instruments. In case of ACME US Insurance, they have outsourced their asset management to a third party. The third-party asset management company executes the trades for ACME US Insurance.

These trades are sent to FAH every night for accounting. In this chapter we will take an example of a stock purchase event and account for it in Fusion General Ledger using the accounting rules.

In this chapter, we will create a configuration to process accounting events for stock purchase for the ACME US Insurance's Asset Management division. You will learn the necessary components required to create and configure a journal. Although the configuration of FAH accounting rules can be done by FAADMIN or users with equivalent roles such as XXFA_FAH_ IMPLEMENTATION_CONSULTANT as shown in Appendix A, you must have access to the data role General Accountant ACME US Insurance Ledger in order to view the journals created by the accounting process.

Create Database Objects

In order to create the database objects, first your database administrators (DBAs) must create a custom schema for the database objects. The following steps can be executed by your DBA by connecting to the SYS schema. Your DBA will most likely create a dedicated tablespace for the user/schema being created.

```
create user xxfah identified by Welcome$$
grant resource to xxfah ;
grant create session to xxfah ;
```

Next, the staging table must be created as shown in the following example. In some organizations, you will use data modeling tools to create and manage these staging tables. It is also very common practice to use ETL tools that prepare data for FAH to process. But for this example, we will create the table manually as shown in the following example:

```
conn xxfah/Welcome$$
    CREATE TABLE XXFAH.XX_FAH_TRADES_STG
        (   BATCH_ID NUMBER,
            FAH_APPLICATION_NAME VARCHAR2(80),
            LEDGER_NAME VARCHAR2(80),
            LEGAL_ENTITY_NAME VARCHAR2(80),
            CREATION_DATE DATE,
            CREATED_BY VARCHAR2(30),
            LAST_UPDATE_DATE DATE,
            LAST_UPDATED_BY VARCHAR2(30),
            EVENT_ID NUMBER,
            ENTITY_TYPE VARCHAR2(80),
            EVENT_TYPE VARCHAR2(80),
            LINE_NUMBER VARCHAR2(30),
            TRADE_CURRENCY VARCHAR2(15),
            TRADE_AMOUNT NUMBER,
            TRADE_DATE DATE,
    TRADE_NUMBER NUMBER,
            EQUITY_NAME  VARCHAR2(240),
            COMPANY_NUMBER VARCHAR2(30),
```

```
      BUSINESS_DIVISION VARCHAR2(60),
      REQUEST_ID NUMBER ) ;
GRANT ALL ON XXFAH.XX_FAH_TRADES_STG TO FUSION WITH GRANT OPTION;
```

After creating the table in a custom schema, next create grant permissions to this table for FUSION schema and create database views, with subsequent grants to FUSION_RUNTIME:

```
connfusion/&password;
CREATE OR REPLACE synonym XX_FAH_TRADES_STG for XXFAH.XX_FAH_TRADES_STG ;
CREATE OR REPLACE VIEW XX_FAH_TRADES_V AS SELECT * FROM XX_FAH_TRADES_STG;
grant all on XX_FAH_TRADES_STG to fusion_runtime;
grant all on XX_FAH_TRADES_V to fusion_runtime;
```

Next, create a PL/SQL package in the FUSION schema. This PL/SQL package will be executed from the Enterprise Scheduler program, which will be registered later in this chapter. For simplicity we are using a package dedicated for trade accounting in this chapter. In a real-life implementation, you will write common FAH feed-processing utilities that can be used across all the incoming feeds. Further, you will create a common set of data models for all incoming feeds with error management integrated with the appropriate error exception management framework of your architecture.

```
CREATE OR REPLACE PACKAGE XX_FAH_TRADE_ACCOUNTING_PKG
AS
   PROCEDURE process_trade(
       p_errbuf OUT NOCOPY  VARCHAR2,
       p_retcode OUT NOCOPY VARCHAR2,
       p_batch_id IN NUMBER );
END XX_FAH_TRADE_ACCOUNTING_PKG;
/

CREATE OR REPLACE PACKAGE BODY XX_FAH_TRADE_ACCOUNTING_PKG
AS
PROCEDURE debug_log(
    p_msg IN VARCHAR2)
IS
BEGIN
  fnd_file.put_line (fnd_file.LOG, p_msg ||CHR (13));
END debug_log ;
PROCEDURE process_trade(
    p_errbuf OUT NOCOPY  VARCHAR2,
    p_retcode OUT NOCOPY VARCHAR2,
    p_batch_id IN NUMBER )
AS
  l_event_id NUMBER;
  l_err_buf  VARCHAR2(4000);
  l_retcode  VARCHAR2(4000);
  l_event_source_info xla_events_pub_pkg.t_event_source_info;
  l_security xla_events_pub_pkg.t_security := NULL;
```

```
BEGIN
  debug_log ( 'Inside Process Trade');
  FOR l_trade_rec IN
  (SELECT trd.ROWID,
    gl.ledger_id,
    xep.legal_entity_id legal_entity_id,
    xst.application_id fah_application_id,
    trd.*
  FROM XX_FAH_TRADES_STG trd,
    gl_ledgers gl,
    xle_entity_profiles xep,
    xla_subledgers_tl xst
  WHERE gl.name              = trd.ledger_name
  AND xep.name               = trd.LEGAL_ENTITY_NAME
  AND xst.application_name   = trd.FAH_APPLICATION_NAME
  AND trd.batch_id           = p_batch_id
  )
  LOOP
    debug_log( 'Processing TradeNumber: '|| l_trade_rec.trade_number );
    l_event_source_info.source_application_id := l_trade_rec.fah_application_id;
    l_event_source_info.application_id        := l_trade_rec.fah_application_id;
    l_event_source_info.legal_entity_id       := l_trade_rec.legal_entity_id;
    l_event_source_info.ledger_id             := l_trade_rec.ledger_id;
    l_event_source_info.entity_type_code      := l_trade_rec.entity_type;
    l_event_source_info.source_id_int_1       := l_trade_rec.trade_number;
    l_event_id := xla_events_pub_pkg.create_event
      (
          p_event_source_info => l_event_source_info
        , p_event_type_code => l_trade_rec.event_type
        , p_event_date => TRUNC(SYSDATE)
        , p_event_status_code => 'U'
        , p_valuation_method => 'DEFAULT'
        , p_security_context => l_security
      );
    debug_log( 'Generated Event ID: '|| l_event_id );
    UPDATE XX_FAH_TRADES_STG
    SET event_id          = l_event_id ,
      last_update_date   = SYSDATE ,
      last_updated_by    = FND_GLOBAL.user_name ,
      request_id         = fnd_job.request_id
    WHERE ROWID          = l_trade_rec.ROWID;
  END LOOP;
END process_trade;
END XX_FAH_TRADE_ACCOUNTING_PKG;
/
```

Configure Fusion Accounting Hub

Table 9-4 lists the high-level steps required for the configuration of accounting rules.
We will implement all the mandatory steps in order to process the journal.

Chart of Account Segment	Derived From
Entity	COMPANY_NUMBER column in XX_FAH_TRADES_STG will contain the Entity segment value. The value in this column will be used as is.
Line Of Business	This will be mapped from the column BUSINESS_DIVISION. We will use the mapping set feature to derive a value in the Line Of Business segment.
Cost Centre	This will default to a constant 0000.
Account	When stocks are purchased, we will debit the trading stock account and credit the cash account.
Intercompany	This will default to a constant 00.
Location	This will default to 1000, which indicates New York. It must be noted that in a real-life project, you will derive a value into this segment from one of the attributes in the source transaction.
Spare	This will default to a constant 00000.

TABLE 9-4. *Business Rules for Chart of Account Derivation*

Create GL Journal Source

In Setup And Maintenance, search and navigate to the task Manage Journal Sources. Click the + icon to create a new journal source with Name: Insurance Trades, Source Key: INSURANCE_TRADES, Description: Insurance Trades, and leave the remaining fields as per the defaults.

Create FAH Configuration Implementation Project

Navigate to Setup And Maintenance and click Manage Implementation Projects. Click the Create icon to create a new project with the following details:

> **Name:** XX_FAH_TRADE_ACCOUNTING
> **Code:** XX_FAH_TRADE_ACCOUNTING
> **Description:** XX FAH TRADE ACCOUNTING

Click Next and expand the offering Fusion Accounting Hub. Enable the check box for Fusion Accounting Hub and all its child offerings, which are Accounting Coexistence, Intercompany, and Intrastat Reporting. Click the Save And Open Project button. Here you will see all the task lists and tasks associated with Fusion Accounting Hub configuration.

Create the FAH Application

To create a new subledger application, perform the following steps in the Task Lists And Tasks screen:

1. Expand the Register Source System Applications Tasks List.

2. Click Select... to the right of Manage Subledger Application as shown in Figure 9-3.

3. Click the circle for Create Subledger Application.

4. Select Create New in the drop-down list.

Use the following information for creating the subledger application: Subledger Application: XX_FAH_TRADE_APPLICATION, Short Name: XX_FAH_TRADE_APPLICATION, Description: XX_FAH_TRADE_APPLICATION, and Journal Source: Insurance Trades. Once this application has been created, all future configurations in FAH for this chapter will be within this application, unless you wish to switch the scope to become another application. After following these steps, a new subledger

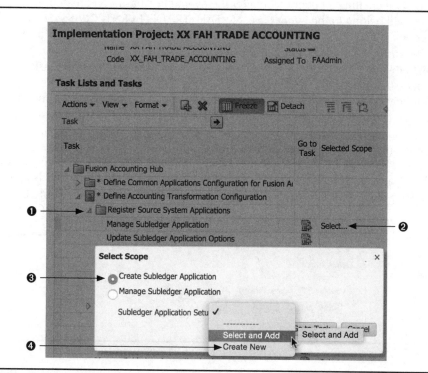

FIGURE 9-3. *Creating a new subledger application for accounting rule configuration*

application named XX_FAH_TRADE_APPLICATION will have been created, with the scope in this project set to this application.

Create the FAH Event Model

In the Manage Subledger Application, click the Create Process Category button. A small window will pop up to create a process category. Enter a name and short name as XX_FAH_TRADE_PRC_CATEGORY and click the Save And Close button.

Create an event model within this process category. Click the + icon as shown in Figure 9-4. Within the event model, create an event class, giving it a name and short name of XX_FAH_TRADE_EVENT_CLASS. In this example, use a Default Journal Category of Miscellaneous. This is a seeded General Ledger category. You will be defining a new journal category for your real implementation project. Attach the database view XX_FAH_TRADES_V to this event class under the System Transaction Identifiers tab as shown in Figure 9-5. Again in the System Transaction Identifiers tab, click the + icon to add a new row for Identifier SOURCE_ID_INT_1 and select TRADE_NUMBER as the View Column. In the User Transaction Identifiers tab, click the + icon to add three records for the identifier and view column combination as shown in Figure 9-5. Map Traded Equity to EQUITY_NAME, Transaction Amount to TRADE_AMOUNT, and Accounting Date to TRADE_DATE.

You will be creating an event type after the event class has been created. This event type will belong to the event class XX_FAH_TRADE_EVENT_CLASS. Select your event class and click the + sign to create the event type, with the name and short name of XX_FAH_PURCHASE_EQUITY.

Now that your event model has been created, you can submit the next task to run a process named Update Subledger Accounting Options. In the parameters, select Application XX_FAH_TRADE_APPLICATION as shown in Figure 9-6 and click Submit. Navigate to the Scheduled Process window and ensure that the submitted process has succeeded.

Next, navigate to the Manage Subledger Application Transaction Objects task and create an entry in the Transaction Objects region with XX_FAH_TRADES_V as the Object Name and Header as the Object Type. Click the Save And Close button, and then submit the task Create And Assign Sources with the parameter Subledger

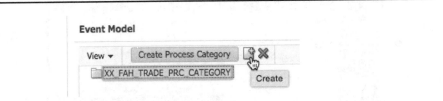

FIGURE 9-4. *Creating an event model for the subledger application*

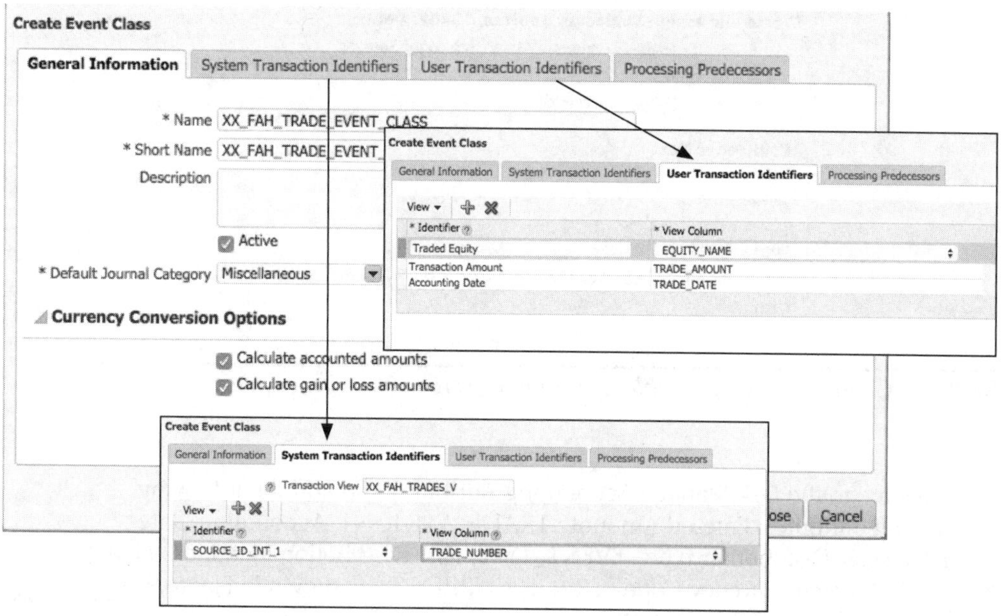

FIGURE 9-5. *Creating an event model for the FAH Trade Accounting application*

Application configured as XX_FAH_TRADE_APPLICATION. At this stage you must ensure that the submitted process has been successful, as shown in the status field of Figure 9-7. You must not proceed with further configuration of accounting rules unless this process has been successful.

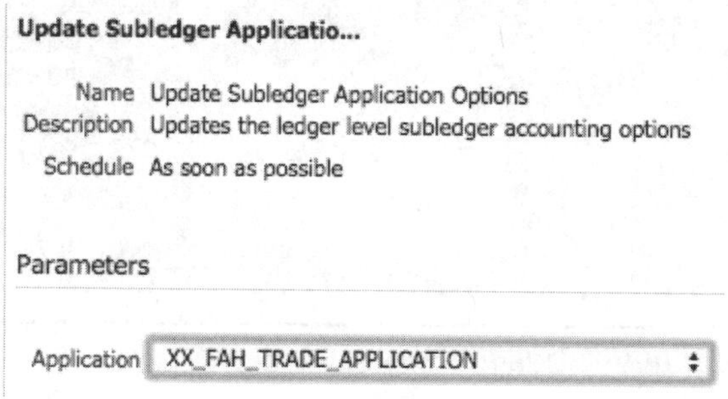

FIGURE 9-6. *Running the Update Subledger Application Options process*

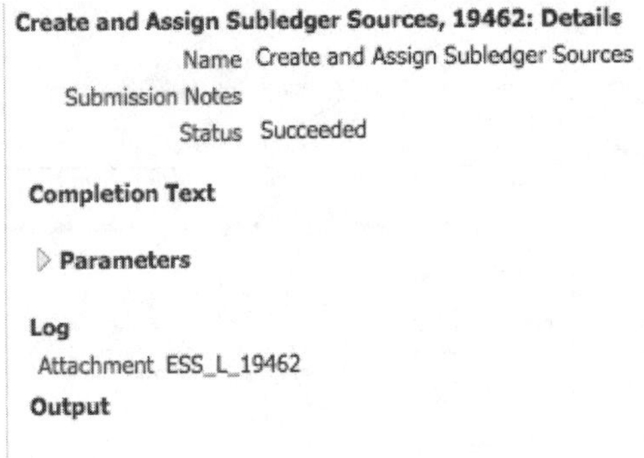

Create and Assign Subledger Sources, 19462: Details

Name Create and Assign Subledger Sources

Submission Notes

Status Succeeded

Completion Text

▷ **Parameters**

Log
Attachment ESS_L_19462

Output

FIGURE 9-7. *Create And Assign Subledger Sources screen showing results*

Navigate to the task Manage Accounting Attributes and add the following accounting attributes: Entered Amount : TRADE_AMOUNT, Accounting Date : TRADE_DATE, Distribution Type : EVENT_TYPE, First Distribution Identifier : LINE_NUMBER, Entered Currency Code : TRADE_CURRENCY as shown in Figure 9-8. Click the Validate Assignments button.

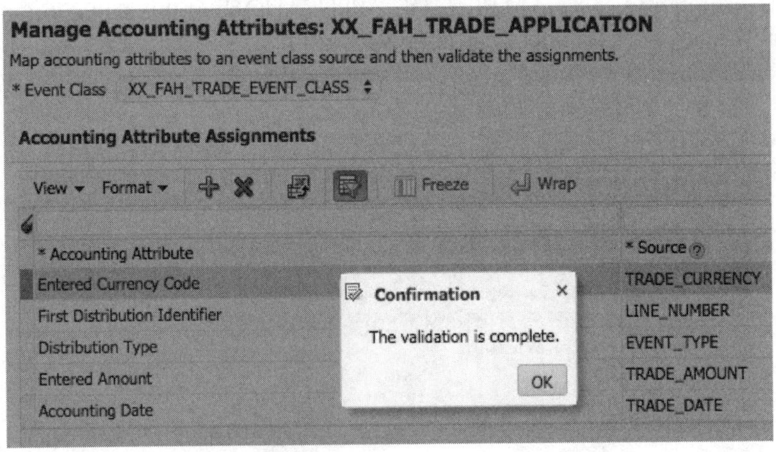

Manage Accounting Attributes: XX_FAH_TRADE_APPLICATION

Map accounting attributes to an event class source and then validate the assignments.

* Event Class   XX_FAH_TRADE_EVENT_CLASS ⬍

Accounting Attribute Assignments

View ▼   Format ▼   ➕ ✖ ⬚ ⬚   ▥ Freeze   ⬕ Wrap

* Accounting Attribute	* Source ⑦
Entered Currency Code	TRADE_CURRENCY
First Distribution Identifier	LINE_NUMBER
Distribution Type	EVENT_TYPE
Entered Amount	TRADE_AMOUNT
Accounting Date	TRADE_DATE

Confirmation ✕

The validation is complete.

OK

FIGURE 9-8. *Accounting attribute assignments*

Configure Accounting Rules

A series of tasks must be performed to configure the accounting rules. These steps are highlighted in Figure 9-9.

Click the Manage Account Rules task and click New. Create a new accounting rule with a name and short name of XX_FAH_COMPANY_SEGMENT. In Chart of Accounts, select ACME Insurance COA Instance, change Rule Type to Segment, and select Company as the segment from the drop-down list. In the Rules region, click the + icon and add a new row with Value Type Source, Value as COMPANY_NUMBER from the drop-down list, and click Validate. This will create an accounting rule for the company segment as shown in Figure 9-10.

Define a mapping set to derive the Line of Business segment value. Using the mapping set, you can map a text value to a predefined value in the value set segment. In this case, we wish to map ACME Life Asset Management division, that is, ALAM, to 104. Navigate to the Mapping Set task and click New to create a new mapping set as shown in Figure 9-11. This value set will map the value in column BUSINESS_DIVISION to the Line of Business segment value.

Click Manage Account Rules and define a new rule named XX_FAH_LOB_SEGMENT, while attaching it to the mapping set created for the Line Of Business segment, as shown in Figure 9-12. Click Validate, and click the Save And Close button.

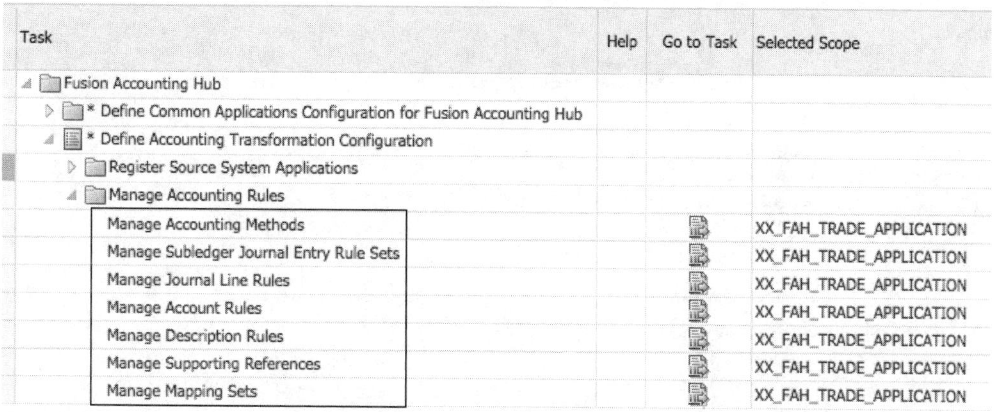

Task	Help	Go to Task	Selected Scope
⊿ ⬜ Fusion Accounting Hub			
▷ ⬜ * Define Common Applications Configuration for Fusion Accounting Hub			
⊿ ⬛ * Define Accounting Transformation Configuration			
▷ ⬜ Register Source System Applications			
⊿ ⬜ Manage Accounting Rules			
Manage Accounting Methods		📄	XX_FAH_TRADE_APPLICATION
Manage Subledger Journal Entry Rule Sets		📄	XX_FAH_TRADE_APPLICATION
Manage Journal Line Rules		📄	XX_FAH_TRADE_APPLICATION
Manage Account Rules		📄	XX_FAH_TRADE_APPLICATION
Manage Description Rules		📄	XX_FAH_TRADE_APPLICATION
Manage Supporting References		📄	XX_FAH_TRADE_APPLICATION
Manage Mapping Sets		📄	XX_FAH_TRADE_APPLICATION

FIGURE 9-9. *Tasks for configuration of accounting rules*

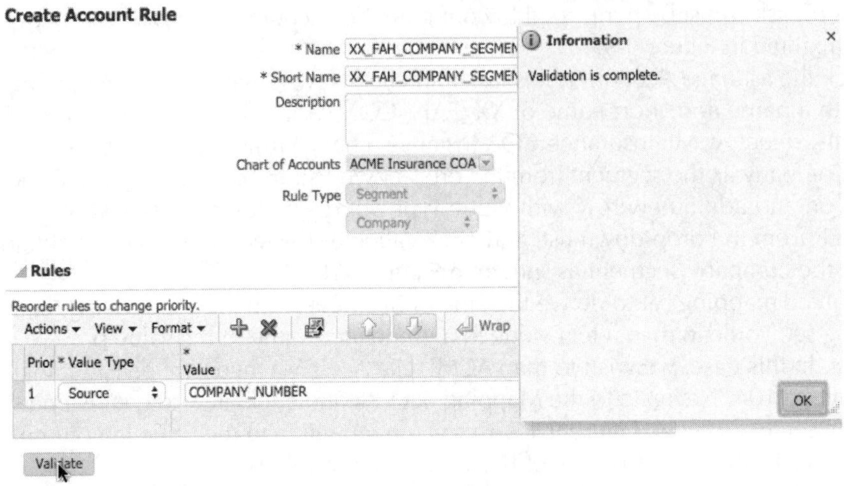

Create Account Rule

* Name XX_FAH_COMPANY_SEGMEN

* Short Name XX_FAH_COMPANY_SEGMEN

Description

Chart of Accounts ACME Insurance COA

Rule Type Segment

Company

Information ×

Validation is complete.

OK

Rules

Reorder rules to change priority.

Actions ▾ View ▾ Format ▾ ➕ ✖ 🗐 ⬆ ⬇ ⤶ Wrap

Prior	* Value Type	* Value
1	Source	COMPANY_NUMBER

Validate

FIGURE 9-10. *The Create Account Rule screen for company segment*

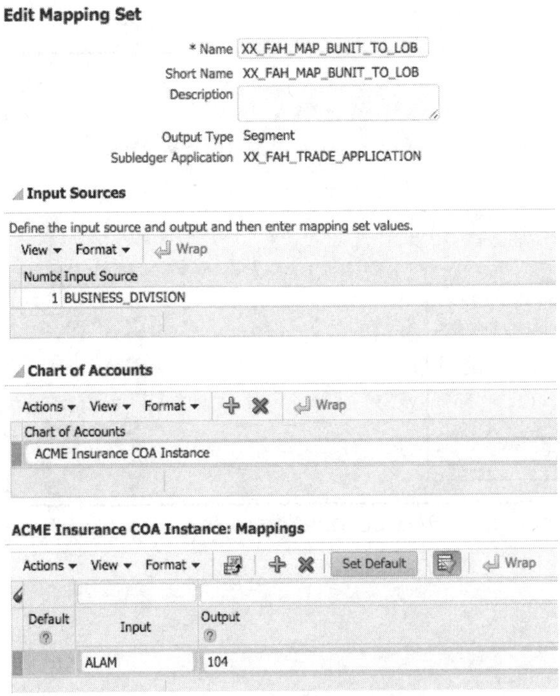

Edit Mapping Set

* Name XX_FAH_MAP_BUNIT_TO_LOB

Short Name XX_FAH_MAP_BUNIT_TO_LOB

Description

Output Type Segment

Subledger Application XX_FAH_TRADE_APPLICATION

Input Sources

Define the input source and output and then enter mapping set values.

View ▾ Format ▾ ⤶ Wrap

Numbe	Input Source
1	BUSINESS_DIVISION

Chart of Accounts

Actions ▾ View ▾ Format ▾ ➕ ✖ ⤶ Wrap

Chart of Accounts
ACME Insurance COA Instance

ACME Insurance COA Instance: Mappings

Actions ▾ View ▾ Format ▾ 🗐 ➕ ✖ Set Default 🗐 ⤶ Wrap

Default ?	Input	Output ?
	ALAM	104

FIGURE 9-11. *Defining a mapping set for the Line of Business segment*

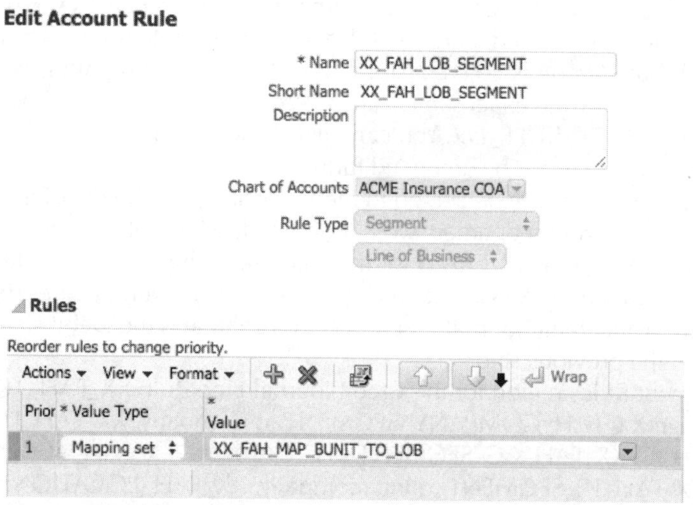

Edit Account Rule

* Name	XX_FAH_LOB_SEGMENT
Short Name	XX_FAH_LOB_SEGMENT
Description	
Chart of Accounts	ACME Insurance COA ▾
Rule Type	Segment ⬍
	Line of Business ⬍

◢ **Rules**

Reorder rules to change priority.

Actions ▾   View ▾   Format ▾   ➕ ✖   🗗   ⬆   ⬇ ↵ Wrap

Prior	* Value Type	✻ Value
1	Mapping set ⬍	XX_FAH_MAP_BUNIT_TO_LOB ▾

FIGURE 9-12.   *Attaching the mapping set to an account rule*

Having created the accounting rules for Entity and Company, next create account rules for the Account, Cost Center, Intercompany, Location, and Spare segments as shown in Table 9-5. The account rules for these segments will be created with constant values. In a real implementation project you will use conditions, mapping sets, or source derivation to derive values for account segments.

Account Rule Name	Segment Applicable	Constant Value
XX_FAH_CC_SEGMENT	Cost Centre	0000
XX_FAH_ACC_SEG_DR	Account	11950 Note: Trading Stock Account
XX_FAH_ACC_SEG_CR	Account	18900 Note: Corporate Bank Account for Third-Party Payment
XX_FAH_IC_SEGMENT	Intercompany	00
XX_FAH_LOCATION	Location	1000 Note: New York
XX_FAH_SPARE	Spare	00000

TABLE 9-5.   *Account Rules for the Remaining Segments*

Navigate to the task Manage Journal Line Rules. This is where the credit and the debit entries will be created. Create a new Journal Line Rule named XX_FAH_TRADE_RULE_CR as shown in Figure 9-13. Ensure that the side is Credit and the Accounting Attribute Group is Entered Currency in the Accounting Attribute Assignments tab. Follow the exact same steps to create a Debit Journal Line Rule named XX_FAH_TRADE_RULE_DR. You can click Action | Duplicate to duplicate the Journal Line Rule that can be amended further.

To create a Journal Entry Rule Set, go to the task Manage Subledger Journal Entry Rule Sets and create a rule set named XX_FAH_TRADE_RULE_SET. Select Event Class XX_FAH_TRADE_EVENT_CLASS for this rule set, with Event Type value All. Assign ACME Insurance COA Instance to this rule set. In the Journal Lines region, click the + sign to attach the Journal Line Rules for Credit and the Debit side that were created in the previous step.

In the Segment Rules region for the Credit Journal Line Rule XX_FAH_TRADE_RULE_CR, assign XX_FAH_COMPANY_SEGMENT to Company, XX_FAH_LOB_SEGMENT to LOB, XX_FAH_CC_SEGMENT to Cost Centre, XX_FAH_ACC_SEG_CR to Account, XX_FAH_IC_SEGMENT to Intercompany, XX_FAH_LOCATION to Location, and XX_FAH_SPARE to Spare. Similarly, for the Debit Journal Line Rule XX_FAH_TRADE_RULE_DR, replicate the same segment rules as that for Credit, but change the Account segment rule to XX_FAH_ACC_SEG_DR. These steps are shown in Figure 9-14. Click Actions and activate the Journal Line Rule Set.

Navigate to the task Manage Standard Accruals, select the Standard Accrual accounting method, and click Actions | Duplicate to create a new accounting method named XX_FAH_ACME_INSURANCE_ACCRUAL. Add the Event Class, Event Type, and Rule Set as shown in Figure 9-15, and activate this accounting method.

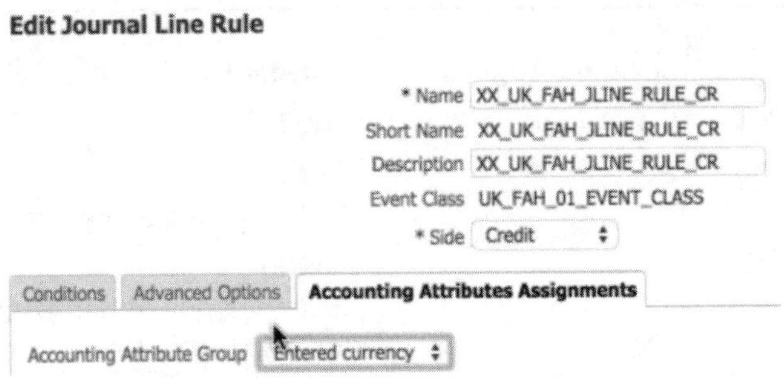

FIGURE 9-13.   *Creating a Credit Journal Line rule*

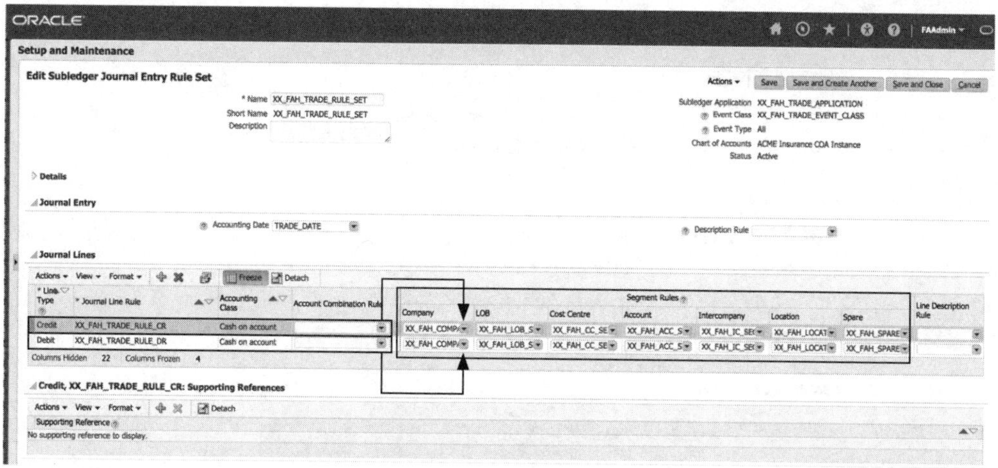

FIGURE 9-14. *Journal Line Rule Set*

After the accounting method has been activated, it can be assigned to the primary ledger ACME US Insurance Ledger. Navigate to the task Specify Ledger Options under Manage Primary Ledgers for ACME US Insurance Ledger, and change the accounting method from Standard Accrual to XX_FAH_ACME_INSURANCE_ACCRUAL as shown in Figure 9-16. This completes the configuration of accounting rules required to implement ACME's requirement.

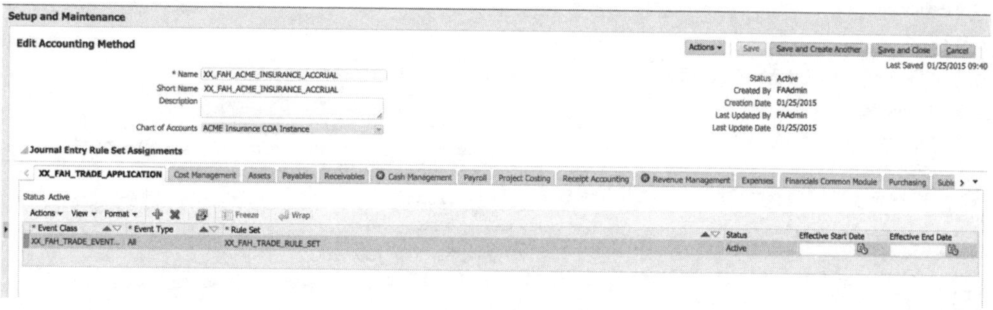

FIGURE 9-15. *Creating an accounting method for the rule set*

Specify Ledger Options: ACME US Insurance Ledger

General Information

* Name ACME US Insurance Ledger

Description ACME US Insurance Ledger

Accounting Calendar

Select a period after the first defined period in the ledger calendar to enable running transla

Accounting Calendar ACME Monthly

First Opened Period ACME-Jan-14

Subledger Accounting

Standard Accrual
Standard Accrual for China
Accounting Metho ✓ XX_FAH_ACME_INSURANCE_ACCRUAL

FIGURE 9-16. *Changing the accounting method of the ledger to use new accounting rules*

Create a System Event and Import Journals

A technical specialist will create a new enterprise scheduler job to process the trades so that accounting can be generated as per your accounting rules. To create this job, go to the task Define Custom Enterprise Scheduler Jobs For Ledger And Related Applications and create a PL/SQL type job as shown in Figure 9-17.

Manage Custom Enterprise Scheduler Jobs for Ledger and Related Applications

Manage Job Definitions | Manage List of Values Sources

Create Job Definition   Save and Close   Ca

Job Definition   Show More

* Display XX FAH ACME Process Trade Journals   * Job Application Name FinancialsEss
  Name
                                                                  ☐ Enable submission from Enterprise Manager
* Name XX_FAH_ACME_PROCESS_TRADE
                                                           * Job Type PlsqlJobType
* Path /oracle/apps/ess/financials/general
                                                           Procedure Name XX_FAH_TRADE_ACCOUNTING_PKG.PROCESS_TRADE
Application General Ledger
                                                           Default Output Format TXT
Description Creates journal entries from ACME's asset management trades
                                                               Report ID
                                                               Priority   4
Retries
                                                           Allow multiple pending False
Job   submissions
Category
                                                                  ☑ Enable submission from Scheduled Processes
Timeout
Period

XX_FAH_ACME_PROCESS_TRADE: Parameters User Properties

Actions ▾ View ▾   ☐ ☐ ✎ ✗ ☐ Copy from Existing Job Definition ⇧ ⇩ ☐ Detach

Parameter Prompt	Data Type	Page Element	Default Value	Read Only	Required
Batch Number	Numeric	Text box		—	✓ Required

FIGURE 9-17. *Creating an enterprise scheduler job to create system events for trades*

After inserting the records into the staging table XX_FAH_TRADES_STG, run this scheduler job, and it should create the events in a table named XLA_EVENTS. Your technical specialist should be able to verify this by querying on this table.

After the event creation, submit a standard enterprise scheduler job called Create Accounting as shown in Figure 9-18.

The Create Accounting process will spawn the journal import program as shown in Figure 9-19.

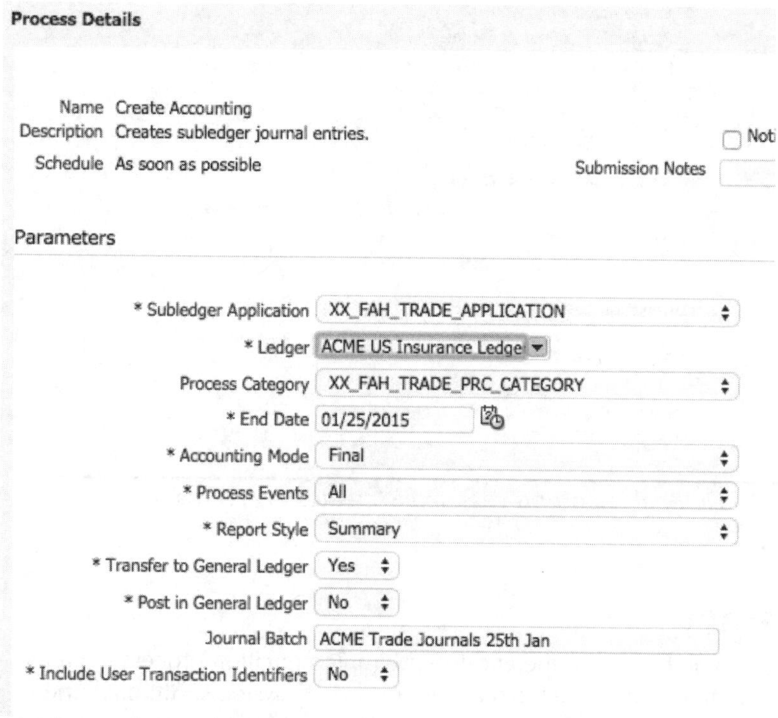

Process Details

Name Create Accounting
Description Creates subledger journal entries.
Schedule As soon as possible

☐ Noti

Submission Notes

Parameters

* Subledger Application	XX_FAH_TRADE_APPLICATION
* Ledger	ACME US Insurance Ledge ▼
Process Category	XX_FAH_TRADE_PRC_CATEGORY
* End Date	01/25/2015
* Accounting Mode	Final
* Process Events	All
* Report Style	Summary
* Transfer to General Ledger	Yes
* Post in General Ledger	No
Journal Batch	ACME Trade Journals 25th Jan
* Include User Transaction Identifiers	No

FIGURE 9-18. *Submitting a Create Accounting job*

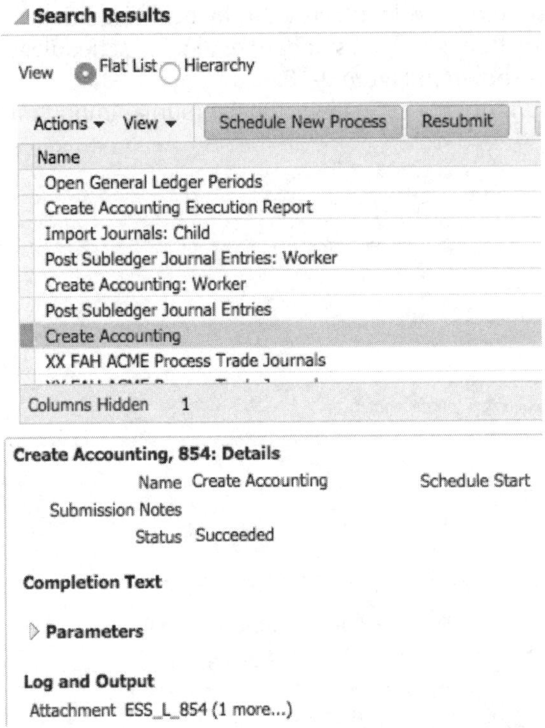

FIGURE 9-19. *The journal import process finally creates the journals from the trading system.*

Summary

In this chapter you have seen the end-to-end implementation process to create accounting for transactions taking place in third-party systems. Although the examples in this chapter perform accounting for investment trades, similar principles can be applied to any other type of system. The example in this chapter creates both a debit and credit side automatically for a single trade event in asset management. However, in some implementations the source system may have its own built-in General Ledger. In those cases, you can implement pass-through accounting so that for each source system transaction line, a corresponding journal line is created in Fusion Accounting Hub.

In this chapter, you have also seen that Fusion Accounting Hub requires teamwork between a business analyst and a technical specialist.

At the time of writing this book, the Fusion Accounting Hub is only available for on-premise or Oracle Private cloud up to Release 9. Oracle may make Fusion Accounting Hub available on public cloud in its future releases.

CHAPTER
10

Consolidation

One of the key activities performed by the finance department is to prepare consolidated financial statements when a company controls one or more other legal entities. Consolidated financial statements are prepared as per accounting requirements (US GAAP, Local GAAP, or IFRS), and the process to prepare the statement for legal reporting of the parent company is called *consolidation*. Determining when to consolidate one entity to another is a complex area of accounting, but generally, if an entity is exposed or has rights to variable return on the investment made on another entity and has the power to control those returns, then the consolidation process should take effect. It is also important to investors because when one entity consolidates another, it reports the other entity's assets, liabilities, revenues, and expenses together with its own, as if they are a single economic unit.

In this chapter, we will explain how to perform consolidation in Oracle Fusion GL. This chapter has been divided into three major sections. The first section will introduce readers to the concept of consolidation. The second section will provide details of different methods of consolidation offered in Fusion General Ledger that can be considered based on the business requirements. The third section provides details about how to apply this knowledge gained to meet the consolidation requirements of ACME Bank. Readers should understand that consolidation is an advanced concept in Fusion Financials and requires many features of Fusion Financials to be configured in the system. So this chapter will have reference to other chapters where those concepts and features are explained in detail.

The Consolidation Process

The consolidation process can be complex based on the percentage ownership of how one entity controls the other, like joint ventures, minority interests, or partially or fully owned subsidiary. When a purchasing company owns (in terms of equity or shareholding) more than 50 percent of the acquired company, then the acquired company is classed as a subsidiary of the purchasing company (also known as the *parent company*). As part of the consolidation process, the following steps are performed to prepare the consolidated financial statements for legal reporting:

- Combine like items of assets, liabilities, equity, income, expenses, and cash flows of the parent with those of its subsidiaries.

- Offset or eliminate the parent portion of equity or investment amount in each of the subsidiaries; for example, joint ventures where only a portion of the business (usually denoted on a percentage basis) is owned by the parent company as part of the joint venture agreement.

■   Eliminate any inter- or intra group balances on revenue, expenses, liabilities, assets and cash flows originating from transactions performed between two legal entities within the parent company (known as *intercompany transactions*) and between two departments under the same legal entity (known as *intracompany transactions*).

Consolidation in a broader sense also refers to the consolidation of results for management information purposes that will help internally to measure Key Performance Indicators, also known as KPI or Key Success Indicators (KSI), and also to aid in making strategic decisions for organic and inorganic growth. Management information will help an organization define and measure progress toward organizational goals. This type of management consolidation is usually based on the organization's internal alignment, that is, based on their service lines or product lines or lines of business, and also largely based on the type of industry that the company operates. Management consolidation also cuts across different legal entities. For example, the company may want to measure the profitability of a product line consolidated at a group level, but this may not be a legal requirement for consolidation.

Consolidation is usually performed at the end of an accounting period on a monthly, quarterly, and yearly basis, and after the subledger accounting entries and feeder system accounting entries have been successfully transferred and accounted for in General Ledger. In large organizations, usually a dedicated consolidation team within the finance department will handle all consolidation/intercompany reconciliations and corresponding adjustments.

Elimination Entries

A parent company and its subsidiaries often engage in a variety of transactions among themselves. For example, manufacturing companies often have subsidiaries that develop raw materials or produce components to be included in the products of affiliated companies. These transactions between related companies or legal entities are referred to as *intercorporate transfers*. All aspects of intercorporate transfers must be eliminated in preparing consolidated financial statements so that the statements appear as if they were those of a single company. Normally, transactions between legal entities within the group company are booked using Intercompany Clearing accounts defined in the Chart of Accounts, like Intercompany Payables and Intercompany Receivables accounts. When Group accounts are reported, these accounts should normally net to zero. The following are a few general scenarios where elimination entries are booked during consolidation for removing the effects of intercompany transactions:

1.   Intercompany transfers of services

2.   Intercompany sales of inventory

3. Intercompany transfers of land

4. Intercompany transfers of depreciable assets

5. Elimination of intercompany debts (such as loans) and ownership interests

In the following section, we will discuss the concept of intercompany transfer of services and intercompany sales of inventory with regard to eliminations between entities, using an example. This will provide readers with a good understanding of the kind of Elimination Journals that are passed during consolidation.

Scenario: Intercompany Transfer of Services

For example, if a parent company called "P Ltd" receives a consulting service from a subsidiary company called "S Ltd" for $50,000, the parent company will recognize $50,000 expenses on its books, and the subsidiary company would recognize $50,000 of consulting revenue. As part of consolidation, an elimination entry would be needed to reduce both consulting revenue (debit) and consulting expense (credit) by $50,000. Even though the income is not affected, elimination is important; otherwise, both revenue and expenses are overstated.

Accounting Entries Booked in Parent Company (Company Code = 01)

	Debit	Credit
01. Expenses Account	$50,000	
01. Intercompany Payables to 02		$50,000

Accounting Entries Booked in Subsidiary Company (Company Code = 02)

	Debit	Credit
02. Sales Account		$50,000
02. Intercompany Receivables from 01	$50,000	

Resulting Elimination Entries

	Debit	Credit
01. Expenses Account		$50,000
01. Intercompany Payables to 02	$50,000	
02. Sales Account	$50,000	
02. Intercompany Receivables from 01		$50,000

Intercompany Sales of Inventory

The Parent Company called "P Ltd" owns all shares of a subsidiary company called "S Ltd," and consolidations need to be performed as of the period March 2014. Assume that on January 1, 2014, P Ltd purchased $10,000 worth of inventory for cash from S Ltd. The inventory had cost S Ltd about $8,000. Let us assume that there is no tax implication on these transactions and the inventory purchased from S Ltd is still in the inventory of P Ltd.

Accounting Entries Booked in Parent Company (Company Code = 01)

	Debit	Credit
01. Inventory	$10,000	
01. Cash		$10,000

Accounting Entries Booked in Subsidiary Company (Company Code = 02)

	Debit	Credit
02. Sales Account		$10,000
02. Cash	$10,000	
02. Inventory		$8,000
02. Cost of Goods Sold	$8,000	

Resulting Consolidation Entries Using Elimination Company Code = 95 as of March 2014

	Debit	Credit
95. Sales	$10,000	
(Sales not made external to group)		
95. Cost of Goods Sold		$8,000
(Not sold external to group)		
95. Inventory		$2,000
(Shown in P Ltd books as $10,000, whereas actually it is $8,000)		

The following points should be considered while creating elimination entries for intercompany transactions:

- For profit and loss accounts like Intercompany Sales and Cost of Goods Sold, elimination entries should be performed using Period To Date Balances (PTD) as the period activity.

- For balance sheet accounts like Intercompany Payables and Intercompany Receivables, elimination entries should be performed using Year To Date Balances (YTD) as the period activity. Because we are using YTD balances, make sure that elimination entries of the previous period are reserved in the current period to avoid incorrect accounting.

- It is common industry practice to define separate elimination company codes for posting Elimination Journal entries. In the scenarios discussed in the preceding tables, the 095 Elimination Company code is used to post Elimination Journal entries, which provides better transparency and auditability. It also helps keep the original legal entity accounting entries untouched.

NOTE
Elimination Company codes are added as additional Company values in the Company Valueset or Segment, and these company codes are directly attached to the ledger (basically, Balancing Segment Values assigned to the ledger).

If both the parent and subsidiary reside in the same ledger, the consolidated statement can be prepared by combining the balances of all three company codes (01, 02, and 95) as shown in Figure 10-1. This method of consolidation

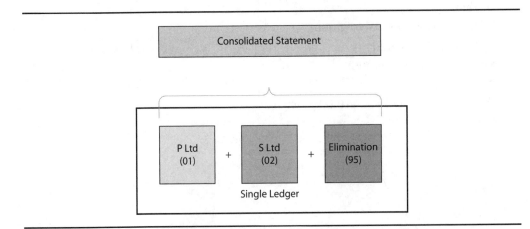

FIGURE 10-1. *Consolidation of single ledger with elimination company*

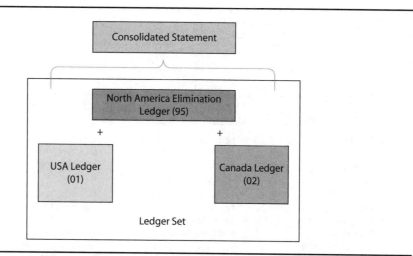

FIGURE 10-2. *Consolidation of multiple ledgers using an Elimination Ledger*

is called Report-Only Consolidation, and we will discuss this in detail in the next section.

If the parent and subsidiary reside in different ledgers, the consolidated statement can be prepared by creating an Elimination Ledger or Consolidation Ledger as shown in Figure 10-2. Prerequisites are that all the ledgers should share the same Chart of Accounts and Calendar so that they can be grouped into a Ledger Set. Using Report Only Consolidation, a consolidated statement can be prepared for the group accordingly.

Different Consolidation Methods

Oracle Fusion Applications supports three types of consolidation methods for handling different scenarios that may arise during the consolidation process, as shown in Figure 10-3. The three consolidation methods are as follows:

- Report-Only Consolidation

- Balance Transfer Consolidation

- Oracle Fusion Hyperion Finance Management (HFM) Consolidation

Choosing a consolidation method depends on how the input consolidation data are currently represented and how the balances need to be aggregated. More often,

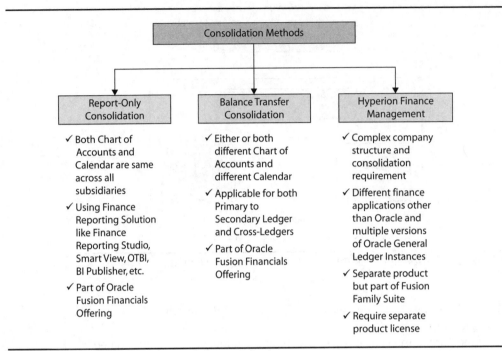

FIGURE 10-3. *Different consolidation methods*

it may be the case that we need to choose more than one consolidation method to meet the legal reporting needs.

Some of the key questions that functional consultants may ask to evaluate the consolidation requirement for all the subsidiaries and the parent company are as follows:

- How many finance systems are involved, and where are the balances of subsidiaries recorded? Do all subsidiaries use Oracle Fusion? Are there any other external non-Oracle ERP systems where balances are recorded?

- How many ledgers are involved, and what is the finance reporting structure (Calendar, Chart of Accounts Structure, and Currency) of each of the ledgers? Do all ledgers share the same Chart of Accounts Structure and Calendar?

- Do all subsidiaries and corporate ledgers have a Globalized Chart of Accounts so that all of their company balances can be easily consolidated?

- If there are multiple ledgers, how are the corporate currency balances recorded? Are there any secondary ledgers or reporting currencies?

■ What are the complexities in the company structure, like joint ventures or fully owned subsidiary, and how are consolidation and elimination performed for these companies?

Report-Only Consolidations

Report-Only Consolidation is the simplest method of preparing consolidation statements using Fusion Reports. This method assumes that all subsidiaries and corporate company balance data required for consolidation reside in a single instance of Oracle Fusion General Ledger, either as a single ledger or multiple ledgers. More importantly, if there are multiple ledgers, all the ledgers should share the same Chart of Accounts and Calendar. We can then create the consolidated statement as a report using Fusion Financial Reporting and Analysis capabilities, such as Smart View, Reporting Center Studio, Oracle Transaction Business Intelligence, and Oracle Business Intelligence Applications, as explained in Chapter 13.

Scenarios Where This Method Is Applicable

The following sections describe common scenarios that you can relate to while making your implementation choice for this type of consolidation.

Scenario 1: Single Ledger   This may be the case where all subsidiaries and corporate group companies (represented as individual balancing segments in COA) operate in a single country or area where they share the same Chart of Accounts, Calendar, and currency as the corporate currency. An example would be a U.S.-based company with diversified business interests and operating within the United States only; however, this company has different legal entities for each of their business interests. All these companies can reside in a single ledger and use Report-Only Consolidation.

Another case may be that a corporation operates across different countries, and each country has its own ledger for its local reporting purposes. For local reporting purposes, you can potentially use Report-Only Consolidation to satisfy the local legal reporting requirements.

Scenario 2: Ledger with Different Currency Other Than Corporate Currency   In this scenario, we have more than one ledger involved in the consolidation process and all use a Global Chart of Accounts; however, each has its own local currency for its Primary Ledger. In this case, we use the Reporting Currency feature to record balances in the corporate currency in addition to the local currency and use the Report-Only Consolidation method to generate the consolidated statement.

Let us consider an example where a company operating in the United States and the United Kingdom only has a need to consolidate corporate earnings at the

U.S. level. Let us assume that there are two ledgers—one for the United States and one for the United Kingdom with Global Chart of Accounts. However, the primary currency for the U.S. ledger is U.S. dollars, and the primary currency for the U.K. ledger is GBP. In this case, the U.K. ledger can use the Reporting Currency feature to record balances in U.S. corporate currency and then subsequently, use the Report-Only Consolidation method to generate the consolidated statement at the U.S. level.

Implementation Steps

In the previous section, we have seen different scenarios where Report-Only Consolidation can be used. We will now look at the high-level steps to perform for this type of consolidation.

Step 1: Create Ledger Set   The first step in this process is to create a ledger set if the balances of the companies are stored in multiple ledgers. A ledger set allows group ledgers to share the same Chart of Accounts and Calendar so that Business Users can manage ledgers centrally for the period-close process, as well as analysis and reporting purposes. Using a ledger set, summarized balances can be generated from multiple ledgers using Fusion reporting capabilities.

Step 2: Translate Balances to the Corporate Currency   As explained in Scenario 2 in the preceding section, translate the local currency balances to the corporate currency so that reporting can be performed using the corporate currency balances. This is accomplished through the Translation process as explained in Chapter 12. Business Users always need to make sure that translation to the consolidation currency is current to reflect all balances.

Step 3: Create Elimination Entries   The next step is to create elimination entries for intercompany and intracompany transactions so as to avoid double counting of income and expenses. Creation of elimination entries can be automated using Allocation Rules Manager as explained in Chapter 11.

Step 4: Create Adjustment Entries   Adjustment entries are performed basically to reclassify certain types of account balances to another for legal reporting needs and to alter the ending balances in various General Ledger accounts. When adjustment entries are created, they are usually booked as Manual Journals via ADFI spreadsheet upload or by using the Create Journal Entry form. You would have seen how to enter manual journal entries in Chapter 8.

Step 5: Report Using Ledger Set and Corporate Currency as Parameter for Consolidated Balances   Use Financials Reporting Center to generate a consolidation report with parameters as Ledger Set and Corporate Currency. Chapter 13 provides detailed steps of how you could build a report using Financials Reporting Center.

Balance Transfer Consolidations

The Balance Transfer Consolidation method will be applicable if Chart of Accounts or Calendar or both Calendar and Chart of Accounts are different between the parent company and the subsidiaries. In this case, the parent and subsidiaries are configured as different ledgers, and either can be associated as a Primary and Secondary Ledger (usually the Primary Ledger will hold subsidiary balances and the Secondary Ledger will represent corporate balances) or a stand-alone ledger with no association between them. Oracle provides a Balance Transfer feature to bring across balances from one ledger to another for consolidation purposes.

Scenarios Where This Method Is Applicable

Balance Transfer Consolidation can be used in the following two scenarios:

- Primary to Secondary Ledger Balance Transfer
- Cross-Ledger Balance Transfer

Primary to Secondary Ledger Balance Transfer

This scenario is applicable where the Primary Subsidiary ledger is maintained in Local COA or Local Calendar and where the Secondary Ledger is maintained in Corporate COA or Corporate Calendar. Balances are transferred from Primary to Secondary Ledger using the Balance Transfer feature. This Secondary Ledger is included in the Consolidation Ledger Set for reporting.

Cross-Ledger Balance Transfer

In this scenario, the Primary Subsidiary ledger is maintained in Local COA or Local Calendar and there is a separate Corporate Ledger, which is maintained in Corporate COA or Corporate Calendar. To consolidate corporate balances, Primary Subsidiary balances are translated to corporate currency using the Report Currency feature (as discussed in Chapter 6), and corporate currency balances are transferred from Primary to Corporate Ledger using the Balance Transfer feature.

Implementation Steps

Let us look at the high-level steps to be performed for this type of consolidation.

Step 1: Translate Balances to the Corporate Currency The first step is to translate non corporate currency Subsidiary Ledger balances to the corporate currency. This allows subsidiary corporate balances to be transferred into the target ledger.

Step 2: Create Chart of Accounts Mapping from Subsidiary Account Values to Corporate Chart of Account Values Create a Chart of Accounts mapping from subsidiary Chart of Accounts values to corporate Chart of Accounts values. This Chart of Accounts mapping information is used within Oracle to transfer amounts and balances from the source (subsidiary) ledger to the target (corporate) ledger. You would have seen an introduction to the Chart of Accounts mapping feature in Chapter 6.

Step 3: Run Balance Transfer Program Oracle provides two programs to transfer balances from one ledger to another to handle both Scenarios 1 and 2 discussed earlier in the Balance Transfer Consolidation section.

- Transfer Balances to Secondary Ledger Program: This program allows balances to be transferred from the Primary Ledger to Secondary Ledger. This program is applicable for the Primary to Secondary Ledger Balance Transfer Consolidation scenario.

- Transfer Ledger Balances Program: This program allows balance transfers from one ledger to another ledger, as long as the Chart of Accounts mapping exists between those ledgers. This is applicable for the Cross-Ledger Consolidation scenario.

NOTE
Balance Transfer Program names are listed as per the Release 8 version of Fusion Applications. If the Balance Transfer Program ran multiple times for a single period from Primary to Secondary/target ledger, make sure that the previously run Balance Transfer Journals are reversed successfully to avoid double booking of balances. The reason is that the Balance Transfer program will select all journals for the given period from Primary Ledger to Secondary/target ledger for transfer.

Step 4: Create Elimination Entries and Create Adjustment Entries The next step is to generate Elimination entries and Adjustment entries as per the reporting needs in the Consolidation ledger.

Step 5: Generate Report Generate a consolidated statement, including Eliminations and Adjustment balances.

Oracle Fusion Hyperion Financial Management Consolidations

Oracle Hyperion Financial Management (HFM), Fusion Edition is a separate software application from Oracle used primarily for the purpose of complex consolidation and reporting. You may choose to use HFM if you would like to take advantage of HFM's powerful feature to consolidate balances from different data sources of General Ledgers, including Fusion General Ledger and previous versions of Oracle E-Business Suite, as well as non-Oracle applications like SAP. HFM also allows drill-down of balances from HFM to source systems. As with Balance Transfer Consolidation, implementation users would need to map the source Chart of Accounts and Hierarchies to HFM to perform advanced consolidation. Standard Oracle Financial Data Quality Management ERP Integrator Adapter can be leveraged to bring balances from Fusion General Ledger to HFM. The setup and configuration of HFM with respect to Oracle Fusion Financials is beyond the scope of this book; however, this section is included in this chapter for completeness of different consolidation options that implementation users can consider.

Comparison of Report-Only Consolidation and Balance Transfer Consolidation

In this section we will explain the advantages and disadvantages of Report-Only Consolidation versus Balance Transfer Consolidation.

Advantages and Disadvantages of Report-Only Consolidation

These are the advantages of Report-Only Consolidation:

■ Provides near-real-time consolidation of balances, as this consolidation doesn't require running of Balance Transfer program steps like the Balance Transfer Consolidation method.

■ Eliminates the need to run additional processes unless the ledgers have a different currency than the consolidation currency.

■ Facilitates a faster period-close process, as the consolidation process is relatively simple.

This is the disadvantage of Report-Only Consolidation:

■ Requires a standardized Chart of Accounts or Global Chart of Accounts and Calendar for the subsidiaries and corporate ledgers in order to group ledgers into a set of ledgers.

Advantages and Disadvantages of Balance Transfer Consolidation

This is the advantage of Balance Transfer Consolidation:

■ Ability to consolidate even when the Chart of Accounts and Calendars of the subsidiaries and corporate ledgers are different.

These are the disadvantages of Balance Transfer Consolidation:

■ May be necessary to define a separate consolidation ledger; or the existing parent ledger can act as a consolidation ledger. Need to transfer subsidiary balances to that consolidation ledger for reporting.

■ If the subsidiary ledger currency is different from the consolidation currency, then we need to run the Translation process first to convert balances to the consolidation currency and then run the Balance Transfer process to transfer subsidiary balances to the consolidation ledger.

■ Additional effort to maintain Chart of Accounts mapping.

■ The Balance Transfer program doesn't send an incremental update of balances from source ledger to target ledger. As a result, every time subsidiary ledger balances are changed, business users need to reserve all the earlier journals in the consolidation ledger and rerun the Balance Transfer process. If the subsidiary currency is different from the consolidation currency, additionally we need to run the Translation process before running the Balance Transfer program.

Consolidation for ACME Bank

In this section, readers will understand how different consolidation methods can be applied to meet ACME Bank's consolidation requirements.

Requirements

Requirement 10.1: ACME Bank has many subsidiary legal entities as part of its reporting structure, as shown in Figure 10-4. ACME Bank Group Company needs to consolidate balances from its subsidiaries from Japan, Latin America, United States of America (USA), and United Kingdom (UK). ACME Bank needs to prepare financial statements in US GAAP and eliminate all intercompany journal entries. In addition, it should include

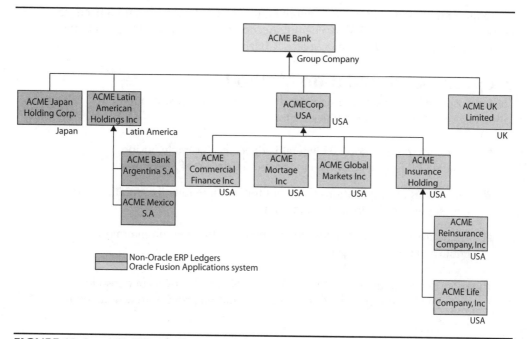

FIGURE 10-4. *ACME Bank Group reporting structure*

financial figures of partly owned companies or non controlling interests (an ownership stake in a company where the held position gives the investor no influence on how the company is run) held under the group company.

Requirement 10.2: Both ACME Japan Holding Corp and ACME Latin American Holdings Inc are using non-Oracle ERP General Ledgers with their own localized Chart of Accounts and Calendar. Balances from these companies need to be consolidated to ACME Bank Group Company on a quarterly basis.

Requirement 10.3: ACMECorp USA (part of Fusion Implementation) needs to consolidate balances of its subsidiaries for both management reporting and legal reporting purposes. This consolidation should include ACME Insurance Holding Company, which has its own ledger with a different Chart of Accounts than the Globalized ACME Chart of Accounts. It has been agreed that this consolidation will happen on a monthly basis inline with a monthly management review cycle. Additionally, consolidated figures of ACMECorp USA in US GAAP (Generally Accepted Accounting Principles) need to be reported to ACME Bank Group company on a quarterly basis.

Requirement 10.4: ACME UK Limited (part of Fusion Implementation) needs to report its balances in US GAAP (Generally Accepted Accounting Principles) to the ACME Bank Group Company on a quarterly basis.

Proposed Consolidation Method

The proposed ACME Bank consolidation should take into consideration the following aspects of the legal entity structure:

- There are multiple source General Ledgers (both Oracle Fusion and non-Oracle ERP ledgers) involved in the consolidation of ACME Bank.

- Within Fusion Applications, legal entities are spread across multiple ledgers with a different Chart of Accounts structure.

- There are local consolidation requirements within certain intermediate legal entities like ACME Corp USA.

The proposed structure for ACME Bank consists of three levels of consolidation as shown in Figure 10-5. The details of the consolidation process are explained in

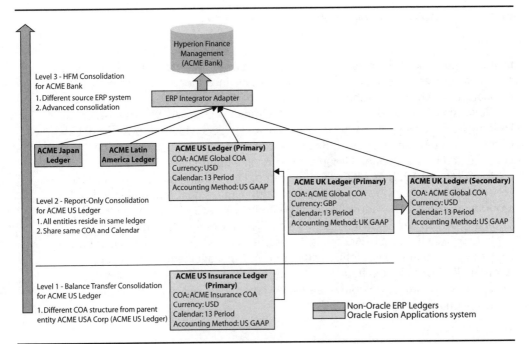

FIGURE 10-5. *Proposed ACME Bank consolidation structure*

the following sections in a bottom-up approach from Level 1 to Level 3, leading to the consolidation of ACME Bank Group Company.

Level 1 Consolidation Using the Balance Transfer Method

The legal entity ACME Insurance Holdings residing in ACME US Ledger needs to bring balances across from ACME Insurance companies. Because both source and target ledgers are using a different Chart of Accounts structure and the requirement is to consolidate on the balance level, the Balance Transfer Method of consolidation will be used. Later in the chapter, we will look at how to set up this type of consolidation in detail.

Level 2 Consolidation Using Report Only

ACMECorp USA represents a consolidated entity of all the companies operating in the United States. Because we have balances from all the U.S. companies in a single ledger, ACME US Ledger, we can easily generate consolidated statements using the Report-Only Consolidation method.

Level 3 Consolidation Using HFM Consolidation

ACME Bank Group Company needs to consolidate balances from different general ledgers (Oracle and non-Oracle ERP) across different countries like the United States, the United Kingdom, Japan, and Latin America. Because not all companies use a Global COA structure, and many entities have complex ownership and accounting requirements, the Hyperion Financial Management Consolidation method is used.

NOTE
This chapter covers only detailed steps of how to perform Level 1 Consolidation using the Balance Transfer method, as Oracle Hyperion Finance Management Consolidation (Level 3) configuration is beyond the scope of this book. Consolidation using the reporting solution (Level 2) is basically the creation of reports using the Fusion Financials reporting tool. Readers will understand how to create reports in Fusion Financials as part of Chapter 13.

Consolidation Using the Balance Transfer Method from ACME Insurance Ledger to ACME US Ledger

In this section, we will look at how to set up and perform consolidation for cross-ledgers.

Requirements

ACME US Ledger needs to consolidate ACME Insurance Ledger balances at the same level of detail as the Global COA. However, for consolidation purposes, they would not require Location Segment details from ACME Insurance Ledger. So the resulting mapping should be as shown in Figure 10-6.

Consolidation Steps

Based on Chapter 6, readers will have already created ACME Insurance Ledger and ACME US Ledger in Fusion. Let us now try to perform the necessary setup steps to consolidate balances between cross-ledgers using the Balance Transfer method.

Step 1: Transfer Balances to the Corporate Currency This step is not applicable in our case because ACME Insurance Ledger is already in the corporate USD currency.

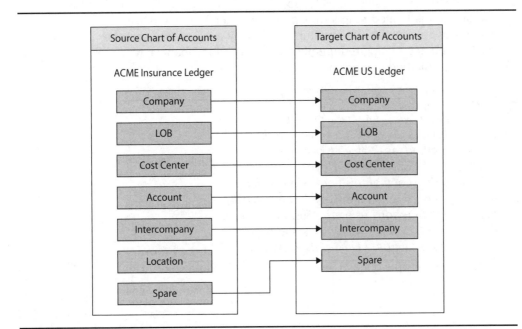

FIGURE 10-6. *Source to target Chart of Accounts mapping*

Step 2: Create Chart of Accounts Mapping from Subsidiary Account Values to Corporate Chart of Account Values   Note: Readers would have already been introduced to the concept of Chart of Accounts mapping in Chapter 6.

Steps to create Chart of Accounts mapping are as follows:

1. Navigate to the Manage Chart Of Accounts Mappings task under Define Chart Of Accounts.

2. Click the Create icon on the Manage Chart Of Accounts Mapping page.

3. Create a mapping from ACME Insurance COA instance (Source Chart of Accounts) to ACME Global COA Instance (Target Instance) as shown in Figure 10-7. We have created Segment Rules for each of the Target Segments and used the Copy Value From Source mapping method, as the segment values used are common across both the source and target COA.

Step 3: Run Balance Transfer Program

1. Create a few journals in ACME Insurance Ledger as described in Chapter 8.

2. Run the Transfer Ledger Balances program from the Scheduled Process page providing parameters for Source Ledger, Target Ledger, and Chart Of Accounts Mapping as shown in Figure 10-8.

3. After successfully running the transfer program, review consolidated journals created in ACME US Ledger. Optionally, create Elimination entries and Adjustment entries to complete the intermediate consolidation.

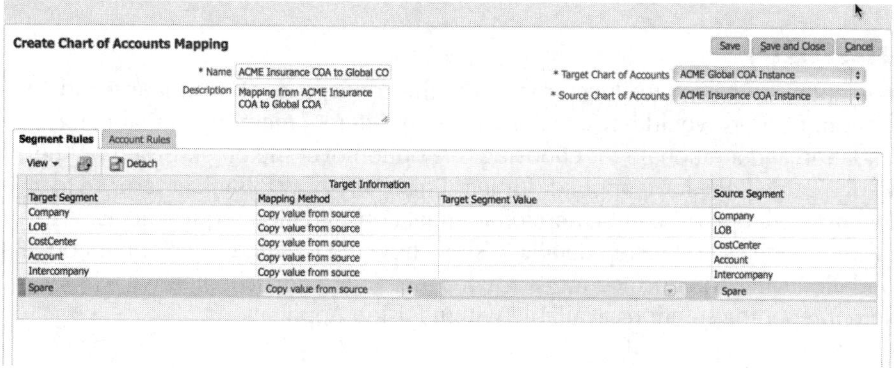

FIGURE 10-7.   *Segment rules mapping*

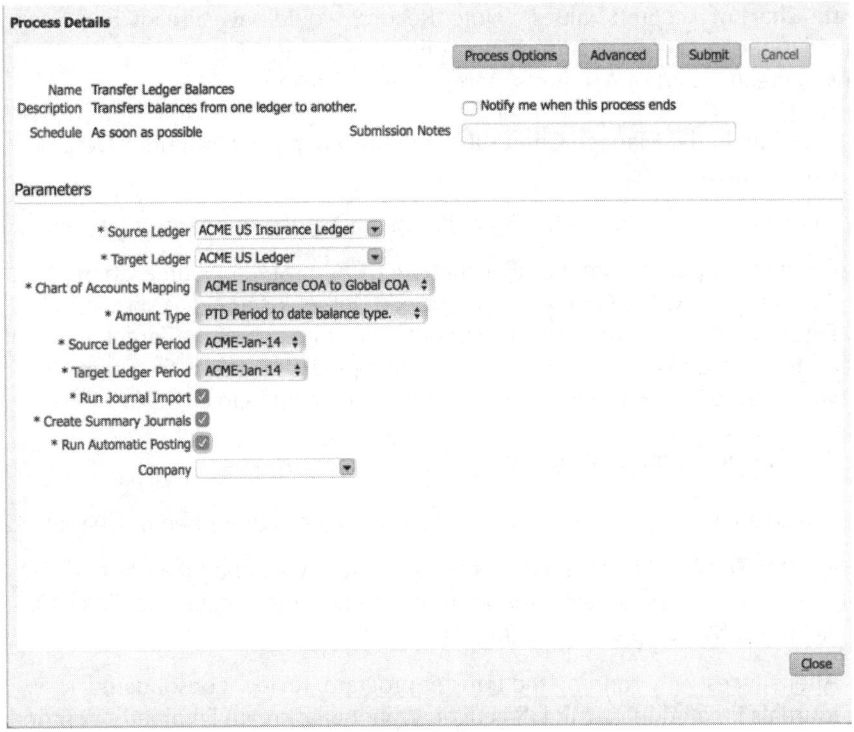

FIGURE 10-8. *Submitting the Transfer Ledger Balances program*

Summary

In this chapter, we have introduced readers to the concepts of consolidation and elimination. Readers would have also understood different methods available for consolidation and a rationale for choosing one option over the other. Based on the knowledge gained, we have applied our learning to the ACME Bank enterprise to see how different options can be applied to meet consolidation requirements. We have also provided step-by-step details to show how the Balance Transfer method of consolidation can be performed for ACME ledgers. In the next chapter, we will look at different reporting solutions available within Fusion Applications.

CHAPTER
11

Allocations Using
Calculation Manager

Geneneral Ledger allocations are components of the financial period closing cycle, along with revaluation, management of historical rates, and other activities that take place before, during, and after period close. Although the period-close process is covered in the chapters that follow, we felt that the readers will benefit from covering the subject of allocations on its own.

To that end, we'll go through an easy-to-follow, step-by-step example, but before we do that, we'll provide an overview of what allocations are and the business motivation for their use, as well as some technical and system architecture background required to understand what is underpinning the allocations' functionality.

Overview of GL Allocations

We often think of allocations as the process of cost sharing. For example, a business might allocate or spread the cost of a large item expense like an advertising campaign across multiple lines of business, departments, or cost centers that benefit from using that item (Figure 11-1). More broadly, in this book we are going to refer to allocation as the process of spreading of expenses or revenues across an organizational hierarchy like a group of cost centers, departments, divisions, and so on.

Here are a couple of examples related to the banking narrative discussed throughout this book. ACME Global Markets, Inc., may decide to bear the cost of development of a trading platform that will be used by its fixed income, foreign exchange, equity, and other trading teams. In our example organization structure, these trading teams belong to ACME Global Markets LOB (line of business) and they

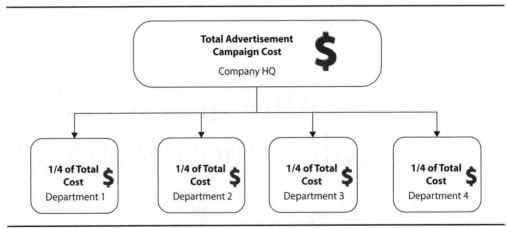

FIGURE 11-1. *Allocation of cost incurred at HQ divided equally across departments*

are also assigned to individual cost centers. In order to hold cost center and LOB managers more accountable for profit and loss, the company's management may decide to track the trading platform development on the cost center level by proportionally allocating the cost of development to individual cost centers associated with different trading teams. The proportionality of allocations can be based on previously agreed criteria such as turnover, headcount, or even a complex formula-based calculation.

The allocations do not necessarily have to be cost related. For example, the previously mentioned trading teams may need to be allocated trading funds at the beginning of each accounting period from a central trading pool of funds. They use these funds to carry out their trading activities, but in order to manage the risks, the management may decide to allocate the trading funds to the individual teams based on the trading team's experience, past performance, volatility of returns, and other criteria, with the aim of reducing the risk. This is a slightly different use case than cost allocation, but the pattern is still the same; we traverse an organizational hierarchy with the aim of allocating the funds based on defined criteria from some account that is controlled centrally.

Business Motivation for Using Allocations

Cost management is an activity typically associated with business operations on LOB, department, and cost center levels. In today's world of somewhat stalled top-line growth, there is an ever-increasing need for efficient cost management, and both finance and IT play important roles in capturing adequate data for analysis.

As we have seen in the previous section, there are also other types of allocations that are good candidates for automation, and business drivers for allocation can vary from risk management to various types of reporting requirements.

The allocation procedures can be very complex, and executing that process manually can be not only just cumbersome and slow, but also prone to errors, which can have a profound impact on business reporting efficiency and accuracy.

Automation of the allocation process can contribute to a greater efficiency, as well as enforcing the governance of applying the allocation rules as per agreed-upon business strategy and goals. IT and finance departments are typically responsible to deploy, make operational, and administer automated allocation processes. The role of technology is very important, and products like Fusion Financials come with out-of-the box tools to help companies avoid relying on offline tools for allocations such as spreadsheets.

Relationship to Allocations' Functionality in Other Oracle Products

Most ERP products out there have functionality to generate recurring and allocation GL journals. In Oracle E-Business Suite (EBS), the corresponding allocation functionality is referred to as Mass Allocations, while in Oracle Enterprise Performance Management (formerly Hyperion EPM), allocations are set up in the Calculation Manager module.

In Fusion Financials, EPM Calculation Manager is incorporated in the technology stack and completely replaces EBS Mass Allocations. In some Oracle documentation and articles, this functionality is also referred to as Allocation Manager; whatever the name, the bottom line is that generation of allocations in Fusion Financials now leverages Oracle Essbase, and from a technology standpoint it is very different in comparison to EBS.

In this chapter we'll go through a detailed example of allocation journal definition and generation, but before we do that, let's brush up on some key technology and Essbase concepts.

The Allocations Process and Oracle Essbase Cube

Fusion General Ledger leverages Oracle Essbase, which was known as Hyperion Essbase, to store balances in a multidimensional database (MDB). MDBs are often used to build analytic applications that support multidimensional queries, often referred to as online analytical processing (OLAP).

However, balances and journal entries are also processed, generated, and stored in Oracle Relational Database using a more traditional online transaction processing (OLTP) approach. In Fusion Financials, most reporting activities are performed against GL Essbase cubes rather than relational tables in Oracle Database.

The reason for this hybrid architectural approach is that balances in Essbase can be preaggregated on every dimension level and hierarchy, which allows accounting data to be analyzed more quickly using numerous analytical tools from the Hyperion product offerings. For example, end users can perform a slice-and-dice type of data analysis using the Hyperion Smart View add-on in Microsoft Excel or directly in Fusion General Ledger application screens.

NOTE
The detailed technical reasoning behind architectural choices is outside the scope of this book. Reporting will be covered in subsequent chapters and will give more insight into how Fusion Financials leverages Hyperion, Fusion Middleware, and the Oracle Database tech stack.

High-Level Allocation Journals Generation Process Flow

In previous chapters we mentioned that when we configure and create a general ledger in the Fusion General Ledger application, an Essbase cube automatically gets created for each combination of CoA instance and Accounting Calendar as defined in the GL setup.

From a technical perspective, the process of generating allocation journals is different than in Oracle E-Business Suite in that it is driven by Hyperion Calculation Manager and Allocation Engine as depicted in Figure 11-2. Preaggregated balances in Essbase Cube serve as the source for generation of allocation journals, and integration with Enterprise Scheduler Service (ESS) jobs to import and post journals back into Oracle Relational Database is seamless and doesn't require manual intervention.

Multidimensional View of GL Balances

In this section we'll just briefly review some key Oracle Essbase concepts applicable for OLAP-oriented databases and relate those concepts to Fusion General Ledger.

Essbase is a general-purpose multidimensional database developed to address the scalability issues associated with spreadsheet software. Figure 11-3 illustrates this concept; for example, we consider financial data like product and/or services

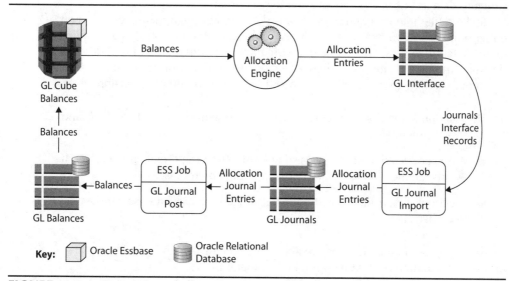

FIGURE 11-2. *Generation of allocation GL journals in Fusion General Ledger*

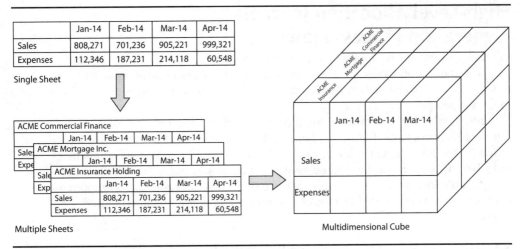

FIGURE 11-3. *Multidimensional view of financial data*

sales and expenses across accounting periods Jan-14 to Mar-14 recorded in a single spreadsheet. If we need to break down the same data across different legal entities like ACME Insurance Holding, ACME Mortgage Inc, and ACME Commercial Finance, then we have multiple spreadsheets, which starts looking like a cube. This gives rise to the idea of multidimensional databases like Oracle Essbase that structure data as the end user uses it in the real world.

In the multidimensional model, data is described through measures based on dimensions that represent facts. The individual values that dimensions are made up of are called *members,* and they can be organized to form hierarchies to describe different structural relationships between members within a dimension.

In our example from Figure 11-3, the cube consists of three dimensions:

- Accounting Periods dimension consisting of Jan-14, Feb-14, Mar-14, and Apr-14 members.

- Legal Entities dimension consisting of ACME Commercial Finance, ACME Mortgage Inc, and ACME Insurance Holding members.

- Account dimension consisting of Sales Account and Expenses Account members.

The measures in the GL cube are account balances, which in Fusion GL are updated in real time by the GL Journal Post program.

Typical operations in a multidimensional data model are

- **Slice and dice**   Defines a subcube data selection; for example, expense account balances for ACME Mortgage Inc company (legal entity) during the Jan-14 and Feb-14 accounting periods. If we select a member from a dimension (for example, ACME Mortgage Inc), the remaining two dimensions (natural account and accounting period in this example) define a spreadsheet, also known as slice. On the other hand, if we select a range of legal entity members like ACME Commercial Finance, ACME Mortgage Inc, and ACME Insurance Holding members along with the remaining two dimensions (natural account and accounting period), the selection defines a subcube, also known as dice, with dimensions restricted to a selected range of members.

- **Roll-up and drill-down**   Defines aggregation of data within the dimension hierarchy. For example, a financial year consists of four quarters and individual accounting period members like Jan-14, Feb-14, and Mar-14, which can be rolled up into Q1-14. Rolling up summarizes the data by walking the dimension hierarchy upward, while drill-down is the reverse of roll-up. In drill-down we walk down the hierarchy from less detailed to more detailed data (for example, Q1-14 -> Jan-14, Feb-14, Mar-14, and so on).

In Table 11-1 we list for reference purposes the GL cube dimensions that are available in Fusion GL and documented in the *Oracle Fusion Applications Financials Implementation Guide* for creating financial reports and allocations using Essbase multidimensional cubes.

In the next section we'll go through a detailed example of sample allocation creation and generation.

Dimension	Description
Accounting Period	Based on the calendar of the ledger or ledger set. Report on years, quarters, or periods.
Ledger or Ledger Set	Used to select a ledger for reporting. Multiple ledgers may be in the same cube if they share a common Chart of Accounts.
Chart of Accounts Segments	Uses a separate dimension for each of the segments from the Chart of Accounts. Organized by hierarchy. A default hierarchy is provided that includes all detail segment values. Hierarchies published in the Publish Account Hierarchies user interface are included.

TABLE 11-1.   *List of Dimensions in GL Cube as Documented in Oracle Product Documentation (Continued)*

Dimension	Description
Scenario	Indicates if the balances represented are actual or budget amounts. Allocation-related dimensions are seeded members and required for allocation solutions. Allocation dimensions are not used directly by end users.
	Budget scenario dimension members are user defined in the Oracle Fusion Applications value set called Accounting Scenario and appear in the cube after running the Create Scenario Dimension Members process.
Balance Amount	Indicates if the value is the opening balance, period activity, or closing balance. Debit, Credit, and Net amounts are available for reporting.
Amount Type	Indicates whether the amounts represent Base, Period to Date, Quarter to Date, or Year to Date.
Currency	Used to select the desired currency for the balances.
Currency Type	Used to select the currency type of the balances (for example, Currency or Statistical).

TABLE 11-1. *List of Dimensions in GL Cube as Documented in Oracle Product Documentation*

Step-by-Step Example

Our example will demonstrate how to create an allocation rule and generate corresponding allocation journals. Before going through the setup, let's define the business requirements for the exercise.

Business Requirements and Accounts Setup

ACME Global Markets USA line of business has four departments that are also separate cost centers along with the Central Trading cost center, which is designated as a central pool:

- Central Trading (Cost Center 8000)

- Fixed Income Trading (Cost Center 8100)

- Foreign Exchange Trading (Cost Center 8200)

- Commodities Trading (Cost Center 8300)

- Equity Trading (Cost Center 8400)

All trading departments use the same software platform for their trading activities, and management decided to divide the license fee cost based on the number of employees in each department. To meet that requirement, the finance department created the following natural accounts: 57360 (Expense Related to Trading Software License), 79000 (Trading Software Licenses), and 19000 (Cash Account).

Account 79000 is defined as a statistical account to hold the department headcount.

NOTE
Fusion General Ledger lets us maintain statistical as well as monetary balances in an account. In our example, the account combination 13.201.8100.79000.00.00000 is assigned Debit (DR) value 10 to represent the headcount in the Fixed Income Trading department.

Finance department accountants came up with the following accounting journal transactions required for allocations:

		Entered		
Line	Account	Debit	Credit	Description
1	13.201.8100.79000.00.00000	10		Licenses used in Fixed Income Trading Department
2	13.201.8200.79000.00.00000	20		Licenses used in Foreign Exchange Trading Department
3	13.201.8300.79000.00.00000	30		Licenses used in Commodities Trading Department
4	13.201.8400.79000.00.00000	40		Licenses used in Equity Trading Department

		Entered		
Line	Account	Debit	Credit	Description
1	13.201.8000.57360.00.00000	300,000.00		License Costs booked to Central Trading
2	13.201.8000.19000.00.00000		300,000.00	Cash paid via Bank

Bottom of Form

Line	Account	Entered Debit	Credit	Description
1	13.201.8000.57360.00.00000		300,000.00	Offset against Central Trading pool account
2	13.201.8100.57360.00.00000	30,000.00		License costs booked to Fixed Income Trading Department
3	13.201.8200.57360.00.00000	60,000.00		License costs booked to Foreign Exchange Trading Department
4	13.201.8300.57360.00.00000	90,000.00		License costs booked to Commodities Trading Department
5	13.201.8400.57360.00.00000	120,000.00		License costs booked to Equity Trading Department

After completing the allocation setup, we should post the following journal entries and test the setup:

Line	Account	Entered Debit	Credit	Description
1	13.201.8000.57360.00.00000	300,000.00		License costs booked to Central Trading
2	13.201.8000.19000.00.00000		300,000.00	Cash paid via Bank

Cost Center Hierarchy Creation Prerequisite

Before creating an allocation rule using Calculation Manager, we need to create a cost center hierarchy to encompass cost centers 8100, 8200, 8300, and 8400 under a parent value that we arbitrarily called "TRAD."

Prior to creating the hierarchy, we create the value TRAD in the ACME Cost Centre value set code.

To do that, we go to the Manage Value Set task, query and select the ACME Cost Centre value set, click the Manage Values button, and make sure that the TRAD value is created with the Summary attribute set to Yes as shown in Figure 11-4.

To define account hierarchies, we use the Manage Trees And Tree Versions task. Here we create the ACME Cost Centre tree as illustrated in Figure 11-5.

After creation the tree needs to be audited (online audit is OK for this exercise) and set to Active status from the Actions menu.

Now we go to the Publish Account Hierarchies task, select ACME Cost Centre (Version1) hierarchy, and publish it to an Essbase cube as shown in Figure 11-6.

We are now ready to proceed with allocation rule creation as per the business requirements.

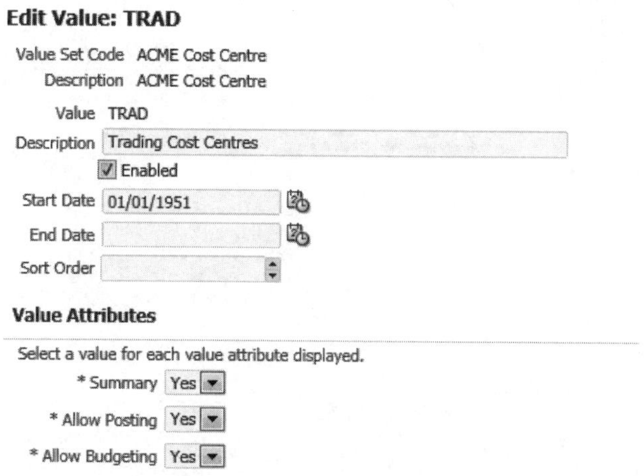

Edit Value: TRAD

Value Set Code   ACME Cost Centre
Description   ACME Cost Centre

Value   TRAD
Description   Trading Cost Centres
☑ Enabled
Start Date   01/01/1951
End Date
Sort Order

Value Attributes

Select a value for each value attribute displayed.
* Summary   Yes ▾
* Allow Posting   Yes ▾
* Allow Budgeting   Yes ▾

FIGURE 11-4.   *Parent value TRAD set up in ACME Cost Centre value set*

Allocation Rule Creation Walkthrough

Allocation rules are created in the EPM System Workspace application, which is fully embedded in Fusion Applications. There are different navigation paths to reach its user interface, and in our installation, we navigate to General Accounting Dashboard | Manage Journals | Create Allocation Rules. Once in EPM System Workspace, we click the Navigate menu item and hover the mouse pointer above the Application item until Calculation Manager appears.

TIP
You have to use Internet Explorer to use EPM System Workspace. In current releases, it is a bit tricky to select the Calculation Manager application; click the Navigate menu item, and hover the mouse pointer up and down until Calculation Manager shows up.

Expand ACMEGlobalCOAInstance as shown in Figure 11-7 and create an allocation rule by right-clicking Rules | New. This should result in the Rule Designer tool being open in your browser. Follow the steps outlined next to create a rule we called Test_Alloc_1 in this exercise:

1. In Rules Designer, in the New Objects section, drag and drop the Point Of View object between Begin and End nodes. Specify values for dimensions as shown in Figure 11-7.

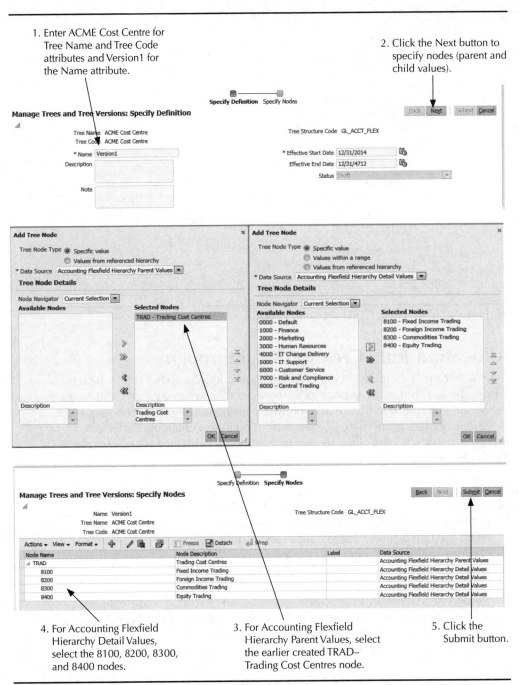

1. Enter ACME Cost Centre for Tree Name and Tree Code attributes and Version1 for the Name attribute.

2. Click the Next button to specify nodes (parent and child values).

4. For Accounting Flexfield Hierarchy Detail Values, select the 8100, 8200, 8300, and 8400 nodes.

3. For Accounting Flexfield Hierarchy Parent Values, select the earlier created TRAD–Trading Cost Centres node.

5. Click the Submit button.

FIGURE 11-5. *Creating the Cost Centre tree hierarchy*

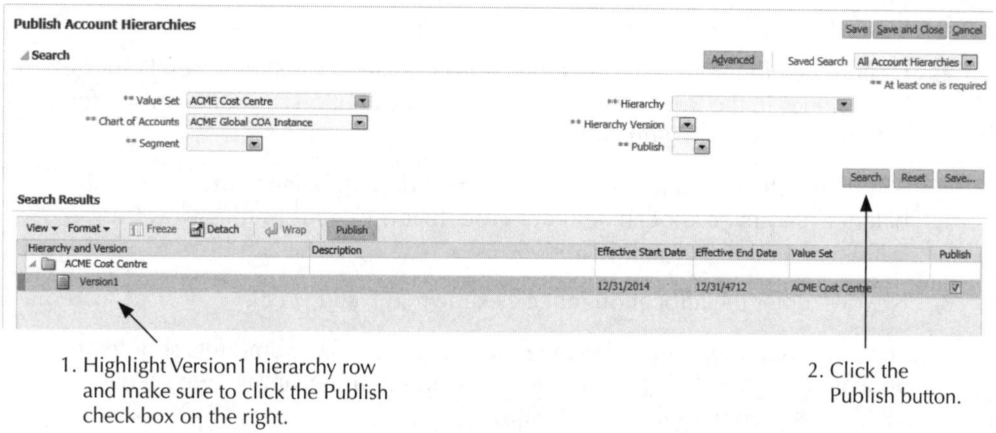

FIGURE 11-6. *Publishing the Cost Centre hierarchy*

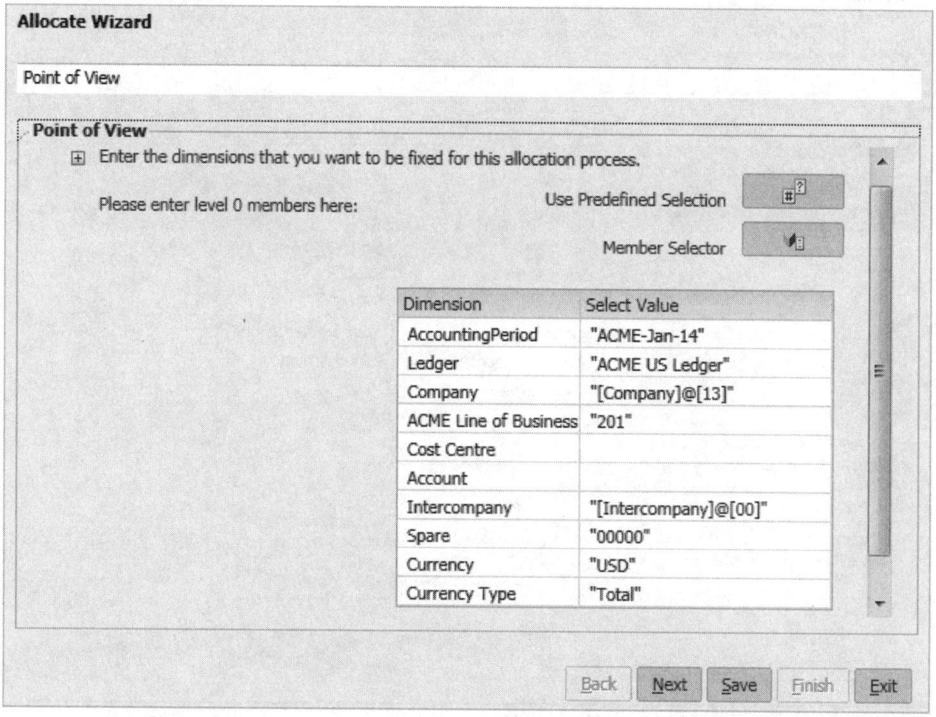

FIGURE 11-7. *Point of View values*

In Point Of View (POV) we define dimension values that remain fixed for this rule (see the previous section on cube operations).

2. Drag Allocation from the New Objects section and drop it between Point Of View nodes in the Rule Designer. Click the Next button and enter values for Source as shown in Figure 11-8.

   Source usually points to the central account or pool balance from which the balance amount is allocated. In our case, that is Central Trading Cost Centre 8000 and natural account 57360.

3. Next we enter the allocation range as shown in Figure 11-9.

   The allocation range specifies the range of values where amounts should be allocated. These values are parent values, and in our example, we specify TRAD Cost Centre as the parent value.

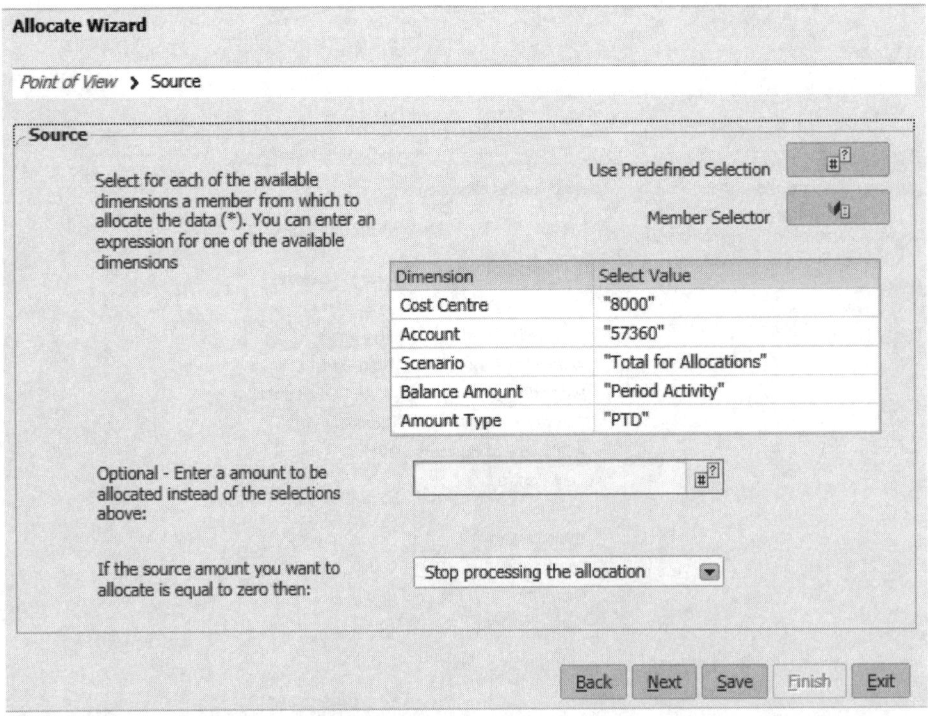

Allocate Wizard

Point of View > Source

Source

Select for each of the available dimensions a member from which to allocate the data (*). You can enter an expression for one of the available dimensions

Use Predefined Selection

Member Selector

Dimension	Select Value
Cost Centre	"8000"
Account	"57360"
Scenario	"Total for Allocations"
Balance Amount	"Period Activity"
Amount Type	"PTD"

Optional - Enter a amount to be allocated instead of the selections above:

If the source amount you want to allocate is equal to zero then: Stop processing the allocation

Back   Next   Save   Finish   Exit

FIGURE 11-8. *Source values in the Allocate Wizard*

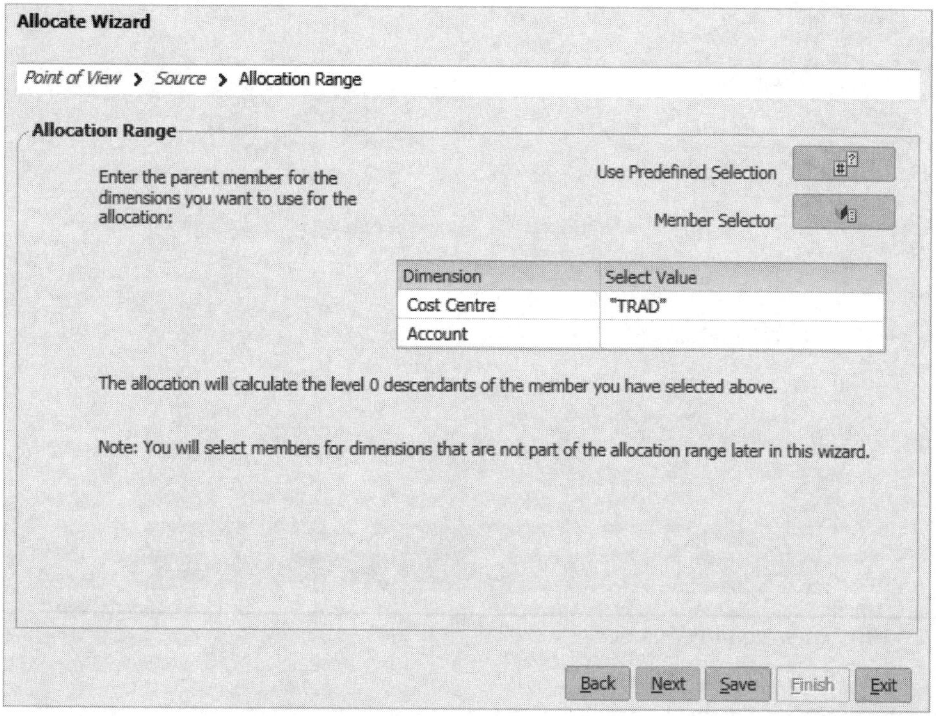

Allocate Wizard

Point of View **>** *Source* **>** Allocation Range

Allocation Range

Enter the parent member for the
dimensions you want to use for the
allocation:

Use Predefined Selection

Member Selector

Dimension	Select Value
Cost Centre	"TRAD"
Account	

The allocation will calculate the level 0 descendants of the member you have selected above.

Note: You will select members for dimensions that are not part of the allocation range later in this wizard.

Back   Next   Save   Finish   Exit

FIGURE 11-9.   *Entering the allocation range*

4. Next, we enter target values as shown in Figure 11-10.

    In our example, the target account is 57360. For expenses, the target is the debit side of the allocation.

5. Next, we enter an offset value as shown in Figure 11-11.

    Offset for expense allocations is the credit side of the transaction.

NOTE
*We are not excluding any members from the
allocation range; therefore, we skip the Exclude step.*

6. Next, we define the basis of the allocation as shown in Figure 11-12.

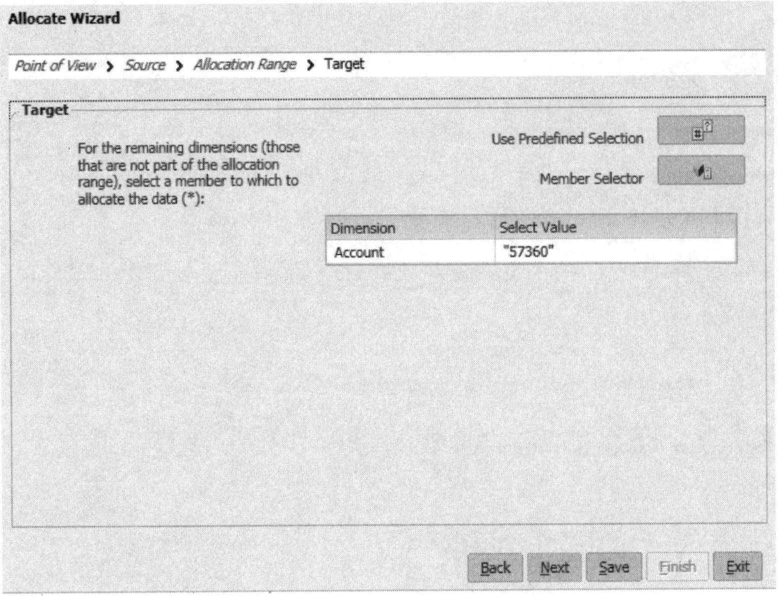

Allocate Wizard

Point of View ❯ *Source* ❯ *Allocation Range* ❯ Target

┌─ Target ──┐

For the remaining dimensions (those that are not part of the allocation range), select a member to which to allocate the data (*):

Use Predefined Selection

Member Selector

Dimension	Select Value
Account	"57360"

Back Next Save Finish Exit

FIGURE 11-10. *Entering target values*

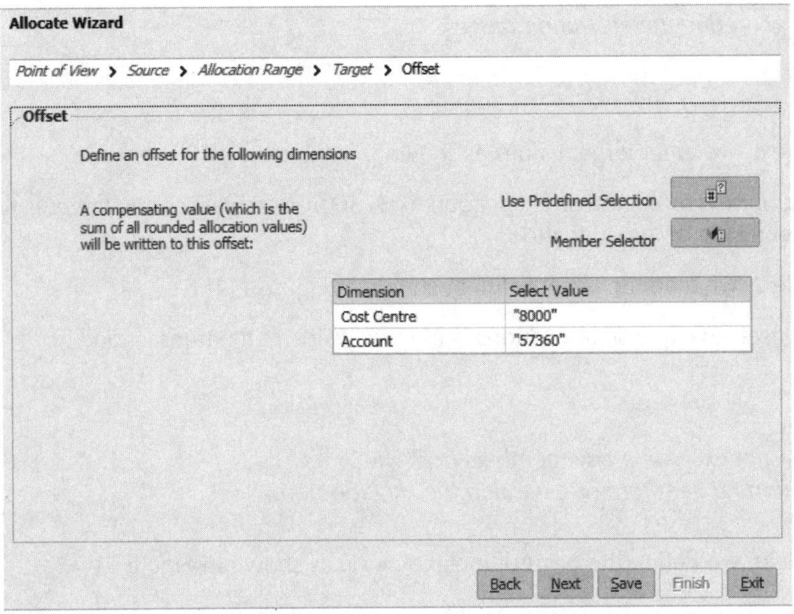

Allocate Wizard

Point of View ❯ *Source* ❯ *Allocation Range* ❯ *Target* ❯ Offset

┌─ Offset ──┐

Define an offset for the following dimensions

A compensating value (which is the sum of all rounded allocation values) will be written to this offset:

Use Predefined Selection

Member Selector

Dimension	Select Value
Cost Centre	"8000"
Account	"57360"

Back Next Save Finish Exit

FIGURE 11-11. *Entering offset values*

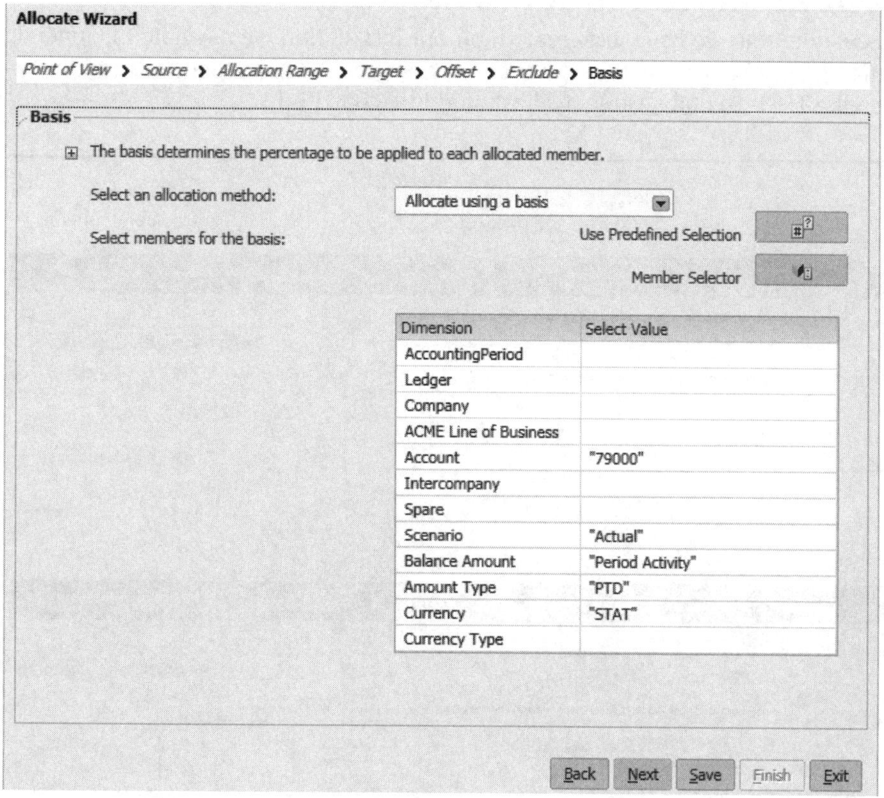

Allocate Wizard

Point of View > Source > Allocation Range > Target > Offset > Exclude > **Basis**

Basis

⊞ The basis determines the percentage to be applied to each allocated member.

Select an allocation method: Allocate using a basis   ▼

Select members for the basis: Use Predefined Selection   [⊞?]

                                                                   Member Selector   [🔳]

Dimension	Select Value
AccountingPeriod	
Ledger	
Company	
ACME Line of Business	
Account	"79000"
Intercompany	
Spare	
Scenario	"Actual"
Balance Amount	"Period Activity"
Amount Type	"PTD"
Currency	"STAT"
Currency Type	

[Back] [Next] [Save] [Finish] [Exit]

FIGURE 11-12. *Entering the basis for allocation*

In our example, the basis for allocation is statistical account 79000, where we keep the department headcount. Please note that Currency is defined as "STAT." We click the Next, Finish, and Save buttons and then Validate And Deploy. If there are no issues, the rule is deployed and ready to be used.

NOTE
We have hard-coded the AccountPeriod value to Jan-14, which is the only open period in our development instance. However, in the real world, you would create a run-time prompt variable that will allow you to pick an accounting period as required at run time.

Generate Allocation Journals

To execute the rule we have just created, on our installation we navigate to General Accounting Dashboard | Manage Journals | Generate General Ledger Allocations and run the TEST_ALLOC_1 rule as illustrated in Figure 11-13.

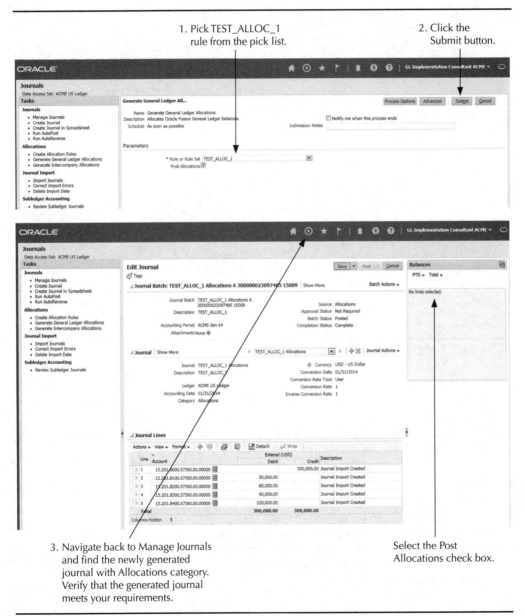

FIGURE 11-13. *Running the allocation rule and system-generated allocation journal*

Summary

In this chapter we provided an overview of allocations and the business motivation for using allocations in Fusion General Ledger. We anticipate that the readers with an Oracle E-Business Suite background will benefit from comparison to the Mass Allocation feature in that product, as well as a gentle introduction to Oracle Essbase basic concepts, as an introduction to the hands-on example at the end of this chapter.

CHAPTER
12

Period Close

I n this chapter we'll look at how we close accounting periods in Fusion Financials as part of the overall accounting cycle. At the beginning of each accounting period, which is typically a calendar month, such as January 2014, or even a calendar quarter or year, accounting departments look into the existing accounting books, put them into order, and close the prior accounting period before opening a new one. Each company or organization typically has its own period-close business process or checklist, which needs to be taken into consideration when implementing Fusion Financials or indeed any other ERP packaged system.

The team implementing Fusion Financials will look at the existing period-close process, optimize it, and agree with the customer on the future process before starting product configuration, taking into consideration the capabilities of the product. In large organizations, customers will usually nominate their own business analysts to work with the implementation team, going through existing spreadsheets and other supporting documents for the period end.

Period Close and Accounting Cycle Overview

Depending on a specific business's complexity during period close, there could be quite a bit of journal adjustments activity, reconciliations, revaluations, GL balances translation, consolidation, and other activities that are collectively referred to as the period-close process. Of course, these activities need to be performed in a certain order, and we'll touch on this at the end of this chapter.

Figure 12-1 illustrates activities part of a typical textbook monthly accounting cycle. Broadly speaking, steps such as Prepare Trial Balance, Journalize and Post Adjusting Entries, and Prepare Adjusted Trial Balance are all part of the month-end close-period process.

In the following sections, we'll provide a quick overview of some of the activities that happen during period close from an accounting perspective.

Trial Balance

The trial balance is a statement (accounting report), which shows balances (debits and credits) for all accounts in the General Ledger. Oracle Fusion Financials is a double-entry accounting system; therefore, every debit has a corresponding credit, and the total of all debits must equal the total of credit entries in the ledger.

Put simply, the trial balance is just a list of balances in all accounts. The purpose of preparing a trial balance report is to check the mathematical accuracy of the ledger accounts and posted transactions, locate deviations and errors (note that not all issues are always detected), and most importantly, provide a good basis for the preparation of final accounts.

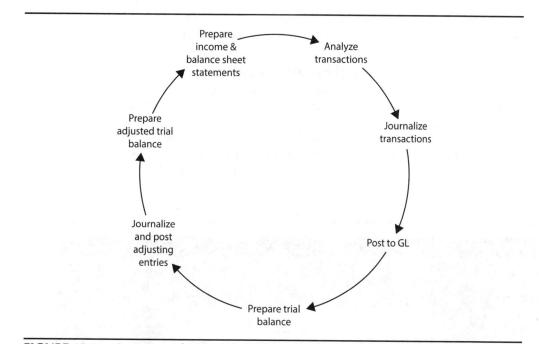

FIGURE 12-1. *Summary of typical monthly accounting cycle activities*

NOTE
In Oracle Fusion Financials, a trial balance report is run to provide summarized account balances and activity by ledger, balancing segment, and account segment value.

Accounting errors may or may not affect the trial balance. For example, a transaction journal that is posted in error to both credit and debit account sides may result in a trial balance that is not affected, and this type of problem can be rectified by posting an adjustment journal. On the other hand, a posted journal that affects one side of the account, resulting in a single-sided error, cannot be fixed by posting an adjustment journal with a single entry. In this situation the problem is fixed by creating a suspense account, which is a special kind of account "used temporarily to carry doubtful receipts and disbursements or discrepancies pending their analysis and permanent classification" (Wikipedia).

Surplus debit in one or more accounts is corrected by crediting the excess amount to the appropriate accounts, and surplus credit is corrected by debiting the excess amount to the respective accounts. Likewise, short debits (or credits) are corrected by "additionally" debiting (or crediting) the respective accounts.

An Example: Running a Trial Balance Report

Just to get a feeling for what the trial balance report looks like in Fusion Applications, we are going to run it for ACME US Ledger and accounting period ACME-Mar-14.

For example, the report can be run by going to Navigator | Tools | Scheduled Processes | Schedule New Process and searching for Trial Balance Report. Figure 12-2 shows the parameters we pass prior to running the report.

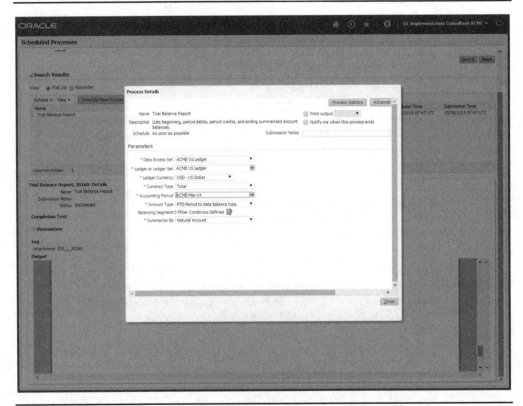

FIGURE 12-2. *Selecting parameters for the trial balance report*

If you recall from Chapter 11 where we discussed allocations, we posted the following journal entries in the period March 2014:

		Entered		
Line	Account	Debit	Credit	Description
1	13.201.8000.57360.00.00000	300,000.00		License Costs booked to Central Trading
2	13.201.8000.19000.00.00000		300,000.00	Cash paid via Bank

Incidentally, the said journal was posted twice, and Figure 12-3 shows the result of running the trial balance report for that period, and a reconciliation of the trial balance to the license costs physically paid would highlight this duplication, which could then be resolved via a journal entry.

Many activities during the period close involve one or more types of adjustments, which are required to be applied for various reasons. In the next section, we'll briefly remind ourselves what the purpose of adjustments is before looking into an example of how to configure and automate the components of the period-close process.

Adjustment Entries

In order for both the revenues and expenses to be recorded in the period in which a business provided services and incurred expenses, some adjustment journal entries need to be made to ensure that the revenue recognition and expense recognition accounting principles are adhered to.

Accounting adjustments are broadly categorized as deferrals and accruals. An example of a deferral is unearned revenue, which is cash received before a business performs services. Likewise, an example of an accrual is accrued revenue, which is revenues for services performed by the business but not received in cash yet.

To illustrate the concept of adjustment entries, let us consider a trading department requirement within our fictional ACME Global Markets USA line of business. It is a common practice by trading firms involved in what is known in financial centers like Wall Street and the City of London as high frequency trading (HFT) to have access to computers physically co-located where trading exchange computers are hosted. This service is often outsourced, and here is how we could account for it.

On this occasion ACME Bank's finance department uses the following accounts: 57361–Expense related to high frequency trading hardware and 79111–Prepaid platform as a cloud service (PaaS). On January 2015, ACME Global Markets USA makes a one-year subscription payment of $120,000 for a cloud service that hosts co-located computer servers required for HFT. Subscription coverage started in January and was paid in advance for a full year. On January 31 the account 79111

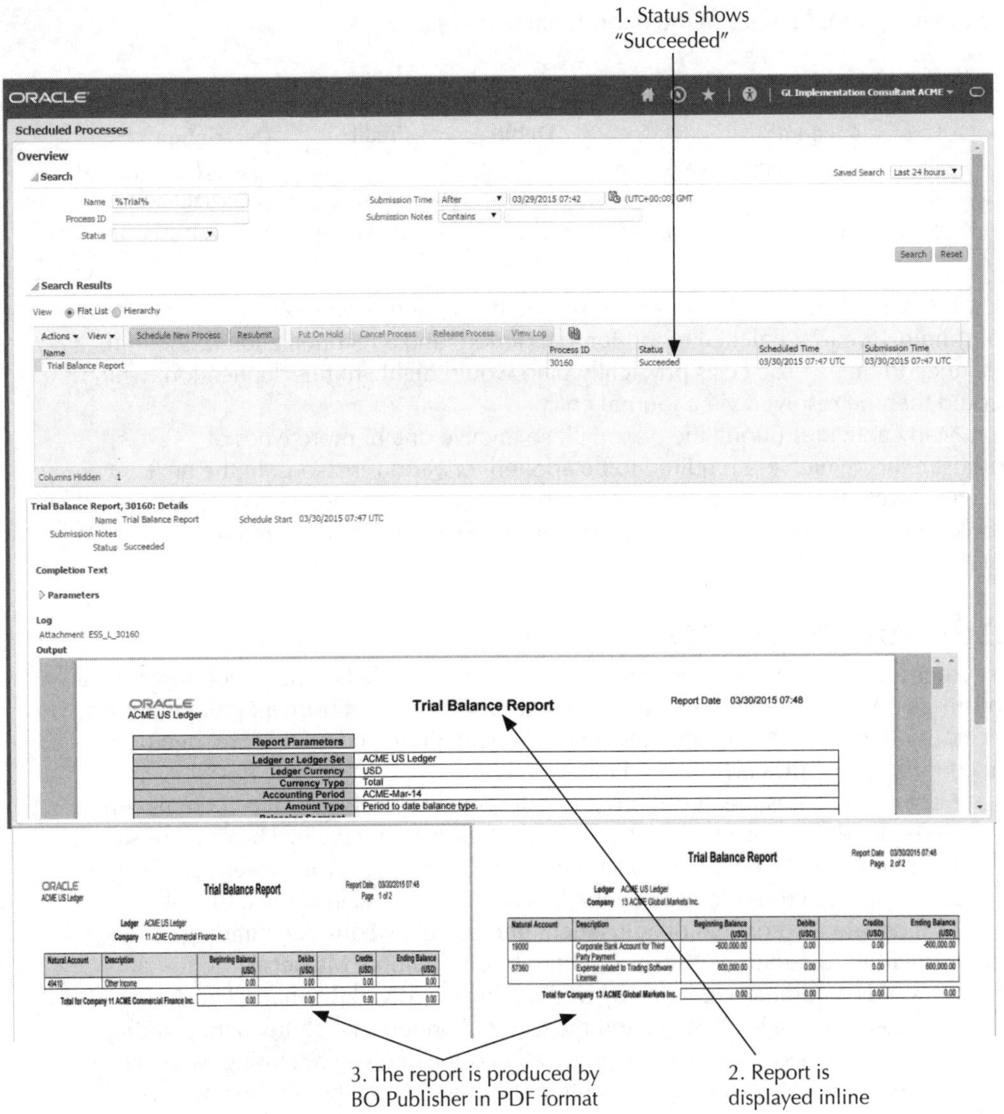

FIGURE 12-3. *Trial balance report for March 2014 period*

shows a trial balance of $120,000. But the actual monthly subscription is $12,000 and needs to be accounted for each month.

The monthly subscription for the prepaid service decreases an asset each month (Account 79111–Prepaid platform as a cloud service). At the same time, owners' equity decreases by debiting expense account 57361–Expense related to high frequency trading hardware. To create an adjustment journal, on January 31 we debit expense account 57361 $12,000 and credit the prepaid PaaS account 79111.

If we didn't perform this adjustment, ACME Global Markets USA would understate expenses in January by $12,000 and at the same time overstate income by the same amount. Additionally, both owners' equity and assets would have been overstated by $12,000 on the balance sheet produced on January 31.

NOTE
The need for adjustment transactions and journals can arise for a vast variety of reasons, but any in-depth accounting is outside the scope of this book. We merely mention the accounting examples to put the components and activities of the period close into context for readers who are either not coming from an accounting background or require a quick refresher on some very basic accounting concepts.

Adjustments can be entered manually using standard Fusion Financials functionality (for example, Manage Journals, Create Journal, Create Journal in Spreadsheet), but can also be automated using Allocations Manager to generate recurring journals and other techniques.

In the following section we'll cover in more detail a particular type of transaction that concerns journals and balances in foreign currencies. These transactions can also require adjustments, and we'll see how this process is automated in Fusion Applications.

Dealing with Foreign Currency Balances: Revaluations and Translations

Generally accepted accounting practices such as SFAS 52 in the United States (SFAS stands for Statement of Financial Accounting Standards, or its international equivalent IAS 21) provide guidelines and mandate how to deal with foreign currency translations and revaluations. The primary objectives of translations and revaluations according to these rules are that they "should provide information disclosing effects of rate changes on enterprise cash flows and equity; should also provide information in consolidated statements as to financial results and relationships of individual consolidated entities measured in their respective functional currencies in accordance with US GAAP" (Wiley CPA Excel Exam Review 2014 Study Guide, Financial Accounting and Reporting).

Put simply, in the context of Fusion Apps, revaluation is a process of adjusting the accounted value of foreign currency–denominated balances as per current conversion foreign exchange (FX) rates. On the other hand, translation is a process of converting the accounted balances from one currency, say USD, to another reporting currency (for example, GBP).

Both revaluations and translations are run as part of the period-close procedure, and the details of how this is done are specific to each organization that implements Fusion Financials. Let us take a look at an example revaluation from a system configuration perspective.

An Example: Configuring Revaluations

The example in this section will assume that some transactions are posted in ACME US Ledger for the period Mar-14. We will illustrate those transactions and show the resulting revaluation journals.

The previous statement implies that revaluation journal entries are a type of adjustments performed at period close. The resulting revaluation adjustment journals are usually reversed at the next accounting period. Because this is done to adjust the accounts that may be overstated or understated at month end, we perform revaluation adjustments usually for reporting purposes and therefore have to reverse the effects of them at the beginning of the next period, which is functionality provided by Fusion Financials.

Figure 12-4 shows a sample journal entered in British Pounds Sterling (GBP). The entered £10,000 debit and credit are converted at the FX conversion rate 1.429,

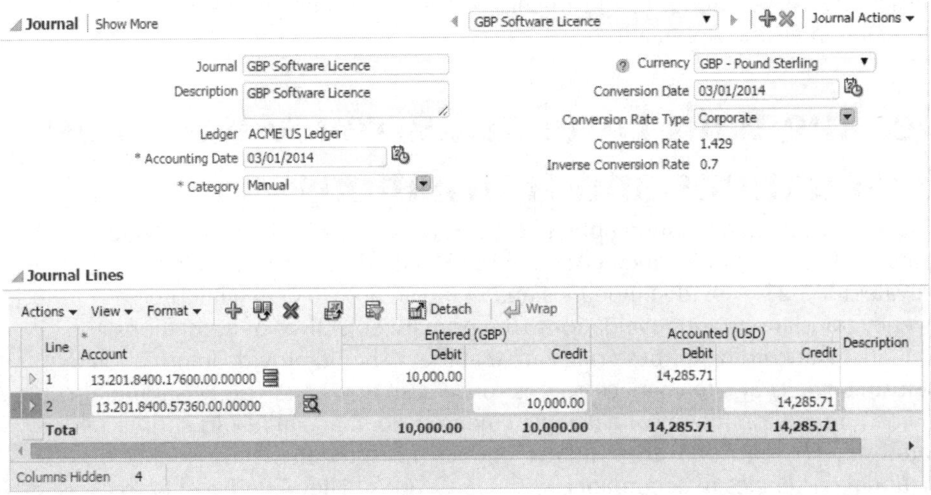

FIGURE 12-4. *Sample journal entered in British pounds (GBP)*

which is the daily rate entered for 03/01/2014 as part of the Manage Currency Rates functionality in Fusion Financials.

By 03/31/2014, the FX conversion rate plummeted to 1.25, and we will perform a revaluation process to account for the FX conversion rate change between those days.

The Manage Revaluations task can be defined as part of the Define Period Close Components | Manage Revaluations task. Figure 12-5 shows an example ACME FX revaluation configuration.

As per the Fusion Financials Implementation Guide, all debit adjustments are offset against the unrealized gain account, and all credit adjustments are offset against the unrealized loss account. If the same account is specified in the Unrealized Gain Account and Unrealized Loss Account fields, the net of the adjustments is derived and posted. In our example, Unrealized Gain Account and Unrealized Loss Account are the same.

NOTE
Realized income or losses refer to profits or losses from completed transactions. Unrealized profit or losses refer to profits or losses that have occurred on paper, but the relevant transactions have not been completed.

In addition to other configuration items such as Name, Description, Chart of Accounts, and so on that are self-explanatory, configuration of revaluations requires accounts of interest to be added by specifying filter conditions (Change Filter Conditions icon) as illustrated in Figure 12-6.

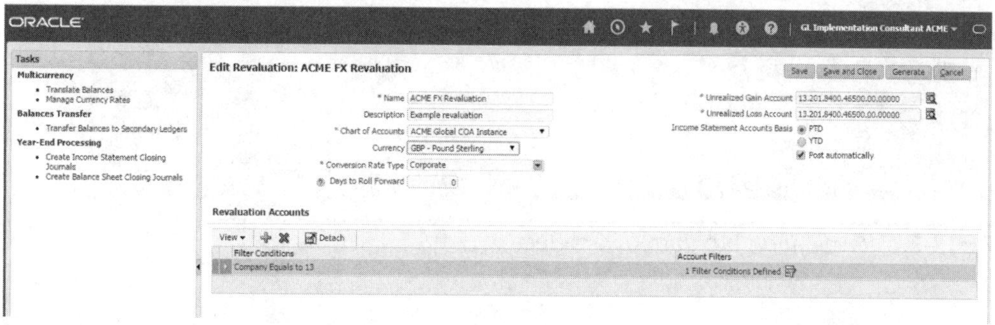

FIGURE 12-5. *Example revaluation configuration*

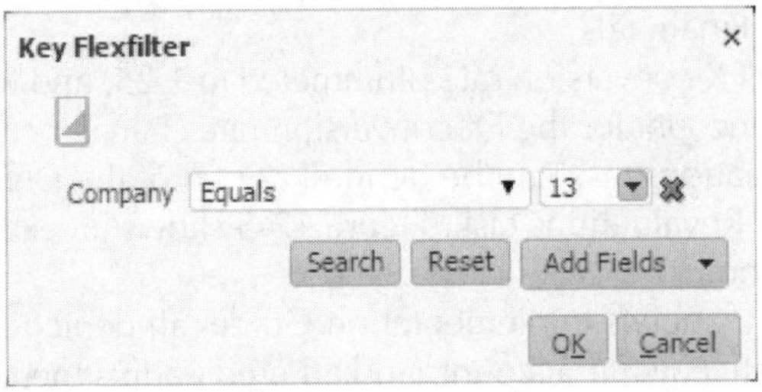

FIGURE 12-6. *Adding an accounts filter condition*

In our example we are looking for all transactions that involve the entity ACME Global Markets (13).

To run our revaluation, we can go to the Period Close work area within the Accounting Dashboard, for example, and run the Revalue Balances job from there. We are prompted to enter parameters as shown in Figure 12-7.

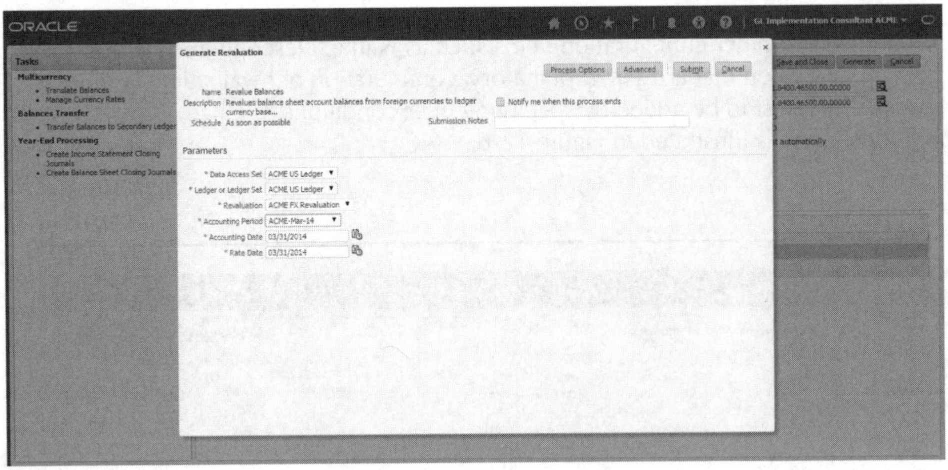

FIGURE 12-7. *Revaluation program parameters*

The submitted revaluation is a scheduled job that produces an output, which can be examined in the browser for validation or troubleshooting purposes. Figure 12-8 shows the output from our example run.

If we examine the program's output, we'll notice that the program has produced a revaluation batch with two journals for amounts of 19,624.85 and 1,785.71. The latter amount relates to revaluation adjustment entries created by the program on our behalf in relation to the journal we entered in GBP currency at the beginning of this example (Figure 12-4). The system-generated revaluation journal is shown in Figure 12-9.

For mathematically inclined readers, unrealized gain/loss account 46500 is credited with USD 1,785.71 as a result of FX fluctuation between 03/01 and 03/31. Our calculator shows:

```
> 1/0.8*10000-1/0.7*10000
  = -1785.714
```

```
ACME US Ledger                          Revaluation Execution Report              Date: 2015-03-31 18:04
                                           ACME FX Revaluation                    Page:              1


Ledger:           ACME US Ledger
Accounting Period:       ACME-Mar-14
Accounting Date: 31-03-2014
Rate Date:       31-03-2014


Revaluation requested for the following currencies:

Currency      Rate                    Status
-------------  ----------------------  --------------------
GBP            1.25


Unrealized Gain Account Template: 13.201.8400.46500.00.00000
Unrealized Loss Account Template: 13.201.8400.46500.00.00000


Revalued Account Ranges:

From Account                                    To Account
----------------------------------------------  --------------------------------------------------
13.....                                           13.....


Journals created:

Batch Name                          Journal Name                     Total Lines   Total Debits   Total Credits
----------------------------------  ------------------------------   -----------   ------------   -------------
Revalues. ACME-Mar-14 31-03-2015 11407  Revalues for GBP balance sheet acco         4       19,642.85      19,642.85
                                    Revalues for GBP income statement a         2        1,785.71       1,785.71
                                                                                 -----------   ------------   -------------
Total                                                                            6       21,428.56      21,428.56


                            ***** End of Report *****
```

FIGURE 12-8. *Output from revaluation program*

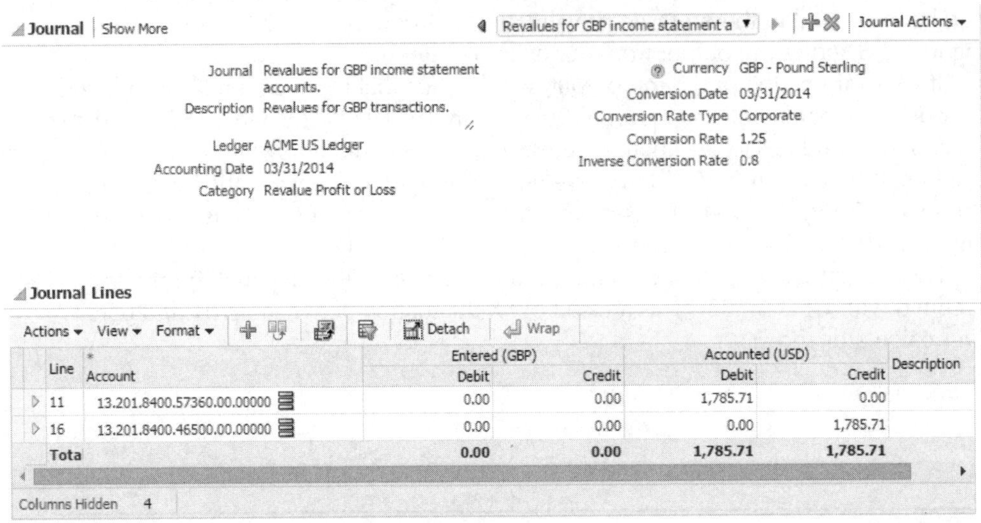

◢ Journal | Show More   ◀ | Revalues for GBP income statement a ▾ | ▶ | ✚ ✖ | Journal Actions ▾

Journal	Revalues for GBP income statement accounts.	ⓘ Currency	GBP - Pound Sterling
Description	Revalues for GBP transactions.	Conversion Date	03/31/2014
		Conversion Rate Type	Corporate
Ledger	ACME US Ledger	Conversion Rate	1.25
Accounting Date	03/31/2014	Inverse Conversion Rate	0.8
Category	Revalue Profit or Loss		

◢ **Journal Lines**

Actions ▾   View ▾   Format ▾   ✚   🗑   🗗   🗒   🖳 Detach   ⤶ Wrap

		Entered (GBP)		Accounted (USD)		Description
Line	Account	Debit	Credit	Debit	Credit	
▷ 11	13.201.8400.57360.00.00000 ▤	0.00	0.00	1,785.71	0.00	
▷ 16	13.201.8400.46500.00.00000 ▤	0.00	0.00	0.00	1,785.71	
Total		**0.00**	**0.00**	**1,785.71**	**1,785.71**	

Columns Hidden   4

FIGURE 12-9. *Revaluation journal generated by the system*

Putting It All Together

Period close is a business process in its own right. It consists of activities performed inside as well as outside of Fusion Applications. The following list is an example of what period close may entail:

■ **Reviewing and posting transactions from subledgers** We need to make sure that the accounting transactions from the subledgers like Receivables, Payables, and others have been completely transferred to the GL.

■ **Performing reconciliation of subledgers** This activity consists of multiple steps, including the validation of subledger transactions transfer to GL and running reconciliation reports. As per Oracle product documentation: "Account Analysis reports include beginning and ending account balances along with all journal entries that constitute the account's activities, and contain activity source, category, and references, which are fully documented to easily trace back to the origin of the balance." After running reports, we need to identify and reconcile any variances, report any adjustments back to the source system, and so on.

■ **Closing period for each subledger** Activity performed from the Fusion Financials front end available as part of the Accounting Dashboard.

■ **Performing allocations**   Any recurring journals and allocations are automated as part of Allocation Manager functionality, which was covered in Chapter 11.

■ **Revaluation of foreign currency balances**   As described earlier in this chapter, accounting practices demand that we revalue account balances to update functional currency equivalents.

■ **Closing the period and opening the next one**   Again, as per product documentation, we can maintain the ledgers' period statuses from the Close Status region in the General Accounting Dashboard. The Close Status region provides real-time visibility into the period-close process from your subledgers to your General Ledger across the entire enterprise.

Figure 12-10 illustrates the BPMN model of an example close-period high-level process. It is quite likely that a real-life procedure will consist of more granular detail and subprocesses. From a technical perspective, it is quite feasible to use Business Process Management (BPM) technology to completely automate the period-close process using tools like Oracle BPM, which is part of the Fusion Applications technology stack.

We covered the subject of integration and BPM in our previous book, *Oracle Fusion Applications Development and Extensibility Handbook* (Oracle Press, 2014).

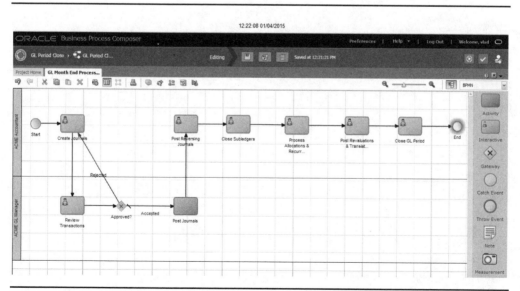

FIGURE 12-10.   *High-level period-close process modeled in Oracle BPM Composer Tool*

For on-premise deployments, most of the functionality is either readily available for integration or can rather easily be exposed to the BPM layer for orchestration. Customers who use Fusion Financials on the cloud need to check with their account manager as to what is available for orchestration as part of the service in their product release.

For cloud implementations, we suggest readers obtain a copy of the Oracle ERP Cloud Period Close Procedures white paper available under the Learn More section on the Oracle Fusion Financials Cloud website. This paper covers the dependencies between the Oracle ERP Cloud application modules, as well as specific procedures for each module.

Summary

In this chapter we provided a 30,000-foot view of the period-close process, which can be quite a lengthy procedure involving accounting and finance departments, external partners, or even system integrators.

We looked at the motivation for the period-close process from an accounting perspective, discussed the Fusion Financials components of the period-close process, and provided an example of how to configure revaluations as part of the period-close process. Finally, we hinted that the whole period-close process is a good candidate for the BPM style of end-to-end automation, with user tasks exposed as web forms and system touchpoints integrated using either the underlying Fusion Applications technology stack or even third-party technology.

CHAPTER
13

Building Financial Reports
and Analysis Dashboards

Oracle Fusion Financials contains different types of reporting tools, such as Fusion Financials Reporting Studio, Smart View, Account Monitor, Account Inspector, Oracle Transaction Business Intelligence (OTBI), and Business Intelligence Publisher (BI Publisher).

It is important to understand the reasons why Oracle has incorporated various reporting methods within the same product and how these methods work while understanding their use cases.

Different Types of Reports in Fusion Financials

Every enterprise can have various different types of roles that want to do reporting. For example, the CFO, Controller, General Accounting Manager, General Accountant, and Financial Analyst would all be the consumers of the financial reports, but each has a different reporting need. Some want reporting to manage day-to-day operations, some want to perform an analysis of how different lines of business within an organization are performing, and some want to publish the financial state of the organization to the regulators.

Broadly speaking, the reports in Fusion Financials can be categorized into the following different types:

Report documents (cannot be changed once published)

- Printed boardroom-ready financial reports

- Local statutory reports

- Printed operational or transaction reports

Interactive reports (published reports to which you can make certain changes)

- Online interactive financial reports

- Exception-based financial reporting

- Transactional reporting

Ad hoc analysis (reports that allow ad hoc queries for retrieving data)

- Excel-based ad hoc analysis (some people like to use Excel)

- Web-based ad hoc financial analysis (some people like to use the Web)

- Ad hoc operational analysis

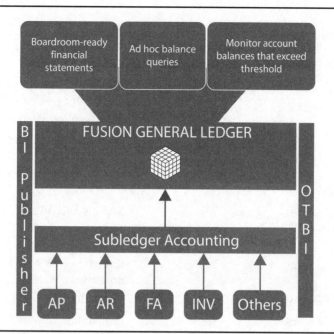

FIGURE 13-1.   *Different types of reports in Fusion Financials*

The usage of these different reports in the context of Fusion Financials is shown in Figure 13-1.

Data Sources in Fusion Financials

Oracle Fusion Financials has primarily two types of data sources. The first are multidimensional cubes, and the second are the traditional relational database tables for operational and transactional reporting. In Fusion Applications, multidimensional reporting is made possible because the GL balances are embedded within Fusion General Ledger, using the Essbase multidimensional cubes. This multidimensional data structure allows the users to perform multidimensional analysis on live data. It allows users to pivot and drill to any level from anywhere within the date-effective hierarchies. The multidimensional balances are updated during the GL Posting process, thus ensuring accurate reporting on live balances. You can also drill down into the underlying journals and transaction details from the multidimensional balances.

The multidimensional cube is automatically set up when you create a Chart of Accounts in Fusion General Ledger. If you add a cost center or modify a hierarchy, then Oracle automatically creates or modifies the cube hierarchy in Essbase. There is no batch program that has to be run to update the cube balances. As when you

Reporting Tool	Can Report on GL Balances	Transactional Reporting	Accessible From
Financial Reporting Studio Fusion Edition	Yes	No	■ Financial Reporting Center ■ Hyperion Workspace
Account Monitor	Yes	No	■ General Accounting Dashboard ■ Financial Reporting Center
Oracle Transactional Business Intelligence (OTBI)	Yes	Yes	Reports and Analytics
Oracle BI Publisher (BIP)	Yes	Yes	Run ad hoc or scheduled processes
Smart View	Yes	No	Excel plug-in
Oracle BI Publisher (BIP)	Yes	Yes	Run ad hoc or scheduled processes
Account Inspector	Yes	No	Financial Reporting Center

TABLE 13-1. *Reporting Tools in Fusion Applications*

post the journals or transactions, Fusion General Ledger automatically posts them to the analytic cube, ensuring that the balances are always in synch. The balances are also pre-aggregated at every possible summarization level. You can analyze real-time balances by slicing and dicing different dimensions. You can pivot from segment to segment and drill into any Chart of Accounts segment from any level in the hierarchy.

Given the different needs of different roles and reporting data sources, Oracle has produced six different tools for reporting in Fusion Applications, as listed in Table 13-1. In this chapter we will learn about each of these reporting tools.

Financial Reporting Studio Fusion Edition

Financial Reporting Studio is a Hyperion suite of tools that is used to produce high-resolution boardroom-ready reports. These reports can be accessed via the Financial Reporting Center in Fusion Applications. You can publish these reports in PDF format or HTML or Excel output. You can either use this tool to report on live data, or you can use this tool to view the data at a specific point in time. You can either make the reports a static PDF, or you can make them interactive in HTML, allowing you to expand from one parent value to another level in the hierarchy and also drill down into transactions.

You can also group the reports into books to view them at the same time, or you can group them into batches to schedule them at different times. For example, you may run the report for different lines of business and send the report to the CFO of that line of business. Likewise, you may want to run some reports at the cost center level so that different cost center managers can receive reports of the financial activities of their team via emails.

Financial Reporting Studio is a client-based report-authoring tool where you can develop the reports for the Financial Reporting Center. This tool needs to be installed on your desktop, following which you can drag and drop to insert titles, logos, graphs, and columns and introduce calculations. The tool allows you to insert rows and columns, with column values being sourced from data, or formulas or static text. You can select dimension members and add calculations or mathematical functions. This is a very easy-to-use tool, and it allows you to create a basic balance sheet or income statement within 15 to 20 minutes.

The reports developed and deployed via this tool can be accessed from the Financial Reporting Center in a browser, which allows you to access all your reports from the repository. The Financial Reporting Center ensures that different people will see different sets of reports to which they have been granted access. You can give access to senior executives, and they can view the reports in PDF or HTML format. In either case, the reports will display the latest balances from Fusion General Ledger.

Some reports can contain multiple components; for example, the first section of the report can contain the Financial KPIs such as Return on Assets (ROA) and Return on Equities (ROE), the second section can display the expense analysis, and a third section can show a graph for profit trends by the line of business.

The reports developed in Financial Reporting Studio will have some default dimensions such as Ledger or Ledger Set, Accounting Period ranges, currency, and the segments in the Chart of Accounts. The Reporting Center gives you the capability to search across any dimension and provides an easy front end to apply further filters on the results via the browser. In addition, a drill-down can be made available out of the box from the balances in the GL cubes to the accounting transactions in Subledger. The Reporting Center also allows further drill-downs from the accounting transactions into the Subledger transactions such as invoices, payments, purchase orders, and so on.

The Financial Reports Center functionality includes

■ Running live reports and books in various formats

■ Viewing published snapshot reports from scheduled batches in various formats

- Creating embedded charts and graphs

- Refreshing report data using run-time points of view or parameters

- Expanding or drilling down from any parent value to the next parent value or to the child value

- Expanding or drilling down from any child value to detail balances, journal lines, and Subledger transactions

- Building multidimensional reports, with multiple hierarchies, using a client-based tool, Oracle Hyperion Financial Reporting Studio, Fusion Edition

- Distributing reports automatically across your organization using email or other distribution mechanisms

- Storing reports in a repository folder structure, using various formats, including PDF, HTML, and spreadsheets

Installing Financial Reporting Studio

You can download the reporting tool from Fusion Applications itself. Navigate to Navigator | Financial Reporting Center | Open Workspace For Financial Reports. In the Workspace, choose Tools | Install | Financial Reporting Studio as shown in Figure 13-2.

At the time of writing this book, the Workspace is compatible only with Internet Explorer and Firefox browsers. After completing the install, launch Financial Reporting Studio and provide your Fusion Applications User ID, Fusion Applications password, and the server URL. Your Fusion Applications administrator should be able to provide the URL for the Financial Reporting Studio Business Intelligence server. Typically this will be http(s)://<hostname>:<PortNumber>. You must contact your administrator for the port number.

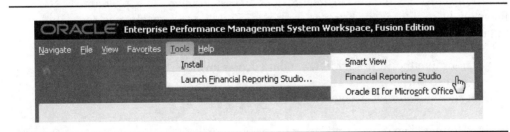

FIGURE 13-2. *Installing Financial Reporting Studio from Fusion Applications*

Compatibility with Internet Explorer

Internet Explorer (IE) Version 9 is supported by Fusion Applications Release 7. IE 10 and above are supported by Fusion Applications Releases 8 and 9. Ensure that the Workspace web server name is added to the list of Trusted Sites in Internet Explorer, using the browser menu: Internet Options | Security | Trusted Sites | Sites.

Compatibility with Firefox Browser

For Firefox, an add-on named Remote XUL Manager must be installed from https:// addons.mozilla.org/en-US/firefox/addon/remote-xul-manager/.

Once this add-on has been installed, navigate to the Developer menu in Firefox, and for Remote XUL Manager, click Add and enter the URL for the Fusion Applications server. For step-by-step instructions, see Oracle Support Note *Using Hyperion Workspace With Recent Firefox Versions (Doc ID 1447453.1)*.

Build GL Report Using Financial Reporting Studio

After the Financial Reporting Studio Fusion Edition has been installed, you need to use your Fusion Applications username and password to log in to the reporting tool, as shown in Figure 13-3, and click OK.

After logging in, right-click anywhere on the tool pane, and select New | Report as shown in Figure 13-4.

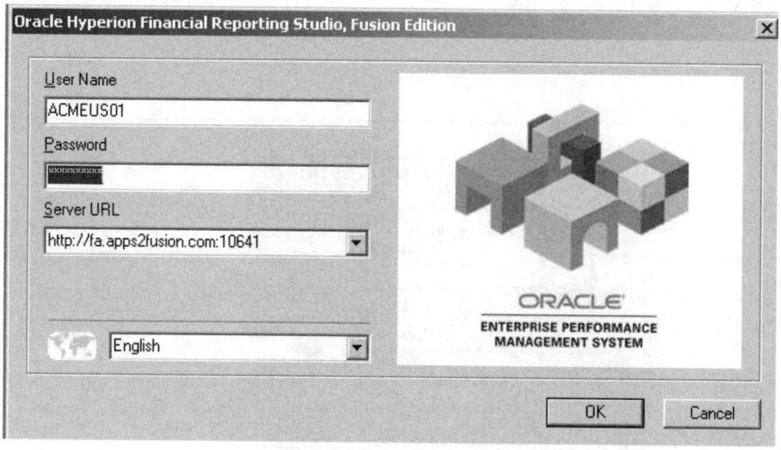

FIGURE 13-3. *Log in to Financial Reporting Studio using your Fusion Applications credentials.*

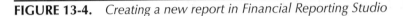

FIGURE 13-4. *Creating a new report in Financial Reporting Studio*

Following the step in Figure 13-4, you will be presented with a blank template where you can define the regions, text, chart, and images as shown in Figure 13-5.

To create a new region, right-click anywhere on the template and select New Grid. Next, click your mouse and drag it to release it so as to create a rectangular area where the region will be built. After the rectangular region has been defined, you will be prompted to enter your credentials and select the database. The database that you select here is the Essbase database that corresponds to your GL Chart of Accounts Instance, as shown in Figure 13-6.

After selecting the Essbase database for your GL Chart of Accounts instance, you can drag and drop components into the pane to build your report, as shown in Figure 13-7.

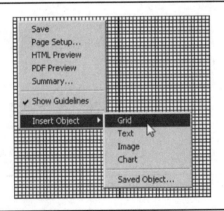

FIGURE 13-5. *Creating a new region by selecting New Grid*

Give any name here.

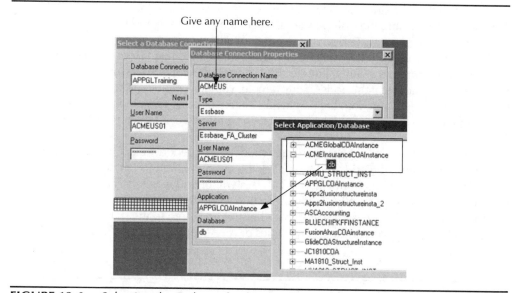

FIGURE 13-6. *Selecting the Essbase database to be used for reporting*

Drag and drop Point of View
dimensions here

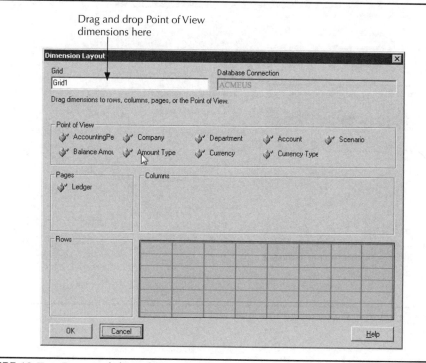

FIGURE 13-7. *Drag and drop dimensions from Point of View into columns, rows, and pages.*

Click and drag the Company into the Pages area, Account into the Rows area, and Accounting Periods into the Columns area. Select the cells in the grid for Account, Company, and Accounting Period. For every cell that you select, its corresponding Heading Row Property window will be displayed on the right-hand side. If you wish to allow drill-down from a cell, then select the check box Allow Expansion to allow drill-downs into the hierarchy nodes. For example, you may want to drill down from Quarter into a period, and from the parent Asset account value to an individual asset account to see the breakdown of the balances. This property can be set as shown in Figure 13-8.

In order to restrict the dimension values shown in the report, select the relevant dimension cell within the grid, and then click the button in the top-left corner, for example, the Account button in Figure 13-8. This will open the Select Members window as shown in Figure 13-9, allowing you to select the member values in that dimension. Bring the dimension values over by shuttling them to the right-hand side. You can select the option All Company Values or All Account Values depending on

Property of a
cell in the grid

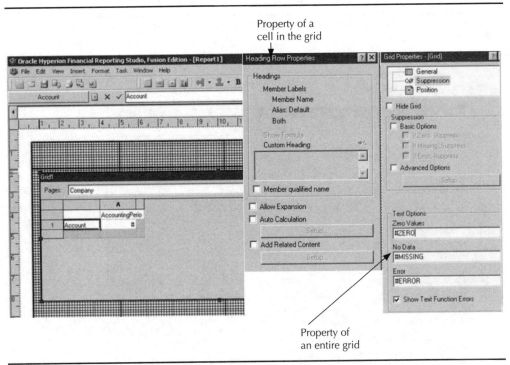

Property of
an entire grid

FIGURE 13-8. *Property grid cell and entire grid*

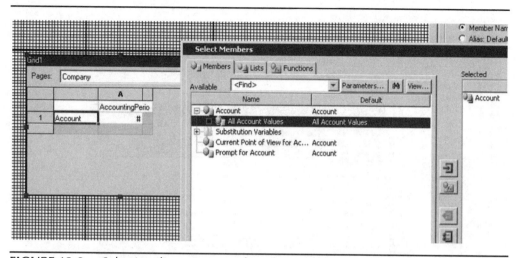

FIGURE 13-9. *Selecting dimension members for reporting*

the dimension for which you are selecting the members. Alternatively, click the + icon within the dimension and select individual members before shuttling them to the right-hand pane. You need to do this step one by one for each dimension of interest as shown in Figure 13-9.

There are many advanced features, such as conditional formatting and suppression of duplicates, which can be set up by selecting the property of the member.

After the report has been developed, click Save and you will be presented with folders to save into. These folders are the folders on the Fusion Applications BI server as shown in Figure 13-10. You can make the report private by saving it into My Folders, or you can save the report within the Custom folder as shown in Figure 13-10.

Once you have developed your report, you can click File | Preview HTML or click the icon as shown in Figure 13-11, and it will run the report and show the report with all the points of view at the top to allow slicing and dicing of the report output. As shown in Figure 13-8, you can select the entire grid and select the property of the entire grid. When you select the entire grid, it then allows you to select Text Options. Here you can override the text that is shown to the user when the balance for an account is zero, or if no balance exists, or the text string seen when in error. It is common for you to replace #ZERO with 0, and #MISSING with 0 in the grid properties.

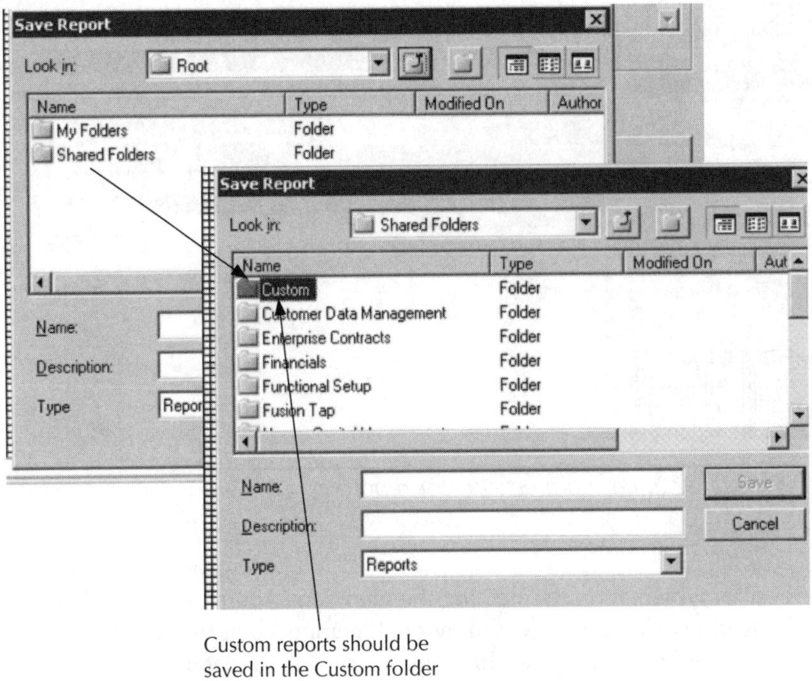

Custom reports should be
saved in the Custom folder

FIGURE 13-10. *Saving a Financial Studio report on the server*

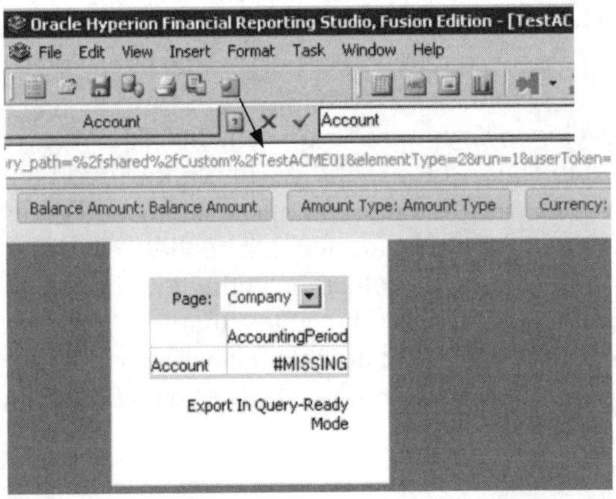

FIGURE 13-11. *Running a Financial Studio report in preview mode*

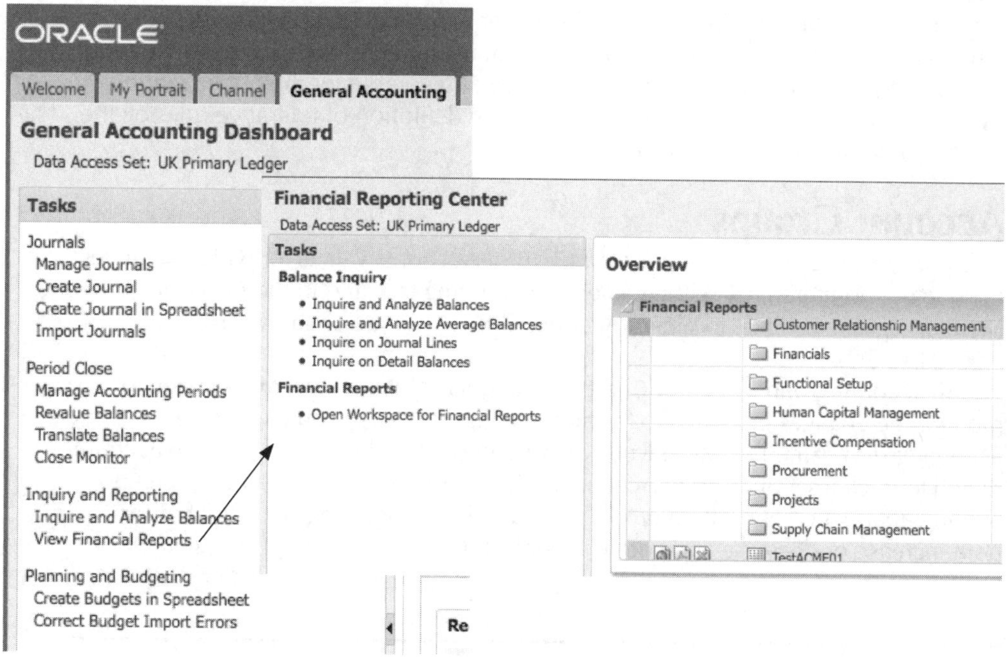

FIGURE 13-12. *Running a Financial Studio report from Fusion Applications*

To view the report from Fusion Applications, first log in to the application, then click the General Accounting tab, and then click View Financial Reports to see the report saved from the tool as shown in Figure 13-12.

Account Monitor

Account Monitor, as the name suggests, allows users to proactively monitor changes to the balances of the key account. You can compare the balances quarter by quarter or year by year without doing any run-time aggregation. The aggregation is done automatically by the Essbase cubes without having to run any background processes. It is common to use this utility for key accounts such as expenses or revenue that is being monitored. For example, the company may have introduced a new travel policy, and you may want to monitor the expenses of flight costs year by year to see if travel-related cost cuts are taking effect in the organization. You can also monitor the exceptions by defining deviations above x percent from last period or last year, or you can monitor expenses going beyond the budgets defined in the system. The drill-down facility allows you to further interrogate the exceptions in account balances by drilling down to the journals and transactions. The system can also automatically mark the deviations in accounts in red or green depending upon whether the deviations in balances are adverse or favorable for the organization. Account Monitor therefore facilitates self-service definition of tolerance rules by the users in order to monitor key accounts.

Account Groups

Account groups can be created for the Chart of Accounts values for which balances need to be monitored. Click the General Accounting tab, and in the Account Monitor region, navigate to View | Account Group | Create as shown in Figure 13-13.

An account group is a set of Chart of Accounts values for which you want to monitor the changes proactively. As shown in Figure 13-14, you can create an account group named ACME Travel Expense Account and add entries in the account region to track a set of Chart of Accounts values for which expenses have gone up by more than x percent. Alternatively, you can also track changes by amount for both increase or decrease and compare against the prior year, or prior quarter, or

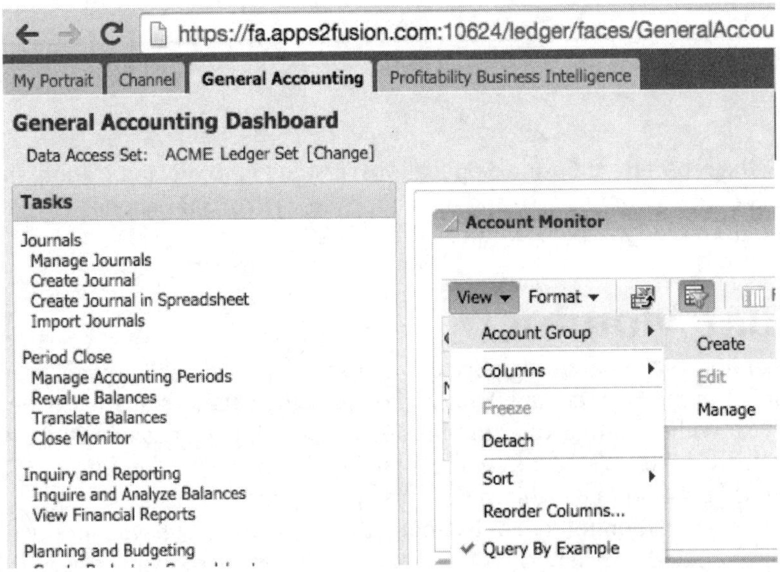

FIGURE 13-13. *The Account Monitor region in Fusion General Ledger*

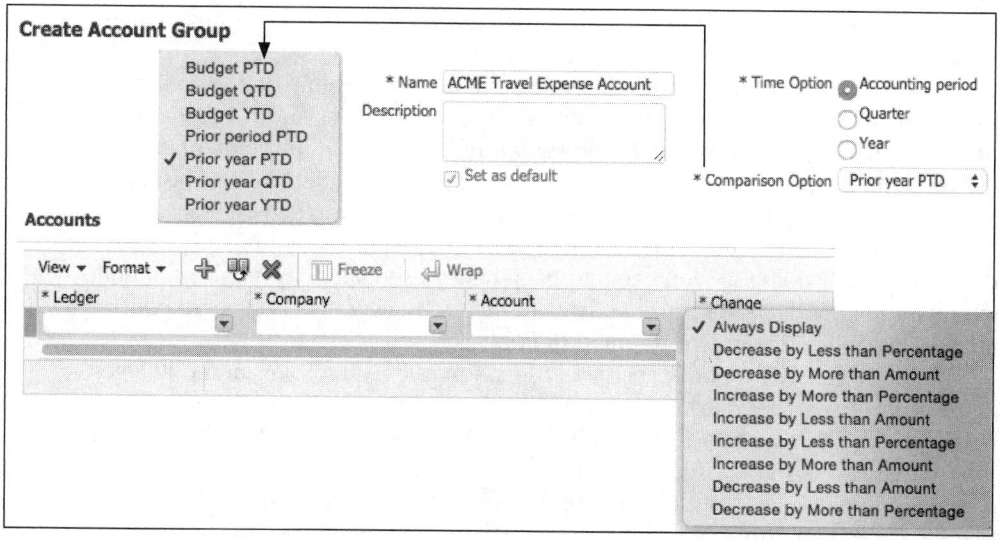

FIGURE 13-14. *Defining an account group with monitoring options*

prior period balances as shown in Figure 13-14. To make account creation easy, Oracle allows you to select values such as All Company values, or All Cost Center values for the record when creating Account Groups. Of course, you can include specific segment values as well for account monitoring.

The system can decide according to the account type whether the changes are good or bad for the organization: for example, increasing sales are a good sign, but increasing expenses are not a healthy sign. Therefore, the system can automatically mark the record in green or red.

OTBI (Oracle Transaction Business Intelligence)

OTBI enables transactional reporting from live data with self-service capabilities. You do not need to develop ETL processes for OTBI reports because this technology does not use a data warehouse. In simple words, OTBI is the OBIEE embedded into Fusion Applications. The question readers may ask is: Why is this so special when many customers already have OBIEE? The key value added by OTBI is that it comes bundled with hundreds of predeveloped reports that users can customize further by dragging and dropping. OTBI inherits all the application and data security features of Fusion Applications. Therefore, you do not need to configure security separately for OTBI. Who can see which data is controlled by the data security policies defined in APM, which is explained in Chapter 7. Thus, OTBI presents a real-time snapshot because the information is prepared on the go when requested by the user via their browser. It supports Fusion extensibility such as flexfields, trees, multilanguage features, and so on.

In the cloud implementations, customizations are not possible on the presentation layer. On SaaS you will have a fixed set of presentation layer and subject areas because you cannot customize the presentation layer in SaaS implementations. However, in the on-premise implementation you can use Oracle's BI Administration tool to do customizations on the presentation layer. Further, you can create your own views of transactional data and present them as subject areas by deploying your development. By doing so, you can introduce new presentation layers. You can build the real-time reports in BI Publisher as well, but OTBI gives self-service ad hoc analysis capability that is not present in BI Publisher.

The OTBI Security model consists of users, job roles, duty roles, and privileges. A user can be assigned to one or more job roles. A job role is descriptive of the user's job function, such as General Ledger Clerk. A user is granted a job role, and a job role has one or more associated duty roles. A job role can span all the applications, whereas a duty role is specific to an application. Job roles are grouped hierarchically to reflect lines of authority and responsibility. Privileges allow specific access to an application or reporting objects and data sets; for example, read access to a report, or read access to a table, and so on. Privileges are associated with duty roles. As soon as a user logs in to Fusion Applications, the system knows the function and data security applicable for that logged-in session. For example, when a finance manager views a list of journals pending approval using an OTBI report, the manager will only see the count of journals that belong to the ledger to which they have access. This is made possible because OTBI respects the data security constraints on the underlying data objects, which are also used by the data entry and inquiry screens in Fusion Applications.

To ensure that the users are enabled for baseline OTBI reporting access, a role named FBI_TRANSACTIONAL_BUSINESS_INTELLIGENCE_WORKER must be assigned to a user. Also, the relevant duty roles can be assigned to the users to grant them access to a group of reports. For example, OTBI Duty Role FBI_ GENERAL_LEDGER_TRANSACTION_ANALYSIS_DUTY has access to the following subject areas:

1. General Ledger - Balances Real Time

2. General Ledger - Journals Real Time

3. General Ledger - Period Status Real Time

4. General Ledger - Transactional Balances Real Time

5. Subledger Accounting - Journals Real Time

6. Subledger Accounting - Supporting References Real Time OTBI Function

Security job roles and their associated duty roles and privileges are assigned to users of Oracle Fusion Applications. The implementation team usually indicates which users can access which application menu or page. This level of security is known as *function security*. This function security also secures access to OTBI reporting objects by assigning BI-specific duty roles to BI-specific job roles. In Fusion Applications, you will find that for every given subject area, usually a single BI duty role is defined, using the naming convention "<xyz>Analysis Duty." Some examples are Account Analysis Duty and Expense Analysis Duty roles. These BI duty roles are mapped to the subject areas using a file known as RPD in the BI Administration tool. The mapping of the BI duty roles to various subject areas comes prepackaged in Fusion Applications. OTBI comes packaged with an Analysis Editor for presenting data in graphs, pivots, tables, and so on, and it is called BI Answers. You also have the BI Composer Wizard, which allows you to quickly create and edit reports. There are multiple subject areas. Within the subject area you have Dimensions, Attributes, and Facts/Measures.

OTBI reports can either be created when logged in to Fusion Applications or from the BI Analytics dashboard. To create an OTBI report from within Fusion Applications, click Navigator and select the menu item Reports And Analytics under the Tools section. Click Create, and you will be presented with all the subject areas available to you based on the roles assigned to your username as shown in Figure 13-15.

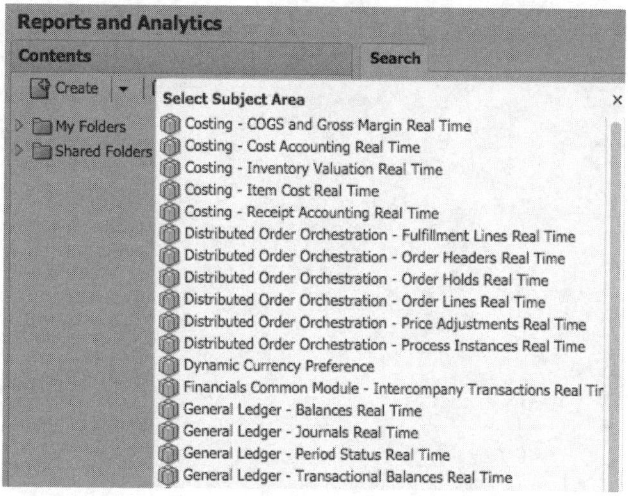

FIGURE 13-15. *Creating a new self-service report dashboard*

As seen in Figure 13-15, the product comes out of the box with General Ledger Balances, Journals, Period Status, and Transactional Balances subject areas. You can select the desired subject area on which the self-service analysis report needs to be developed. Each subject area consists of various facts and dimensions as shown in Figure 13-16. You can shuttle the desired dimensions and facts into the report that you want to build. It is also possible to enable drill-down to the journals and transactions using the drop-down list Interaction.

After selecting your dimensions, click Next, and in the Select Views section, enter a title and select the option of Tabular or Graphical format. Apply sort and filter conditions as desired, and save your report. The report can either be saved in your personal area, which is named My Folder, or it can be saved in a shared area under Shared Folders. A good video demonstration for this can be found at https://goo.gl/ct7mu1.

When saving your custom reports that you want to share, you must create them under a subfolder within a custom folder. This will ensure that your reports are easily accessible and will never be overwritten by Oracle patches.

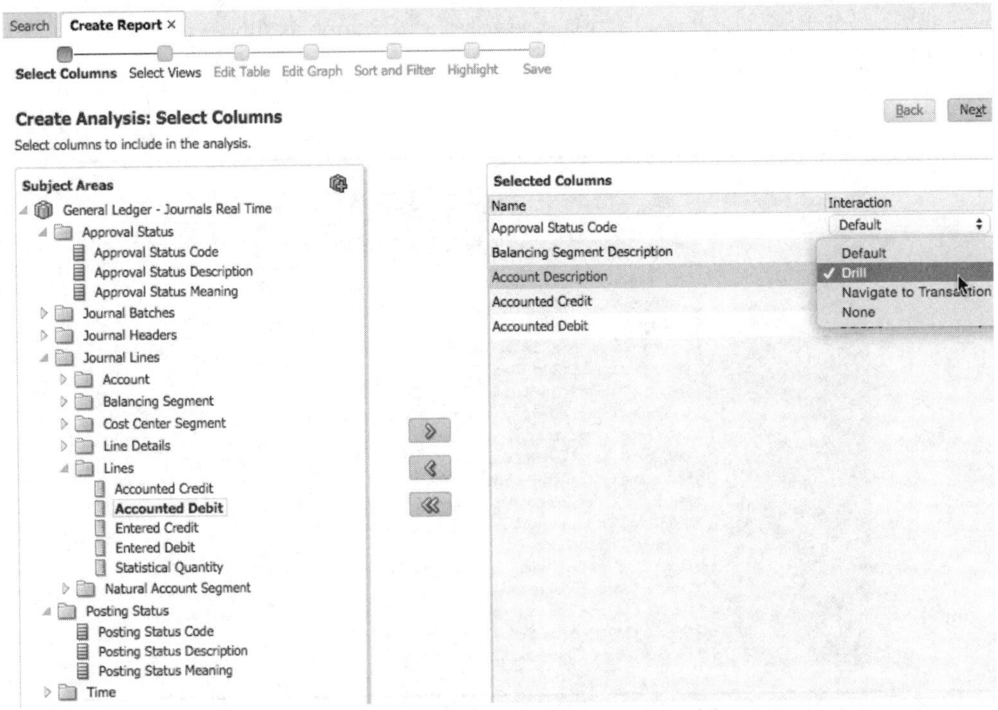

FIGURE 13-16. *Selecting dimensions and facts for reporting*

Create a Simple OTBI Report

Let us assume that you as a user want to send the list of journal batches created on a daily basis straight into your mailbox. In order to implement this requirement, first you have to set your default delivery profile. Log in to Analytics Dashboard using the URL http(s)://host:port/analytics. Click your login name in the top-right corner, then My Accounts, and navigate to the tab Delivery Options. Select Email from the drop-down Devices list and click the + sign to create a new device with Name Send to myself, Category Email, and Device Type HTML Email, followed by the preferred email address, as shown in Figure 13-17. Click OK and set this device to be the default. In OTBI, the term "device" simply means a medium used to deliver content to the users. The contents of an agent can be delivered to devices such as an email or SMS message.

Next, define a new report. Click Analysis under Create as shown in Figure 13-18 and then scroll down to select General Ledger – Journals Real Time in the pop-up window titled Select Subject Area.

Double-click Journal Batch Description under Journal Batches | Batch Details as shown in Figure 13-19. Double-click Accounting Date, Currency, Journal Status, and Period Name underneath Journal Headers | Header Details. Click Save and give this

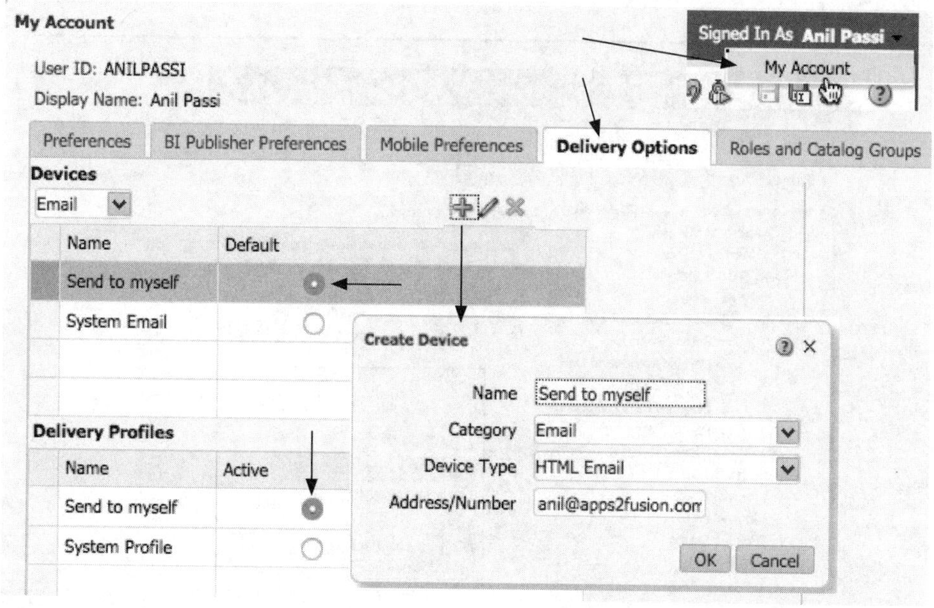

FIGURE 13-17.   *The end users can set their default delivery preferences.*

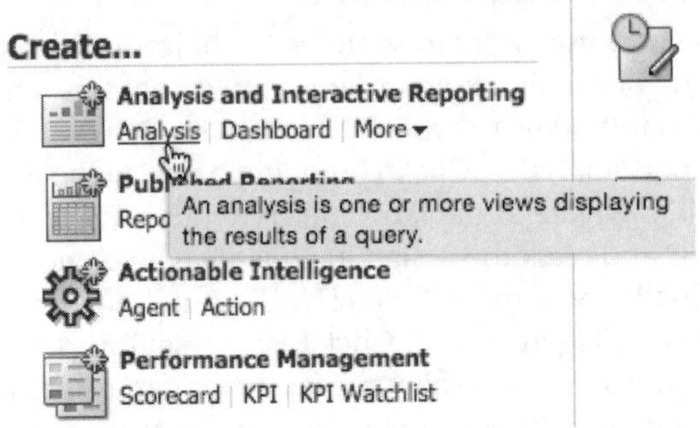

FIGURE 13-18. *Creating an analysis for interactive reporting using OTBI*

self-service report a name: ACME Journal Batch Listing. The path for saving this report is /Shared Folders/Custom/Financials.

OTBI has a component named Agents, which delivers analytics to users based on scheduled or triggered events. Delivery can be a pop-up message on Dashboard via Alerts or as email. To deliver this report either to the Dashboard or via email to

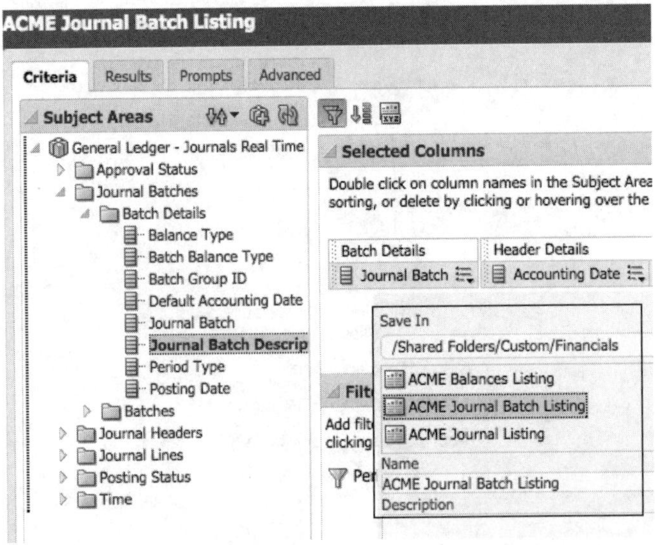

FIGURE 13-19. *Creating a new OTBI report for Journal Batch Listing*

FIGURE 13-20. *Creating a new agent for delivering the report to yourself*

yourself, click New | Agent as shown in Figure 13-20. Click the Schedule tab and select the agent's delivery frequency, such as Never or Daily or Weekly or Monthly.

Click the Delivery Content tab and give this delivery agent a Subject "Journals created today." Click Browse to select the report that was created for the journal listing, as shown in Figure 13-21.

Click the Recipients tab and chose your default username. In the Agent's Actions tab, select the radio button Specific Devices, with the Email check box enabled. Click the Save button, and save this under My Folders, giving it the name My Scheduled Journal Batch Emails. Click OK and as per the schedule, you will receive an email in your mailbox with the journal listing as shown in Figure 13-22.

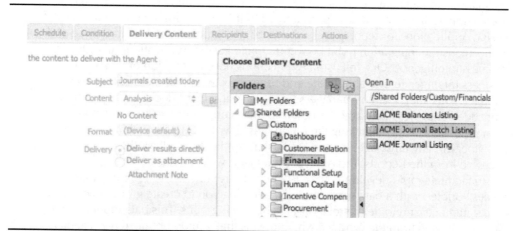

FIGURE 13-21. *Selecting the report that will be delivered by this agent*

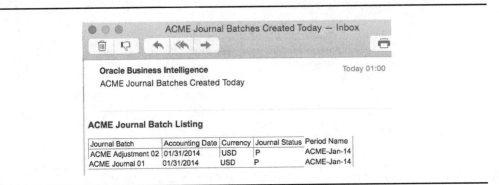

FIGURE 13-22. *Journal listing delivered automatically to your mailbox*

BI Publisher Reports in Fusion Applications

The BI Publisher Reports tool is for high-resolution, pixel-perfect reports. You can customize the output by changing the template to produce a PDF or in Excel or HTML or DOC format, and so on. This report is also good for high-volume transactional data reporting. Fusion comes out of the box with many BI Publisher reports. You will typically use BI Publisher reports for documents that are meant to be printed.

The traditional financial landscape used a separate and independent work area for Business Intelligence and reporting. However, in Fusion Applications, both the operational and analytics reports are available directly within Fusion Applications itself. Further, these integrated reports adhere to the underlying security principles of Fusion Applications for report access and data. The Reports And Analytics pane and work area is the integration point between Oracle Fusion Applications and Oracle Business Intelligence. Oracle Fusion Applications does a good job of making the Business Intelligence available to the end users directly in their application user interface. This allows senior management to make informed decisions based on the embedded analytics and dashboards. It also drastically improves BI participation from the casual users by making the report launch with just one click. The BI reports are either directly embedded within the Fusion Applications UI, or they are accessed from the Reports And Analytics pane and work area.

To facilitate rapid development of BI Publisher reports, Fusion Applications comes bundled with a data model builder, allowing you to create groups based on SQL statements and to define relationships between groups. This data model builder can be accessed from the browser, which means that you do not need the database connection credentials for developing reports because SQL queries can be designed straight into the browser-based data model editor. The key difference with OTBI is that with OTBI, you as a user will be agnostic to the SQL statements that are executed on database tables. In the case of OTBI, the SQL statements are hidden under the hood of the subject areas model within the RPD file. Another key difference is that the data model builder in Fusion Applications can source the data from a variety of sources as listed in Table 13-2.

Data Source Type	Data Source Description for Reporting
SQL Query	This is a traditional approach to writing SQL statements that can be either simple or complex. It is common that only expert users will be creating data models. Relations can be built between the results of various SQL statements.
LDAP Query	Allows you to query LDAP directories such as Active Directory, Oracle Internet Directory, and so on, by specifying the attributes of interest.
MDX Query Against an OLAP Data Source	Allows you to write queries against multidimensional cubes such as Essbase.
Oracle Endeca Query	Endeca is a tool from Oracle that allows you to collate and query both structured and unstructured data such as social media, emails, presentations, web contents, and documents. This option allows you to write Endeca Query Language (EQL) queries against the Oracle Endeca Server.
Oracle BI Analysis	This option allows you to use the subject areas available in OTBI as your data source. The only reason you will use this option is when you want to build reports using data from subject areas with output formats and layouts that you control.
HTTP XML Feed	This option allows you to build and publish reports that consume data from RSS and XML feeds over the Web.
View Object	You will almost never use this option as a functional implementer. The OTBI standard reports fetch data via something known as view objects. View objects are wrappers around the database tables. The view objects are built using XML and Java technology, and these can be made available to BI Publisher.
Web Service	At the time of writing this chapter, the web services returning XML can be used as a source for building reports. Functional implementers will very rarely use this option.
CSV File	Administrators can create folders on Fusion Applications Server and add them as data sources. The desired roles can be granted access to this data source. CSV files that are dropped in this folder can be used as a source for building reports.
Microsoft Excel File	Administrators can create folders on Fusion Applications Server and add them as a data source for Excel as well. At the time of writing this chapter, only the XLS files are supported. It is possible to report data from multiple sheets.
XML File	Administrators can create folders on Fusion Applications Server and add them as a data source for XML as well. XML files in that directory can then be browsed and used as a source for BI reporting.

TABLE 13-2.   *Different Data Sources for Building BI Publisher Reports*

As seen in Table 13-2, in order to report on a piece of data, it needs to be defined as a data source. The BI Publisher engine converts the results of the data source to XML and passes them to a BI report template. This template contains the design and presentation logic to achieve the desired layout and formatting of the final output.

Scheduling Capabilities in BI Publisher

The scheduling capabilities of BI Publisher reports are the same as for OTBI reports. You can conditionalize the execution of a scheduled report based on an event. To implement this option, you can define an event trigger of type=Schedule. This event trigger can be associated with a SQL query. If this SQL query returns no record, then a scheduled run of the report will not be executed. Therefore, just prior to running the scheduled job, the associated SQL query in the event trigger will be executed. If no data is returned from the SQL query, then the job instance report is not run. If data is returned, the job instance runs as scheduled. One example of this feature is where you want to email the exceptions in Financial Accounting Hub of a nightly batch process after the import process is completed. If there are no exceptions in the exception tables, then you can skip running of the exception listing report. On similar lines, you may want to skip the execution of a scheduled import process for journals if there is no data in the corresponding GL_INTERFACE table.

For on-premise implementations, the technical developers in your team can also write custom PL/SQL code snippets to be executed before or after the execution of a data source. The Before Data trigger is executed before the data set is fetched, and the After Data trigger is executed after the BI Publisher engine has generated the XML from all the data sets within the data model. The PL/SQL function used for these triggers must return TRUE or FALSE. In a SaaS-based environment, the customers are not allowed to write their own PL/SQL, and therefore there is a restriction on the usage of before and after event triggers for SaaS customers for their custom reports. As an example, this feature can be useful in scenarios where you want to create an audit entry specific to your needs after the exceptions have been reported.

Bursting the Report Output with Multiple Delivery Options

The BI Publisher reporting engine also has a feature known as *bursting*. This is used to split data into smaller pieces based on specified criteria. After the split of data has been achieved, you can then deliver those smaller pieces of data to multiple locations. Bursting definitions contain instructions for splitting data, generating a document in the desired format for each split section, and then delivering the output to the desired destination using a desired mechanism. For example, you can split the manual adjustment journals created by cost center to advise each cost center manager via email that adjustment journals have been created for their respective cost centers. Using bursting, each cost center manager will then see the affected balances for just their cost center, even though the data source of the BI Publisher report will return adjusted values for each cost center. Also, bursting gives you the option of applying a different layout template and delivery mechanism to each split section of the XML generated by the data model.

Templates for Formatting the Output

Reporting templates are used to format the data for presentation. Oracle BI Publisher provides an add-in for Microsoft Office to facilitate the coding of layout instructions into Office documents. Most of the templates delivered in Oracle Fusion Applications are RTF templates. An RTF template is a Rich Text Format file that contains the layout instructions for BI Publisher to use when generating the report output. RTF templates are created using Microsoft Word. Oracle Fusion Applications also comes with an embedded template builder tool that can be used for generating interactive HTML-based reports.

Report Output

A report is the final output where the user can view the data in the desired format. Some of the key output formats supported by BI Publisher are listed in Table 13-3. The complete list can be found in Oracle product documentation, as Oracle can add new supportable formats.

Output Format	OUTPUT_FORMAT in Bursting SQL Query
Interactive	Not supported for bursting
HTML	HTML
PDF	PDF
RTF	RTF
Excel	Excel for MHTML, Excel2000 for HTML, XSLX for XSLX
PowerPoint	PPT or PPTX
PDF	PDFA for PDF/A, PDFX for PDF/X, and PDFZ for zipped PDF
FO Formatted XML	XSLFO
XML	XML
Comma Separated	CSV
Text	Text
Flash	Flash

TABLE 13-3. *Formats Supported by Oracle BI Publisher*

Create a BI Publisher Report
to List Journal Batches for the Last Day

In this section you will find a step-by-step approach to create a data model, template, and report with an example. The Fusion Applications BI Publisher environment can be accessed using a URL similar to https://<host:port>/analytics//. This is the same URL that was used to develop an OTBI report. In this simple example, a report will be developed to list the journal batches that were posted during the last day. The steps for developing this report are as follows:

1. First, we need to create the data model. Click the menu item New and then the menu item Data Model under Published Reporting, as shown in Figure 13-23.

2. To extract the data for journal batches, you need to know the relevant tables, which can be found in the standard Oracle documentation. Create a new set using the SQL statement shown in Figure 13-24. You can click the menu item View Data to see the sample results of this query in tabular format. Click the Save button to save the data model. At this point the system will prompt you to select the data model location. Given that this is a custom data model, select the folder structure /Shared Folders/Custom/Financials, giving it the name XXACME_LAST_DAY_BATCHES_DM. Don't save your data model in My Folders, as it will only be visible to the user who created it.

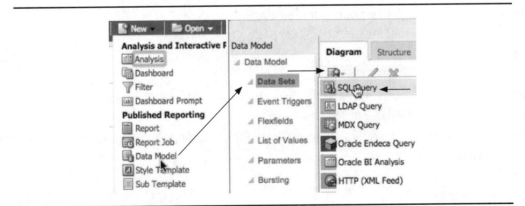

FIGURE 13-23. *Creating a new data model*

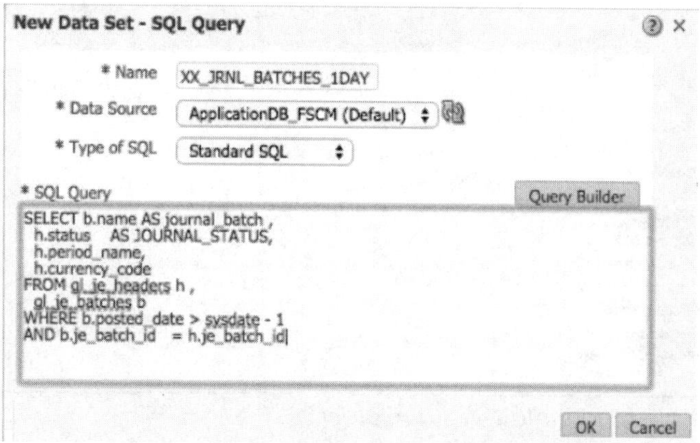

FIGURE 13-24. *Creating a data set for a journal batch listing*

3. Next, we need to create a BI Publisher report that uses this data model. Click the New Report button, select the data model created in the previous step, and then click the Use Report Editor radio button as shown in Figure 13-25 and click Finish.

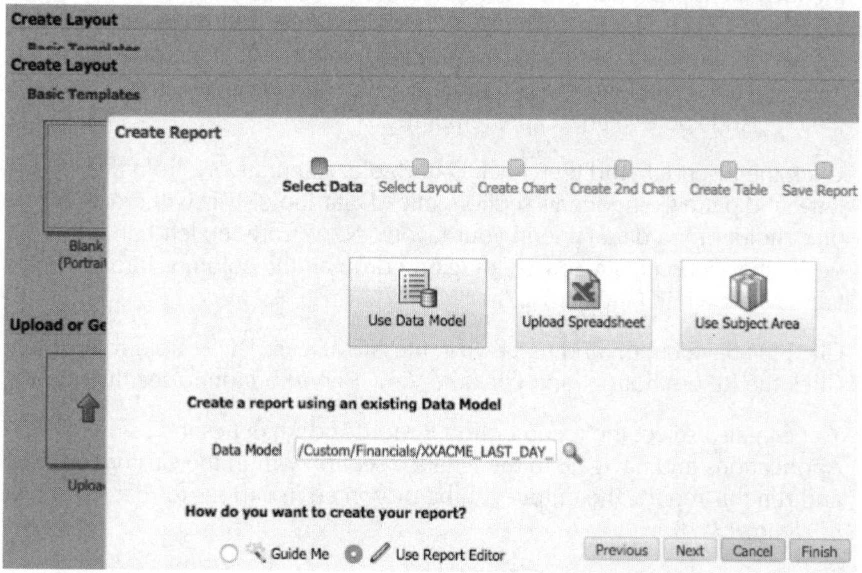

FIGURE 13-25. *Creating a new layout using an existing data model*

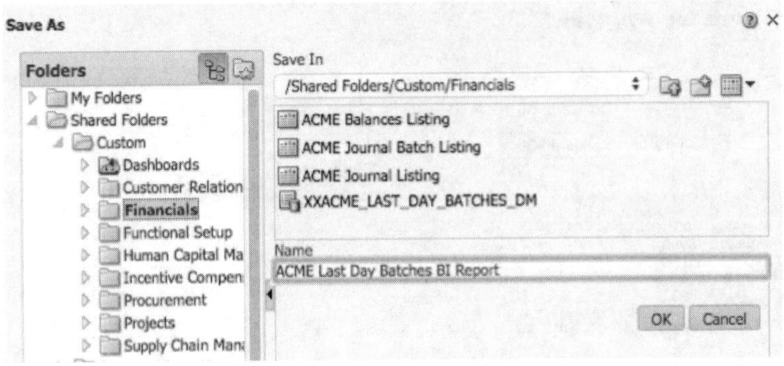

FIGURE 13-26. *Save the report into a custom folder.*

4. When you click Finish, you will be prompted to save the report. In this example, we will save the report in the same directory where we saved the data model, giving this report a name, ACME Last Day Batches BI Report, as shown in Figure 13-26.

5. When you click the OK button, you will be presented with a window for creating or uploading a template. You can use one of the template designs to develop your layout in the built-in editor. Alternatively, you can upload the layout template that you develop offline in third-party tools such as Microsoft Office. The Basic Templates provide a few built-in basic layout formats for building the report. In this example we will first create the template using the Embedded Template Builder. In order to do so, click the Header And Footer (Landscape) template.

6. Click the Insert tab and then click Data Table. Alternatively, from the left-hand pane Components section, click Data Table. This will create a placeholder for a data table in your layout. Now, from the left-hand pane under the section Data Source, drag and drop all the columns into the data table as shown in Figure 13-27.

7. Click the Save button and name your file ACME Last 1 Day Role Template. Click the Return button, and click the View Report button to see the output.

8. You can also select the menu option Report And Analytics in Fusion Applications and navigate to the Finance section within the Custom folder and run this report. The output can be presented in various formats as shown in Figure 13-28.

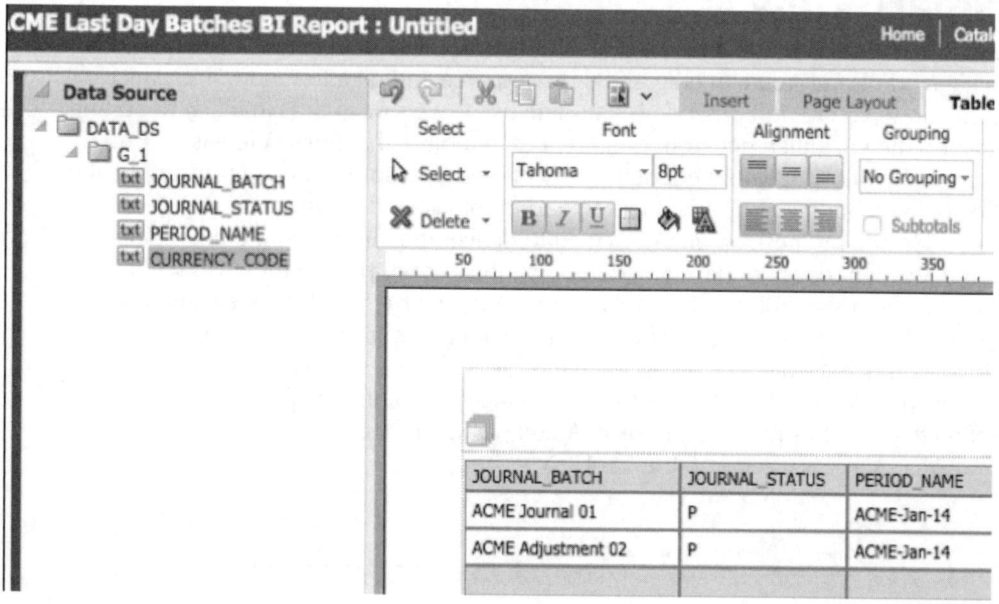

FIGURE 13-27. *Drag and drop columns from the data set into the data table.*

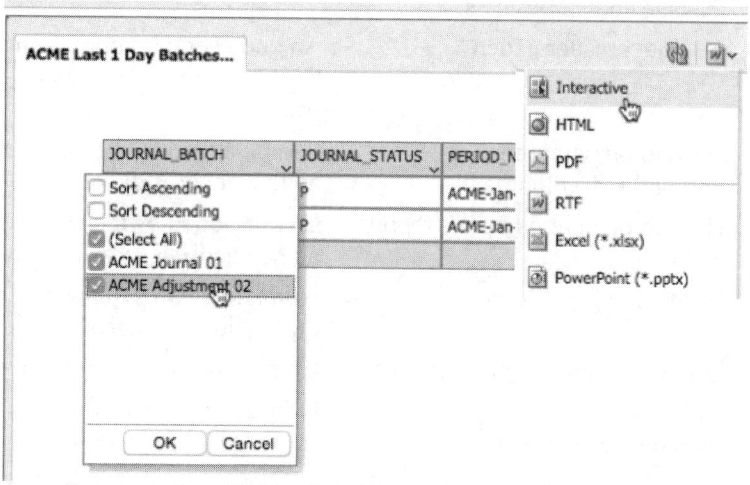

FIGURE 13-28. *Viewing output of the report in various formats*

Smart View

Smart View is an ad hoc analysis tool. It allows you to view General Ledger balances in Excel. You can drag and drop and slice and dice to report on balances. It also allows you to drill down into transactions, as we saw in the Financial Reporting Center. The key difference from other reporting tools is that Smart View is an Excel-based tool, allowing you the functionality offered by a spreadsheet, for example, the flexibility to build graphs, pivot tables, add formulas, and so on. You can save the Excel file on your desktop and use email to deliver the information to the recipient. If the recipient does not have Smart View on their desktop, then they will see this Excel file as a static piece of data. However, if they have Smart View installed with appropriate access, they can refresh the Excel balances from their desktops. If any of the balances have been changed since the Excel file was saved by the sender, then the recipient can still see the up-to-date balances. Also, the recipient can further refine the report using slice and dice. A comparison of the Financial Reporting tool and Smart View is listed in Table 13-4.

	Financial Reporting Studio Tool	**Smart View**
Audience	Senior executives who are not aware of the dimension hierarchies and so on, or casual users who manage lines of business	Used by financial analysts and power users
Developed by	A subject matter expert	An end user who understands the GL Chart of Accounts structure
Calculations	Have to be within the report during the development	Can be added by the end user via ad hoc analysis directly in Excel
Graphs	Have to be defined by the report author	Can be added by the end user via ad hoc analysis directly in Excel
Formatting	Formatting is predefined	Formatting can be changed during ad hoc analysis in Excel
Data source	Uses GL balances in Essbase cube	Uses GL balances in Essbase cube
Drilldown	Drill-down is possible to subledger transactions	Drill-down is possible to subledger transactions

TABLE 13-4. *Comparison of Financial Reporting Tool and Smart View*

Building a Simple Report Using Smart View

In order to build reports using Smart View, you first have to install a Smart View plug-in for Excel from the Oracle website. A quick way to find this plugin is to search for Oracle Smart View for Office Downloads. Alternatively, type in this URL: http://www.oracle.com/technetwork/middleware/epm/downloads/smart-view-1112x-2412371.html

Next, you need the URL of the Smart View workspace on your Fusion Applications instance. Typically this will be https://<host>/<port>/workspace/SmartViewProviders. You must speak to your administrator to obtain the port number because this port will be different from your normal port used for application access.

After you have installed the Smart View plug-in, you will see a tab named Smart View in Excel as shown in Figure 13-29. Click Options, and under the Advanced settings, enter the Smart View workspace URL in the Shared Connections URL drop-down. Click OK.

In your right-hand pane you will now find a Smart View window. Click the drop-down option Shared Connections as shown in Figure 13-30. This will prompt you to log in using your application login and password. Authentication at this stage ensures that Smart View can report on those Chart of Accounts values for which you have access. Next, select Oracle Essbase as shown in Figure 13-30. This will show a list of all the Essbase cubes in your Fusion Applications instance. Expand Essbase_FA_Cluster and select ACMEInsuranceCOAInstance and double-click db. This will open the Essbase tab in Excel.

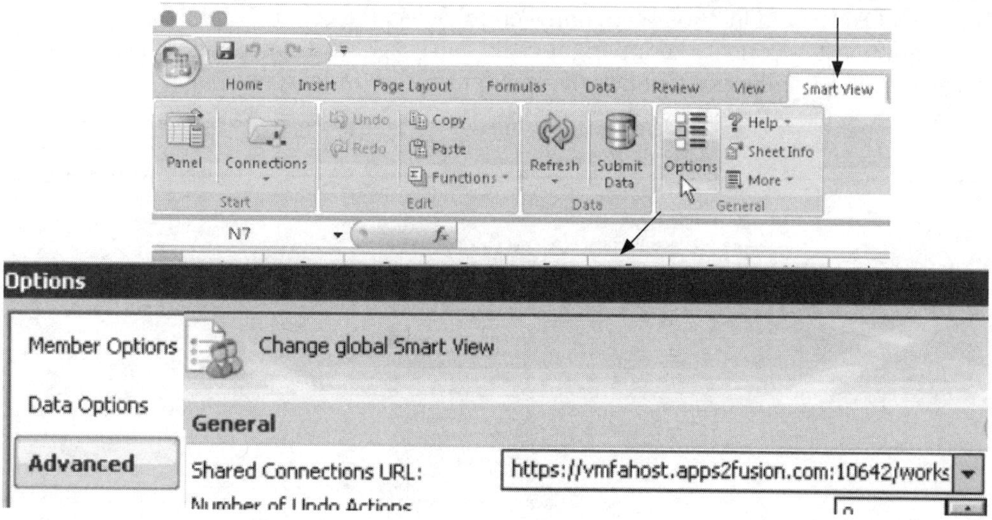

FIGURE 13-29. *Smart View Options, Advanced settings*

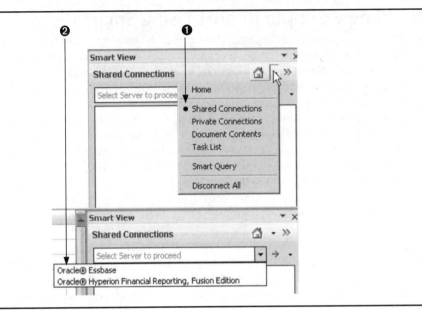

FIGURE 13-30. *Opening the Essbase tab in Excel*

Click POV (Point of View) under the Essbase tab in Excel, and drag Account Dimension in front of AccountingPeriod. To drag from POV to Excel, hover the mouse over POV Dimension until you see the mouse arrow, and then drag the Account POV entry in front of AccountingPeriod. Select the cell in Excel that contains the text AccountingPeriod, right-click, and drag over Ledger. Right-click Ledger in Cell B1 and move that into the POV pane. Your Excel screen should then look similar to the image shown in Figure 13-31.

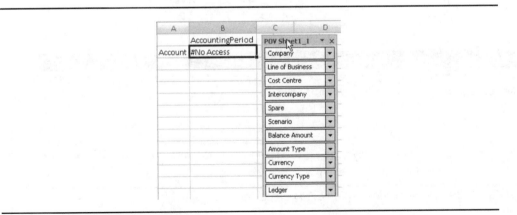

FIGURE 13-31. *Smart View cells*

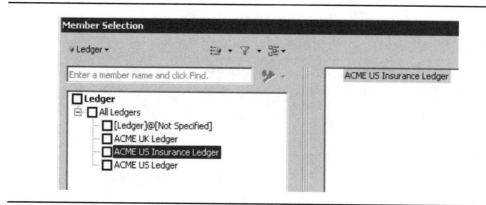

FIGURE 13-32. *Selecting values for dimensions in POV*

Click the Ledger drop-down and shuttle ACME US Insurance Ledger to the right as shown in Figure 13-32. Click the small drop-down beside the text Ledger below the window title Member Selection, again shown in Figure 13-32. Select Scenario, and shuttle Actual to the right, because we want to show actual GL balances. Next select POV member Balance Amount and shuttle Period Activity to the right. Select Amount Type and shuttle Base to the right. Select Currency and shuttle USD to the right. Select Currency Type and shuttle Total to the right-hand pane.

Navigate to the Essbase tab in Excel, highlight the AccountingPeriod cell, click Member Selection, and select the periods ACME-Jan-14, ACME-Feb-14, and ACME-Mar-14 on the right. Select the Account cell and click the Member Selection menu item again to shuttle 10020 and 10010 to the right. Click the Refresh menu item within the Essbase tab, and this will show the GL balances as shown in Figure 13-33.

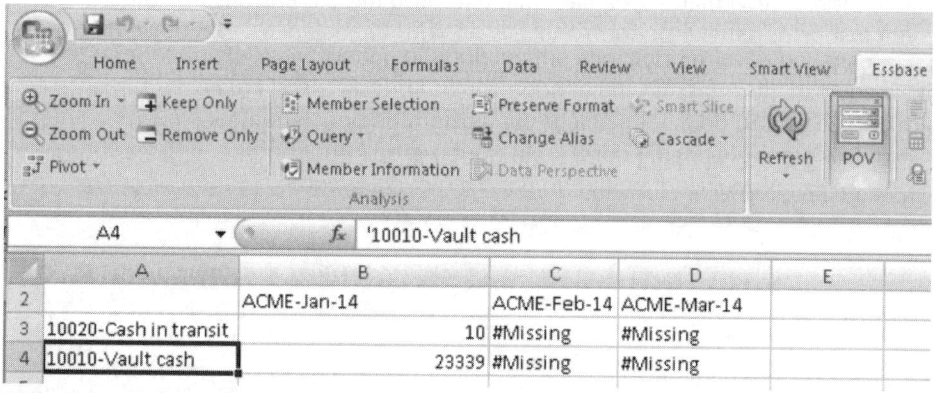

FIGURE 13-33. *Balances in Smart View*

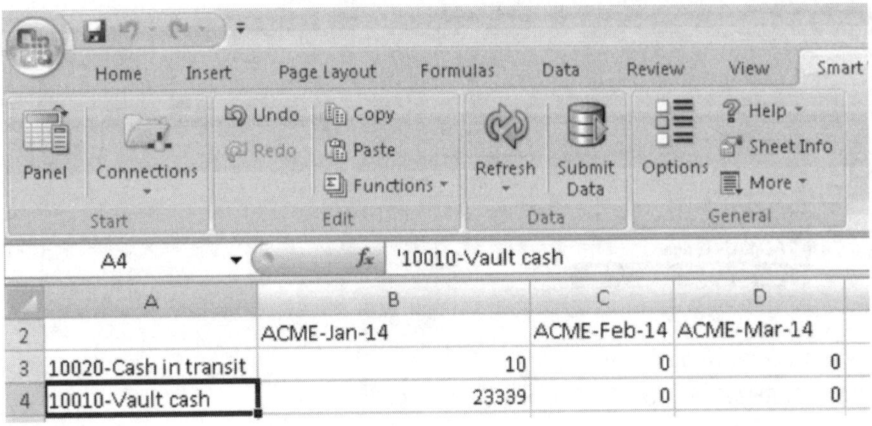

FIGURE 13-34. *Smart View report output*

You will notice that periods that have 0 balances show the text "#Missing" in those cells. In order to replace #Missing with 0, click Options in the Smart View tab, and then select Data Options, and in the Replacement section, select a value of #NumericZero for field #NoData/Missing Label:. Refresh the Smart View, and this will show the final output as per Figure 13-34.

Account Inspector

The Account Inspector tool is similar to Smart View, but it runs on the browser to explore GL account balances. Some people prefer to stay in the browser rather than going to Excel, and they can use this tool. The features in Account Inspector are similar to Smart View; that is, you can drag and drop the dimensions into the Account Inspector pane to perform analysis on your GL balances. Of course, you will not get the features that are native to Excel in Account Inspector.

To access Account Inspector, log in to the application, click General Accounting Dashboard in the Navigator, and select the menu item Inquire And Analyze Balances. Expand the Account Values, and you will see the account values as shown in Figure 13-35.

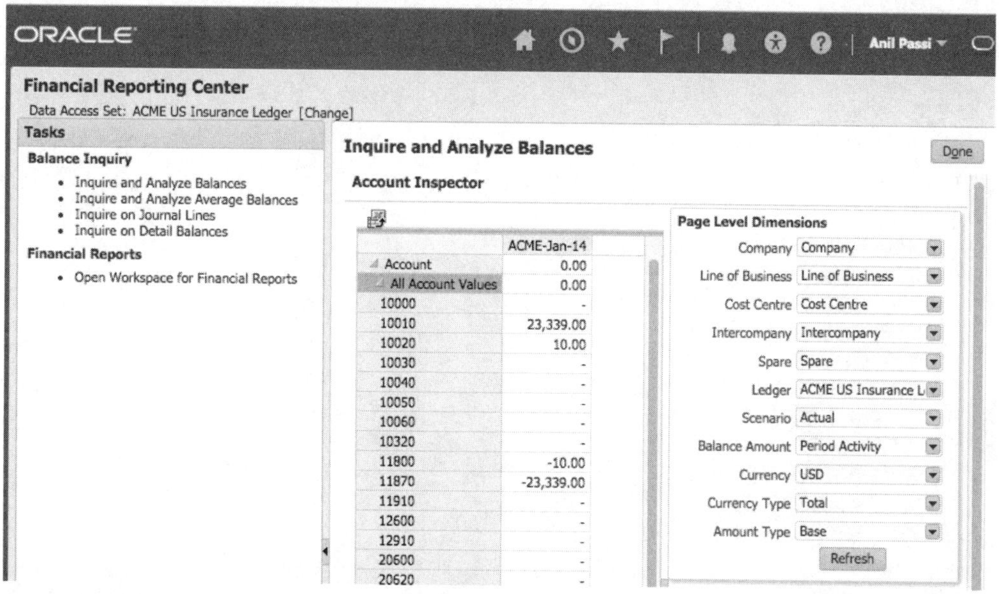

FIGURE 13-35.   *Account Monitor in Fusion Financials*

Summary

In this chapter you have learned about various reporting tools in Fusion Financials and their usage. You have also learned the steps to build simple reports using a variety of toolsets. The architecture implemented in Fusion Applications reporting ensures that the central data security policies are applied across all reporting tools, regardless of the nature of the tool used for reporting in Fusion Applications.

Oracle Fusion Financials delivers a feature-rich reporting platform that is built on top of an analytic data model. Fusion Financials delivers a multidimensional reporting and analysis platform that provides real-time access to financial information at your fingertips. End users can build their own reports and dashboards very quickly by leveraging the self-service BI capability of the product.

APPENDIX
A

Create Implementation Users

This appendix will provide a step-by-step guide for creating an Oracle Fusion Applications user login and assigning necessary roles to the users to start the ACME Bank implementation. The exact steps listed in this appendix are specific to Fusion Applications Release 8, but should largely remain applicable for future releases as well. We recommend readers refer to support.oracle.com for any version-specific steps.

As discussed in Chapter 3, we need to create the following three application users as per Table A-1.

#	Implementation Application User Login Name	Business Type User	Seeded Role in Fusion	Description
1	XXFA_IMPLEMENTATION_ MANAGER	Project Manager	Application Implementation Manager	Responsible for overall delivery of the project
2	XXFA_FIN_GL_IMPLEMENTATION_ CONSULTANT	Functional User	Application Implementation Consultant	Responsible for setting up Fusion Financials Core General Ledger
3	XXFA_FAH_IMPLEMENTATION_ CONSULTANT	Functional User	Application Implementation Consultant	Responsible for setting up Fusion Accounting Hub

TABLE A-1. *Application User List*

Steps to Create an Application User

Follow these steps to create an application user:

1. Log in to Oracle Fusion Applications using FAADMIN or User with both IT Security Manager job role and Application Implementation Consultant roles. **Note:** Make sure that the following Oracle Identity Management (OIM) roles are part of the IT Security Manager job role's role hierarchy:

   a. Identity User Administrators

   b. Role Administrators

2. Click Navigator | Setup And Maintenance link.

3. Navigate to Define Implementation Users | Create Implementation Users task. The Oracle Identity Manager Self Service console page will open.

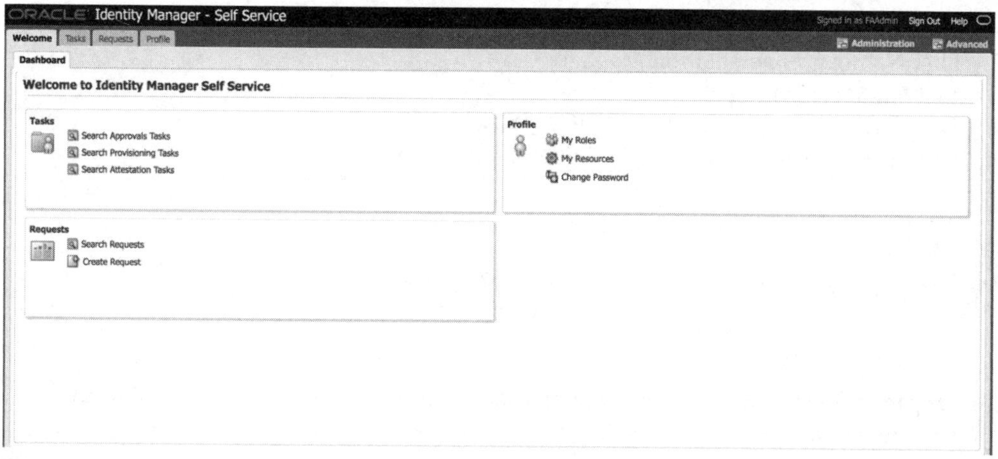

FIGURE A-1. *Oracle Internet Manager – Self Service page*

> **NOTE**
> *Alternatively, you can log in to Oracle Identity Manager directly using the OIM Console URL.*

4. As shown in Figure A-1, click the Administration link.

5. Click the Create User link under the Oracle Identity Manager Delegated Administration section as shown in Figure A-2.

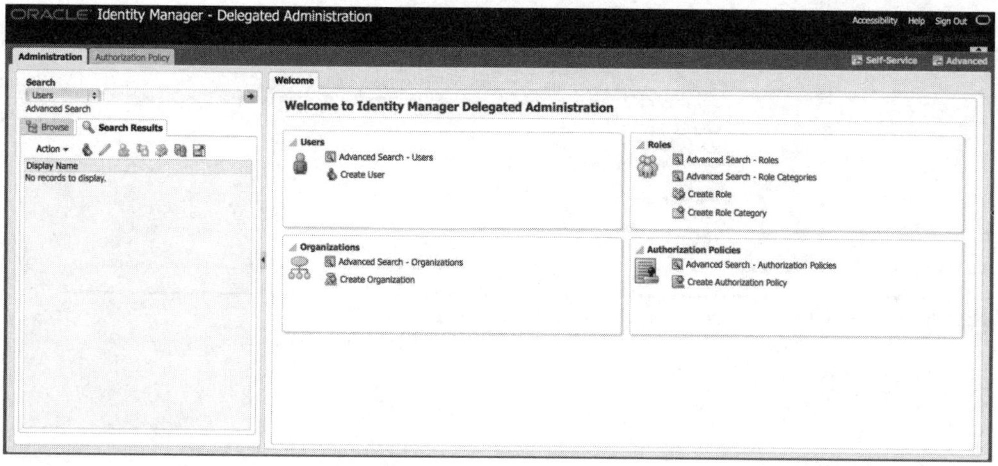

FIGURE A-2. *OIM Create User link page*

6. Enter the following minimum details in the Create User screen:

First Name: Implementation Manager
Last Name: ACME
User Login: XXFA_IMPLEMENTATION_MANAGER
Password & Confirm Password: <Enter Password to Set>

NOTE
*You will be prompted to reset the password after the
first successful login using the password you entered.*

Organization: Xellarate Users (Seeded Organization name provided with Fusion)
User Type: Other

7. Click Save and you will receive confirmation that the user has been created
    successfully as shown in Figure A-3.

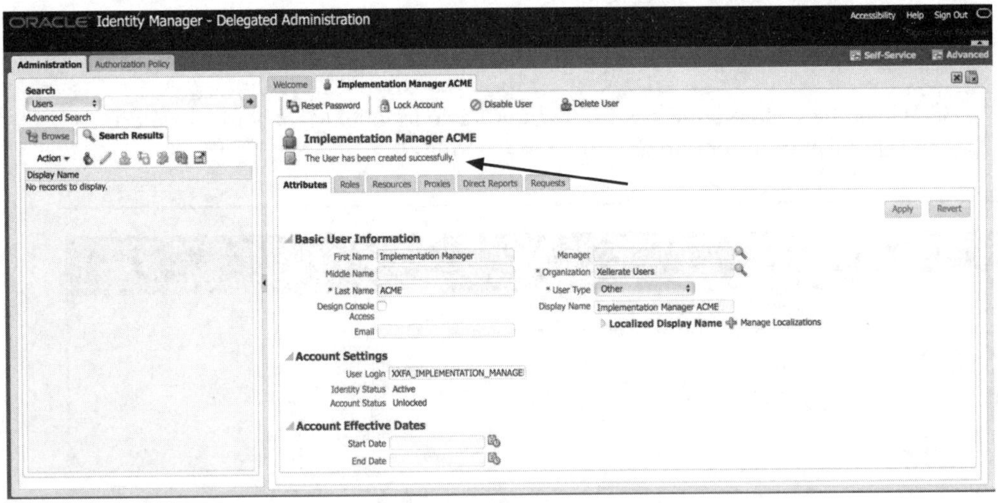

FIGURE A-3. *OIM Create User confirmation message*

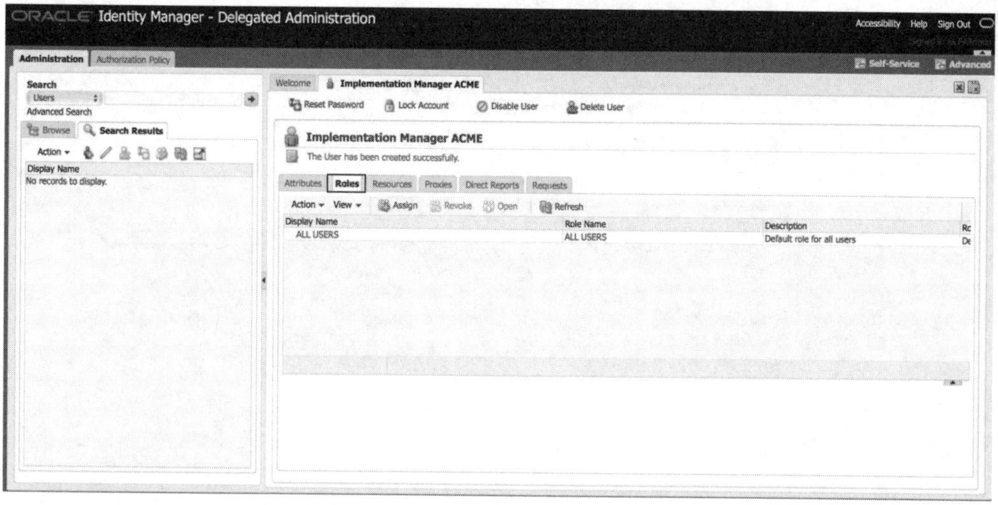

FIGURE A-4. *Assigning roles to the user*

8. Click the Roles tab and then click Assign as shown in Figure A-4.

9. Add the Application Implementation Manager Role as shown in Figure A-5.

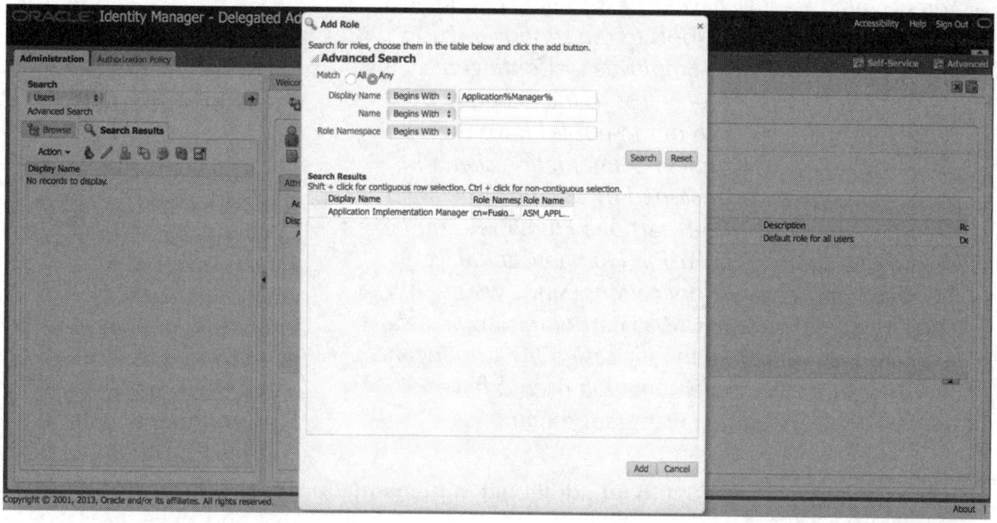

FIGURE A-5. *Assigning the Application Implementation Manager role to the user*

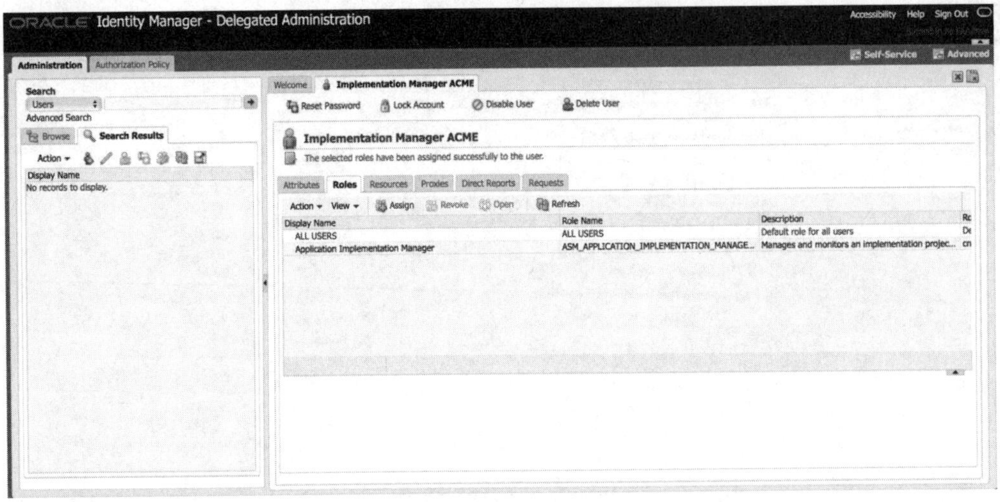

FIGURE A-6. *Assign role confirmation page*

10. You will receive a confirmation message once the selected role has been assigned successfully to the user as shown in Figure A-6.

NOTE
You will also need to have access to the Scheduled Processes menu under Tools to run reports in Fusion Applications. Either the Employee or Contingent Worker role can provide access to the Scheduled Processes menu, as both of these roles have the Worker Duty. In a normal implementation scenario, these roles will be provisioned by default if the login for the users is created as part of a Human Resource record through Oracle Fusion Human Capital Management (HCM) Applications. Since we are not implementing Fusion HCM as part of this book, as a workaround, we can manually assign the Contingent Worker role to the Implementation user to have access to the Scheduled Processes menu.

11. Repeat steps 1 through 8 for additional implementation users. Make sure that for XXFA_FIN_GL_IMPLEMENTATION_CONSULTANT and XXFA_FAH_IMPLEMENTATION_CONSULTANT, you assign Application Implementation Consultant roles in step 7.

Changes to Security Model in Fusion R10

Starting from Release 10, role definitions for security reference implementation have been simplified. The simplified roles reduce the complexity of role administration.

There are four main changes in the simplified reference role model of Release 10, as follows:

■ The seeded reference roles have the ORA prefix, and these roles must not be changed.

■ The role hierarchies delivered in Release 10 are simplified, and the hierarchies are much flatter with fewer duty roles.

■ Prior to Release 10, each job role was implemented as an enterprise role that could be viewed through OIM. In Release 10, job roles and abstract roles are now implemented as two different roles: enterprise job roles, as in prior releases, will be visible in OIM, and application job roles will be visible in Authorization Policy Manager (APM). Starting from Release 10, duty roles and privileges will be granted to application job roles rather than to enterprise job roles.

■ Aggregated privileges have been introduced in Release 10. These privileges are similar to function security privileges in prior releases, but they have data security policy associated with them.

Customers that implement Release 10 directly will have the new set of roles. Customers that upgrade from Release 9 to Release 10, however, will have two sets of roles. They will have the old roles that existed prior to the upgrade, and they will have the new reference roles delivered with Release 10. Immediately following the upgrade, users will continue to be assigned to the old Release 9 roles, and the new Release 10 roles will be inactive.

Release 10 also introduces a copy role functionality. You may create a new role by copying an existing role, and then editing the copy. If so, you have the option of copying only the "top" role (the role itself) or the top role and its inherited roles. If you choose to copy only the top role, your copy shares its role hierarchy with the source role. That is, the source role inherits subordinate roles, and your copy inherits the same roles. Subsequent changes to those inherited roles will affect not only the source role, but also your copy. If you choose to copy the top role and its inherited roles, the copied top role inherits new copies of all subordinate roles. This option insulates the copied role from any changes to the original versions of the inherited roles.

Index

C

M

N

S

T

Join the Largest Tech Community in the World

 Download the latest software, tools, and developer templates

 Get exclusive access to hands-on trainings and workshops

 Grow your professional network through the Oracle ACE Program

 Publish your technical articles – and get paid to share your expertise

**Join the Oracle Technology Network
Membership is free. Visit oracle.com/technetwork**

🐦 @OracleOTN   f facebook.com/OracleTechnologyNetwork